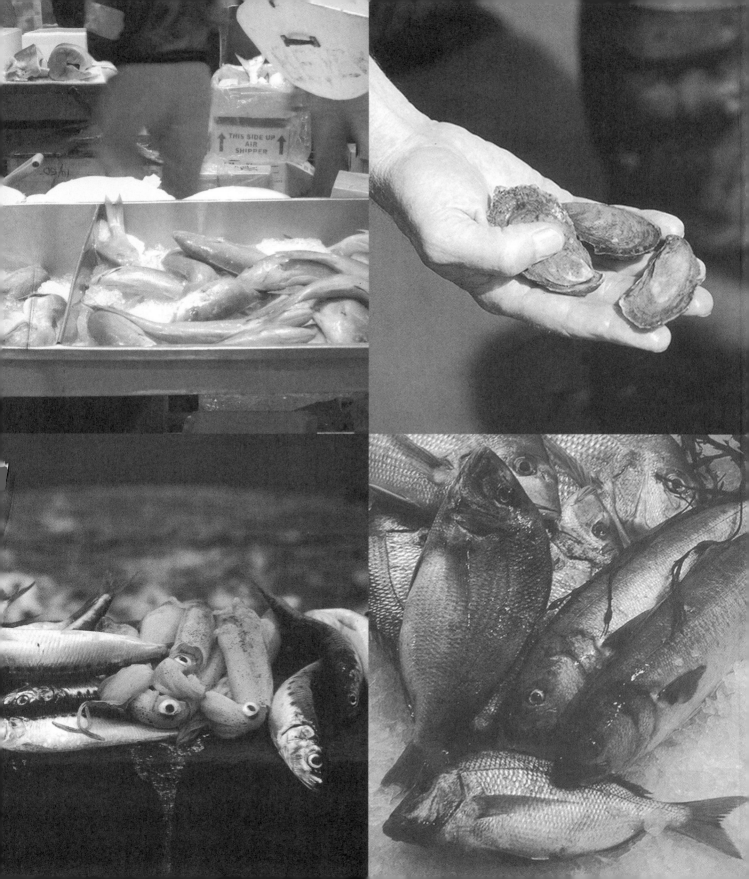

# FISH FOREVER

■ ■ ■ ■ ■ ■ ■ ■ ■ ■ ■ ■

THE DEFINITIVE GUIDE TO UNDERSTANDING, SELECTING,
AND PREPARING HEALTHY, DELICIOUS, AND
ENVIRONMENTALLY SUSTAINABLE SEAFOOD

## PAUL JOHNSON

PHOTOGRAPHY BY KARL PETZKE

BICENTENNIAL
1807
WILEY
2007
BICENTENNIAL

JONN WILEY & SONS, INC.

This book is printed on acid-free paper. ♾

Copyright © 2007 by Paul Johnson. All rights reserved
Photography © Karl Petzke

Published by John Wiley & Sons, Inc., Hoboken, New Jersey
Published simultaneously in Canada
Wiley Bicentennial Logo by Richard J. Pacifico

For general information on our other products and services or for technical support, please contact our Customer Care Department within the United States at (800) 762-2974, outside the United States at (317) 572-3993 or fax (317) 572-4002. Wiley also publishes its books in a variety of electronic formats. Some content that appears in print may not be available in electronic books. For more information about Wiley products, visit our web site at www.wiley.com.


Library of Congress Cataloging-in-Publication Data

Johnson, Paul, 1948-
Fish forever : the definitive guide to understanding, selecting, and preparing healthy, delicious,
and environmentally sustainable seafood / Paul Johnson.
      p. cm.
ISBN 978-0-7645-8779-5 (cloth)
1. Cookery (Seafood) I. Title.
      TX747.J63 2007
      641.6'92—dc22

                        2006027627


INTERIOR DESIGN AND COMPOSITION BY DEBORAH KERNER DESIGN
FOOD STYLING BY DAN BECKER

Printed in the United States of America
10 9 8 7 6 5 4 3 2 1

To my wife, Joan,
and daughter, Kelley,
with love

# CONTENTS

# ACKNOWLEDGMENTS

THANKS TO:

Tom Worthington, Dave Stern, and Carlos Trujillo for doing my job as well as their own while I wrote. Connie Lenoir for making sure the office ran right. The entire Monterey Fish Market staff, both at the pier in San Francisco and at the retail market in Berkeley, for doing a great job.

Kitty Cowles for her confidence, Patty Unterman for her encouragement, Ed Ueber for his pragmatism, and Alice Waters for inspiration.

Karl Petzke for his great photography, Vanessa Barrington for unfailing attention to detail as a recipe tester, Alexis Lipsitz for her editorial skills, and Dan Becker for food styling.

My editor Justin Schwartz and, of course, Natalie Chapman, and everyone at John Wiley & Sons whose efforts made this book so much more than it would have been otherwise: Ava Wilder, Christine DiComo, Jacqueline Beach, and Brent Savage. Also, Deborah Kerner for an incredible job on the interior design, and copyeditor Helen Chin for her hard work.

Dr. Judy Sakinari and Dr. Robert Price for answering my many questions and providing advice on seafood health issues.

All the chefs I've worked with through the years, and especially those who answered my questions: Jean-Pierre Moullé, Wendy Brucner, Maggie Pond, Catadanori Chio, Aki Nagata, Giovanni Scorzo, Russell Moore, Freddy Fong, Paul Canalis, Mike Tusk, David Rosales, and Judy Rodgers.

All the small-boat, sustainable-minded fishermen still on the water, especially Donnie Pemberton and Marc Alley for letting me get in the way while they worked, and Howell Boone for his stories.

Anthony Tringali in Monterey, California, and John Finger at Hog Island Oyster Co. for help with location photos.

Nicholas Ralston, Joyce Nettleton, Harold McGee, ODFW biologist John Norris, Mike Toussaint at Marin Oyster Co., Brenda Thomas at Mctompkin Seafood, Harry Yoshimura at Mutual Fish, Jerry Ivers of Lafayette Caviar, Amelia Bucci and her partners, Paul and Les, at Bucci's restaurant.

Finally, and most importantly, to Joan and Kelley, who put up with me and ate more fish than they would have thought possible.

ix

THE STAFF AT MONTEREY FISH MARKET, FROM LEFT TO RIGHT:
DAVE STERN, CARLOS TRUJILLO, CONNIE LENOIR,
PAUL JOHNSON, AND TOM WORTHINGTON

# TIMES HAVE CHANGED

Times have changed in the seafood market. Not too long ago, most of the seafood sold in America was caught and eaten locally. Today, seafood is a much greater part of our diet: The average American consumes two and a half times more seafood than he or she did twenty years ago, and seafood is shipped to American markets from around the world. It is not unusual to find Vietnamese tuna in New York City, Alaskan king salmon in Boston, or New Zealand snapper in St. Louis. As a result, American seafood cooking is far more interesting and diverse today than it was just two decades ago and today's cooks are far more sophisticated than in the past, demanding not only quality but also assurances that the seafood we eat is healthy. Additionally, there's a growing awareness that the choices we make at the market have a direct effect on the environment, and that our individual decisions on what to buy can make a difference in the future of the world's fisheries.

## GOOD NEWS, BAD NEWS

One reason for the growing popularity of fish and shellfish is that seafood has proven to be one of the most beneficial foods we can eat. The omega-3 fatty acids found in seafood are essential to optimal childhood development. Medical research indicates that children born to mothers who consume higher quantities of omega-3-rich fish are healthier at birth, exhibit higher IQs, and have better health later in life. For adults, the benefits of regularly eating seafood include reducing the risk of heart disease and stroke, remedying arthritis and depressive symptoms, strengthening the immune system, and possibly preventing Alzheimer's disease.

For all the health benefits of fish, however, the public has recently become aware that eating seafood may also carry risks. Well-publicized cautions regarding the potential danger of everything from cholera to mercury in seafood have some consumers unsure if the risk of eating fish is worth the reward. The very safety of our seafood has fallen under suspicion.

*Fish Forever* strives to present a clear and balanced explanation of the advantages and dangers of eating seafood. I explain how to eat a wide variety of fish safely and without worry, as well as how people at greatest risk can avoid potential dangers. Health rewards and risks are profiled for each and every species, and where appropriate, the reader is referred to a health appendix at the back of the book for further information. High-profile public concerns such as mercury and PCBs in fish and the risks involved in eating raw fish are covered in detail. You'll discover which tuna has the lowest levels of mercury, how to detect chemical additives in seafood, and why eating lobster tomalley and crab butter may not always be a good idea. All the information you need to ensure that the seafood you and your family eat is safe and healthy can be found in these pages, including a chart that details mercury and omega-3 levels in seafood.

Healthy eating is a personal and immediate concern, but the ocean's health is also of concern to our children and their future. Over-fishing and pollution have laid waste to once-productive fishing grounds. The Grand Banks, once considered the richest fishing grounds in the world, have yet to fully recover from rampant overfishing by foreign factory trawlers decades ago. Increasingly, the bad news is borne out in newspaper headlines: "Ninety Percent of All the World's Large Predatory Fish Depleted" and "Pollution from Mississippi Responsible for 70,000-Square-Mile Dead Zone in Gulf of Mexico." Aquaculture, once touted as the savior of the world's fisheries, has turned out to be something of a Pandora's box: Salmon farms pollute, threaten native stocks, and breed disease, while shrimp farming has been responsible for the destruction of ecologically important coastal wetlands. Meanwhile, trawlers mine the seas to feed the ever-growing demand for fish food.

The ocean and its resources are clearly in crisis. Codfish, bluefin tuna, Chilean sea bass, and red snapper are just a few of the fish species that have fallen victim to overfishing and mismanagement—and many types of turtles, seabirds, and marine mammals are threatened as well. Fortunately, there are glimmers of light shining through the clouds: The Pew Oceans Commission and the congressionally funded U.S. Commission on Ocean Policy have both recently released long-term studies defining the state of our ocean resources. These reports outline very real solutions to the problems and give hope for the future stewardship of our seas. Congress has recognized the importance of sustainable fisheries, and fishing and environmental groups claiming millions of members have made ocean conservancy and sustainable fisheries a primary objective for the future.

## FISH TALES

Ten years ago, we were bombarded with stories about how healthy it was to eat seafood. Never a caution was aired, and seafood consumption skyrocketed. Today, the pendulum has swung to the opposite extreme, with the media sending out sensationalistic chronicles on the risks of eating fish and shellfish.

We need to strive for a better and more balanced understanding of the issues involved with eating seafood while still continuing to encourage improvements in the environment. Lately, too much emphasis has been placed on the negative aspects of consuming fish, which has worked largely to scare people away from the benefits of seafood as part of a well-balanced diet. For example, recent stories of reported high levels of PCBs in salmon are misleading; wild salmon often have no detectable levels of PCBs, while even farmed salmon test at levels two hundred times below government standards—chicken, dairy products, and beef are a far greater source of PCBs in our diet than fish.

Another example: Only recently has the type of mercury most prevalent in fish even been identified and it appears that it is less harmful to human cells than previously believed. Additionally, the latest studies show that the high levels of selenium found in fish may act to sequester mercury and interfere with its absorption. The dangers of cholesterol in squid, shrimp, and other shellfish have proven unfounded, and it's now known that the sterols found in oysters, clams, and mussels, once thought to be harmful, are actually beneficial plant sterols that *prevent* the uptake of cholesterol.

The mainstream medical community overwhelmingly believes that the benefits of eating seafood far outweigh the risks, the most recent studies by Harvard School of Public health and the National Academy of Sciences agree with this, yet the sensationalism of the negative garners headlines. Yes, there are dangers to eating seafood, just as with all foods, but those dangers can be identified and either avoided or mitigated.

## WISE CHOICES

Jacques Pépin wrote about sustainable seafood choices in the *New York Times* Op-Ed page on July 3, 2001: "Chefs make choices every day— choices that are not related solely to the presentation of the finest culinary creations one can imagine. Now more than ever, it is clear how our choices can affect the environment." But it is not only chefs who are making these decisions; the average home cook must make these choices as well. Making an informed decision at the market no longer means simply vying for the freshest-looking piece of fish; it can also mean choosing wild salmon over farmed, substituting haddock for cod, and including in our diet many of the formerly scorned small, fatty fish such as anchovies, mackerel, sardines, and smelt—all of which have been found to be among the healthiest and most environmentally friendly seafood choices.

As consumers, the most available, meaningful, and valid action we can take to encourage sustainable fisheries is to *choose wisely at the market*. If the public starts questioning how and where their seafood is caught or raised, it will reverberate throughout the supply chain: Purveyors, fishermen, and the entire seafood industry will come to learn that promoting sustainable fishing is economically beneficial for everyone concerned.

*Fish Forever* profiles the sustainability and resource considerations of each individual species, pointing out not only the best choice, but the better choice as well. From a marine conservation perspective, it's important to identify and support not only those perfect "green choices," but also those fisheries that are striving to make meaningful improvements.

Being a wise consumer is about coming up with real solutions for real-world concerns.

Trap-caught spot shrimp may be the "perfect choice" alternative to aquacultured shrimp, but they're seldom available to the average consumer. On the other hand, wild American shrimp are a very good choice and are readily available—providing a real-world option that makes a difference to the environment.

Interspersed throughout the text are stories such as Bobby's Bluefin: The Last Fish (page 374), Too Much of a Good Thing (page 268), and Buy American (page 294), all of which strive to introduce the broader issues of sustainable fishing and encourage the reader to stay interested and informed. Among other topics, these stories tell why it is important to support the good fishermen in a bad fishery, the danger of fishing down the food chain, and what's good and not so good about aquaculture.

The seafood species chosen for this book don't all belong on an environmental "green list"; many—including monkfish, grouper, and cod—are here largely because they are among the most popular species in the marketplace. Some species are included because they're associated with vital issues such as the importance of supporting good fishermen in a bad fishery. Still others, like butterfish, mackerel, sea robin, and wreckfish, are here because they are underutilized and should be promoted. The "green lists" I leave to the more dynamic venue of the Internet; my favorite is the Monterey Bay Aquarium's Seafood Watch program at www.mbayaq.org.

Aside from ensuring that the food we eat is healthy and placing a high priority on making seafood a sustainable resource, we face an additional —and, to many, a daunting—challenge: how to find fresh, top-quality seafood and then come up with simple, foolproof seafood recipes that really work. The average cook who walks into the local fish market may yearn to try an unfamiliar fish or a new way of cooking it, only to hesitate for fear of risking disaster in the kitchen.

Hesitate no longer. *Fish Forever* is the seafood cook's ideal resource, offering insider tips on how to choose the best seasonal and regional seafood found in American markets today. These tips will tell you what to look for in a healthy fish, and help you gain the confidence to select good fish even in a bad market. *Fish Forever* goes beyond the clichés of clear eyes, red gills, and the briny smell of the ocean to uncover the secrets of the experts. Learn how to read the color and markings of seafood, what each species should look and feel like when fresh, and the best season for each species.

Once the preferred fish finally does find its way into the kitchen, the current trend toward simple, healthy recipes with plenty of flavor will continue. The seafood of the future will more likely be dressed with a simple Italian salsa verde of parsley, capers, and olive oil rather than complex preparations calling for butter and cream. The recipes in this book, in one way or another, are all inspired by the many great cooks I've worked with over the years. When I sell a piece of fish, it often comes with the question, "What are you going to do with it?" Sometimes I get back an immediate answer, but just as often I find myself being used as a sounding board for recipe development: "Maybe I'll poach it in a coriander-scented broth . . . hmm . . . or maybe I'll put it in the pizza oven and give it an aïoli." The chefs who have influenced me the most are those who cook honest, simple food, and are concerned that those foods remain sustainable.

The recipes in *Fish Forever* favor fresh seasonal ingredients that are as healthful as the seafood. Butter and cream are used with a restrained hand, while good oils, citrus juices, vinegars, and herbs take front and center. The recipes are inspired by a variety of cuisines, but execution remains consistent. Using basic kitchen equipment, even a modestly competent cook can achieve spectacular results. These are simple recipes that convey the creativity and verve of a contemporary professional kitchen, but are completely accessible to the home cook.

In addition to the recipes, the In the Kitchen section found in each entry suggests a range of cooking techniques and a variety of sauces and seasonings that marry particularly well with that species. My hope is that, as you thumb through this book, you'll be inspired to do a little creative experimenting on your own, blending technique, sauce, and seafood from throughout the book as you see fit.

Today's retail consumer and restaurant chef alike are faced with a confusing array of choices at the market. *Fish Forever* is your indispensable guide to buying and preparing healthy, sustainable seafood. It tackles health and environmental concerns head-on, and explains everything you need to know about how to maneuver confidently from market to kitchen: what to buy, where to find it, how best to prepare it—and how to do it all with a good conscience.

# FROM COOK
# TO FISHMONGER

■ ■ ■ ■ ■ ■ ⋙ ■ ■ ■ ■ ■ ■

The one question I'm asked more than any other is how I started in the seafood business. I was born in Rhode Island, where life revolves around the sea. Fishing is a big part of the economy, everyone knows a commercial fisherman or two, and seafood seems to be a part of every memorable event.

As a child, I spent my summers at the family beach house at Point Judith. After a day on the beach, we would walk down to the harbor to watch the procession of tuna boats steam into the channel. Crowds gathered around to see giant bluefin tuna tip the scales at one thousand-plus pounds. In those days, the greatest concern we harbored for the future of seafood was whether Uncle Emil had caught flounder or bluefish for dinner.

In 1978, I was working as a cook in the Inn Season in Berkeley, California. The tiny restaurant was owned by a U.C. Berkeley professor who supported his passion for the stove with grant money from awards in astrophysics, not that unusual for the early days of Berkeley's

"gourmet ghetto," the small area of shops and restaurants in north Berkeley where the "California food revolution" first took hold. Our seafood was provided by Doctor Jerry, a friend of Alice Waters of Chez Panisse, whom she had convinced to travel to the docks in San Francisco in search of fresh fish. As Inn Season was only two blocks from Chez Panisse and Doctor Jerry was an ex-colleague of the owner, he sometimes bought fish for our restaurant as well.

After several months of buying fish at the docks, Doctor Jerry had become decidedly unenthusiastic about the early morning hours (a commitment the job entailed). He no longer wanted the job himself but felt responsible for finding a replacement. He repeatedly tried to convince me to take over, saying I had a natural talent for recognizing fresh seafood. I, on the other hand, thought of myself as a career chef and refused. That is, until an incident with the local fish wholesaler changed my mind.

We had booked an important event at the

restaurant that was to feature first-of-the-season king salmon. Doctor Jerry was, as he put it, on a short sabbatical; I suspected that the sabbatical might be permanent, so I tried to establish a relationship with the local fish wholesaler by placing several orders. When it came time to order the salmon for our special event, I called the wholesaler, letting him know both the situation with our fish buyer and the importance of the event to me. He assured me that he bought only the best and would personally oversee my order; I, in turn, promised all my future business for a job well done.

## SOUTH BY SOUTHEAST: THE BERING SEA MOVES

On the day of the event, the seafood delivery was later than usual, but I wasn't all that worried after the wholesaler's personal assurances. When the driver finally did arrive, he was carrying a soggy cardboard box with Cyrillic lettering on the side. *That* made me nervous. With a grunt, the driver hefted the box off his hip and slammed it down on the countertop. He wiped sweat from the end of his nose, handed me the bill, and said "Here sign this, I'm really late." I ignored him and cautiously peered in the box. Inside were partially thawed salmon fillets with the tortured appearance of having been frozen far too long. My promised local salmon seemed to have come from a Russian factory trawler somewhere out on the Bering Sea. I was astonished. *"What . . . is . . . this?"* I hissed.

The driver mumbled something about running out of local fish, then changed tack and tried to assure me that the Bering Sea was "up north," just off the coast of California. He pushed the bill at me again. In a frenzy I tore it into the tiniest little pieces imaginable; then offering him the door, I said, "Please, get out and take your garbage with you!"

In a panic, I sent a dishwasher off to Chinatown for ducks. We turned up the ovens and pulled some old red wines from the depths of the cellar. The guests were understanding and even a little flattered to hear that the salmon hadn't been good enough to serve to such discriminating palates. The event was a success, the food and wine enjoyed by all. Everyone went home happy—everyone, that is, except me. I had no idea where I would buy my seafood in the future.

## FISH ALLEY

The next morning, it came to me. I called Doctor Jerry and told him I would be willing to take over his job as fish buyer for Chez Panisse. A few nights later, Alice, her chef, Jean-Pierre Moullé, and I sat at a table in the kitchen of Chez Panisse. We talked about seafood and cooking and, after several glasses of wine, we were able to laugh about how the Bering Sea had become a local body of water.

We agreed that better fish was out there; it was just a matter of finding it. And the task would be up to me: I would begin buying seafood for Chez Panisse as well as the Inn Season. Alice insisted I start the very next morning. She pushed the following night's menu and a handful of cash on me before locking the doors. Once on the street, I realized I had just agreed to start a new business with two customers—one of whom was me.

A few hours later, I crossed the Bay Bridge and found my way to the docks. A bent and rusted street sign welcomed me to Fish Alley: two rows of dingy, low warehouses separated by greasy, broken asphalt. The warehouse walls were battered and dull; entire sections of gray clapboard had been gouged out by roughly stacked bins of fish, and in places fish parts and blood textured the walls like a mosaic. Broken pallets and garbage were stacked everywhere.

It was 4 a.m., and the gulls and sea lions were already screeching and barking for their fair share. A huge stinking tallow truck partially blocked the entrance to the alley. Its engine roared and bucked; gears screeched trying to grind up the fish bones and guts being dumped into its maw.

I avoided being run over by a flatbed truck stacked high with wooden crab crates, only to get sprayed with filthy black water. A speeding forklift hit one of the many potholes in the alley and lost its purchase on a huge overloaded bin of fish. A loud crash was followed by a tsunami of fish and ice spilling across the alleyway. Curses and catcalls came from scurrying figures dashing for doorways trying to avoid the oncoming wave of fish.

Everything was filthy, everyone was rude. The language was Italian, but the only words I understood were the curses. I was overwhelmed, intimidated, and giving serious thought to heading back home. But an image of myself came to mind, with glass of wine in hand, glibly assuring Alice and Jean-Pierre that I'd be bringing them everything they needed for the evening's menu. I waded back in.

When the sun began to brighten the sky, I worked my way through stacked-up crab pots and broken-down fencing to get a better look at the bay. What I came upon next in the clear light of day was the exact opposite of everything I had seen so far. A spotless seventy-foot trawler, with *St. Francis* painted on her bow, was tied up at the dock. Still dripping seawater, her net was neatly rolled up on the spool; boots, shovels, and lines were all neatly organized. Wooden boxes filled with beautifully fresh fish were stacked on the deck. Tied up beside the trawler were a dozen or more brightly painted little Monterey double-enders, fashioned after the Sicilian felucca. Most were powered by diesel but some still carried the lateen sail of times past.

Salmon as fresh as I had ever seen were being carefully handed up to the dock. Halibut and flounder lay glistening in the morning sun. A wolf eel slithered out of a box of skates and headed for the water. On the deck of the smaller boats were woven baskets full of rockfish, still stiff with rigor: chile-pepper red, emerald green, brilliant orange—their dazzling colors, gaping mouths, and gleaming eyes a study in still life.

The Golden Gate Bridge and the misty Marin headlands lay across the water, and the air was filled with the briny smell of fresh fish. Suddenly, Fish Alley seemed like a much friendlier place.

Not long after that first day at the wharf, Bay Wolf Restaurant began buying their fish from me, and when friends opened the Hayes Street Grill in San Francisco I was forced to give up any pretense of being a cook. I quit my job at Inn Season and became a full-time fishmonger.

I spent the next twenty-five years working out of Fish Alley. The first couple of years I drove a broken-down old truck and cut fish outside in all sorts of weather on a nearby abandoned pier. Eventually, I leased a space in the alley and became one of those characters who had so intimidated me that first morning.

## MONTEREY FISH

When I first began selling fish in San Francisco, the seafood industry seemed carefree. Fishermen worked the local waters from a fleet of colorful double-ended Italian-style fishing dories. At day's end, an open-air fish market on the wharf gave San Francisco the look of a vibrant working port, and the only worry was whether we'd have enough ice on hand for all the fish being landed. Today, a mere glimmer in time later, the bluefin tuna is in danger of commercial extinction, the artisanal San Francisco fisherman has left the wharf to become a fireman or an electrician, and I spend much of my day dealing with issues that have little to do with the freshness of fish.

I work the wholesale fish market from the docks at Fisherman's Wharf in San Francisco, while my wife Joan and her sister Kim run our retail fish market, Monterey Fish Market, across the bay in Berkeley. Most of my days are spent trying to glean information from suppliers, fishermen, and seafood industry experts, then making sure that information is passed on to chefs and retail customers. For the retail market in Berkeley, we've printed brochures that explain the issues of sustainability and suggest ecologically sound choices. We also supply handouts that address health issues of current concern, and the counter holds stacks of recipe cards for the taking. It all flows out the door in a steady stream, along with advice and encouragement from the staff.

At Monterey Fish Wholesale on the wharf in San Francisco, everyone knows the drill: The crew has worked together for years, and mornings rush past in a blur of buying, selling, and negotiations—selling the fish in the house today, anticipating tomorrow's needs, and searching the supply lines.

11

On a typical morning, my brother-in-law Tom, who manages the wharf along with Dave and Carlos, is helping Michael Mina choose the seafood for the spring menu of his restaurant on Union Square. Meanwhile, Andrew from Café Boulud in New York calls to order Dungeness crabs; Dave takes the order, and then finishes describing a Jardinière sardine recipe to Patty Unterman at the Hayes Street Grill. Carlos is directing the fish coming in one door through a labyrinth of cleaning, cutting, and packaging before it goes out the other door to be delivered to restaurants and markets. I'm simultaneously taking a phone order from Charles Phan at the Slanted Door, on hold at the Gloucester fish auction, and listening to the repeated rings of two other lines that no one is answering. Judy Rodgers wants to know if there is still a boycott against swordfish, and Paul Bertolli calls to ask what to tell his customers about the article on mercury in seafood in today's *New York Times*.

My staff and I talk to chefs and seafood professionals throughout the country every day, and the consensus is the same everywhere: Consumers are being more careful in choosing the seafood they eat; they want assurances that their seafood is healthy and safe; they want more information on how to choose seafood and cook it at home; and they have greater concern than ever for the environment and for seafood's future as a sustainable resource.

The pages ahead are filled with twenty-five years of accumulated experience and knowledge garnered from fishermen, seafood buyers, scientists, and great cooks. It is my hope that the information found in this book will help you enjoy the adventure of selecting, preparing, and, most of all, eating the best the seas have to offer, and to do it with confidence. Equally as important, I hope it inspires you to make the wise choices that will ensure we have *Fish Forever*.

# SELECTING, STORING, AND COOKING SEAFOOD

■ ■ ■ ■ ■ ■ ⋖🐟 ■ ■ ■ ■ ■ ■

To achieve the goal of eating delicious, healthy, sustainable seafood we may sometimes need to travel somewhat turbulent seas. The directions below for selecting, storing, and cooking seafood will ease the journey.

## SELECTING FRESH SEAFOOD

Short of catching your own top-quality fresh fish, the best way to find it is to buy it from a store that specializes in seafood. All the fish in the display case should have a moist, clean appearance. The store should smell like fresh fish, and the counter should be busy and staffed with knowledgeable people who can explain how and where each variety was caught, describe the taste of the fish, and readily offer suggestions about handling and preparing them.

Here are a few pointers that can help you:

**LEARN TO RECOGNIZE FRESH SEAFOOD** • Whole fish should have clear eyes, firm flesh, and red gills; fillets should have a lustrous shine; and live shellfish should be active and feel heavy for their size. The signs I give in each entry in this book are all-important. But fresh seafood has a bright and lively appearance that is easier to recognize than define. Stop by the seafood counter often to try to get a feel for which fish is fresh without analyzing. After a while, it becomes second nature.

**BE FLEXIBLE** • Fresh seafood doesn't come in uniform shapes and sizes, and not every kind is always available. Seasons change; fish gather or disperse for their own reasons. It's unrealistic a cook who goes to the market demanding only large scallops or small halibut and expecting the best fish at any time of year. Instead, plan your meal around what's fresh at the market that day.

**FOLLOW THE SEASONS** • Begin your search for seafood by finding out what is local and what is in season—always the criteria for ensuring the best flavor and price while impacting the environment the least.

**KNOW YOUR SOURCES** • Choose seafood caught by sustainable methods of capture such as hook and line or trap. Seafood caught selectively by small-boat fishermen is brought onboard quickly, so is subject to fewer flavor-sapping stress hormones. The fish is cleaned, bled, and iced immediately after capture, and the flesh is not bruised from nets or the weight of other fish, all of which leads to superior-flavored seafood.

**CULTIVATE YOUR FISHMONGER** • Take the advice of the person behind the counter; he or she should be well versed on what's fresh that day, what's likely to be coming in off the docks tomorrow, and which fish are in season.

## STORING FRESH SEAFOOD

Seafood should always be kept as cold as possible; bacteria and enzymes that have evolved with fish and shellfish in a cold environment remain active when temperatures are low. Even the objective signs of freshness (clear eyes, firm flesh, and so on) are as much a product of good handling as of how long the fish has been out of the water. Shellfish that are kept alive and fish that are conscientiously iced will always have the best flavor and texture.

At home, I keep my fish in a cooler in a shady spot outside; that way, there is never a spill in the refrigerator and I know it will stay cold. Bring your cooler with you to the fish market and ask for crushed ice.

Pack whole fish directly in the ice, belly-side up, and fill the belly cavity with ice. Put fish fillets, scallops, squid, and shrimp in a plastic bag, squeeze the air out, tie the bag tightly, and bury it in the crushed ice, leaving the top of the bag out of the ice so that no water seeps into the bag.

Clams, mussels, and oysters get the same treatment as fish fillets—only don't tie the bag; leave the top open and out of the ice.

For live crustaceans such as lobster, crabs, or crayfish, fill the cooler partway with ice, place wet newspaper on top of the ice, then place the live shellfish on top of the newspaper. Cover them with more wet newspaper and sprinkle a thin layer of ice over the top.

## STORING SEAFOOD IN THE REFERATOR ■ ■ ■

For whole fish, fish fillets, scallops, squid, and shrimp: Unwrap or remove the fish from the plastic bag it came in; rinse, dry, and place on a clean plate. Cover, and place in the back of the lowest shelf (the coldest part) of your refrigerator.

For clams, mussels, and oysters: Place in a bowl and cover with a wet towel; place one or two ice cubes on the towel so it stays damp, and put the bowl in the coldest part of the refrigerator. Drain the bowl if any water accumulates.

For crabs, lobsters, and crayfish: Place the shellfish in a plastic bag; place wet newspaper or a damp towel on top of them and leave the top of the bag open. Store them in the coldest part of the refrigerator.

## COOKING SEAFOOD

Cooking seafood is no more difficult than cooking other foods. There are techniques to learn that are specific to seafood; opening clams, cleaning squid, and so on, but that is true of all foods. Any cook has to learn the secrets and intricacies of cooking vegetables or pork or chicken; think how difficult it is to bone out a chicken. It's just a matter of familiarity; all it takes to get good at cooking fish is to cook fish.

The most important thing to remember about cooking fish is that fish proteins and collagen react to heat at lower temperatures than do those in terrestrial animals; medium-rare in seafood is just above 120°F, while a medium-rare steak is approaching 140°F. This calls for gentler cooking over more moderate heat, allowing the heat to penetrate the deeper layers of flesh without overcooking and drying the outer layers.

Most seafood is best either completely raw or thoroughly cooked. I love the crisp texture and simple flavor of raw seafood (see Raw

Seafood: How to Stay Safe, page 408). But when seafood is cooked rare, it loses its crisp texture and doesn't have time to develop the full flavors of cooked seafood. Thoroughly cooking seafood firms the texture and breaks down cell walls, allowing fats, sugars, and flavor compounds to mix into a savory stew that best shows the full flavor of seafood.

That said, most seafood should be removed from heat when medium-rare, that is, the center is still slightly translucent, so that the ambient temperature of the surrounding flesh allows continued cooking to doneness by the time the fish is served. In the recipes I refer to this state as "almost opaque throughout."

Some moderately dense, rich-flavored fish, such as salmon or striped bass, can be cooked so they remain slightly rare, or translucent, in the center when served, but only tuna, whose muscle structure and flavor profile are so similar to beef, is able to stand up well to the mixed message of a seared outside and a fully rare interior.

## HOW TO KNOW WHEN IT'S DONE ▪ ▪ ▪

Cooking by the clock is a good place to start, but it's far from an exact science—there are simply too many variables. Although the standard is ten minutes per inch, a thick piece of fish takes less time per inch than a thin piece. For example, a half-inch-thick piece of sole will take all of five minutes to cook, while a two-inch-thick piece of salmon will be cooked long before twenty minutes have passed. Fat fish are slower to cook than lean fish, even within the same species. Fish with bones take more time per inch than those without. Fillets require less time than steaks to cook, and a whole fish often needs more than ten minutes per inch. The starting temperature of the fish and the actual heat of the fire also affect cooking times.

How, then, to tell if a piece of fish is done? The poke-and-prod method is probably the most reliable. As fish cooks, it firms and develops a springy texture. To get a feel for the texture of raw versus cooked fish, press lightly on a piece of fish before it goes onto the heat, then every couple of minutes while it cooks. When it starts to feel firm and a little springy, insert a thin-bladed knife to force the flakes at the center apart, in order to see how much of the flesh has changed from translucent to almost opaque. Use a flashlight for a better view. Take the fish off the heat while it is still "almost opaque throughout." Don't worry: After a little practice, you'll be able to determine doneness by feel alone. And finally, better to undercook than overcook; undercooked fish can go back on the heat but overcooked fish is overcooked fish.

## Seafood Advice for Pregnant or Nursing Women, and Young Children

My wife and I recently went to a restaurant with friends. They ordered raw oysters and smoked salmon for appetizers, and as we sat and talked our female friend told us she was pregnant. I let them know that raw oysters and smoked salmon were right at the top of my list of seafood that pregnant women should not eat and came up with a quick list of other seafood dos and don'ts for pregnant women. Here is the list I gave our friends that night; it is a compilation of advice from Omega-3s, Mercury, and Pregnancy (page 407); Raw Seafood: How to Stay Safe (page 408); and Persistent Organic Pollutants (page 417).

**AVOID:**

- Raw or lightly cooked mollusks such as clams, mussels, or oysters
- Cold smoked fish such as salmon (including lox) or sturgeon
- Eating the internal organs of fish or shellfish including fish liver, lobster tomalley, or crab butter
- Wild freshwater fish
- Fish and shellfish from bays and inshore estuaries in urban areas
- Swordfish, marlin, shark, Gulf of Mexico tilefish, king mackerel, and large-sized tunas
- Striped bass, bluefish, grouper, and jacks over ten pounds.
- Deep-fried seafood
- Canned white-meat albacore tuna

**CHOOSE:**

- Seafood high in omega-3s two to three times a week as per FDA guidelines (see Omega-3 chart, page 404)
- Seafood low in mercury (see Mercury chart, page 405)
- A variety of seafood from different locations
- Hot smoked fish
- Canned light-meat tuna or Pacific Coast low-mercury certified white-meat albacore tuna
- Sushi and other raw finfish dishes are okay; just avoid the large fatty tuna
- Spiny lobster, crab, shrimp, squid, octopus, sea snails, and abalone may all be eaten cooked or raw
- Mollusks of which only the muscle and not the viscera is eaten; sea scallops, geoduck clam, and surf clam (hokiga) are okay

# SEAFOOD BY THE SEASONS

The seasons have a much greater influence on seafood than on terrestrial animals. Creatures of the sea are completely dependent on the food made available to them by a natural environment that is based on cycles of abundance and scarcity. And unlike domestic land animals that burn only fat to fuel the next generation, fish and shellfish use their own proteins as well as fats to create offspring, depleting not only energy reserves but their very selves.

Early-season salmon are lean and delicate; their flesh is a brilliant red from feeding on tiny shrimplike krill. Later in the year, the same salmon have fattened on anchovies and sardines; their orange-hued flesh is muscular and firm, their flavor complex and robust. By year's end, after entering their river of birth, they are completely spent, their flesh pale, soft, and flavorless. No other food is so dependent on season and environment, so variable in fat and flavor, or so delicious when everything is right.

## SEASONAL
## SEAFOOD CHART

In truth, a seasonal chart for wild seafood can be only a general guideline. Changing oceanic and climatic conditions cause cyclic changes. Management regulations and economic factors affect the availability of wild seafood from year to year and season to season. In this chart, black represents the most likely peak season of availability while dark grey indicates a larger time period in which the peak season sometimes falls. Light grey represents times when a species is sometimes available but not at its peak of availability and white indicates regulatory closures or times when the species is generally not available.

Individual entries in the text contain more complete information on seasonal availability.

## Seasonal Availability of Wild Seafood

| Species | January | February | March | April | May | June | July | August | September | October | November | December |
|---|---|---|---|---|---|---|---|---|---|---|---|---|
| Anchovy | | | | | | | | | | | | |
| Black Sea Bass | | | | | | | | | | | | |
| Bluefish | | | | | | | | | | | | |
| Bream, Daurade* | | | | | | | | | | | | |
| Bream, Scup | | | | | | | | | | | | |
| Bream, Tai Snapper | | | | | | | | | | | | |
| Butterfish | | | | | | | | | | | | |
| Catfish* | | | | | | | | | | | | |
| Clam | | | | | | | | | | | | |
| Cod, Atlantic | | | | | | | | | | | | |
| Cod, Haddock | | | | | | | | | | | | |
| Cod, Hake | | | | | | | | | | | | |
| Cod, Pollack | | | | | | | | | | | | |
| Crab, Blue | | | | | | | | | | | | |
| Crab, Dungeness | | | | | | | | | | | | |
| Crab, Soft-Shell Blue | | | | | | | | | | | | |
| Crab, Stone | | | | | | | | | | | | |
| Crayfish* | | | | | | | | | | | | |
| Croaker, Atlantic | | | | | | | | | | | | |
| Dory, John | | | | | | | | | | | | |
| Grouper | | | | | | | | | | | | |
| Halibut, Alaska | | | | | | | | | | | | |
| Halibut, California | | | | | | | | | | | | |
| Jack, Amberjack | | | | | | | | | | | | |
| Jack, Hamachi* | | | | | | | | | | | | |
| Jack, Yellowtail | | | | | | | | | | | | |
| Lobster, Maine | | | | | | | | | | | | |
| Lobster, Spiny | | | | | | | | | | | | |
| Mackerel | | | | | | | | | | | | |
| Mahimahi | | | | | | | | | | | | |
| Monkfish | | | | | | | | | | | | |
| Mussel* | | | | | | | | | | | | |
| Octopus | | | | | | | | | | | | |
| Ono or Wahoo | | | | | | | | | | | | |

| Species | January | February | March | April | May | June | July | August | September | October | November | December |
|---|---|---|---|---|---|---|---|---|---|---|---|---|
| Opah | | | | | | | | | | | | |
| Oyster* | | | | | | | | | | | | |
| Rockfish, Pacific | | | | | | | | | | | | |
| Sablefish | | | | | | | | | | | | |
| Salmon | | | | | | | | | | | | |
| Salmon, Steelhead | | | | | | | | | | | | |
| Sandab | | | | | | | | | | | | |
| Sardine | | | | | | | | | | | | |
| Scallop, Bay, wild | | | | | | | | | | | | |
| Scallop, Sea | | | | | | | | | | | | |
| Sea Robin | | | | | | | | | | | | |
| Shad | | | | | | | | | | | | |
| Shrimp, Bay, Maine | | | | | | | | | | | | |
| Shrimp, Bay, Pacific | | | | | | | | | | | | |
| Shrimp, White, wild | | | | | | | | | | | | |
| Shrimp, Spot | | | | | | | | | | | | |
| Skate | | | | | | | | | | | | |
| Smelt | | | | | | | | | | | | |
| Snapper* | | | | | | | | | | | | |
| Sole or Flounder | | | | | | | | | | | | |
| Squid | | | | | | | | | | | | |
| Striped Bass | | | | | | | | | | | | |
| Striped Bass, hybrid* | | | | | | | | | | | | |
| Sturgeon* | | | | | | | | | | | | |
| Swordfish | | | | | | | | | | | | |
| Tilapia* | | | | | | | | | | | | |
| Trout or Char* | | | | | | | | | | | | |
| Tuna, Albacore | | | | | | | | | | | | |
| Tuna, Bigeye | | | | | | | | | | | | |
| Tuna, Bluefin | | | | | | | | | | | | |
| Tuna, Yellowfin | | | | | | | | | | | | |
| Weakfish | | | | | | | | | | | | |
| Whelk or Periwinkle | | | | | | | | | | | | |
| White Sea Bass | | | | | | | | | | | | |
| Wreckfish | | | | | | | | | | | | |

* Indicates aquacultured seafood, which experience little variation of availability.

**Legend:**
- Regulatory closure or times when species is generally not available
- Species is sometimes available but not at peak of availability
- Larger time period of availability
- Most likely peak season of availability

In the fall of 2006, two studies comparing the benefits and risks of seafood consumption, one by the Harvard School of Public Health ("Seafood Choices: Balancing Benefits and Risks") and the other by The Institute of Medicine of the National Academies ("Fish Intake, Contaminants, and Human Health: Evaluating the Risks and the Benefits"), came to the same conclusion: The health benefits of eating seafood far outweigh the risks. Fish consumption was shown to be associated with myriad health benefits, from reduced risk of cardiac death to improvements in child brain development.

The risk from chemicals found in fish from environmental pollution, including mercury, PCBs, and dioxins were put in perspective: 90 percent of the PCBs and dioxins in the U.S. food supply come from foods other than seafood and no evidence was found linking low-level mercury exposure from seafood consumption to harmful effects on healthy adults.

Dariush Mozaffarian, the lead author for the Harvard study, which compiled data from hundreds of studies concerned with seafood and health, said, "The benefits of eating fish greatly outweigh the risks . . . It is striking how much greater both the amount of the evidence and the size of the health effect are for health benefits compared with health risks. Seafood is likely the single most important food one can consume for good health."

That said, not all fish are created equal and common sense tells us that some segments of society, pregnant or nursing mothers and those trying to become pregnant (see Omega-3s, Mercury, and Pregancy, page 407), young children, and those with compromised immune systems should be extra cautious. Seafood is one of the safest and healthiest foods we can eat, but by following the checklist below we can ensure that we are making a healthy choice even healthier.

Here is a checklist to choosing healthy seafood:

- *Choose seafood from the bottom of the marine food web:* Mollusks such as clams, mussels, oysters, and scallops that filter their food from the sea are nutritionally well balanced and accumulate plant sterols that interfere with the uptake of cholesterol. Some finfish are also filter feeders: Sardines, anchovies, herring, menhaden, shad, and sockeye salmon are rich in heart-healthy omega-3 fatty acids and do not bio-accumulate pollutants.

- *Choose seafood that is one step up the food web:* soles and flounders, haddock, skate, squid, crabs and shrimp, farmed catfish, and tilapia. While many of these "whitefish" species contain only low to moderate amounts of omega-3s, they are less apt to bio-accumulate pollutants.

- *Choose short-lived fish:* examples include mahimahi, salmon, mackerel, sardines, herring, anchovies, squid, farmed rainbow trout, and the short-lived tunas (skipjack, bonito, and young Pacific albacore). When eating long-lived predatory fish from the top of the food web, such as yellowfin and bigeye tuna, swordfish, striped bass or grouper, choose smaller, younger individuals.

- *Choose a variety of species from different locales:* When eating seafood from freshwater lakes, streams, and urban estuaries—waters favored by recreational fishermen—do not repeatedly eat the same type of fish taken from the same area. Seafood that comes from clean offshore waters far from industrialized areas are a good choice: Alaska pollock and cod, hake, whiting, king crab, Pacific salmon, sablefish, haddock, and mackerel.

- *Choose fatty fish high in heart-healthy omega-3s:* salmon, sardines, sablefish, mackerel, smelts, herring, shad, anchovies, small tuna, arctic char, and rainbow trout.

## THE SEARCH FOR SUSTAINABLE SEAFOOD

In less than the span of a lifetime we've seen the world's oceans transformed from pristine wilderness teeming with fish to shopworn waters that are overfished and battered by pollution. The reasons are many and varied but the greatest culprit has been industrialization. More than 50 percent of the world's population lives within a few miles of the sea and more are moving there every day. Filled wetlands and dammed rivers are unable to absorb the constant load of chemical fertilizer and animal waste flowing to the sea from industrialized agriculture. The resulting algal blooms and subsequent die-off (eutrophication) have created huge oxygen-depleted dead zones in the ocean. Every eleven months the equivalent of an Exxon-*Valdez* worth of oil is washed from our streets and millions of pounds of mercury and other pollutants are washed from the air.

The development of highly efficient fishing technologies combined with government subsidies for bigger and ever more powerful boats and the modern fishery manager's imperative of "maximum sustainable yield" fisheries has created industrialized fishing, which is simply not sustainable. The ocean's biodiversity and the world's food supply are threatened.

Ominous sounding? Yes. But, at the same time, I feel more positive about the future of the oceans and our fisheries than I have for years, because we have begun to recognize the problems and are talking about the solutions. In recent years there has been a powerful surge of interest in ocean conservation and sustainable fisheries. Seafood lovers, fishermen, divers, surfers, environmentalists, and even legislators have come to realize the importance of good stewardship of our seas and the rebuilding of healthy fisheries. Millions of individuals and hundreds of organizations have recognized healthy oceans and sustainable fishing as being vital to the health, happiness, and safety of our children and the world they will live in.

The seas are resilient and if given the chance will return to their former purity and riches. But we need to work together to do the things it will take to save our oceans. As citizens there are many steps we can take to protect the ocean and its diverse fish and plant life. As consumers the most important step we can take is to encourage sustainable fishing by making a wise choice at the market, choosing sustainable seafood.

## THE WISE CHOICE ■ ■ ■

While we can all agree that some fisheries are sustainable and some are not, the fact is the choice is often not a simple one. Choosing sustainable seafood is complicated by more factors than can be listed. Thousands of species that are caught in hundreds of ways pass through many different hands to come to market from all over the world.

The Choosing Sustainable Seafood sections of *Fish Forever* answer the questions that make choosing wisely easier: How was it caught or raised? Where was it caught? Does it reproduce quickly? Are fishery managers doing a good job? In some cases making the wise choice is simple, but in other instances the wise choice is a difficult one—a seafood population may be healthy but the method of fishing is bad for the environment, or populations are well managed in the South Atlantic but not in the Gulf of Mexico. At times like these I may encourage only buying a species when it is caught by sustainable methods, or from an area where stocks are healthy. At other times, I simply let the information speak for itself. By providing guidance rather than a "green list" of choices I hope to give the reader the tools to make their own wise choices at the market.

Here is a list of things we can do to support and encourage sustainable fisheries, both in the market and in our daily living:

- Choose seafood that is caught by sustainable fishing methods, which do not harm reefs and other important areas where fish live and breed (essential fish habitat) or kill a lot of juvenile fish, birds, turtles, and marine mammals (bycatch) that just happen to be in the neighborhood. Hook and line, trap, pot, and harpoon are almost always good; others may or may not be. (See Fishing and Aquaculture Methods Appendix, page 418.)

- Choose seafood that is raised by sustainable aquaculture methods that do not spread disease, pollute, or use wild fish for food. (See Fishing and Aquaculture Methods Appendix, page 418.)

- Support small-boat fishermen, who use sustainable methods of fishing. These fishermen have an interest in seeing local fisheries remain sustainable.

- Shop at stores that label their seafood. New country-of-origin labeling rules mandate that all seafood sold in supermarkets be labeled as to origin and whether it is wild or aquacultured. Any good fish market should label its seafood as to how and where it was captured or cultured and if it is wild or aquacultured.

- Buy seafood that carries the Marine Stewardship Council or FishWise point-of- purchase sustainable seafood label.

- Eat more seafood that is short lived and reproduces quickly: Squid, clams, mussels, oysters and scallops, anchovies, herring, sardines, smelts, mahimahi, and wild salmon are a few.

- Try something new: A handful of species make up most of the seafood we eat. Consumer demand plays a big part in overfishing and encouraging nonsustainable aquaculture. Chilean sea bass and orange roughy stocks were crushed by consumer demand and the reason we have so many shrimp and salmon farms is because most of us eat the same seafood day after day.

- Ask the person behind the counter or on the phone selling fish questions: How and where was it caught, are populations healthy, and is it considered a sustainable fishery? If they answer your questions satisfactorily, you have a good fishmonger; if not, keep asking and you'll drag him or her into the arena.

- Learn as much as you can: Join Seafood Choices Alliance, a group of chef's consumers, seafood professionals, and fishermen dedicated to supporting sustainable fisheries (www.seafoodchoices.com). Visit Monterey Bay Aquarium's Seafood Watch Program at www.mbayaq.org or any of the other sustainable seafood lists sponsored by various organizations.

- Vote for legislators that support good ocean and fishery policy. Seafood lovers, fishermen, divers, surfers, environmentalists, and others make up a huge constituency that has the power to persuade Congress and state legislatures to take action to protect our oceans. The Marine Fish Conservation Network's web site at www.conservefish.org is a good place to learn about the issues and Ocean Champions at www.oceanchampions.org is a nonpartisan organization that supports legislators on either side of the aisle who favor good ocean and fishery policy.

- Prevent global warming. The ocean environment is fragile; the effects of global warming threaten important coral habitat and the phytoplankton and other tiny marine organisms that are food for all the creatures of the sea.

- Don't pollute. Lawn, household, and automotive chemicals end up in the ocean if not used and disposed of properly.

- Support organic and other agricultural practices that promote good land use and don't use chemical fertilizers and pesticides.

- Encourage fisheries that are making improvements in how they fish. Innovations are legion. Trapdoors on shrimp nets save turtles, longliners avoid birds, and pingers on swordfish gill nets protect marine mammals.

- Support aquaculture that is making improvements in how they raise fish. Farmers who follow "best practices" reduce their effect on the environment and wild fish.

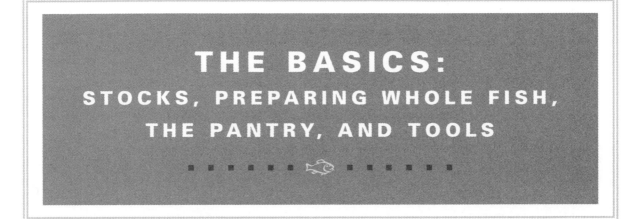

# THE BASICS:
## STOCKS, PREPARING WHOLE FISH, THE PANTRY, AND TOOLS

The basics will carry you through the recipes in this book and further. Making stocks and preparing whole fish for cooking are relatively simple skills that will stay with you and be helpful always. More detailed seafood technique requires a dedicated work of its own, such as Rick Stein's book, *Complete Seafood*.

The pantry is unusual in that it is not full of ingredients but rather it is full of basic ingredient techniques you'll find helpful in the kitchen, from hints as simple as how to mince garlic and make fresh bread crumbs to recipes for mayonnaise and curry powder. The section on tools is just that—a look at seafood and kitchen tools that will make preparing and cooking seafood easier.

## STOCKS

Good stocks are the basis of great soups, stews, chowders, and sauces. They can be as complex as a fish and shellfish stock with twenty ingredients or as simple as a few mussels steamed in water and wine. The more you make fish stocks, the easier it becomes and the more you'll appreciate their versatility. Make extra and freeze some for convenience. If the ingredients are fresh, most of the work is done.

# FISH STOCK

The secret of good fish stock is to be sure the bones are fresh and to use plenty of vegetables, seasonings, and aromatics. A pound or two of mussels or clams, or a few leftover crab, shrimp, or lobster shells added to the stock will greatly enrich the flavor. Remember that fish stock should only be simmered; the calcium in fish bones easily dissolves, and if boiled the stock can become cloudy and taste chalky.

3 pounds fish bones and heads, gills
    removed

2 tablespoons olive oil

2 leeks, white and light green parts only,
    rinsed and chopped

1 onion, chopped

3 stalks celery with tops, chopped

1 carrot, peeled and chopped

½ small fennel bulb, trimmed and chopped,
    or a few fennel seeds

Stripped zest of 1 lemon and 1 orange

1-inch piece fresh ginger, peeled
    and chopped

6 or 8 coriander seeds, cracked

6 peppercorns, cracked

10 parsley stems

1 thyme sprig (optional)

2 cups dry white wine

8 cups cold water

Salt and freshly squeezed lemon juice
    to taste

1. Clean the bones well; scrape out the blood line, which lies along either side of the backbone. I sometimes use a handful of coarse salt to scrub out the nooks and crannies in the belly cavity. Rinse the bones well to remove any salt, residual blood, or slime. Set aside.

2. In a large nonreactive stockpot, heat the olive oil over medium heat and sauté the leeks, onion, celery, carrot, and fennel until soft, about 5 minutes. Turn off the heat and allow the vegetables to cool for several minutes. Add the citrus zest, ginger, coriander seeds, peppercorns, parsley, and optional thyme. Place the well-cleaned and -rinsed bones on top and cover with the white wine and cold water.

3. Bring to a simmer over medium heat, skimming off any foam that rises to the top. Gently simmer, uncovered, for 20 to 25 minutes. Strain the stock through a fine-meshed sieve, leaving behind the last bit of cloudy liquid. Season with salt and lemon juice. Store for up to 2 days in the refrigerator, bringing the stock to a boil every 2 days if kept longer, or freeze for up to 2 months.

# SHELLFISH STOCK

A stock made of crab, shrimp, crayfish, or lobster shells is a great base for a bisque, chowder, risotto, or gumbo. (See also Quick Lobster Stock, page 28.) Use whatever vegetables and aromatics happen to be on hand—it can be as simple and quick as sautéing the shells with a few vegetables, then simmering in water. Or try the more flavorful stock below.

2 tablespoons olive oil or unsalted butter

3 pounds crab, shrimp, crayfish, or
   lobster shells

2 leeks, white and light green parts only,
   rinsed and chopped

1 onion, chopped

1 carrot, peeled and chopped

3 stalks celery with tops, chopped

1 pound mussels and or clams (optional),
   scrubbed and debearded if necessary

3 tomatoes, chopped (about 1 cup)

Chunk of fresh ginger, chopped

6 or 8 coriander seeds, crushed in a mortar

A few fennel seeds, or 1 star anise pod

6 peppercorns, cracked

Stripped zest of 1 lemon

2 cups dry white wine

4 cups water

Salt and freshly squeezed lemon juice
   to taste

1. In a nonreactive stockpot, heat the olive oil or melt the butter over medium heat and sauté the shells for 5 minutes. Add the leeks, onion, carrot, and celery and cook until they begin to soften, about 5 minutes. If using mussels or clams, add them here; they really give depth of flavor. Add the tomatoes, ginger, coriander, fennel, peppercorns, and lemon zest and cook for 5 minutes.

2. Cover with the white wine and water and bring to a simmer over medium heat, skimming off any foam that rises to the top. Simmer, uncovered, for 30 minutes. Strain the stock through a fine-meshed sieve and season with salt and lemon juice. Store for up to 2 days in the refrigerator, bringing the stock to a boil every 2 days if kept longer, or freeze for up to 2 months.

# QUICK LOBSTER STOCK

2 tablespoons unsalted butter

Reserved lobster shells from two
   1¼-pound Maine lobsters

1 onion, chopped

1 carrot, chopped

1 stalk celery, chopped

½ cup chopped tomato

4 cups water

1 cup dry white wine

Salt and freshly squeezed lemon juice
   to taste

1. In a nonreactive stockpot, heat the unsalted butter over medium heat and sauté the shells for 5 minutes. Add the onion, carrot, and celery and cook until they begin to soften, about 5 minutes. Add the tomato and cook for 5 minutes.

2. Cover with water and wine and bring to a simmer over medium heat, skimming off any foam that rises to the top. Simmer, uncovered, for 30 minutes. Strain the stock through a fine-meshed sieve and season with salt and lemon juice to taste.

# QUICK CLAM OR MUSSEL STOCK

Bottled clam juice is a poor substitute for fish stock; most brands taste downright bad. It's better to use chicken stock, vegetable stock, or even wine and water rather than chance ruining your stew or chowder. That, or make a quick stock from mussels or clams or a combination of the two. The mussel or clam meat, if not overcooked, can be used in other recipes.

Use whatever vegetables and aromatics happen to be on hand. Your stock can be as simple and quick as just steaming shellfish open in wine and water with a few aromatics, or you can make the more flavorful Mediterranean-influenced shellfish stock below.

This is a very concentrated stock that can be diluted with water by as much as half when using.

2 tablespoons olive oil

1 leek, white and green parts only,
   rinsed and chopped

1 onion, chopped

2 stalks celery, chopped

Outer leaves and feathery tops of
   1 small fennel bulb

Stripped zest and juice of ½ orange

½ cup chopped tomatoes

1 cup dry white wine

2 cups cold water

2 pounds clams or mussels, scrubbed and
    debearded if necessary, or 1 pound each

Freshly squeezed lemon juice, salt, and
    freshly ground pepper to taste

1. In a nonreactive stockpot, heat the olive oil
   over medium heat and sauté the leek, onion,
   and celery until soft, about 5 minutes. Add
   the fennel, orange zest and juice, and tomatoes. Increase the heat to high and cook for 5
   minutes.

2. Add the white wine and cold water and bring
   to a boil. Reduce the heat and gently simmer,
   uncovered, for 15 minutes. Add the mussels
   and clams; simmer for 10 minutes. If you want
   to use the meats for another dish, take them
   out just after the shells open so they do not
   overcook. Strain the stock through a fine-
   meshed sieve and season with lemon juice,
   salt, and pepper. Store for up to 2 days in the
   refrigerator, bringing the stock to a boil every
   2 days if kept longer, or freeze for up to 2
   months.

## VEGETABLE STOCK

MAKES 6 CUPS

A light vegetable stock can be used as the base for a quick and easy stew of fish and vegetables, bringing all the ingredients together, or for simply braising or poaching fish. It works particularly well with stronger flavored fish such as salmon, tuna, or shad, which can easily clash with a fish or shellfish stock.

2 tablespoons olive oil

1 large onion, coarsely chopped

1 leek, including green parts, rinsed
    and chopped

3 stalks celery, with leaves, coarsely
    chopped

2 carrots, peeled and coarsely chopped

½ bulb fennel, trimmed and coarsely
    chopped, or ½ teaspoon fennel seeds

2 garlic cloves, smashed

8 cups water

½ cup coarsely chopped fresh flat-leaf
    parsley

½ teaspoon black peppercorns, cracked

2 thyme sprigs

1 teaspoon salt

In a large, heavy pot, heat the oil over medium
heat. Add the onion and cook until soft,
about 5 minutes. Add the leek, celery, carrots,

fennel, and garlic; cook for 4 or 5 minutes more, stirring occasionally. Add all the remaining ingredients and bring to a boil. Skim any foam that rises to the top. Reduce the heat and simmer, uncovered, for 45 minutes. Pour the stock through a fine-meshed sieve, pushing on the vegetables with the back of a wooden spoon to extract all the liquid. Cover and store for up to 2 days in the refrigerator, bringing the stock to a boil every 2 days if kept longer, or freeze for up to 2 months.

## COURT BOUILLON, OR POACHING LIQUOR

MAKES 6 CUPS

Court bouillon is typically used to impart flavor to seafood when poaching or braising. The resulting liquid left over after cooking was traditionally used as the basis for flour and egg–based sauces that were often finished with cream. Contemporary cooks are more apt to thicken the court bouillon after cooking with pureed sorrel, watercress, herbs, tomatoes, or mushrooms to make vegetable-thickened sauce. Because a court bouillon is very acidic it can be used in emulsified sauces where oils and acidic ingredients, such as verjus, flavored vinegar, or citrus juice, are beaten together until thickened.

8 cups water

½ cup white wine vinegar

1 leek, white part only, rinsed and chopped

2 onions, chopped

2 stalks celery with tops, chopped

1 carrot, peeled and chopped

1 teaspoon salt

Pinch of cayenne pepper

1 thyme sprig

A few parsley sprigs

6 or 8 coriander seeds

A few fennel seeds

Stripped zest of 1 lemon

Freshly squeezed lemon juice and
   salt to taste

In a nonreactive stockpot, combine everything except the lemon juice and salt. Bring to a boil, reduce the heat, and simmer for 30 minutes. Pour the court bouillon through a fine-meshed sieve, pushing on the vegetables with the back of a wooden spoon to extract all the liquid, and season with the salt and lemon juice. Cover and store for up to 2 days in the refrigerator, bringing the stock to a boil every 2 days if kept longer, or freeze for up to 2 months.

A perfectly cooked fillet of fish can be exquisite—but eating the whole fish is a completely different affair.

Serving whole fish at the table slows down the pace of the meal, creating a more relaxed, friendly atmosphere. It beckons us to share and to eat with our hands. It brings to mind a gathering of friends on a warm, sunny day in the Greek Isles or Turkey, where whole fish is often found at the table.

With a fish fillet, the texture, flavor, and doneness is usually pretty much the same from start to finish, whereas the texture of a whole fish may range from soft and succulent to crispy and crunchy; the flavor is mild and sweet in places and darkly intense in others. Yes, it's messy, and it has to be eaten more carefully, but it's delicious.

When a whole fish is cooked over charcoal or fried, the skin becomes crisp, like that of a well-roasted chicken. Deliciously chewy, overdone pieces of meat can be stripped away from the flanks near the tail. The fins, crisped from the heat, break apart into crunchy bits that taste like a cross between dried nori and bacon scraped from the bottom of a cast-iron pan.

The muscular tenderloin near the shoulder of a whole fish is always moister than the same cut could ever hope to be when cooked as a fillet. The belly meat, usually lost in filleting, slides away from the bones, greasy and delicious, slippery with fat.

Then there are the fisherman's favorites, the "tongues," a misnomer really, for they're not really tongues but two small muscular morsels, dark and intense, nestled under the chin, and the cheeks with their scalloplike texture. For the adventuresome, the sounds (the air bladder) are surprisingly crisp and toothsome.

All that remains are a pile of bones and scraps. But don't throw them out just yet. Surprising little nuggets of flesh are hidden in nooks and crannies, so delicious it would be a shame to miss them. Suck the last juices from the bones and your fingers.

Cooking a whole fish can be intimidating the first time or two, but the effort is well worth the reward. Just as cooking whole lobster or crab is a part of every good cook's repertoire, so should be cooking whole fish.

### PREPARING
### WHOLE ROUND FISH ▪ ▪ ▪

Most fish shops will scale, gill, and gut your fish if you ask. Some will charge for the service. If you catch your own or just want to try your hand at preparing a fish for cooking whole, here is the technique: Scale the fish first; to keep scales from flying all over the kitchen, fill the sink with water and scale the fish underwater.

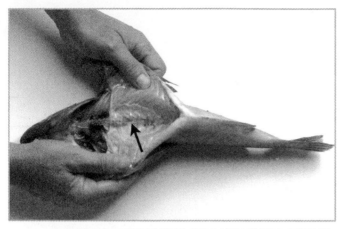

A. A WHOLE ROCKFISH WITH GILLS AND VISCERA REMOVED. ARROW INDICATES THE LOCATION OF THE FISH'S KIDNEYS, WHICH MUST STILL BE REMOVED.

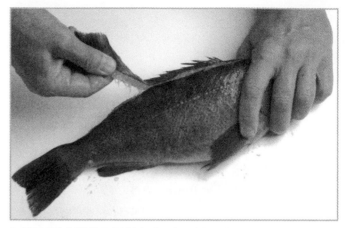

B. PULLING OUT THE DORSAL FIN, WHICH HAS BEEN INCISED FOR EASY REMOVAL.

C. A WHOLE ROUND FISH, READY FOR COOKING. DORSAL AND ANAL FINS HAVE BEEN REMOVED TO ALLOW EASY REMOVAL OF THE FLESH AFTER COOKING. THE DIAGONAL SLICES IN THE FLESH ENSURE EVEN COOKING.

With a curry comb or fish scaler (see page 40), scrape repeatedly from the tail toward the head. Be sure to scrape every nook and cranny: under the pectoral fins, next to the dorsal spines, and all around the tail area.

To remove the gills and viscera, insert the tip of a boning knife in the anal vent; slit the belly open all the way to the chin. With a pair of scissors, snip the gills at the collarbone and throat, where they are anchored. Pull out the gills and viscera and discard.

If your fishmonger cleaned your fish for you, this is probably as far as he will go, but there is still more to do. Inside the belly cavity you will be able to see what looks like two ropes of dark-colored blood, one on either side of the backbone. These are the kidneys (see photo A above). Slice open the thin, translucent membrane on either side of the backbone to expose the kidneys and scrape them away with the tip of a knife or a metal spoon and rinse well.

Next, remove the large dorsal fin that runs the length of the fish's back. Use a small sharp knife to make two quarter-inch-deep incisions along the entire length of the fin, one on either side. Grasp the dorsal fin at the tail end and pull toward the head, removing the entire fin with spines (see photo B above). Repeat the same process for the anal fin located on the ventral side in front of the tail (see photo C at left). This allows the meat to be easily and completely lifted off the bone when cooked.

Check the entire fish for any remaining scales, paying particular attention to the area where the dorsal and anal fins were. Rinse the entire fish well, including the belly cavity.

Cut three or four diagonal slices one quarter to one half inch deep at one-inch intervals into the thickest part of the flesh on either side of the fish (see photo C on page 32). This will ensure even cooking.

### PREPARING
### WHOLE FLATFISH ■ ■ ■

There is no need to remove the extremely fine scales of small flatfish. Begin to clean the fish by making one decisive cut from just behind the head to behind the anal vent, removing the head, gills, and viscera (see photo A below).

If you prefer to leave the head on, follow the directions for removing the gills and viscera without cutting off the head in the second paragraph of the Preparing Whole Round Fish section (page 32).

Inside the belly cavity, slit open the membrane on either side of the backbone to expose

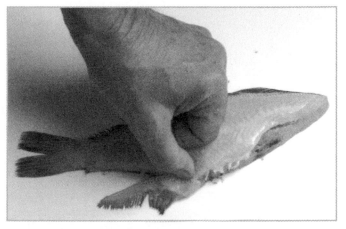

B. PROBE TO FEEL FOR THE NATURAL SEPARATION BETWEEN THE SMALL BONES, WHICH CONTROL THE VENTRAL FIN, AND THE LARGER SKELETAL BONES.

A. ONE DECISIVE CUT REMOVES THE HEAD, GILLS, AND VISCERA OF A SMALL WHOLE FLATFISH.

C. A PAN-READY FLATFISH, TRIMMED FOR COOKING. PROPER REMOVAL OF THE DORSAL AND VENTRAL FINS ALLOW FOR EASY, BONE-FREE REMOVAL OF THE FLESH AFTER COOKING.

the dark-colored blood line (kidneys); scrape them away with the tip of a knife or a metal spoon. Rinse the entire fish well, including the belly cavity.

The dorsal and ventral fins that run the entire length of the body on both sides of the fish must be properly removed to ensure that the fish will be free of bones when cooked. Probe with your finger to find the natural separation between the small bones, which control the dorsal and ventral fins, and the larger skeletal bones, which connect to the backbone (see photos B and C on page 33). Cut at this natural separation to ensure that all the bones can be removed with ease when the fish is cooked.

Once cooked, the top fillet can be easily lifted off and turned over on the plate. The exposed skeleton, which will remain intact, can be easily lifted away, leaving two boneless fillets on the plate.

## THE PANTRY: BASIC INGREDIENTS AND TECHNIQUES

This pantry is not about choosing ingredients—for the most part I leave that up to you—but rather it is mostly simple techniques that will help you work smarter and more efficiently in the kitchen.

BREAD CRUMBS, FRESH • Fresh bread crumbs that don't come in a box are a revelation; it's like comparing canned green beans to fresh. To make, simply remove the crust from good country-style bread or even a commercial white bread, cut into one-inch cubes, and grind in a small food processor or a blender.

BUTTER, CLARIFIED • In a small saucepan, melt unsalted butter. Bring the melted butter to a boil over medium-low heat and cook for ten to fifteen minutes. The water will bubble and crackle until it evaporates; then the milk solids will begin to fry and stick to the bottom of the pan. Skim off any foam that rises to the top. Gently pour off the golden clarified butter, leaving any milk solids in the pan. Clarified butter will keep, covered, in the refrigerator for several weeks.

CRÈME FRAÎCHE • Put one cup heavy cream (not ultrapasteurized) and two tablespoons buttermilk in a clean jar. Set the jar in the sun for two or three hours, or gently warm in a water bath to 85°F; leave at room temperature overnight. The next morning, it will be thick and tangy and can be used in place of sour cream or Mexican crema. In cooler climates, the cream may take longer to thicken; if in the morning the cream has not thickened, leave it in a sunny window or warm place for several more hours. Refrigerate for up to two weeks.

**CITRUS, TO SEGMENT** • With a sharp, thin-bladed knife, cut off both ends of the fruit. Place the fruit, cut-side up, on a cutting board. Following the contour of the fruit, cut from top to bottom to remove the skin and white inner membrane down to the pulp. Free the segments by cutting along both sides of the membrane that separates each segment from the next. Do this over a bowl to collect any juices. With a little practice, you'll find you need only to cut one side of a segment, then turn the knife away from you and push to make the segment jump out of the fruit. Squeeze what's left of the fruit over the bowl to collect the juice.

**CURRY POWDER** • Indian cooks toast and grind custom spice mixtures for every meal. It really isn't very difficult and doesn't take that long, but I'm lazy and not Indian. When I prepare my own curry spice mixes, I always make extra so I have a little around the house for when I'm in a rush but want a little Southeast Asian flavor.

## CURRY SPICE MIX NO. 1

MAKES ½ CUP

This mixture is great for spicing cauliflower or other vegetables to be roasted in the oven. It's also a flavorful and fragrant seasoning for quickly sautéed mild-flavored fish such as sole. To sauté, dredge the fish in the dry spices; for broiling, grilling, or baking, make a thick paste by adding olive oil and lemon juice to the spices, then smear the paste on the fish before cooking.

1 tablespoon mustard seeds

1 teaspoon cardamom seeds (from 8 to 10 green cardamom pods)

3 tablespoons ground turmeric

1 tablespoon sweet paprika

1 teaspoon cayenne pepper

1 tablespoon salt

1. In a cast-iron skillet over medium heat, toast the mustard and cardamom seeds until fragrant, about 1 minute. Grind to a powder in a spice grinder and mix with the turmeric, paprika, cayenne, and salt.

2. Put the mix in an airtight container, shake well, and store in a cool, dry place for up to 1 month.

THE BASICS

35

# CURRY SPICE MIX NO. 2

This mixture is more complex than No. 1 and is perfect for a stew, or for broiling a more assertive-flavored fish like salmon, amberjack, opah, or mackerel.

1 tablespoon mustard seeds

1 teaspoon cardamom seeds (from 8
   to 10 green cardamom pods)

1 teaspoon cumin seeds

½ teaspoon fennel seeds

3 tablespoons ground turmeric

1 tablespoon sweet paprika

1 teaspoon cayenne pepper

1 tablespoon salt

1. In a cast-iron skillet over medium heat, toast all the seeds together until fragrant, about 1 minute. Grind to a powder in a spice grinder and mix with the turmeric, paprika, cayenne, and salt.

2. Put the mix in an airtight container, shake well, and store in a cool, dry place for up to 1 month.

**DRIED CHILES, TO TOAST** • Dried chiles should be shiny and pliable. Rinse off any dust and pat the chiles dry with a towel. Cut them open and discard the stems and seeds. In a dry cast-iron skillet over medium heat, toast the chiles, turning them frequently, for several minutes until they darken and become crisp and aromatic. Or roast dried chiles on a baking sheet in a preheated 350°F oven, turning them a few times, until crisp. This could take as little as five minutes.

**GARLIC, TO MINCE** • Smash the peeled clove to a smear with the side of a French chef's knife. If there are green shoots in the center of the clove, be sure to remove them or the garlic will be bitter. Sprinkle on a little coarse salt, and mince. When using garlic in blender or food processor recipes, always mince it in this manner or mash it with salt in a mortar with a pestle before continuing with the recipe.

**MAYONNAISE, TO MAKE** • We all have a jar of commercial mayonnaise in the cupboard and in a pinch it works well, In less than a minute commercial mayonnaise can be turned into Red Pepper Mayonnaise (page 118) or Chipotle Mayonnaise (page 267). But homemade mayonnaise is delicious on its own terms and surprisingly easy to make; it will really make a Tartar Sauce (page 273) shine. The same technique can be used to make any of the aïolis found throughout the book. It's a skill well worth mastering.

# MAYONNAISE

1 large egg yolk

1 teaspoon dry mustard

Pinch of kosher salt, plus more to taste

1 teaspoon warm water

¼ cup mild olive oil

½ cup refined peanut or other mild-
    flavored oil

Warm water as needed (optional)

1 tablespoon freshly squeezed lemon juice

¼ teaspoon cayenne pepper

Start with all the ingredients and utensils at room temperature. In a medium bowl, combine the egg yolk, dry mustard, the pinch of salt, and the water; whisk until smooth. Gradually whisk in the oils, starting with just a few drops at a time; as the sauce begins to thicken, add the rest of the oil in a slow, fine stream. If the mayonnaise becomes too thick, thin it with a bit of warm water. Whisk in the lemon juice and cayenne; season with salt to taste. Store in a clean jar in the refrigerator for several days.

## NUTS:

**ALMONDS, TO BLANCH OR TOAST** • To blanch almonds, drop raw almonds in boiling water for one minute, then drain in a sieve. Working quickly while the nuts are hot, pinch the pointed end of each almond, which will cause it to slip out of its skin. To toast almonds, either blanched or those that still have their skins, spread them on a baking sheet and bake in a preheated 300°F oven for twenty minutes, or until light brown in the center. Stir once or twice during cooking so they cook evenly.

**HAZELNUTS AND PEANUTS, TO SKIN** • Toast as for almonds, above, then wrap in a terrycloth towel and rub vigorously to remove the skins.

**PINE NUTS, TO TOAST** • Toast the nuts in a preheated, lightly oiled cast-iron skillet over medium heat, shaking the skillet frequently so they toast evenly. Cook for three to four minutes, or until golden.

**WALNUTS, TO TOAST** • Spread the walnuts on a baking sheet and toast in a preheated 275°F oven for ten minutes, or until they are light golden and begin to smell toasty. Walnuts burn easily, so it is better to err on the side of undercooked. Stir once or twice during cooking so they cook evenly. Or toast them in a dry cast-iron skillet over medium heat for five minutes, shaking the pan frequently.

**OILS** • For sautéing, making mayonnaise, vinaigrette, or other sauces, I often call for "mild-flavored olive oil." My local store sells an extra-virgin olive oil from Sicily whose flavor is good but not overpowering, and it is relatively inexpensive. I save my spicy, expensive extra-virgin Tuscan oil for finishing a dish by adding a drizzle of oil at the end. For high heat cooking, such as deep-frying or panfrying, and at times when mild-flavored oil is called for, I favor *refined* peanut oil, an oil with a nice, fresh flavor and good stability. Refined peanut oil is considered safe for those allergic to peanuts. The *unrefined* peanut oil called for in many Asian recipes is too rich in peanut flavor for most of the recipes in this book. However, note that today, most widely available oils, including canola, corn, peanut, and soy, are genetically modified. And refined oils are not as healthy as unrefined oils. If you are concerned about these issues, choose organic and unrefined oils.

**OLIVES, TO PIT** • Place olives between clean kitchen towels and pound lightly with a mallet or the bottom of a saucepan. Pick out the pits and discard.

**PEPPERS, TO ROAST AND PEEL** • Completely blacken the pepper over an open flame or under the broiler. Place the pepper in a bowl, cover with a plate, and let cool for ten minutes. Remove the pepper from the bowl; peel and wipe away most of the blackened skin. Seed and stem the pepper.

**PEPPERCORNS, TO CRACK** • Cracked pepper provides a surprisingly hot bite to a dish, and just like freshly ground pepper, freshly cracked peppercorns are far superior in flavor to "prepared" cracked pepper. Crack peppercorns in a mortar by lightly pounding with a pestle, or put the peppercorns on a cutting board and roll over them with the bottom of a heavy saucepan. With one hand on the far rim to steady the pan, use the handle for leverage to push down and crack the peppercorns while rolling over them.

**SALT, TO SEASON** • Kosher salt, traditionally used for "koshering," or curing, foods, contains no iodine or other additives. Its large, flaky grains do not cling together, so it is easy to sprinkle evenly over food and it measures consistently. The unique structure of kosher salt makes it very light and thus less salty. Kosher salt, by volume, is about one half as salty as table salt or sea salt. Trace amounts of minerals found in sea salt provide flavors not found in table or kosher salt; coarse sea salt added to taste at the end of a recipe provides a burst of flavor.

**SPICES, TO TOAST** • Spices are always best when toasted and freshly ground. Toast them in a dry cast-iron sauté pan or skillet over medium heat until the smell of spices fills the air, then let cool. Use a mortar and pestle to crack spices such as black peppercorns or coriander for a mixture of fine, medium, and coarse grains. Use a spice grinder for a finer, more consistent grind.

**TAMARIND WATER** • The six- to eight-inch-long brown tamarind pods, resembling fat broad-bean pods, contain large seeds and a very tart pulp, which is used as a souring agent in South-east Asian, Indian, and Latin cuisines. Whole pods can often be found in ethnic markets. To prepare: Peel, soak the pulp in hot water, and press the softened pulp and liquid through a strainer. Otherwise, buy bottled concentrate or block pulp and dilute in hot water.

**TOMATOES, TO PEEL, SEED, OR SHRED** • The easiest way to peel a single tomato is to spear it with a long-handled fork and hold it over an open gas flame until the skin splits. It can then be easily peeled. To peel and seed a quantity of tomatoes, cut a small cross through the skin on the bottom of each tomato. Blanch the tomatoes in boiling water for thirty seconds, or until the skin begins to peel away at the cut in the bottom of the tomato. Remove the tomatoes from the water and quickly peel them while still hot. To seed: Core and cut the tomato in half horizontally. Hold the tomato half, cut-side down, and give it a squeeze and a hard shake at the same time to remove the seeds. To shred: Cut the unpeeled tomato in half, squeeze out the seeds, and shred the flesh side on the largest holes of a box grater; discard the skin.

## BASIC TOOLS

Most of the tools listed below are probably already found in the average well-equipped kitchen, but there are also some helpful seafood-specific tools that one may want to consider purchasing.

**BLENDERS AND FOOD PROCESSORS** • These are found in nearly all kitchens today; I know many people are wizards with them and use them for everything. I use a blender for making tomatillo or red chile salsa and I use my three-cup food processor for making fresh bread crumbs.

**KNIVES** • The most important tools of all in any kitchen are a good French chef's knife, a paring knife, a thin-bladed fillet knife for fish, and a cleaver for bones; buy a sharpening stone and steel and learn how to use them.

**MANDOLINE** • Mandolines are great for making juliennes of green mango or slicing potatoes or other vegetables the same thickness so they cook evenly. An inexpensive Japanese mandoline is fine, though the more expensive French version stays sharp longer.

**MICROPLANE** • These fine kitchen rasps are perfect for adding a bit of lemon zest, garlic, or ginger to a dish.

**MORTAR AND PESTLE** • Indispensable for quickly mashing garlic, ginger, and chiles; cracking black pepper or other spices; and making pesto or nuoc cham. A mortar that holds two or three cups is sufficient for home use. I like the coarse texture of wood for wet ingredients such as garlic or chiles, while stone seems to work better for hard spices.

**NEEDLE-NOSE PLIERS** • Use these to remove pinbones from fish.

**SPICE GRINDER** • Freshly toasted and ground spices make a great difference in flavoring a dish. Use a regular spice grinder, or keep an electric coffee grinder just for this task.

## SOME SEAFOOD-SPECIFIC TOOLS ▪ ▪ ▪

Seafood tools specific to the task are available through fisherman's supply stores, restaurant supply stores, or Morty the knife man, who specializes in seafood tools and protective clothing at www.mortytheknifeman.com. (This web site is a great place to browse for ideas; check out the steel-mesh protective glove for opening oysters.)

**CLAM AND OYSTER KNIVES** • These knives are made for the task; using other knives, screwdrivers, or beer can openers is dangerous and probably won't work.

**CRAB HAMMER AND BLOCK** • A wood or aluminum block measuring four by four inches, plus an aluminum hammer for cracking crab are just right to do the job. Check with Morty the knife man (www.mortytheknifeman.com).

**FILET KNIFE** • Thin-bladed, fish fillet knives make the job of filleting fish easy. They are similar to a boning knife but longer and more flexible.

**FISH SCALER** • Use a curry comb purchased from a feed supply store, or buy a fish scaler for three times the price.

# THE FISH

# ANCHOVY

S ea green above and silvery below, the anchovy is one of the most prolific and widespread fish in the sea. Schools of anchovies that appear as no more than a flash of silver may number in the millions. Grazing on microscopic plankton, each anchovy filters hundreds of gallons of water a day to strain out its food.

The anchovy ranges over all the temperate and tropical seas of the world. Of the more than 130 varieties of anchovies, sixteen are found in U.S. waters. The only commercial fishery in the United States that targets anchovies for food is located on the Pacific Coast. The **northern anchovy** (*Engraulis mordas*) is sold there mostly as live bait and to a lesser extent as food. The **bay anchovy** (*Anchoa mitchilli*), found on eastern shores, is often one of a mixture of juvenile fish taken as whitebait, but no targeted fishery exists for adults in the east.

For the best quality, go with live anchovies, which are available from March through September, with the height of the season from June through August. In fishing ports on the Pacific Coast, anchovies are kept alive in net pens to be used as bait for salmon and halibut. To get fresh anchovies, have the local party-boat skipper direct you to one of the anchovy pens, often located in some hidden corner of the docks, or simply ask your seafood purveyor to order the fish for you.

Anchovies sparkle when they are fresh from the sea, but after only a few hours out of the water they lose their luster and turn dark. Within a day, they begin to blush on the gill plate, ashamed of their age. Anchovies with entrails hanging from broken bellies are good for nothing but chum.

Of greater importance from a culinary standpoint are two anchovies from distant shores. The **Mediterranean**, or **true anchovy** (*Engraulis encrasicholus*), found along the Mediterranean Sea and southern European coastline, is salt-cured and sold worldwide in cans or bottles. The **Buccaneer anchovy** (*Encrasicholina punctifer*) of Asia is salted and fermented into fish sauce, a fundamental seasoning in the cuisines of Thailand, Vietnam, Cambodia, Burma, Laos, and the Philippines.

## CHOOSING SUSTAINABLE SEAFOOD

Anchovies are very resilient to fishing pressure. An individual anchovy matures quickly and may spawn multiple times in a year. Schools of tightly packed anchovies swim in the upper-water column, making bycatch and habitat destruction easily avoidable. Purse seine is the preferred method of capture (see page 420).

Huge schools of anchovies common to inshore areas are the most abundant source of food for essentially every predatory fish, bird, and mammal in the sea. Although human consumption and the use of anchovies as bait has very little impact on populations, commercial fishing fleets that "fish down the food chain," targeting small pelagic fish for fertilizer, fish oil, and animal feed, can be a threat to this critical part of the marine food web.

## CHOOSING HEALTHY SEAFOOD

Small, fatty fish, such as anchovies, mackerel, and sardines. are rich in heart-healthy omega-3 fatty acids, and health professionals advise eating them on a regular basis to help avoid chronic heart disease. Anchovies are a good source of B vitamins and minerals, particularly selenium, and a natural source of DMAE (dimethylaminoethanol), a compound sold in natural foods stores for boosting brain power. Tinned sardines are particularly rich in calcium.

The bio-accumulation of pollutants is not an issue with the short-lived filter-feeding anchovy. Much like shellfish, however, filter-feeding fish may accumulate naturally occurring marine toxins during algal blooms (see "Red Tide" Marine Toxins, page 415).

## IN THE KITCHEN

Fresh anchovies are mildly sweet, with a vastly different flavor than that of cured anchovies or fermented fish sauce.

To clean fresh anchovies: Remove the scales by rinsing the fish under running water while gently scraping away the scales with a fingernail. While grasping the head of the fish firmly with the fingers of your right hand use the fingers of your left hand to pinch through the flesh just below the collar (see photo A), then gently and evenly pull toward the tail. With a little gentle persuasion and some practice, two boneless fillets will strip away from the backbone (see photo B). Discard the head with attached backbone and entrails.

Anchovy curing is a complex process whereby naturally occurring enzymes act on the fish. Temperature, humidity, oxygen levels in the drums, overall duration of the cure, and an artisanal skill in balancing these factors produce the characteristic flavor of cured anchovies. A well-cured anchovy or fish sauce should have some of the flavor attributes of a good cheese or cured olive and no overt fishiness.

Umami, described as the savory taste of protein, has long been considered by many in Asia to be the fifth flavor after sweet, sour, salt, and bitter, and it is gaining recognition in Western kitchens. It is particularly abundant in fish sauce and cured anchovies, giving a flavor boost to any dish.

The list of familiar dishes based on or sea-soned with anchovies is endless, among them Green Goddess dressing and Caesar salad, bagna cauda (a warm dip served with vegetables), anchoïade (a Provençal vegetable spread), tapenade, and pasta puttanesca.

Cured anchovies and fish sauce should be staples in every kitchen pantry. Packed in salt or oil, salt cured anchovies are not submitted to high temperatures so are considered semi-preserved; enzymatic action continues to take

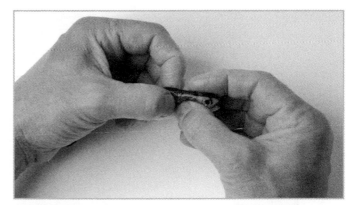

A. TECHNIQUE FOR CLEANING ANCHOVIES: WHILE HOLDING THE HEAD FIRMLY, PINCH THROUGH THE FLESH JUST BEHIND THE COLLAR AND PULL TOWARD THE TAIL.

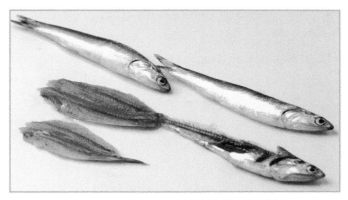

B. ANCHOVY FILLETS PEELED AWAY FROM THE BACKBONE.

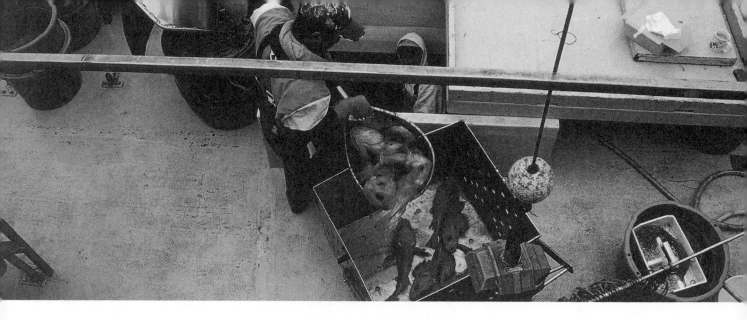

place in the can or bottle. A popular and good-quality brand of salt-cured anchovy, packed in either salt or oil, is Agostino Recca, but many other fine brands are available.

Whole salt-packed anchovies should be rinsed of excess salt. Split them open with your fingers and remove the backbone. The backbone itself makes a delicious finger snack when fried in olive oil. Oil-packed anchovies can be used as they are; open tins or jars should be stored in the refrigerator.

**White anchovies** are pickled in an acidic liquid (lightly salted water, vinegar, and lemon); although they can be used in the same manner as salt-cured anchovies, their flavor is more refined. White anchovies are perishable, so they should always be refrigerated and kept for no more than thirty days.

In southern Italy, the amber-colored liquid fish sauce, *flos gari*, produced as a by-product of curing anchovies, is beaten with olive oil and used as a sauce for pasta. The process and the flavor are little different from Asian fish sauce (see below) or the ancient Roman anchovy sauce garum.

Fish sauce is as common to the Southeast Asian table as salt is to the Western table. Asian fermented fish sauces such as Vietnamese **nuoc mam** and Thai **nam pla**, which closely resemble ancient Roman garum, are becoming ever more popular in the West. The same care must be taken in the production of fish sauce as in curing anchovies.

If you're looking for quality Vietnamese fish sauce, keep in mind that fish sauce from the Vietnamese island of Phu Quoc bearing the words *nhi* ("best quality") and *ca com* ("made of anchovies only") on the label is widely considered by connoisseurs to be definitive of quality fish sauce. Lighter-colored fish sauces, such as the widely available Thai Kitchen brand, are milder in flavor.

# NUOC CHAM (VIETNAMESE DIPPING SAUCE)

Nuoc cham is the basic condiment at the Vietnamese table. It is used for dipping seafood, vegetables, and meat or for simply drizzling over rice. It is a good accompaniment to charcoal-grilled oily fish such as mackerel. This sauce should be made fresh each time it is used, as it does not keep well.

2 garlic cloves

1 or 2 Thai bird, Fresno, or other red chiles, seeded and minced

Juice of 2 limes (shells reserved)

1 tablespoon sugar

¼ cup fish sauce

¼ cup water

Using a mortar and pestle, mash the garlic and chile to a paste. (Some cooks prefer to mince the chiles.) Add the lime juice, then scrape the pulp from the lime shells with the tip of a knife and add. Stir in the sugar, fish sauce, and water, mixing until the sugar is completely dissolved.

# SPAGHETTI WITH ESCAROLE, ANCHOVIES, AND BREAD CRUMBS

This is my idea of fast food, perfect for a quick lunch or midnight snack. Be sure the anchovies are new, the olive oil top quality, and most of all the garlic is fresh and hasn't begun to sprout (sprouted garlic will ruin this dish with bitterness). Fresh bread crumbs, fried in a little of the olive oil, with a good squeeze of lemon at the last moment, make a perfect finish to the dish.

1 pound spaghetti

5 to 6 tablespoons olive oil

4 garlic cloves, minced

4 packed cups chopped escarole

12 anchovy fillets, chopped

Pinch of red pepper flakes

2 tablespoons chopped fresh flat-leaf parsley

½ cup fresh bread crumbs

Lemon wedges for garnish

1. In a large pot of salted boiling water, cook the spaghetti until al dente. Drain, reserving a little of the water.

2. In a large sauté pan or skillet, heat 4 tablespoons of the olive oil over medium heat and

sauté the garlic until soft but not browned, about 2 minutes. Add the escarole and sauté until bright green and wilted, about 2 minutes. Add the anchovies, red pepper flakes, and spaghetti. Add 2 or 3 tablespoons of the reserved cooking water.

**3.** Toss the ingredients together well and cook over high heat until the water has evaporated and the spaghetti is sizzling hot and completely coated with oil. Mix in the parsley.

**4.** In a small sauté pan or skillet, heat the 1 or 2 remaining tablespoons olive oil over medium heat and sauté the bread crumbs until crispy and golden, 3 or 4 minutes.

**5.** Divide the spaghetti among 4 bowls and top with the bread crumbs. Serve with lemon wedges.

## Fishing Down the Food Chain

Ski week, and five kids scramble to find seats at the kitchen table of a rented cabin on the slopes of Mount Blackcomb in Whistler, Canada. The adults are still getting dressed, readying to hit the slopes. I pile scrambled eggs on paper plates and pass them out to the kids with a "Hurry up, let's eat; it's ski time!" One of the boys takes two quick bites and gives me a funny look but doesn't say anything. My twelve-year-old daughter Kelley is more direct. "Dad, did you wash the pan before you cooked the eggs?" she asks. "They taste like old fish, they're disgusting." A chorus of "yucks" and "eeyews" follow, and everyone demands cereal instead.

Almost a third of the seafood landed in the world is used to feed poultry, pigs, and farmed fish, as pet food, and for industrial purposes. Fish oil is used to make varnish, cosmetics, pharmaceuticals, lubricants, and most of all, fish meal for livestock. Fifty-five percent of all the forage fish landed in the United States is used to feed chickens and pigs. And that's why our eggs tasted like old fish that morning—someone had fed old fish meal to their chickens.

The fish that have been found to be most productive for fish meal and other industrial purposes are small, fatty fish high in protein and oils, such as capelin, anchovies, sardines, and menhaden. These fish are extremely abundant and only small amounts are used for human consumption. At first glance, using them for fish meal would seem to be a good thing, but what needs to be emphasized is that these fish are a vital link in the marine food web. They eat algae and plankton for food, and then they themselves become food for larger, more desirable carnivorous fish such as salmon and striped bass. When industrial fisheries for oil and meal first began in the 1930s, the impact of removing large amounts of forage fish from the bottom of the food chain was largely ignored. Each species was managed as a "stand-alone" species. In other words, fish were managed as if they didn't interact with their environment and other fish. Today, fishery managers are finally beginning to take into account the fact that prey and predator fish are interdependent and that all fish require a healthy ecosystem to thrive. It's incredible to think that something so basic to nature could be ignored.

If we want to preserve our fish, we can't do so one fish at a time; we must look at the entire ecosystem. One example of this is the menhaden, a type of herring that is particularly abundant in the Chesapeake Bay area. Although hardly anyone eats menhaden, it represents America's second largest fishery. Last year, an astounding 375 million pounds of menhaden was ground up into fish meal for chickens, hogs, and aquaculture operations. Many people feel, and it only makes sense, that removing this much menhaden from the ecosystem is taking its toll on the Chesapeake Bay.

Predatory fish such as striped bass can't find enough menhaden to eat and as a result are becoming less productive and more susceptible to disease. "Dead zones" have become prevalent in the bay. Nutrient pollution from industrial agriculture upriver create vast algal blooms that choke the bay of oxygen. Without the abundant filter feeding menhaden to graze on these algal blooms, the bay is being overwhelmed. Clearly, without menhaden to clean the bay of algae and provide food for larger fish, the bay has become less hospitable to all the species that call the Chesapeake home—including humans.

A disturbing trend has developed as demand for fish meal and oil grows. "Fishing down the food chain" even further, we've begun training our sights on krill, a shrimplike zooplankton that forms one of the most basic building blocks of the marine food web.

Fishing down the food chain and its impact on the marine food web will surely be one of the most important ocean conservation issues to face us in the future.

# BLACK
# SEA BASS

One of the best-tasting fish in the sea, the **black sea bass** (*Centropristis striata*), like its close relation the grouper, is a true sea bass. While most members of the Serranidae family prefer warm tropical waters, the black sea bass prefers the cooler, more temperate seas from Cape Hatteras, North Carolina, to Cape Cod, Massachusetts.

Black sea bass winter off the coastal reefs of the Carolinas and mid-Atlantic states. In the spring, they migrate north, taking up residence on the banks of New York and New England. Although black sea bass are closely regulated and availability is determined by management strictures, they are at their best quality and most abundant in the fall and winter, when the fish are fat and have yet to begin their spring spawning run.

A mature black sea bass is striking in appearance. Its gleaming black skin reflects an indigo blue sheen along the back, and a quilted pattern of tiny, perfectly spaced white diamonds adds sparkle. The dorsal hump on the shoulders of the mature male gives a daunting appearance of power, much like a male buffalo or lion, despite the fish's diminutive size, seldom over two pounds.

Black sea bass are most often sold as whole round fish. Their small size at maturity is ideal for the whole-fish preparations favored in Chinese cuisine. This makes them one of the most popular fish in Chinese markets on the East Coast, where they are sold alive or iced. Whole black sea bass should be firm-fleshed, with a bright appearance and red gills. Live sea bass should look lively and healthy, and the tank they are in should appear clean.

Ethnic restaurants and markets on the West Coast prefer the local rockfish species for whole fish. Black sea bass is more likely to be sold in upscale markets as fillets or whole fish. The fillets should be pinkish to pure white, with no red bruising or other discoloration.

Two closely related and nearly indistinguishable species of sea bass, the **rock sea bass** (*C. philadelphica*) and **bank sea bass** (*C. ocyurus*) are found from south of the Carolinas into the Gulf of Mexico. These fish are all so similar that at one time they were thought to be the same species. Indeed, from a culinary standpoint, all can be treated alike.

## CHOOSING SUSTAINABLE SEAFOOD
The depletion of Georges Bank cod stocks in the 1960s by foreign trawlers led both recreational party-boat and commercial fishermen to turn their focus to black sea bass. Without a sound management plan, stocks were overfished, and landings rose as high as 21 million pounds a year. When landings fell to less than 5 percent of historic levels, fishery managers realized they had a crisis on their hands. A conservative quota of 3 million pounds a year, with minimum size regulations, has set the resilient black sea bass on the road to recovery. Stocks have improved steadily since 1997.

The principal commercial fishing gear used to catch black sea bass in the mid-Atlantic is trawls and fish traps. The New England fishery prefers to use rod and reel and, to a lesser degree, traps.

## CHOOSING HEALTHY SEAFOOD
The black sea bass is an excellent, low-fat, high-protein source of antistress B vitamins and minerals, particularly selenium, and most of its fat is of the heart-healthy polyunsaturated variety. The fish is not noted for accumulating organic pollutants and is seldom parasitized.

## IN THE KITCHEN
The black sea bass averages one to three pounds, making it the perfect candidate for whole-fish cookery. (To learn how to clean a whole fish, see page 31.) Commercially, sea bass are graded as pins (¾ to 1 pound), medium (1 to 1¼ pounds), large (1¼ to 2 pounds), and jumbo (2 pounds and up).

Feeding primarily on shrimp, crabs, squids, and razor clams, the sea bass has flesh that is intricately flavored, finely textured, and delicate yet firm. The skin is edible, as is the liver and any roe or milt. The bones make a delicious stock. The black sea bass is rarely parasitized, making it an excellent choice for raw fish dishes.

Steaming, deep-frying, roasting, or grilling over a hot charcoal fire are all popular methods of preparation for whole black sea bass. Fillets are equally versatile and take to any method of cooking. Poach sea bass fillets in a white wine broth spiked with scallions, fresh ginger, coriander, and tomatoes, or sauté skin-on fillets, starting skin-side down, until crispy and nearly cooked through before turning them over for just a minute to finish cooking.

## GRILLED WHOLE BLACK SEA BASS IN HERB–BREAD CRUMB MARINADE

SERVES 4 AS A MAIN COURSE

In my twenties, I was hired as the "chef" of the century-old Metacomet Country Club in Providence, Rhode Island. Most of the membership and all the cooks were Italian; the menu was heavy on pasta and fish. The kitchen crew were all long-time employees and far more knowledgeable than I was. I learned far more than I taught.

At the Metacomet, fish destined for the grill was marinated in a mixture of olive oil, lemon juice, and herbs, which was then thickened with dry bread crumbs. The thick marinade was pushed into cuts, crevices, and the belly just before the fish went on the fire. The olive oil and lemon–soaked bread crumbs would slowly release their marinade during cooking, basting the fish as it cooked.

Unlike thin marinades that simply run off during cooking, this bread crumb marinade binds the flavor of the herbs and lemon to the fish. The fish stays moist and the bread crumbs become crusty and brown. I use rosemary, sage, and thyme because that is what I have in my yard, but any flavorful herb such as oregano or marjoram will work fine.

Two 1½- to 2-pound whole black sea bass, prepared for cooking (see page 31)
½ cup olive oil
½ cup freshly squeezed lemon juice
⅓ cup fine dry bread crumbs

3 tablespoons minced mixed fresh herbs
1½ teaspoons kosher salt
Freshly ground black pepper to taste
4 small heads loose-leaf radicchio

1. Put the fish on a large platter and pour the olive oil and lemon juice over it; turn the fish several times to coat it well. Sprinkle the bread crumbs, herbs, salt, and pepper over the fish. Turn the fish until it has an even coating of oil-soaked bread crumbs. Marinate for 1 or 2 hours at room temperature, turning and basting the fish from time to time. As the bread crumbs absorb the marinade and thicken, push them into cuts, crevices, and the body cavity.

2. Prepare a medium fire in a charcoal grill, or preheat a gas grill to 350°F. Oil the grill rack well and place the fish on the rack. Cook for 10 to 12 minutes per inch of thickness at the thickest part. Cook two thirds of the time on the first side to really crisp the skin, then turn the fish and finish on the other side for the remaining cooking time.

3. Rinse the radicchio, drain, brush with oil and vinegar, and grill alongside the fish as it cooks. Serve with a loaf of good bread.

## BLACK SEA BASS FILLETS BRAISED WITH LEMON, OLIVES, AND ARTICHOKES

SERVES 4 AS A MAIN COURSE

I love the flavor of olive and lemon in this recipe. I make it a lot, and if I'm in a rush I leave out the artichokes. I like to serve it with a crusty Potato Galette, which is easy to make (recipe follows).

8 small artichokes

1 cup good-quality green olives, such as lucques or picholines

2 lemons, preferably organic, scrubbed

4 tablespoons olive oil

2 garlic cloves, minced

1 teaspoon minced fresh thyme

1 tablespoon minced fresh flat-leaf parsley

½ cup dry white wine

Seasoned flour: ¼ cup all-purpose flour mixed with 1½ teaspoons kosher salt and ¼ teaspoon freshly ground black pepper

Four 5-ounce black sea bass fillets

Splash of extra-virgin olive oil

1. Bring a medium saucepan of water to a boil. Snap off the tough outer leaves of each artichoke and trim off the top inch of the remaining leaves. Remove the stems and trim the artichoke bottoms. Add to the boiling water and cook until tender, about 10 minutes. Drain, cut the artichokes in half, and scrape out the furry choke with a teaspoon. Cut the artichokes in half again if larger than bite-sized.

CONTINUED

2. Place the olives between clean kitchen towels and pound lightly with a mallet or the bottom of a saucepan. Pick out the pits and discard.

3. Trim the ends off one lemon and cut it in half from end to end. Slice the lemon as thinly as possible into half-moon shapes, removing any seeds as you go.

4. In a small sauté pan or skillet, heat 2 tablespoons of the olive oil over high heat. Pat the artichokes dry and sauté them for 2 or 3 minutes, or until browned and crispy at the edges. Reduce the heat to medium, add the garlic, and cook for 1 minute. Add the lemon slices, olives, thyme, and parsley, and then add the juice from the second lemon and the white wine. Simmer for a minute or two and set aside.

5. In a large sauté pan or skillet, heat the remaining 2 tablespoons olive oil over high heat. Dredge the sea bass fillets in the seasoned flour and sauté for a minute or two on one side to brown. Turn the fish over and add the artichoke mixture to the pan. Reduce the heat to low and simmer gently for about 5 minutes while spooning the liquids over the fish. Just before serving, add a good splash of your best extra-virgin olive oil.

## ▪ ▪ ▪ POTATO GALETTE ▪ ▪ ▪

Put 2 tablespoons olive oil in an 8-inch cast-iron skillet. Peel and slice 3 large russet potatoes and arrange them, one slice overlapping the next, to cover the bottom of the pan. Press down firmly and season with salt and pepper.

Roast for 1 hour in a preheated 400°F oven. When turned out on a plate, the potatoes will be crispy and stuck together. Cut the potatoes into 4 pie-shaped pieces.

# BLUEFISH

The benignly named **bluefish** (*Pomatomus saltatrix*) has a reputation for being the most ferocious and bloodthirsty fish in the sea. It's a reputation that's well earned: Passing schools of blue-fish are known to leave a trail of dead and mangled prey in their wake. Experienced East Coast fishermen can testify to the legendary voraciousness and superb fighting qualities of the bluefish: They know to keep out of their range when the fish are snapping and thrashing; fingers have been lost trying to retrieve hooks.

The bluefish, found in U.S. Atlantic coastal waters from Maine to Florida and into the Gulf of Mexico, is a migratory species that travels northward up the eastern seaboard in the spring and heads back south in the fall. As huge schools of bluefish make their annual migra-tion up the Atlantic seaboard, smaller schools leave the

migration route to remain near chosen coastal bays and inlets along the way. When they appear along the mid-Atlantic and New England coast in early June, they are fat and prime from feeding on schools of herring, menhaden, and other small fish.

Although bluefish can grow to twenty-five pounds, the smaller fish of less than six pounds are the healthiest and most desirable to eat; many people consider the one- to two-pound juvenile "snapper blues" the best eating of all.

Whole fresh bluefish will have tight, shiny scales and will feel reptilian; that is, they shouldn't be overly slippery or slimy. The eyes should be bright and clear, not clouded or sunken in their sockets. Check that the gills are clean and tinged with pink or red.

With fresh fillets, look for a lustrous sheen and a dense, firm appearance. They should not appear soggy or waterlogged or have visible bruising, tears, or gaps. The flesh should be blue-gray, with a translucent quality. The darker red, hemoglobin-rich muscle tissue should be intensely red. The two rows of red dots, one on either side of the fillet marking the muscle fibers that control the fins, should be tightly formed and intense; the color should not have bled into the surrounding lighter-colored flesh.

June through September is the ideal time to enjoy bluefish. Eating this fish during the summer months is a long-held tradition in New England and the mid-Atlantic states. Fish markets along the shore are the best place to find fresh bluefish. Bluefish is particularly appreciated in Turkey, Brazil, and Vietnam, so it may show up in local Vietnamese fish markets. Otherwise, when bluefish are "running"—fiercely chasing prey as they migrate close to the shore—your own rod and reel may yield a bluefish faster and more efficiently than any other resource.

## CHOOSING SUSTAINABLE SEAFOOD

The availability of bluefish over the years is a tale of extreme cycles, with periods of tremendous abundance followed by times of relative scarcity. Currently, we seem to be entering a period of ascendancy after years of scarcity during the 1990s.

In past years of abundance, bluefish were often wastefully discarded by fishermen interested in catching bluefish for sport rather than food. A new federal fishery management plan restricts bag and size limits for recreational fishermen, and conscientious sport fishermen now practice "catch and release."

Commercially, bluefish are primarily caught with gill nets and bottom trawls. Better still is the use of pound nets, traps, seines, and rod and reel, which offer the dual benefit of producing better-quality fish with less environmental impact.

### CHOOSING HEALTHY SEAFOOD

Bluefish are an excellent high-protein source of B vitamins and minerals, particularly selenium, which may help reduce mercury absorption. They are rich in omega-3 fatty acids, which have been shown to lower blood cholesterol, have an anti-inflammatory effect, and enhance brain function.

In the past, consumer advisories have been issued for bluefish from areas known to have sedimentary accumulation of persistent organic pollutants such as PCBs and dioxin (see page 417). Though conditions have greatly improved in the last thirty years thanks to the Clean Water Act, avoid large fish, particularly those from industrialized areas prone to pollution.

To reduce the risk of exposure, choose smaller fish of five pounds or less, trim away the darker-fleshed fatty areas, and grill or cook by any method that allows the dissolved fats to drain away (see Persistent Organic Pollutants, page 417). Do not eat the liver or other viscera of the bluefish. Small "snapper blues" of one to two pounds are less than a year old and have yet to migrate to inshore areas—and as a result are most assuredly unaffected by pollutants.

### IN THE KITCHEN

The polyunsaturated fats in the flesh of the bluefish start to deteriorate almost immediately after death, resulting in the strong flavors so often identified with this fish. But properly handled, bluefish can be sweet, mild, and delicious. To guarantee fresh flavor, bluefish must be cleaned and iced immediately after capture.

Bluefish should be cooked fully to ensure good texture; when undercooked, the texture can be unpleasantly soft. Its rich, distinctive flavor stands up well to assertive ingredients. Citrus, vinegar, or other acidic ingredients such as rhubarb, unripe wine grapes, or beach plums can be used to cut the inherent oiliness. Brining, salting, or marinating before cooking or using this fish raw helps guarantee a firm texture and bright flavor. A light pickle of equal parts rice wine vinegar and water with a touch of sugar and salt works well. Smoked bluefish, an East Coast favorite, is delicious on pumpernickel bread with a vinegared horseradish sauce.

# PAN-GRILLED BLUEFISH
# WITH A GREEN TOMATO RELISH

Fatty-fleshed shad, mackerel, and salmon are also particularly good with this recipe. The Green Tomato Relish is the perfect foil for the oily and rich-flavored bluefish. Check at your local farmers' market for the green tomato if you don't have a personal garden. Serve this dish with corn on the cob or roasted new potatoes and a salad of avocado, jícama, roasted pumpkin seeds, and greens.

**GREEN TOMATO RELISH**

**1 large green tomato (unripe red tomato), cut into ¼-inch dice (about 1 cup)**

**1 white onion, cut into ¼-inch dice (about ½ cup)**

**½ cup freshly squeezed orange juice**

**½ cup cider or white wine vinegar**

**2 teaspoons sugar**

**½ teaspoon minced fresh oregano, or 1 teaspoon coriander seeds, toasted and crushed**

**1 serrano chile, seeded and minced**

**¼ cup finely diced red bell pepper**

**Pinch of salt**

**½ cup ice cubes**

**Four 5-ounce bluefish fillets**

1. For the relish: Put the green tomato and onion in a bowl and add boiling water to cover; let stand for 2 minutes. Meanwhile, in a medium bowl, combine the orange juice, vinegar, sugar, oregano or coriander, chile, bell pepper, and salt. Drain the tomato and onion, and while still hot add them to the bowl with the orange juice mixture. Add the ice cubes to crisp the relish and decrease the acidity. Cover and refrigerate for at least 2 hours or up to 5 days.

2. Preheat a grill pan over medium-high heat until it is smoking hot. Wipe the raised ridges with a paper towel dabbed in oil. Cook the fish until the grill marks are distinct, turning once halfway through the cooking process, a total of about 10 minutes per inch of thickness.

3. Drain the relish and serve with the bluefish.

NOTE: In Spain, when fish is cooked *a la plancha*, it is started on a ridged area to one side of the griddle before being finished on the flat grill plate. This gives the fish the appearance of having been on a charcoal grill and allows excess oils to drain away. It's a particularly healthy way to cook the fatty bluefish. At home, you can achieve similar results with a grill pan, a cast-iron skillet with raised ridges on the bottom. Look for Lodge cast-iron pans in stores or on the Internet.

# BLUEFISH TARTARE WITH RHUBARB

Every spring, Alan Glidden sets his fish trap out off Point Judith in Rhode Island. Bluefish, scup, sea trout, and striped bass are put into air-freight boxes and covered with ice while still flopping in protest. They arrive in San Francisco merely hours out of the water, consistently some of the freshest fish we get all year.

Though seldom used as sashimi or in other raw preparations, fresh bluefish is surprisingly crisp and delicate flavored. Small mild-flavored snapper blues of less than 2 pounds are best for this recipe. Larger fish tend to be stronger flavored from feeding on menhaden. Substitute mahimahi or mackerel if the bluefish isn't perfect.

The flavor of rhubarb goes particularly well with bluefish, even more so when its mouth-puckering tartness is tempered by a quick salting, as it is here.

2 small stalks young rhubarb, cut into
  ¼-inch dice (about ½ cup)

½ teaspoon kosher salt

1 small seedless Japanese or English
  cucumber, cut into ¼-inch dice
  (about ½ cup)

12 ounces very fresh bluefish fillets

1 teaspoon dry mustard

1 teaspoon freshly squeezed lemon juice

2 tablespoons olive oil, plus more
  for brushing

2 tablespoons minced fresh mint

½ teaspoon coarse sea salt

1 bunch arugula or watercress, stemmed
  for serving

Diced red radishes for garnish

12 slices baguette cut on a 45-degree
  diagonal

1 garlic clove, halved

1. In a small bowl, toss the rhubarb with the kosher salt and let stand for a few minutes. Quickly rinse and dry the rhubarb, then put it in a clean bowl with the cucumber.

2. With a sharp knife, remove the dark blood line that runs down the center lateral line of the bluefish fillets. Discard the dark flesh. Trim away the thinnest edges and the belly flap, being sure to include the fine pinbones that reside just to the center of the belly meat. Each fillet has now been turned into 2 relatively uniform blocks.

3. Cut each block crosswise into ⅜-inch-thick slices, cut the slices into ¼-inch julienne, and then ¼-inch dice. Cut away and discard any dark red muscle as you prepare the fish. Add the diced fish to the bowl with the rhubarb and cucumber.

4. In another small bowl, make a paste of the dry mustard and lemon juice, then whisk in the 2 tablespoons olive oil. Add the mint, then add to the bluefish mixture, sprinkle in the coarse sea salt, and toss well to coat. Serve on a bed of arugula or watercress and garnish with the diced radish.

5. Brush the bread on both sides with olive oil, grill or broil on both sides until lightly golden, and then rub the toast with the cut side of the garlic, which will melt into the bread. Place the toasts around the tartare so everyone can help themselves.

# BREAM

S ea bream, distributed throughout the tropical and temperate seas of the world, has long been among the most popular and esteemed species in the Mediterranean and Indo-Pacific. But it's only recently that the fish has gained acceptance in the United States. Three varieties of bream—the **European daurade** (*Sparus aurata*), the **New Zealand tai snapper** (*Pagrus auratus*), and our own **Atlantic Coast scup, or porgy** (*Stenotomus chrysops*)—are now finding their way into many U.S. markets.

## ATLANTIC COAST SCUP

The scup, or porgy, drawn from our own Atlantic Coast, is an excellent-flavored but much underappreciated fish. Often maligned as too strong flavored and bony, the scup has never achieved mainstream popularity in this country. Its small size, seldom larger than one pound, may be the real reason for its lack of acceptance at the market—and to me, that's a shame. I actually prefer its wild flavor to that of the far more expensive daurade royale. The scup is favored by those who appreciate a full-flavored fish that is the perfect size for cooking whole. They are often one of the least expensive choices at ethnic markets. Most scup are taken from April until November in inshore waters between Cape Cod and Cape Hatteras.

## EUROPEAN DAURADE

The European, or gilthead bream, marketed as daurade (in France) or orata (in Italy), is indigenous to the Mediterranean Sea and the eastern Atlantic from England to northern Africa. Although populations in the wild have been greatly depressed from overfishing, this highly regarded bream is extensively aquacultured—Greece, Turkey, Italy, and Spain are some of the major producing countries. Aquacultured daurade are popular with chefs in the finer restaurants of major metropolitan areas, and may sometimes be found in upscale fish markets.

## NEW ZEALAND TAI SNAPPER

The New Zealand tai snapper was first named by the eighteenth-century Pacific explorer Captain James Cook, who mistook it for a member of the Lutjanidae, or true snapper, family, with which he had become familiar in American waters. This wild-caught sea bream is a beautiful exception in an often unremarkable-looking family of fish. The body is pale pink with golden hues and a scattering of iridescent powder-blue spots on the back and flanks, with hot-pink tail and fins that burn with an almost neon intensity. Tai snapper average between one and five pounds but may occasionally grow to twenty pounds; smaller fish are common in shallow waters.

Tai snapper is New Zealand's most popular fish, both for local consumption and export. More than thirty thousand tons of tai snapper are landed annually off New Zealand shores, but the fish is at its best during the cold New Zealand winter months of June through October, when it's fat and meaty but not yet inclined to spawn. Live tai snappers are regularly flown from New Zealand to Hong Kong and Japan, where they often take center stage as whole fish at the celebratory table. Indeed, tai snapper is one of the most popular fish in Japanese cuisine.

Fortunately, the tai snapper's popularity on our own shores has grown, and fish-lovers in the United States now have access to the finest-quality tai snapper year-round at many fish markets. One key to quality is a hook left in the fish's mouth: Tai snapper that is caught by hook and killed immediately with a probe to the brain brings the highest price at market. The hook is left in the mouth to verify this preferred method of capture.

## CHOOSING SUSTAINABLE SEAFOOD

Overfishing and pollution have greatly depleted wild stocks of the European daurade. When the fish is sold in the United States, it is nearly always aquacultured. Even on the shores of its home, the Mediterranean and eastern Atlantic, the daurade is seldom seen as wild fish, having become prohibitively expensive. Pollution and the other problems inherent to open-sea aquaculture methods are quite problematic in many areas of the Mediterranean where daurade are grown. Wild tai snapper or scup are far more environmentally sound choices.

The New Zealand quota-management system has earned the country a reputation as a leader in the advance of sustainable fisheries. A minimum legal size allows tai snapper at least one spawning season before it can be legally caught. Again, hook-caught tai snapper are the best choice. Concerns include fishing pressure on the most productive older fish.

Atlantic Coast scup populations seem to be rebounding nicely from previous low levels, and signs are positive for the future. Fishery managers have been very cautious about increasing quotas, taking under consideration the shortage of older, more productive fish.

## CHOOSING HEALTHY SEAFOOD

The sea bream is a very good low-fat, high-protein source of antistress B vitamins and minerals, particularly potassium and selenium. Most fats are of the heart-healthy polyunsaturated variety. Breams are seldom susceptible to infective parasites, though care should always be exercised when eating raw seafood (see Raw Seafood: How to Stay Safe, page 408). Aquacultured sea bream are always parasite-free.

## IN THE KITCHEN

The daurade is considered an essential ingredient in the classic Provençal fish stew bouillabaisse. As an aquacultured fish it is generally mild and unassuming, a vehicle for other flavors rather than the star of the dish. The stronger-flavored wild tai snapper and scup are far more interesting. The off-white flesh of the tai snapper has a distinctive flavor reminiscent of shellfish; the scup, its flavor even more pronounced, tastes similar to pompano or other jacks.

All sea breams can be cooked in the same manner. Smaller fish are the perfect size for whole-fish preparations, while the very largest fish can be filleted. Whole fish can be herb stuffed and charcoal grilled, baked in rock salt, or steamed. When charcoal grilling or sautéing fillets, leave the skin on—it is incredibly delicious when cooked crispy. Breams are ideal for any raw-fish preparation (witness the tai snapper's popularity as sushi and sashimi in Japanese and Korean restaurants). Steaming or simmering in a sake-based stock is also a popular Japanese cooking method.

# BROILED SEA BREAM FILLETS WITH CHIMICHURRI SAUCE

Chimichurri is an Argentinean sauce most often served with grilled meat, particularly flank steak, but it has the bright, fresh flavors I really like with seafood. Made with fresh herbs, vinegar, lemon, and olive oil, it's delicious and healthy, too, and great with either fish or shellfish. Use it as a marinade before grilling, a base for braising, or as a table condiment to spoon over cooked seafood. It is very good with oily or meaty fish, such as any of the jacks, swordfish, or tuna; it is also good with grilled lobster and is one of my favorite sauces for pan-seared scallops. Use it as a topping for steamed shellfish, or mix it with rice and cold cooked shellfish to make a salad.

I like to chop the ingredients by hand to give it a relishlike consistency. But if you prefer to make it in a blender or food processor, be sure to mash the garlic in a mortar with a pestle before processing with the rest of the ingredients.

When broiling thin, delicate fish fillets such as snapper or flounder, I use a flat-bottomed cast-iron griddle (not a grill pan) without sides rather than a broiler pan. The heavy bottom slows the cooking enough so that the fish can brown well before overcooking, and the fillets don't fall apart as they often do on a ridged broiler pan. These inexpensive pans come in round, oval, square, or rectangular shapes, and are easily found in cookware stores.

Serve this dish with Bulgur Pilaf and simple steamed zucchini squash; the Chimichurri Sauce goes well with both.

- - - - - - - - - - - - - - - - - - -

**Four 5-ounce tai snapper, scup, or daurade fillets**
**Olive oil for coating**
**Salt to taste**
**Chimichurri Sauce (recipe follows)**
**Bulgur Pilaf (recipe follows)**

Preheat the broiler. Lightly oil the griddle and arrange the fillets on the pan. Coat the fillets with a little oil and lightly season with salt. Place the fish 4 or 5 inches from the heat source and broil for 6 to 8 minutes, or until the top is nicely browned. There is no need to turn the fillets. Serve with Chimichurri Sauce.

# CHIMICHURRI SAUCE

This sauce may seem sharply acidic at first, but trust me, it is addictive—you'll soon find yourself going back for more.

1 large bunch flat-leaf parsley, stemmed
and minced, about ⅔ cup

¼ cup loosely packed fresh oregano leaves,
minced

3 garlic cloves, minced

1 teaspoon kosher salt

½ teaspoon freshly ground pepper

½ teaspoon ground pure chile or
cayenne pepper

¼ cup olive oil

¼ cup good sherry or red wine vinegar

3 tablespoons freshly squeezed lemon juice

In a medium bowl, simply mix everything together.

# BULGUR PILAF

Bulgur, especially popular in the Middle East, where it is used to make tabbouleh and pilaf, is whole wheat that has been steamed, dried, and then cracked. It is a wonderful, nutty-flavored grain that needs little or no cooking.

Sauté half a diced onion in oil until it softens and begins to turn golden; add 1½ cups bulgur and cook for 1 minute more. Add 1½ cups stock or water, cover, and cook for 5 minutes, or until the liquid is absorbed. Set aside, still covered, to steam for 5 minutes before serving.

# WHOLE TAI SNAPPER BAKED IN SALT

This is a really easy recipe and only intimidating the first time you try it. It presents beautifully at a party and is the most foolproof way to get spectacular results cooking a whole fish. Coarse sea salt is best for this recipe; you can find inexpensive sea salt in the bulk section of natural foods stores for less than a dollar a pound. I have a twenty-five-pound bucket of Sicilian sea salt in my cellar that cost fifty cents a pound, and honestly, I like it as well as most French salt at twenty times the price.

Serve this with broccoli rabe that has been blanched and sautéed in garlic and olive oil. Or serve with oven-roasted potatoes, carrots, turnips, and beets tossed in a little oil and sea salt and roasted in the hot oven for forty-five minutes. Turn the vegetables over halfway through cooking.

One 3- to 4-pound whole tai snapper or
    other fish, fins removed, cleaned,
    and scaled (see page 31)
1 tablespoon black peppercorns, cracked
    in a mortar with a pestle
1 lemon, washed and finely sliced
1 fennel bulb, trimmed, cored, and
    finely sliced
Handful of any fresh aromatic herb,
    such as thyme, oregano, or rosemary
2 large egg whites
¼ cup water
6 cups coarse sea salt
Extra-virgin olive oil and lemon wedges
    for serving

1. Preheat the oven to 450°F. Thoroughly rinse the fish with cold water, removing any trace of blood, and pat dry. Season the cavity with the cracked peppercorns and stuff the fish with the sliced lemon, fennel, and herbs.

2. In a large bowl, whisk together the egg whites and water. Add the salt and mix thoroughly.

The mixture will feel like coarse, damp sand and look like slushy snow. On a large oven-proof platter, spread a base of salt about ¾ inch thick and the size of the fish. Place the fish on the salt mixture and cover with the remaining salt mixture. With your hands and a rubber spatula, smooth the salt over the fish so that it's completely enveloped.

3. Bake for 20 minutes, then remove from the oven and let rest for 5 minutes. Rap the salt crust sharply with the handle of a chef's knife; the crust will crack into large pieces and can be removed and discarded. Brush away any excess salt with a pastry brush (the skin may stick to the crust here and there). Serve with a cruet of your best extra-virgin olive oil and lemon wedges.

NOTE: For larger fish in the six- to eight-pound range, such as salmon or striped bass, double the salt mixture and increase the cooking time to forty minutes, with a five-minute rest.

## Loup de Mer: A Sheep in Wolf's Clothing

Loup de mer—"wolf of the sea"—evokes an image of a voracious pack of canine-toothed predators roaming the sea in search of helpless prey to rip to shreds. But in reality, the ferocious-sounding loup de mer are closer to sheep than wolves.

At one time, the **loup de mer**, or **European sea bass**, along with the European daurade, a sea bream discussed above, were among the most prized wild fish to be found in all of the Mediterranean and eastern Atlantic. The few wild captured fish that are still available command astronomical prices in Paris and in London.

Today, the vast majority of both of these fish are tame both in nature and in flavor. Aquacultured throughout Greece, Turkey, Italy, Spain, and other countries, today's farmed European sea bass and daurade have won the hearts of chefs worldwide (including the United States). They are consistently available and always fresh, making them a busy restaurateur's dream, though to be honest, they've lost something in flavor along the way.

I've heard these fish described as amazingly flavorful and succulent—but in reality that's the sizzle, not the steak, being sold. These fish developed their reputation for exquisite flavor when wild fish were abundant; today's aquacultured sea bass and daurade are more dependent on the chef's skill than inherent flavor. Farmed fish are fed a manufactured feed that has been dried, pelletized, and uniformly formulated to optimize growth for the least amount of cost. A lack of off flavors is of more concern than the presence of distinct flavors. Aquacultured fish are fine for what they are—fish from the farm—but don't be fooled into thinking their flavor is comparable to that of real wild fish.

# BUTTERFISH

The underappreciated and underutilized—but healthy and delicious—**butterfish** (*Peprilus triacanthus*) arrives fresh from the sea wrapped in a skin of silver filigree. Its occasional yellow and blue highlights bring to mind the larger and better-known pompano.

Butterfish are named for their high fat content and slippery coating, and average four to six ounces each. They range the entire Atlantic Coast and to a lesser extent the Gulf of Mexico. A similar species, the **Pacific pompano** (*Peprilus simillimus*), is found on the West Coast.

Atlantic butterfish are most plentiful during the late spring and late fall; Pacific pompano are available in spring and summer. Most of the commercial catch of butterfish is frozen and shipped to Japan, China, and India. In the United States, fresh butterfish can be found in shoreside fish markets as well as in Caribbean, Chinese, and other specialty markets.

When buying butterfish, look for fish that are brilliant silver, and avoid those that have darkened to gunmetal gray. Closely smell the gills for off odors.

### CHOOSING SUSTAINABLE SEAFOOD

The highly resilient and abundant butterfish is an underutilized resource in the United States. Because of the low market demand, most of the butterfish caught as bycatch in other fisheries are discarded at sea.

### CHOOSING HEALTHY SEAFOOD

The short-lived butterfish spends a good deal of its time in the open ocean and feeds close to the bottom of the food chain, a very healthy choice for both the fish and those who eat it. Butter-fish, like other small, fatty fish, are rich in heart-healthy omega-3 fatty acids.

### IN THE KITCHEN

Butterfish is said to melt in the mouth like butter. It is an excellent pan fish, with dark, oil-rich meat that when cooked turns white and opaque. Butterfish are usually just gilled and gutted with the head and skin left on. You don't have to completely remove the scales—a quick rub under running water is enough. Butterfish can be dredged in seasoned flour and sautéed, or breaded and deep-fried. They are very good grilled or broiled and can also be baked in sauce or steamed. The richness of butterfish, similar to that of pomfrets and jacks, calls for pairing with something piquant. Tamarind, tomatillos, yogurt, chutneys, and salsas all go well with butterfish.

### In the Company of Jellyfish

Juvenile butterfish often lurk in the vicinity of large jellyfish. When potential danger threatens, they dive into the protective confines of the stinging tentacles. Some jellies may harbor an entourage of a dozen or more butterfish.

## PAN-CHARRED BUTTERFISH
## WITH GREEN CHUTNEY AND RAITA

Similar in flavor and texture to pomfret, which is very popular in India, butterfish goes nicely with Indian-style chutneys and raitas. This recipe also works well for scup, porgies, and even some of the milder-flavored, thin-bodied whole fish, such as John Dory, tai snapper, sand dabs, or other small, whole flatfish.

Serve this with basmati rice pilaf and Roasted Cauliflower Curry (page 72).

**8 whole butterfish, prepared for cooking**
  **(see page 31)**
**4 garlic cloves**
**1-inch piece fresh ginger**
**Pinch of ground cumin**
**¼ teaspoon cayenne pepper**
**¼ teaspoon salt**
**Freshly squeezed lime juice to taste**
**½ cup refined peanut oil or another**
  **high-heat oil for frying**
**Green Chutney (recipe follows)**
**Raita (recipe follows)**

**1.** Rinse and dry the butterfish. Cut an X in the flesh to the bone on both sides. Using a mortar and pestle, make a paste of the garlic, ginger, cumin, cayenne, and salt with a little lime juice. Rub the paste into the cuts in the fish.

**2.** In a large sauté pan or skillet, heat the oil over medium-high heat. As soon as the oil starts to shimmer, carefully lay the butterfish in the pan and cook for 3 or 4 minutes on each side, or until golden brown. Transfer to a wire rack to drain and pat dry with a paper towel to remove any excess oil.

**3.** Serve Green Chutney atop the fish and Raita alongside as an accompaniment.

# GREEN CHUTNEY

2 cups fresh cilantro leaves

1 cup fresh mint leaves

1 bunch scallions, white part only, chopped

1-inch piece fresh ginger, peeled and chopped

3 green serrano chiles, seeded or not

½ cup tamarind water (page 39), or juice of 2 lemons and enough water to make ½ cup

½ teaspoon kosher salt

In a blender, puree all the ingredients together until smooth.

# RAITA

Frying the spices in oil before adding them to the yogurt enhances their flavor and fills the room with a wonderful perfume that sparks the appetite.

1 cup whole milk yogurt

¼ teaspoon cayenne pepper

Large pinch of kosher salt

1 cucumber, peeled, seeded, and chopped

2 tablespoons refined peanut or another mild-flavored oil

1 tablespoon mixed black mustard seeds, cumin seeds, and fennel seeds

Pinch of ground turmeric

In a small bowl, whisk the yogurt until smooth and light. Stir in the cayenne, salt, and cucumber. In a small sauté pan or skillet, heat the oil over medium-high heat and add the mixed seeds. Fry for 1 minute, or until the mustard seeds begin to crackle and pop; add the turmeric and cook for another 30 seconds. Remove from the heat and let cool a bit, then pour over the yogurt. Just before serving, stir the spices and oil into the yogurt.

# ROASTED CAULIFLOWER CURRY

Make a paste of 1 tablespoon olive oil and 2 tablespoons Curry Spice Mix No. 1 (page 35). Toss 2 cups cauliflower florets with the curry paste and roast for 10 minutes in a preheated 375°F oven.

## Everything but the Lips

The first time I had whole butterfish, it was a revelation. I came downstairs to find our friend Yolanda and my wife in the kitchen. Yolanda was standing over a black cast-iron frying pan that was sizzling away. "I thought I would make us some lunch," she said. "I found these in the refrigerator." In the pan were three fat blue and silver butterfish I had brought home that morning.

Yolanda fried the butterfish on both sides until they were crispy and brown. She put them on paper plates next to some cold rice she had sprinkled with vinegar and hot sauce. "Lunch is served," she said.

I looked at the crispy brown fish. The head was still there, which didn't bother me, as were the fins and tail. But what struck me was that the entire belly was intact and hadn't been cleaned. "Hey, you didn't clean them," I said.

"They're fine," Yolanda said. "We do this in Peru all the time with small fish."

Yolanda was right when she said "they're fine"; in fact, not only were they fine, they were some of the most delicious fish I'd ever eaten: moist, crispy, and chewy all at once and packed with flavor. The flesh was moist and mild, the skin chewy and savory. The fins and tail were crispy from the heat, like bits of bacon scraped from the bottom of a cast-iron pan. And the belly with its innards was rich and sweet, and full of tasty roe.

We were able to enjoy Yolanda's delicious butterfish without cleaning them because young butterfish and even many small adult fish, such as smelts, anchovies, and sardines, are filter feeders. They eat microscopically small plants and animals (plankton) that are quickly digested and impart only richness to the flavor of the fish. After all, eating one of these filter-feeding fish without cleaning it is not much different than eating an oyster, a clam, or a mussel, which also filter plankton for food and are not traditionally cleaned before being eaten.

Most fish, including larger, adult-sized butterfish, must be cleaned before cooking. Directions for preparing and cleaning a whole fish for cooking so it will tumble off the bone can be found on page 31.

# CATFISH

With its white, firm, delicately flavored flesh, the ubiquitous **channel catfish** (*Ictalurus punctatus*) is considered an excellent food fish and one of the best-tasting freshwater fishes in the country. This once-scorned "trash fish" has been transformed into a nationwide best seller, thanks to an aggressive catfish-farming aquaculture industry centered in the Mississippi Delta states of Alabama, Arkansas, Louisiana, and Mississippi.

The bane of catfish in the past has been "muddy" flavor. Catfish and other freshwater fish absorb water through their skin to hydrate, or "drink," so algal blooms or muddy runoff in the water where they live is reflected in the flavor of their flesh. Today's catfish are grown in clean, closed-system freshwater ponds, and samples of catfish are taste-tested five or six times throughout their life cycle by specially trained testers to guard against "off flavors."

When catfish are mature, they are delivered live to high-tech processing plants, where they are processed for shipment to stores, markets, and restaurants throughout the country. While this approach is somewhat industrialized, the result is a consistent supply of reasonably priced, mild-flavored, white-fleshed catfish, to the tune of some 650 million pounds a year.

Smaller regional catfish farms supply live, dressed, and freshly filleted catfish to local markets. You can also find dressed and filleted catfish at seafood markets and grocery stores throughout the country. Ethnic markets often carry live catfish.

Although catfish fillets have a coarse, rough-textured, almost homely exterior (they don't "present" as well as most saltwater-fish fillets), the freshest ones are appealingly pink-to-beige-colored and have a moist appearance. Fillets should not be bruised, torn, or spotted with blood; there should be no musty odor or brown discoloration along the edges. Whole fish should be firm-fleshed and sweet-smelling. The naturally occurring protective coating of slime should be clear and viscous. As whole fish age, the slime turns yellow, coagulates into clumps, and takes on an odor. The complete absence of slime may indicate repeated washing to hide the age of the fish.

In 1994, when import restrictions against Vietnam were lifted, one of the first items to make real inroads into U.S. markets was catfish grown in the waters of the Mekong Delta. Imported **Vietnamese catfish** (*Pangasius bo-courti*), known as *basa*, has taken a big share of the U.S. market, not only because it's inexpensive, but because its flavor is comparable to U.S. catfish. A second, easier-to-grow species known as *swai* (*P. hypophthalmus*) is not as highly regarded.

## CHOOSING SUSTAINABLE SEAFOOD

Raised with little impact on the environment and on wild fish, U.S. farm-raised catfish are grown in closed-system freshwater ponds and fed a diet based almost entirely on vegetable protein; less than 10 percent of their diet is made up of wild fish. The industry regularly earns accolades from environmental groups for its solid ecological standards.

## CHOOSING HEALTY SEAFOOD

Catfish are an excellent low-fat source of protein. Although aquacultured catfish are lower in omega-3s than wild and carnivorous seafood, they are low in saturated fats and free of environmental pollutants and parasites.

NOTE: Catfish do not have scales, so they should be avoided by those with religious-based culinary restrictions.

## IN THE KITCHEN

Gone are the days of menus featuring simply "fried catfish" or "Cajun-style catfish." Today, catfish is being used in everything from quenelles to Laotian-style catfish soup and clay-pot cookery.

Catfish fillets are always sold skinless, and

even dressed catfish are usually sold with the skin removed. If you're cooking a whole catfish at home, it's best to remove the skin before cooking, but it can also easily be removed afterward. Whole catfish can be peeled in a process similar to peeling a green eel: Nail the head to a board and cut through the skin at the neck all the way around just below the head. Then grasp the skin at the nape with a pair of pliers and peel downward toward the tail. Better yet, have your fishmonger do it.

## CATFISH TACOS WITH SHREDDED CABBAGE AND RED CHILE SALSA

SERVES 4 AS A MAIN COURSE

Fish tacos are great for everyone; even the kids like them. Dredge the catfish in cornmeal, then panfry it to give it a nice crunch—but if you want to avoid the calories, simply braise the catfish (or any other fish, for that matter) in a little Red Chile Salsa (recipe follows). The salsa is also good with grilled or sautéed fish and makes a nice sauce in which to braise shrimp.

2 cups finely shredded cabbage
   (use a mandoline if possible)
¼ cup coarsely chopped fresh cilantro
Juice of 2 limes
½ cup yellow cornmeal
½ cup all-purpose flour
1 tablespoon kosher salt
½ teaspoon cayenne pepper
Refined peanut or another high-heat oil
   for frying
1½ pounds catfish fillets, cut into strips
2 dozen corn tortillas
Mexican crema, crème fraîche (page 34),
   or sour cream for drizzling
Red Chile Salsa (recipe follows)

1. In a medium bowl, mix the cabbage, cilantro, and lime juice together and set aside.

2. In a shallow bowl, combine the cornmeal, flour, salt, and cayenne. Stir with a whisk to blend. In a large sauté pan or skillet, heat 1 inch oil over medium-high heat until shimmering.

3. Meanwhile, rinse the catfish strips and allow them to drain well. Roll the catfish strips in the cornmeal mixture; be sure they are well coated. Cook the catfish in the hot oil until brown and crispy on all sides, 3 to 4 minutes. Using tongs, transfer them to a wire rack to drain.

**4.** Wrap the tortillas in a damp towel and warm them in a preheated 350°F oven for 15 minutes, or put them in a glass or ceramic bowl, cover the bowl with a plate, and heat them in a microwave oven on high for 1 minute.

**5.** Fold the fish in a corn tortilla and top with the cabbage followed by a drizzle of Mexican crema, crème fraîche, or sour cream and Red Chile Salsa.

## RED CHILE SALSA

MAKES 1 CUP

3 dried red New Mexico (California) chiles

2 unpeeled garlic cloves

1 onion, cut into ½-inch-thick slices

1 tomato

½ teaspoon dried Mexican oregano, toasted in a dry sauté pan or skillet until fragrant

Pinch of ground cumin

Large pinch of kosher salt

Grated zest of ½ orange

2 tablespoons cider vinegar

2 tablespoons freshly squeezed orange juice

**1.** Use a cast-iron skillet, griddle, or Mexican *comal* to dry-roast the chiles, garlic, sliced onion, and tomato: First, split the dried chiles lengthwise and remove the seeds. Heat the pan over medium heat until hot. Flatten the chiles out in the pan by pressing them with a metal spatula, and cook for 1 minute on each side, or until a smoky chocolate aroma rises up and the chile becomes brittle. Transfer the chiles to a plate.

**2.** In the same pan, roast the garlic and onion slices until brown and soft, 4 to 5 minutes. Peel the garlic and transfer it and the onion to the plate with the chiles. Lastly, dry-roast the tomato until it is a dark, brownish-black color and soft, 4 to 5 minutes. In a blender, combine all the roasted vegetables and the remaining ingredients and blend to a lightly coarse puree, adding enough water to keep everything moving. The sauce will be thick and red, with flecks of chocolate brown chile and tomato throughout.

# CRISPY FRIED CATFISH WITH RÉMOULADE SAUCE

SERVES 10 AS AN APPETIZER

These delicious little fried catfish nuggets make great hors d'oeuvres to serve at a party. Plus, just because these catfish nuggets are breaded doesn't mean they have to be fried; they can be baked in a hot oven, broiled, or even grilled over a charcoal or gas fire.

For something different, marinate shrimp and catfish (doubling the oil in the marinade) and thread them on skewers to make brochettes. Roll the brochettes in the bread crumbs and grill over a medium-low charcoal or gas fire. By the time the bread crumbs are toasted and brown, three to four minutes per side, the fish will be cooked.

4 garlic cloves

2-inch piece fresh ginger, peeled and
minced

¼ teaspoon coarse sea salt

¼ teaspoon dry mustard

¼ teaspoon cayenne pepper

1 tablespoon cider vinegar

2 tablespoons refined peanut or another
high-heat oil, plus more
for frying

1½ pounds catfish fillets, cut into
1-inch pieces

2 cups dried bread crumbs

Lemon wedges or Rémoulade Sauce
(recipe follows) for serving

1. Using a mortar and pestle, mash the garlic cloves, ginger, and salt to a paste. Pound the dry mustard and cayenne into the garlic-ginger paste. Stir in the cider vinegar and oil. Pour into a baking dish, add the catfish, and turn to coat well. Let stand at room temperature for up to 1 hour, or refrigerate for 1 or 2 hours.

2. Put the bread crumbs on a baking sheet and toss the catfish in the crumbs until thoroughly coated. In a large cast-iron pan, heat ¼ inch oil until shimmering. Add the catfish and cook in batches, without crowding, until brown and crispy on all sides, 4 to 5 minutes. Serve with lemon wedges or Rémoulade Sauce.

# RÉMOULADE SAUCE

MAKES 2 CUPS

¾ cup refined peanut or another mild-
  flavored oil
¼ cup freshly squeezed lemon juice
¼ cup chopped onion
¼ cup chopped scallions, including light
  green parts
¼ cup chopped celery
¼ cup chopped green bell pepper
2 tablespoons prepared horseradish
¼ cup whole-grain mustard

¼ cup chopped fresh flat-leaf parsley
2 tablespoons chopped fresh tarragon
  or chervil
1½ teaspoons kosher salt
¼ teaspoon cayenne pepper
Pinch of freshly ground black pepper

In a food processor or blender, combine all the ingredients and process for 30 seconds to make an almost-smooth sauce.

# CLAM

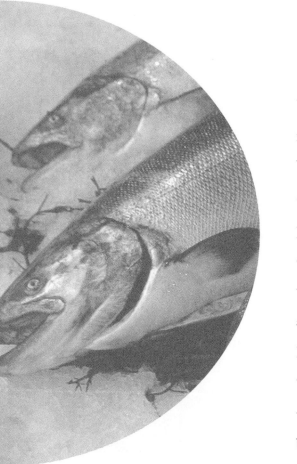

Clams come in hundreds of unique varieties. The selection is ever-changing; new clams come to market and others fall out of favor. Visit any seafood business today, and you may find boring clams, which drill into solid rock for protection; blood clams, so named for their blood-red meat; the ocean quahog, which can live more than two hundred years; or the geoduck clam, which inspires graphic comparison to the male anatomy. Clams range from the tiny **bean clam**, the smallest edible clam, which averages more than seventy per pound, to the **South Pacific giant clam** (*Tridacna gigas*), which at up to 750 pounds is not only the largest edible clam but also the most colorful, its flesh a startlingly vibrant electric blue-green and gold.

Clams can be divided into hard-shell or soft-shell varieties. Hard-shell clams are completely encased in a very hard shell that is resistant to all but the most persistent predators. Soft-shell clams carry a thin, brittle shell that can easily be cracked or broken. This type of clam is unable to completely withdraw into its shell; its siphon, or "neck," remains partially exposed outside the shell. Soft-shell clams make up for their lack of a completely protective shell by being able to burrow rapidly into the substrate in order to avoid predators.

Some of the more common commercial species of both hard-shell and soft-shell varieties available in the United States are detailed below.

## HARD-SHELLED CLAMS

■ ■ ■

### MAHOGANY CLAM

Small-sized Ocean quahogs (*Arnica icelandic*) from the near-shore waters of the Gulf of Maine are sold as **mahogany clams**. The mahogany clam has a rich mineral flavor and high salt content. Mahogany clams, particularly smaller ones, are delicious both on the half shell and cooked; larger mahoganies are less consistent in flavor and are best used in recipes, such as tomato-based dishes, where they will not overpower.

Ocean quahogs harvested from deep offshore clam beds are processed into frozen and canned clam products labeled "ocean clams."

### MANILA CLAM

Twenty years ago, the **Manila clam** (*Tapes philippinarum*) was a mere curiosity on the West Coast, an interloper that had stowed away in shipments of oyster spat from Japan in the 1930s. The Manila clam quickly spread up and down the entire Pacific Coast but was not commercially harvested until the 1980s. Until that time, the most commonly eaten clams on the Pacific Coast were the native Pacific littleneck and the butter clam.

Once consumers were introduced to the Manila clam, they quickly found the mild-flavored, sweet, and tender bivalve delicious raw or cooked. As a result, Manila clams now dominate the West Coast clam market. The quick-growing clam has taken particularly well to aquaculture—farmed Manila clams are indistinguishable in flavor from wild clams. Today, nearly 100 percent of the Manila clams on the market are grown on farms, where freshness and environmental impact are easily controlled.

Not only is the Manila clam the most popular clam used in the West Coast, but it's also beginning to get a foothold on the East Coast, the traditional bastion of the quahog. Because the clam is small and steams open in a minute or two, much like the *vongole* of Italy, many Italian restaurateurs in New York and New England are finding the ease of cooking and authenticity of presentation to their liking.

The **Pacific littleneck** (*Prothaca staminea*) and the **butter clam** (*Saxidona giganteus*) have been pushed aside in the marketplace by the Manila clam, but in nature they are still abundant. Their fall from favor was hastened by a very short shelf life, but these meaty, excellent-flavored clams can still be found in a few West Coast fish markets and restaurants.

## NEW ZEALAND COCKLE

The **New Zealand cockle** (*Austrovenus stuchbury*) is an attractive clam found throughout New Zealand waters. Its delicately ridged shell is a coffee-cream color that fades to a soft green blush at the hinge. Curiously, both the New Zealand mussel and cockle have evolved a green-colored shell, a pattern seen in no other bivalve.

New Zealand cockles, along with many other New Zealand seafoods, have become commonplace in the U.S. marketplace. Less expensive than domestic clams, cockles are suitable to all methods of preparation, whether raw or cooked. They make a particularly good substitute for Manilas or other small clams during the summer months, when domestic clams may be spawning. Cockles are best from April through August (the southern hemisphere's winter). Cockles should be tightly closed or, if gaping, react immediately when touched.

A popular New Zealand method of cooking cockles is to place them in a tight-fitting hinged wire basket and roast them over an open fire, which imparts a nice smoky flavor and aroma. Open the basket over a bowl to catch all the sweet juices. Like all clams, cockles will toughen if overcooked and should be cooked just until the shells have opened and the cockles are firm.

## QUAHOG

The **quahog**, or **common hard-shell clam**, is the most abundant clam found in U.S. waters and has been a popular component of American cuisine since the first European set foot on the shores of the New World. The word *quahog* (pronounced *co-hog*) was first derived from the Narragansett Indian word *poquaûhock*. Its Latin name (*Mercenaria mercenaria*) originated from the fact that its polished shell, known as *wampum*, was the most common medium of exchange used by Native Americans and pilgrims alike well into the eighteenth century.

A somewhat confusing array of names has developed over the years to designate various sizes of quahog clams. Often the generic term "littleneck clam" is used to describe any size of quahog. But the specific legal size designation is as follows: The traditional **littleneck**, at six to ten per pound, is prized for eating on the half shell. **Cherrystones**, at four to six per pound, are most often used in pasta sauce or other quick-cooking dishes. The largest quahogs (at more than four per pound) are designated **chowder clams** and are often used for stock when making chowder or ground up for long-cooking dishes.

To further the confusion, aquacultured quahogs may legally be sold at smaller sizes than wild clams. In addition to the traditional sizing metric for wild clams, aquaculture clams are sold at twelve to fifteen per pound, fifteen to eighteen per pound, or even eighteen to twenty-two per pound.

When buying quahogs, which are available in just about every market in the United States, look for tightly closed shells or, if gaping, shells that close immediately when touched. The shells should not be cracked, chipped, or feel slimy. The flavor of a clam as well as the color of its shell is determined by the mineral content of the waters in which it is grown. Quahogs vary from a brittle chalky white to tan, amethyst, and almost black. When choosing clams, I find those with a tan or amethyst color to be the most balanced in flavor: not too sweet and with a nice mineral tang.

## SURF CLAM

The **Atlantic surf clam** (*Spisula solidissima*) averages five to nine inches in length when mature. Found from Maine to North Carolina, the clam favors the surf line and is often seen washed up onshore after being dislodged by heavy winter surf. Traditionally hand-harvested for use in chowder or fritters, the surf clam is an excellent sweet-flavored ocean clam.

Today's commercial fishery focuses on large clam beds found in deeper water off the mid-Atlantic states. Commercially caught surf clams are always processed before selling, either cut into strips for frying or chopped up for chowders and sauces. The best-quality processed surf clams are labeled "sea clams" and are frozen without the addition of sodium tripolyphosphate, a preservative.

The closely related **Arctic surf clam**, or **Stimpson's clam** (*Sipsula polynyma*), is found from Cape Cod north. The commercial harvest is taken by hand with rakes from a well-managed Canadian fishery. The digger, or foot, of the Arctic surf clam is tinged a bright "Japanese red" (in Japan, the clam is known as *hokkigai*). It is particularly desirable for sushi, sashimi, and other raw preparations.

## SOFT-SHELLED CLAMS

## ATLANTIC RAZOR CLAM

The **razor clam** (*Ensis directus*) is common to the tidal flats of New England and the mid-Atlantic states, and is found in the waters from Labrador to the Carolinas. Its preference for the cool, saline waters of ocean beaches is reflected in its good, briny flavor. Razor clams are able to burrow quickly into the sand or dart away in a free-swimming manner much like scallops to avoid predators. Long, narrow, and slightly curved, the olive-green to gold elongated shell resembles an old-fashioned straight-edge razor. The razor clam is often gaping slightly in the market; if it doesn't shut quickly when touched, don't buy it.

American razor clams successfully invaded European waters in the past century, in the process displacing the native clam. The seafood-loving Spanish enthusiastically embrace the American razor, often cooking them *a la plancha*: on a griddle.

## GEODUCK

The **geoduck clam** (*Panopea abrupta*), pronounced *gooeyduck*, found along the Pacific Coast from California north through British Columbia and into southeast Alaska, is the largest burrowing clam in the world. It may reach a weight of fourteen pounds. It is also one of the longest-living animals in the world; one specimen captured off the Queen Charlotte Islands in British Columbia was found to be 168 years old, its age determined by the number of rings on its shell. Geoducks reach maturity at five years and continue to reproduce for more than one hundred years.

The geoduck has been commercially harvested since 1976; in the United States, it's most often found in Chinese and Japanese markets but is also widely available in the Pacific Northwest. The siphon, the most desirable part of the geoduck, has a sweet, fresh sea flavor and a crunchy texture that reveals itself best when eaten either raw or very quickly cooked. When you are buying live geoducks, look for plump, full, firm-looking siphons that will stand at attention. Light beige—colored siphons are preferred.

## PACIFIC RAZOR CLAM

Large and much more rectangular in shape than the Atlantic razor clam, the delicious **Pacific razor clam** (*Siliqua patula*) is one of the most highly regarded of native West Coast clams. The clam was widely available until the appearance of a parasitic disease in the 1980s; it is now highly regulated. The season is open from September to May, with the best harvest times coinciding with extreme low tides.

The Pacific razor clam is commercially harvested by the Indian tribes of Washington state, and is also available from Canadian waters. Razor-clam beds around Cordova and the Cook Inlet area of Alaska produce healthy harvests as well, but because of the great distance to market, the clams usually arrive already shucked and frozen.

## SOFT-SHELL "STEAMER'" CLAM

The **soft-shell clam** (*Mya arenaria*), a mainstay of New England cuisine, is the common "steamer" or "fryer" of New England shores. It can also be used to make chowder, as is traditional in Rhode Island and parts of Maine. Although the soft-shell clam is found along the entire Atlantic Coast, the main commercial areas are Maine and southern New England. The very best soft-shell clams are reputedly drawn from the mudflats of Ipswich, Massachusetts, and the surrounding environs of Cape Ann, an area famous for its extensive clam beds.

Accidentally introduced with shipments of seed oysters into San Francisco Bay, the soft-shell clam has spread from Monterey Bay to

Alaska; in European waters, the soft-shell clam has been recorded from Norway to the Bay of Biscay, France. Surprisingly, the soft-shell clam is not a highly sought-after species either on the West Coast of the United States or throughout shellfish-loving Europe.

### CHOOSING SUSTAINABLE SEAFOOD

Inshore wild-clam fisheries are regulated by the states; regulations vary but usually include minimum harvest size and rotational harvesting. Most states restrict inshore clam fisheries to traditional artisanal methods of harvest such as hand-raking, which minimizes impact on the sandy substrate these clams enjoy.

Filter-feeding clams and other bivalves improve water quality by filtering algae and other nutrients from the water where they are grown. Clam aquaculture is environmentally friendly and in some instances may be preferable to wild fisheries. Interest in clam aquaculture is growing quickly; already the commercial supply of Manila clams is 100 percent aquacultured. The Atlantic quahog is extensively aquacultured in Florida, the southeast Atlantic shore, and even Cape Cod, with new farms coming on line every year. The aquaculture of the **South Pacific giant clam** has recently begun, and aquacultured razor clams will soon be available; their fragile nature and difficulty of capture make them the perfect candidate for aquaculture.

Nutrient pollution, which encourages algal blooms, from the industrialized use of fertilizers, anmal waste, and shoreline development, is the greatest threat to both wild clams and their habitat (see Too Much of a Good Thing, page 268). The recent collapse of the Chesapeake Bay soft-shell clam fishery was brought about by a combination of nutrient pollution and the use of an industrial fishing method, the hydraulic dredge. Ocean quahogs and surf clams are also fished by hydraulic dredge, a method that unfortunately has a good deal of impact on fishery habitat.

### CHOOSING HEALTHY SEAFOOD

Clams were once thought to contain high levels of cholesterol. It is now understood that mollusks that filter plant-based phytoplankton from the water for food contain very little cholesterol or saturated fat. Rather, they contain cholesterol-like plant-based sterols, which actually *interfere* with the uptake of cholesterol. As a result, clams are no longer excluded from a typical low-cholesterol diet and are considered a heart-healthy low-fat source of protein. Clams contain incredibly high amounts of vitamin $B_{12}$ and are an excellent source of iron, zinc, and selenium.

Clams may harbor potentially harmful pollution-related or naturally-occurring pathogens. Commercial shellfish beds are monitored and tested for pathogens by state and federal auth-

orities under the auspices of the National Shellfish Sanitation Program, and clams from those beds should be displayed with their NSSP harvest tag. To be completely safe, pregnant women, young children, and those with compromised immune systems should refrain from eating raw clams at any time (see Raw Seafood: How to Stay Safe, page 408).

### IN THE KITCHEN

Hard-shelled clams—such as littlenecks, mahogany, Manila, New Zealand cockles, and Pacific littlenecks—are all commonly eaten in their entirety raw on the half shell. The large surf clam's firm, bright-red foot may also be eaten raw—it is sliced on the bias and referred to as *hokigai* in sushi bars.

Hard-shelled clams can be opened with a clam knife, sprinkled with seasoned fresh bread crumbs, and baked or broiled. They can be shucked or steamed open and chopped for use in pasta sauce. Manilas, cockles, and small-sized littleneck and mahogany clams steam open in only a minute or two. They can be eaten from the shell or removed to be used in quick-cooking recipes. They are perfect as a last-minute addition to paella or seafood stews.

To shuck a hard-shelled clam: Cup the clam in the palm of your left hand with the hinge against the heel of your thumb. Align the edge of a clam knife between the lips of the shell. While steadying the knife with your right hand, use the fingers of your left hand on the back of the blade to draw the knife into the clam between the lips of the shells (see photo). Slide the knife in far enough to sever the two abductor muscles, one on either side. Pry back the top shell, and run the knife across the inside of the shell to cut the abductor muscles from the top shell. Run the tip of the knife around the edge of the shell to release any meat that has come away with the top shell. Twist off, and discard the top shell. Run the knife across the inside of the bottom shell to cut the abductor muscle free. Run the tip of the knife around the edge of the bottom shell, to completely free the meat.

Soft-shelled clams may be eaten raw or cooked.

The easy-to-shuck Atlantic razor clam has excellent flavor raw or cooked. The entire clam may be eaten on the half shell, or it may be removed from the shell and used in sauces or such raw preparations as ceviche. Steamed or grilled over charcoal or on a griddle—*a la plancha*—they are delicious seasoned with Persillade (page 173), Charmoula Marinade (page 396), or Romesco Sauce (page 346).

The common soft-shell "steamer" clam is almost always cooked, usually either steamed or fried. The siphon of a soft-shell "steamer" clam has a sheathlike covering that must be stripped off and discarded before it can be eaten. When serving soft-shell clams as steamers, the removal is usually left to the diner. Soft-shell clams sold as "fryers" have the siphon cover removed. The high labor cost of prepar-

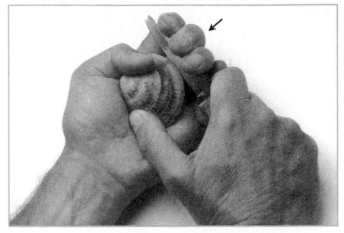

HAND POSITION AND TECHNIQUE FOR SHUCKING A HARD-SHELL CLAM: USE THE FINGERS OF YOUR LEFT HAND TO DRAW THE KNIFE BLADE INTO THE CLAM AS INDICATED BY THE ARROW.

ing these clams has made the essence of my youth, a fried clam roll and chocolate soda at the beach, an astronomically expensive gourmet treat.

Large, meaty Pacific razor clams are removed from their shell, split open, and cleaned of the dark interior belly sac. They can be used in raw preparations but are most often simply dusted in flour and panfried in the style of meunière.

Geoduck is very popular raw in sushi bars. When cooked it toughens quickly, so it is best used in fast-cooking stir-fries, as a last-minute addition to soup, or to dip into a Chinese hot pot. The large siphon of the geoduck, the most desirable part, is covered by a thick, protective sheathlike covering just as the smaller but closely related soft-shell "steamer" clam is. The skinlike covering must be removed before using

the clam in either cooked or raw preparations. To prepare a geoduck: Cut the abductor mussel to remove the clam from its shell, then cut away and discard the dark egg-sized belly sac. To remove the sheathlike skin covering the siphon, place the siphon under the hottest running water your hands can tolerate. After thirty seconds, the skin will bubble and begin to loosen. It can then be easily peeled away to expose the creamy-smooth edible flesh underneath. Split the siphon lengthwise in half and cut each half into paper-thin slices on a sharp diagonal.

### STEAMING CLAMS

Atlantic hard-shelled littleneck clams are the most stubborn clams to steam open; reduce the cooking times below by half for other hard-shelled clams such as Manilas and cockles, or the soft-shelled Atlantic razor and soft-shell "steamer" clam. Start with a heavy saucepan and one inch of liquid at a full boil. Put the clams in the pot not more than two or three layers deep. Put the cover on tight and hold it in place to create extra steam pressure; after two or three minutes it will become difficult to hold the cover in place from the pressure of the steam inside. Give the pan a rough shake but don't look inside. Continue to shake the pan once every thirty seconds for the next three minutes; only then can you remove the cover and look inside. Any clams that have not completely opened may need a little help from a knife slipped between the shells. The old saw advising that unopened clams need to be discarded applies to clamshells that are full of mud instead of clam, a rare occurrence.

# STEAMED CLAMS
# WITH LEMONGRASS AND GINGER

Clams simply steamed in white wine and water are delicious—and even better if the liquid they are steamed in is seasoned first. They make a quick and easy meal when served over pasta, fregola, couscous, or rice.

2 tablespoons refined peanut oil or another
   high-heat oil for frying

1 tablespoon minced fresh ginger

1 tablespoon minced garlic

1 tablespoon minced Thai bird
   or other chile

1 stalk lemongrass, white part only,
   peeled and chopped

2 tablespoons minced fresh basil
   (Thai if available)

1 cup dry white wine

½ cup water

3 pounds clams, scrubbed

In a large, heavy saucepan, heat the oil over medium-high heat. Add the ginger, garlic, chile, and lemongrass and sauté for 2 or 3 minutes; add the minced basil for the final 15 seconds. Add the white wine and water, turn the heat to high, and bring to a full boil. Add the clams, put the cover on tight, and hold it in place to create extra steam pressure; after 2 or 3 minutes, it will become difficult to hold the cover in place from the pressure of the steam inside. Give the pan a rough shake but don't look inside. Continue to shake the pan once every 30 seconds for the next 3 minutes; only then can you remove the cover and look inside. Any clams that have not completely opened may need a little help from a knife slipped between the shells.

# STEAMED CLAMS
# WITH PROSCIUTTO AND GARLIC

SERVES 4 AS AN APPETIZER OR 2 AS A MAIN COURSE

This simple Italian-inspired steamed clam recipe is one of my favorite quick and easy meals when served over spaghetti, vermicelli, or linguine.

¼ cup olive oil

4 ounces prosciutto, diced

3 tablespoons minced garlic

1 tablespoon red pepper flakes

2 tablespoons minced fresh flat-leaf parsley

1 cup dry white wine

½ cup water

3 pounds clams, scrubbed

In a large, heavy saucepan, heat half the olive oil over medium-high heat. Add the prosciutto and sauté for 3 or 4 minutes until crispy and brown around the edges. Add the garlic and cook for another minute until the garlic becomes clear but has not started to brown.

Stir in the red pepper flakes and minced parsley to cook. Add the white wine and water, increase the heat to high, and bring to a full boil. Add the clams, put the cover on tight, and hold it in place to create extra steam pressure; after 2 or 3 minutes, it will become difficult to hold the cover in place from the pressure of the steam inside. Give the pan a rough shake but don't look inside. Continue to shake the pan once every 30 seconds for the next 3 minutes; only then can you remove the cover and look inside. Any clams that have not completely opened may need a little help from a knife slipped between the shells.

# PORTUGUESE CLAM BOIL
# WITH CHOURIÇO AND KALE

As I was wandering the docks of New Bedford last summer, it struck me that despite the fact it had been well over a century since the last whaling crews from the Azores had collected their pay in New Bedford, all the signs were written in Portuguese.

At a small fisherman's café, over chouriço and eggs, the cook told me that many of the crew members now fishing the New Bedford scallopers are recent emigrants from the Portuguese Cape Verde Islands. Much like the whaling crews of old, these fishermen seek the familiarity of language and cuisine in the new world: Spicy chouriço and linguiça sausages are served for breakfast, lunch, and dinner; caldo verde is a favorite; and Portuguese clam boil is served wherever you go in New Bedford.

Portuguese clam boil is a spicy stove-top version of a clambake, a rustic dish often served at large gatherings; lobsters, potatoes, corn, and boiling onions may find their way into the mix. This recipe is more suited to serving a small family at home, but the flavors are authentic. Packed with lean pork and spices, the chouriço provides all the seasoning you'll need. Serve this with country-style bread and corn on the cob, if you like.

¼ cup olive oil

8 ounces Portuguese chouriço or linguiça sausage, or Spanish chorizo sausage

1 onion, diced

1 red bell pepper, diced

1 pound tomatoes, peeled, seeded (see page 39), and chopped, about 2 cups

1 cup dry white wine

1 tablespoon white wine vinegar

1 pound young kale, chopped

1 large garnet yam, peeled and cut into ½-inch dice (about 1½ cups)

3 cups water

4 pounds small hard-shell clams, scrubbed

Lemon wedges and minced fresh cilantro for garnish

In a large, heavy pot, heat the oil over medium-high heat and brown the sausages well on all sides, about 3 or 4 minutes. Transfer to a plate. Add the onion and bell pepper to the pot and sauté for 2 or 3 minutes. Add the tomatoes, white wine, and vinegar; cook for 3 or 4 minutes. Add the kale, yam, and water. Bring to a simmer and cook for 10 minutes. Add the clams to the pot. Return to a simmer, cover, and cook until the yams are tender and the clams open, about 5 minutes. Slice the sausages into ½-inch coins and return them to the pot. Serve in bowls, garnished with a lemon wedge and cilantro.

# C O D

The cod family represents one of the most important sources of food fish in the world. Wherever cod and its close relatives pollock, hake, whiting, and haddock are found, they are heavily exploited. Nearly 40 percent of all the seafood captured in the United States last year—three and a half billion pounds—was from one species of the cod family, the Alaska pollock.

## ATLANTIC COD

Most **Atlantic cods** (*Gadus morhua*) average between five and fifteen pounds, and although the giant fifty- and sixty-pounders of the past are gone, it is not unusual to see twenty- to thirty-pound fish come onboard. Whole cod vary from a bright, rich mahogany color to a deep sea green with dark marbling. Avoid fish with dull or faded color, usually a sign that they have been repeatedly washed to remove odors.

Fillets should be resilient and bright looking: uniformly white with no visible blood spots or bruising. A silvery subcutaneous fat layer on the back side of the fillet distinguishes the Atlantic cod from its less desirable cousin, the Pacific cod.

Although codfish is available year-round, the fattest, best quality codfish are caught in chilly New England waters during fall and winter. Hook-and-line–caught cod from New England's Georges Bank are not only the best-quality cod, but the best environmental choice as well. The largest concentration of hook fishermen work from Cape Cod and belong to the Cape Cod Commercial Hook Fisherman's Association (CCCHFA), selling their catch locally or through the Gloucester fish auction.

## HADDOCK

Since Georges Bank haddock stocks were reported at their lowest recorded levels in 1991, they have rebounded tenfold to become one of New England's healthiest groundfish species. The haddocks' rebound is in part due to favorable ocean conditions, but has also been brought about by the resiliency of this fish.

New England fishery managers have declared the 2003-year class of haddock to be the largest ever recorded, possibly numbering as high as one billion fish. As these fish enter the fishery in 2006, haddock is becoming more widely available and less expensive, a great alternative to the slower-recovering Atlantic cod.

The **haddock** (*Melanogrammus aeglefinus*) can be distinguished from other closely related members of the cod family by its distinctive black lateral line and the large thumbprint-sized spot above its pectoral fin. The flanks are a dusky purple-gray tinged with pink, fading to white on the belly. Haddock fillets, which average three fourths of a pound to two pounds, are always sold skin on, so that the distinctive identifying thumbprint can be used to distinguish it from cod.

Removing the skin reveals a beautiful silver coating of fat on the back side of the fillet. Fresh haddock fillets are snowy white and finer textured than cod. Avoid fillets that are bruised, lack translucency, or have yellow or brown discoloration along the edges. A yeasty or musty odor is the first sign of age in the haddock.

## HAKE OR WHITING

Hake, or whiting, as it is often called in the United States, is among the most highly regarded of all fish in Spain, Portugal, South America, and South Africa. Of the fifteen or so species of hake fished commercially throughout the world, some are beautiful, great-eating fish with sweet flavor and fine texture, while others, such as the Pacific whiting, have little to recommend them but price.

Found from New England to Georgia, **silver hake** (*Merluccius bilinearis*) and **red hake** (*Urophycis chuss*) are both sold as whiting. They are fine-textured, delicious fish. From December to March, more hake is landed in New York and New Jersey ports than any other fish. Larger, better-quality "top of the load" hake are shipped to Europe, where they are much appreciated, while small fish are sold in Caribbean, Latino, and other urban ethnic markets as whiting. Farther south in the Carolinas and Georgia, whiting is among the most popular of all fish at the market. Fillets average less than a pound.

Two very good-eating imported hakes, the South African Cape Capensis and the New Zealand Antarctic queen, both certified as sustainable fisheries by the Marine Stewardship Council, until recently were marketed only in Europe, but are beginning to find acceptance in the United States.

## POLLOCK

**Atlantic pollock** (*Pollachius pirens*) is a firm-textured, flavorful fish, even preferred by some to cod. Unfortunately, it lacks visual appeal. The flesh of pollock has a blue cast, and the fat layer on the back is deep gray; when cooked, the fish tastes delicious but turns a completely dull and unappealing deeper gray. Marketers have tried to dress it up with names such as blue cod, blue snapper, Boston bluefish, and, most recently, the Norwegian saithe—but the fish has never been well accepted in the market.

Most pollock is landed as bycatch to other fisheries, so it is often of undistinguished quality and much of it is discarded. The time to try this delicious but underutilized fish is during the fall when a directed gill-net fishery in the Gulf of Maine targets schools of migrating pollock.

### CHOOSING SUSTAINABLE SEAFOOD

All members of the cod family are extremely fecund, maturing early and producing many millions of eggs every year, which should allow them to support substantial fishing pressure— as they did from the beginning of commercial fishing around the year a.d. 800 until the development of the modern factory trawler in the mid-twentieth century.

The impact that small-boat fresh-fish fishermen have on the overall Atlantic cod resource is trifling when compared with that of the fish taken for the frozen market. Unfortunately, because fishery management policies favor large-production boats over the small artisanal, conservation-minded fisherman, the hook fisherman continues to pay for the sins of the factory trawler. Even though Atlantic cod stocks are stressed, I believe it is important to support the small-boat fisherman by buying fresh hook-caught cod. Without the small-boat fisherman, there'll be no choice at the market.

Silver and red hake are completely recovered from past overfishing, but white hake found from the Gulf of Maine north are considered overfished. The bycatch and discard of juvenile hake within the fishery is of concern, and the habitat where hake are caught is not particularly resilient to the damage caused by trawl gear used to catch these fish.

The Marine Stewardship Council has certified Alaska pollock as a sustainably managed species.

### CHOOSING HEALTHY SEAFOOD

All the cods are extremely low in fat and high in protein. They are a good source of B vitamins and minerals (particularly selenium), and a low-to-moderate source of the omega-3 fatty acids said to lower blood cholesterol and have an anti-inflammatory effect.

Cod and other saltwater fish may be susceptible to the infective parasites known as cod worms. Immediately cleaning fish after it is caught removes most parasites. Cod that are caught by small boats that fish sustainably and clean each fish as it comes onboard rarely contain cod worms. Care should always be exercised when eating raw or undercooked seafood (see Raw Seafood: How to Stay Safe, page 408).

## Alaska Pollock

Stroll through the freezer section of any supermarket in America, and you will be virtually surrounded by Alaska pollock. Nearly every breaded fish stick, nugget, portion, fillet, and burger in the freezer case is made from pollock. The myriad surimi-based imitation-seafood "analogs" that resemble crab, lobster, squid, and scallops are made from pollock. But the likelihood of finding Alaska pollock in the fresh seafood section of that same supermarket is virtually nil.

The numbers for Alaska pollock are staggering: Nearly 40 percent of all the fish caught in U.S. waters is Alaska pollock—and last year alone, three and a half billion pounds of Alaska pollock came across the dock. But Alaska pollock itself is virtually invisible, never sold fresh, and seldom if ever seen in the grocery store as anything other than an ingredient in "value-added seafood products." Look behind the scenes at Gorton's, Unilever, McDonald's, or H. Salt Esquire or any supermarket in the world and you'll see plenty of Alaska pollock. Like Poe's purloined letter that was hidden in plain sight, pollock is all around us but impossible to find.

## IN THE KITCHEN

The coarse-textured cod and pollock, the delicately flaky haddock, and the gossamer-textured hake or whiting are all similar in that they are lean, white, and adaptable to a host of recipes. The delicate nature of these fish lends itself to gentle cooking methods such as steaming, baking, or sautéing—but they may also be charcoal-grilled if first wrapped in pancetta, prosciutto, fig leaves, cabbage, or other leaves.

Broiled scrod, a market term for the smallest haddock, has always been a New England favorite. After being marinated in olive oil and lemon, then dredged in bread crumbs thick with paprika, the smallest, most delicate haddock fillets are broiled until toasty. Any type of cod is perfect for frying; from the classic fish and chips to frying in tempura batter and serving with citrus-soy ponzu sauce. Poached or steamed and served with a salsa verde, persil-lade, or other herb sauce, baked in *papillote*, or simply sautéed, cods are always delicious. They made a perfect addition to chowders and stews, and their rich natural gelatins make them a fine addition to fish sausages.

The roe and milt, cheeks, and the throat piece (or the "tongue") are all considered delicacies and may be simply cooked in butter with garlic, parsley, and a splash of lemon, vinegar, or verjus. The edible liver was once considered a valuable medicinal aid in the form of cod-liver oil. Isinglass, a very pure form of gelatin, made from the cod's air bladder, is still considered the very best natural gelatin and is used in refining beer and wine.

Though cod skin is usually removed before cooking, it is delicious if sautéed until crisp; be sure to first scrape away the fine scales. The bones are superb for creating a stock that is rich in flavor and thick with natural gelatins.

# MEDITERRANEAN BAKED COD

The Mediterranean flavors of this baked dish are familiar and homey. Any member of the cod family will work well in this recipe, which is easy to put together; preparation takes just a few minutes.

Serve this with the garlic-rubbed Bruschetta (recipe follows) to soak up the juices. For something more substantial, roasted potatoes or couscous also soak up the broth nicely. For a vegetable, artichokes come to mind, but squash, green beans, or some simply sautéed greens, such as chard, kale, or spinach seasoned with vinegar, would pair nicely as well.

4 tablespoons olive oil

3 to 4 saffron threads

1 or 2 leeks, white part only, rinsed and chopped (about ½ cup)

1 small bulb fennel, trimmed, cored, and finely sliced (reserve fennel fronds for garnish)

¼ cup dry white wine

Juice of ½ lemon

Four 5-ounce cod, pollock, hake, or haddock fillets

3 tomatoes (about 1 pound), quartered

Kosher salt and freshly ground black pepper to taste

Bruschetta (recipe follows)

**1.** Preheat the oven to 400°F. Pour 2 tablespoons of the olive oil into a 9-inch-diameter casserole, add the saffron, leek, and sliced fennel, and toss with the olive oil. Cover the casserole and bake for 10 minutes, or until the leek and fennel are sizzling and beginning to brown at the edges.

**2.** Remove the casserole from the oven, pour in the wine and lemon juice, and let cool for a minute or two. Place the fish on top of the vegetables. In a small bowl, season the tomatoes with plenty of salt, pepper, and the remaining 2 tablespoons olive oil. Pour the tomato mixture over the fish. Cover the casserole and return to the oven for 10 minutes more.

**3.** There will be plenty of golden-hued broth, spiked with chunks of braised tomato. Serve in shallow bowls garnished with minced fennel fronds, accompanied by Bruschetta.

## BRUSCHETTA

Brush slices of country bread with olive oil, then toast both sides; over a charcoal or wood fire is the ideal, but under the broiler or in a toaster oven is fine. Peeled garlic cloves rubbed over the toasted bread will melt into the bread, creating a heady garlic bruschetta to dip in the broth.

## CLASSIC NEW ENGLAND FISH CHOWDER

SERVES 4 AS AN APPETIZER

Chowder has been a mainstay of New England cookery since the early nineteenth century. Every New Englander has an opinion on the right way to make chowder, and seldom do two cooks agree. Herman Melville devoted an entire chapter of *Moby-Dick* to chowder. He writes of the Try Pots, a chowder house in Nantucket, Massachusetts, which served only cod or clam chowder: "Fishiest of all fishy places was the Try Pots, which well deserved its name; for the pots there were always boiling chowders. Chowder for breakfast, and chowder for dinner, and chowder for supper, till you began to look for fish-bones coming through your clothes."

Good fish chowder can be made with any mild white fish, black sea bass, striped bass, Pacific rockfish, halibut, or any of the cods. If you have neither the time nor the inclination to make a fish stock, you can whip up a quick shellfish stock by steaming open two pounds of clams in white wine and water. Another option is to buy frozen fish stock from your local fish market or specialty store.

Although most New England–style chowders call for salt pork, I prefer to use just a small amount of bacon to add a bit of smokiness. That way, it tastes as if it were cooked over the wood fires at the Try Pots. A green salad and country bread as accompaniment is enough to make a meal.

2 slices bacon, cut into ⅛-inch matchsticks

2 tablespoons unsalted butter

1 cup ¼-inch-diced onion

½ cup ¼-inch-diced celery

½ cup ¼-inch-diced carrot

4 cups Fish Stock (page 26) or Quick Clam or Mussel Stock (page 28)

**12 ounces potatoes, peeled and cut into
½-inch dice (about 2 cups)**

**½ cup heavy cream**

**1½ pounds haddock fillets, cut into
1-inch cubes**

**2 tablespoons minced fresh dill**

**2 tablespoons minced celery leaves**

**Sea salt and freshly ground black or white
pepper to taste**

1. In a heavy soup pot over medium-low heat, cook the bacon until crisp. Transfer to paper towels to drain. Pour off all but 2 tablespoons of the bacon grease. Add the butter to the pot with the diced onion, celery, and carrot and sauté for 3 or 4 minutes over high heat while stirring. Add the stock and bring to a simmer. Add the potatoes and cook until almost cooked through, about 5 to 10 minutes. (Adjust the time for the variety of potato. Floury russets will cook quickly; new potatoes and waxy varieties such as red will take longer.) Turn the heat off, and add the cream, haddock, dill, celery leaves, and bacon. Season with salt and pepper.

2. Let stand for 1 hour. Just before serving, reheat over low heat while giving the chowder an occasional gentle stir.

NOTE: It is always best to make a chowder at least an hour before it is to be served to let the flavors meld and the texture become richer.

# FISH AND SHELLFISH MINESTRONE
# WITH PESTO

Add squid, mussels, shrimp, or octopus to this recipe to make it even grander, if you wish. It's really at its best with the addition of about six ounces of squid or baby octopus. Serve this with lots of fresh country-style bread and a green salad.

2 cups dry white wine

2 pounds littleneck clams, scrubbed

4 tablespoons olive oil

2 leeks, white part only, halved, rinsed,
    and sliced

2 garlic cloves, minced

1 pound ripe tomatoes, diced (about 2 cups)

1 red bell pepper, roasted, peeled
    (see page 38), and diced

5 ounces Italian green beans (Romanos),
    trimmed and cut into 1-inch sections
    (about ¾ cup)

2 cups water

1¼ pounds haddock or other white-fleshed
    fish fillets, cut into 1-inch cubes

Pesto (recipe follows)

1. In a large pot, bring the white wine to a full boil. Put the clams in the pot, put the cover on tight, and hold it in place to create extra steam pressure; after 2 or 3 minutes, it will become difficult to hold the cover in place from the pressure of the steam inside. Give the pan a rough shake but don't look inside. Continue to shake the pan once every 30 seconds for the next 3 minutes; only then can you remove the cover and look inside. Remove the clams when they are just cooked, and reserve them and the stock.

2. In a large, heavy saucepan, heat the oil over medium heat and sauté the leeks for 2 or 3 minutes, then add the garlic and cook for another minute. Add the tomatoes, red pepper, green beans, the reserved clam stock, and the water; simmer for 10 minutes. (If adding squid or octopus, give them a quick sauté in olive oil and add to the pot now.) Add the fish and cook just until almost opaque throughout, 2 or 3 minutes; return the clams to reheat. Divide among 4 bowls and stir a spoonful of Pesto into each.

# PESTO

Not only is pesto delicious in dishes, it's also great for marinating fish destined for the grill—simply drizzle over cooked fish, or stir into a pot of steamed clams at the last minute to make a pasta sauce.

Although it is much easier and quicker to make pesto in a blender, the flavor and texture of pesto made with a mortar and pestle is incomparable. If you do opt to use a blender or food processor, crush the garlic and pine nuts in a mortar before adding all the ingredients to the processor. One trick I've found in making pesto more manageable is to finely chop the basil with a knife before adding it to the mortar. This extra step in the beginning reduces the time spent pounding with a pestle to no more than 5 minutes, allowing the cook to experience the satisfaction of a handmade pesto in a reasonable amount of time with less work.

1 bunch basil, stemmed
(about 1 cup packed)
1 to 2 garlic cloves
½ teaspoon coarse kosher salt
1 tablespoon pine nuts, toasted
(see page 37)
¼ cup olive oil
Juice of ½ lemon
2 tablespoons grated Parmesan cheese
(optional)

1. Wash and thoroughly dry the basil leaves. Stack the basil leaves, 10 or 15 at a time, one on top of another and cut them into julienne, then cut crosswise into fine dice. (The idea is to cut the leaves fine but not work them excessively, preserving the essential oils for the pesto.)

2. Using a large mortar and pestle, pound the garlic and salt until crushed; add the pine nuts and pound to a paste. Add the basil a tablespoon at a time while pounding with the pestle. Continue pounding to work in the olive oil. Season with lemon juice and add the Parmesan, if desired, although I prefer to let the flavor of garlic and basil shine through for this dish.

3. Pesto is always best made fresh but extra pesto can be stored in the refrigerator for several days; pour a thin film of olive oil on top to prevent discoloration and cover well.

## Good Fisherman in a Bad Fishery

When my father-in-law lived on Long Island, he was friends with Peter Matthiessen, a well-known author and commercial fisherman, who wrote a book about Long Island fishermen entitled *Men's Lives*—the title comes from a Sir Walter Scott quote: "It's no fish ye're buying—it's men's lives." The book tells of the culture and history of fishing on Long Island and how progress, changing times, and government regulations have eaten away at tradition and the small-boat fisherman's economic and social well-being. It was written about times past but it is completely apropos to the plight of the small-boat fisherman today.

Everyone interested in the issues of ocean conservation speaks of the importance of encouraging sustainable fisheries and the need to support sustainable fishermen. But the actions of both fishery management and environmental groups don't always support these goals.

### THE PLIGHT OF SMALL-BOAT FISHERMEN

Federal fishery policy often favors big boats and industrialized fishing over small-boat sustainable fishermen. Here's why: When a species of fish is deemed overfished, the law dictates that fishing levels must be reduced to sustainable levels. The problem lies in the way in which this mandate is implemented. What usually happens is that fishery management reduces fishing quotas across the board according to historic catch levels. Since small boats that traditionally fish by sustainable methods have caught fewer fish in the past, they are given a smaller portion of a reduced quota of fish. The hook-and-line fisherman who brought home 1,000 pounds of fish a day can no longer make expenses when his quota is cut to 100 pounds a day. Meanwhile, the trawler that caught 100,000 pounds of fish can still eke out a living on 10,000 pounds of fish. It soon becomes economically unfeasible for the hook-and-line fisherman to continue to fish, and the trawler is the only boat left on the water.

It baffles me to see 3 percent of the Atlantic cod resource be allotted to small-boat hook-and-line fishermen that fish selectively and have little or no impact on habitat, while 97 percent of the fish is given to trawl and other nonselective boats. Plus, it exasperates me to look out on the Pacific and see trawlers still working for rockfish while it is almost impossible to find a hook-and-line—caught rockfish any more. This is exactly the opposite of what should be happening. Federal policy should be supporting sustainable fisheries by giving more of the fish to those who use sustainable methods of fishing, not less.

## CONSUMER BOYCOTT BEWARE

But it isn't only federal fishery policy that hurts the sustainable fisherman. Consumer boycotts of an entire species, such as the widely publicized swordfish boycott of 1998, can have the same effect on the sustainable fisherman.

Two of the most important criteria in choosing sustainable fish are how and where a fish is captured, something the boycott of an entire species of fish fails to take into account. Boycott swordfish and you also boycott the "good fisherman": the harpoon swordfisherman. Boycott codfish and you also boycott the hook-and-line cod fisherman. Boycott all rockfish and you boycott even the sustainably managed rockfish fisheries. With broad-based consumer boycotts, it's the same scenario all over again: Because the small-boat sustainable fishermen work closer to the edge economically, they are the first to be forced off the water.

Consumer choice at the marketplace is a powerful tool that can be used to support sustainable fisheries, but it has to be wielded with care. It's important to keep in mind that the choices we make at the market affect not only the fish and the environment, but the community of people involved in fishing as well. If we lose the sustainable fisherman, we lose the voice of reason and a strong advocate for conservation. That's why it is so important to continue to buy from the "good fisherman," even in a bad fishery.

The Monterey Bay Aquarium's Seafood Watch program at ww.mbayaq.org/cr/seafoodwatch.asp provides not only popular regional pocket guides to sustainable seafood, but the site is chock-full of educational resources as well. This easy-to-use, well-organized site contains detailed and up-to-date information on everything from which cod to eat and who to buy it from (the Cape Cod Hook Fishermen's Association, www.ccchfa.org) to scientific reports on the effects of bottom trawling.

# C R A B

Hundreds of varieties of crabs are found worldwide, but nowhere are they as important a part of the cuisine as in the United States.

The Atlantic and Gulf Coast **blue crab** (*Callinectes sapidus*) and the Pacific Coast **Dungeness crab** (*Cancer magister*) are the most versatile varieties and of the greatest culinary interest. Florida **stone crab** claws, **king crabs**, and **snow crabs** are all delicious, but come to the market largely in cooked form.

### BLUE CRABS: HARD-SHELL AND SOFT-SHELL

Hard-shell blue crabs are fat and meaty and at their peak of quality in late summer and fall. The customs and culture surrounding generations of crabbing has created more names for the blue crab than I will ever know or understand: sponge, sally, peeler, jimmie, buster, green crab, punk, swamp, and bucky crab are just a few of the names used to indicate a blue crab's sex, size, or other characteristics. Live blue crabs are sold as No. 1 "jimmies": the largest hard-shell males; No. 2 "jimmies": smaller males; and "sooks": the smaller and less-expensive females. Sooks, with their distinguishing red-tipped claws, are often preferred by the locals for their sweet meat.

Live crabs should be snapping lively. Carefully pick one up from behind to be sure it's not a recently shed "bucky crab"; it needs to be heavy for its size, with a hard shell—pinch a leg to be sure. Depend on the integrity of a busy shop for quality steamed crabs.

The soft-shell blue crab—a distinctly American food—is available in spring and summer. Warming water temperatures encourage crabs to molt, or shed their shell, in order to accommodate summer growth. The estuaries and marshes of the Gulf and southern Atlantic states produce the first soft-shell blue crabs of the season, which are usually consumed locally. By the first full moon of May, Chesapeake Bay crabs have begun to shed, and soft crabs are being shipped to markets and restaurants throughout the country.

Watermen with a practiced eye identify "buster crabs"—those that are ready to shed their shells—and isolate them in shoreside saltwater tanks until they have finished shedding. Monitoring soft-shells is a twenty-four-hour-a-day job: The actual shedding of the shell can take anywhere from one to three hours, and crabs must be removed from the water as soon

as they finish. Otherwise, they harden up and turn into just another common hard-shell crab, losing much of their market value.

Because of the extremely fragile nature of a soft-shell crab, it takes only a little rough jostling in transit to kill some of them, so the greatest care is taken to make sure soft-shell crabs arrive at the marketplace alive. They are carefully arranged in straw-lined flats that are packed in shock-resistant boxes marked "Fragile." They are then quickly flown or trucked to market.

But be aware some shippers will leave their crabs in the water for a little while after they have shed, which allows the shells to partially harden. These hardened "soft-shell crabs" are stronger and more likely to arrive at their destination alive—but they will be disappointing at the table, tough and chewy. I would choose a recently deceased but soft crab over a lively but partially hardened soft-shell crab. A recently deceased crab will still be plump, full of seawater, and odorless when smelled at the apron, which covers the stomach on the underside. A crab that has been dead too long (more than twelve hours) appears flattened, dull, and wrinkled, and smells at the apron. The most important criteria for all soft crabs, even live ones? The undersides, when sniffed at the apron, should smell like fresh seawater.

Soft-shell crabs are graded into five sizes, starting with the smallest, euphemistically named *mediums*, progressing through the *hotels, primes,* and *jumbos* to the largest, *whales*. Some say smaller is softer, and others say bigger is fatter, but all are delicious, and, like anything wild, the taste varies from crab to crab. Hotels and primes make convenient serving sizes: You only need one per person for a first course and two per person for a main course.

## DUNGENESS CRABS

A chill in the air, bright blue rain-washed skies, and steaming pots of crabs cooking on the wharf mark the coming of winter for me now as surely as the first snowfall of New England did when I was a child. The opening of San Francisco's Dungeness crab season on November 15 is not only the harbinger of a changing season but also represents the best of seasonal and sustainable seafood.

The Pacific Coast Dungeness crab fishery is considered the most sustainable crab fishery in the world. Crabs are caught in environmentally friendly traps and are managed by size, season, and sex. Only male crabs are harvested; females are returned to the sea to reproduce for years to come.

Dungeness crabs are found along the entire Pacific Coast from central California to Alaska. Most Dungeness crabs, about 65 million pounds, are caught from December through February in California, Oregon, and Washington. The fisheries of Southeast Alaska and British Columbia are most productive in June and July.

Although some Dungeness crabs grow as large as four pounds, those between one and a half and three pounds have been available either live or cooked in Pacific Coast markets since the first days of the fishery in the early twentieth century. It's only been the last several years, however, that the rest of the country has caught on to the meaty, succulently flavored Dungeness. Traveling the country, I've seen live Dungeness crab in the Chinese markets of Boston, New York, and Chicago; I've seen cooked Dungeness in St. Louis and Minneapolis supermarkets; and I've seen Dungeness crabmeat just about everywhere.

Live crabs should be lively. A listless or dead crab will be mushy textured and bitter flavored. When I choose a Dungeness crab, I first look for a rich violet-purple on the back and a nice cream-colored belly—not too yellow or white, but cream. This tells me that the crab is in its prime. Avoid crabs with black spots or barnacles on the shell; regardless of their size, large or small, black and barnacled crabs are at the end of their lives and won't be sweet.

Avoid crabs that have recently shed their shell; they will feel light and the shell will be soft and spongy. Both live and cooked crabs should seem heavy for their size when hefted; pinch a leg to be sure the shell is hard.

A cooked crab should have its legs tightly pulled up to the body, which indicates that it was cooked alive; the shell should not be broken or cracked. Cooked crabs that have a black discoloration at the leg joints or where the leg joins the body have not been cooked long enough and will soon become mushy and unpalatable.

## STONE CRABS, KING CRABS, AND SNOW CRABS

Fresh-cooked Florida stone crab claws are available from October to May. Alaskan king crabs come in three species: red, blue, and golden, with red being the largest and most sought after. Live king crab is occasionally sold in Chinese restaurants in major cities—but be prepared to pay more than two hundred dollars for a single crab. Most king crab is sold as cooked or raw frozen section, and because only live crabs are cooked, the quality is consistently high. King crabs are unique in that they only have six legs unlike most crabs, which have eight, but they make up for their lack of legs with size. A king crab may span six feet from tip to tip and weigh fifteen to twenty pounds.

Snow crabs from Alaskan and Atlantic Canadian waters provide inexpensive frozen crabmeat and are sold in supermarkets as frozen sections or legs.

## CRABMEAT

Little matches the succulent sweetness of fresh crabmeat. To me, the best fresh crabmeat is the meat you pick yourself from crabs you have just boiled in your own kitchen. However, picking your own crabmeat is labor-intensive and expensive: It takes seven pounds of cooked blue crabs, six pounds of rock crabs from Maine (for peekytoe crabmeat), and four pounds of Dungeness crabs to produce just a pound of crabmeat. So, just the cost of buying live crabs from the market will usually make your own home-picked crabmeat more expensive than commercially picked meat. For those times when you have neither the will nor the way to pick your own, some very good commercially picked fresh crabmeat is available.

The first rule when choosing crabmeat is to buy seasonally. Dungeness crabmeat is best in the winter, peekytoe in spring and summer, and blue crab in the late summer and fall. Buy from a reputable dealer with a clean shop; the greatest danger of illness associated with crabmeat is cross-contamination. Check the quality while you're still in the shop: Fresh crabmeat should smell sweet, with no off-ammonia odors. Once you arrive home, taste and feel the crabmeat to be sure it's not slimy, salty, stringy, or dry. If the crabmeat passes all tests, store it on ice in the coldest part of the refrigerator for no more than a day.

Fresh Pacific Coast Dungeness crabmeat is always hand-picked and never pasteurized. During the height of the season (December through February), prices are low and the quality is very good across the board. As crabs become scarce later in the season, some processors continue to produce top-quality crabmeat from fresh crabs. Other, more price-oriented processors thaw and pick lower-priced, previously frozen crabs. So, as with all things, you get what you pay for. But the problem is that no one labels crabmeat picked from previously frozen crabs—euphemistically called "refreshed crabs"—as frozen crabmeat. It is only labeled as frozen crabmeat when the meat is picked and then frozen. That's a shame, really, because crabmeat picked from previously frozen crabs is vastly inferior to fresh crabmeat. This practice gives Dungeness crabmeat a bad name, which is unfair to quality processors and hurts the entire industry. If your crabmeat is salty, stringy, or dry, that's a sure sign that "refreshed" crabs have been used.

Blue crabmeat is graded as jumbo lump (the fattest and sweetest unbroken pieces of white meat from the body), backfin (broken pieces of lump and milder-flavored flake meat), and claw meat (dark and stronger flavored). Quality blue crabmeat is always hand-picked.

Fresh blue crabmeat from the Chesapeake Bay area and Carolinas, where the industry has a long tradition of quality, is at its peak in late summer and early fall. During the winter months, blue crabmeat is available from the Gulf of Mexico states of Louisiana, Texas, and Florida. The quality can be very good, but most of the blue crabmeat produced in the Gulf states is consumed locally.

Most of the blue crabmeat sold during the rest of the year is pasteurized crabmeat, a canned product with an unrefrigerated shelf life of up to eighteen months. Some pasteurized blue crabmeat is produced in the United States, but the majority of it is **Pacific blue crab** (*Portunus pelagicus*), produced in the Indo-Pacific. Labeling is often purposely obtuse, so read the label carefully if you prefer domestically produced blue crabmeat.

"Peekytoe" is simply Down East terminology for the Maine rock crab's resemblance to a picket fence when it lies on its back, pointy toes in the air. Say "picket-toedcrab" five times quick and you get *peekytoe*. **Peekytoe crabs** (*C. irroratus*) were once considered a lobster-bait-stealing nuisance, but today are served in the best Manhattan restaurants. Hand-picked peekytoe crab is at its highest quality in spring and summer.

A similar species from Maine but more difficult to pick is the **Jonah crab** (*C. borealis*), which produces a less flavorful and lower-priced crabmeat. It is often machine picked, so it's usually broken up and may still contain residual shell and fin.

### CHOOSING SUSTAINABLE SEAFOOD

Most crab fisheries are dependent on traps that allow for the release of bycatch, undersized crabs, and females. Crab traps today are constructed so as to minimize so-called ghost fishing when lost. Release doors are sewn in with cotton twine that quickly rots and falls apart to ensure that the trap does not fish endlessly after being lost.

Although the Dungeness crab stock is healthier than ever, the fishery has grown threefold since 2002. Fishermen who were bought out of other fisheries have entered the crab fishery, and the demand for Dungeness crabs has expanded explosively. It's time to think about limiting the size of the fishery to ensure a sustainable future.

Blue crabs are short lived and very prolific; most populations are healthy, but some less so. Nutrient pollution (see Too Much of a Good Thing, page 268) from fertilizer, animal waste and development has put parts of the Chesapeake Bay ecosystem under great pressure. Although Chesapeake blue crabs are still at healthy levels, they are undergoing a down cycle. Fishermen believe this is a natural occurrence and that the crabs will return on their own. A practice that has possibly contributed to a reduced Chesapeake Bay crab population is the long-held tradition of allowing the dredging of mature female crabs in winter months. These crabs are picked for meat—so I avoid fresh-picked blue crabmeat in the winter.

Florida's stone crab fishery has long been considered sustainable. No crabs are ever killed; instead, one claw is removed and the crab is released, alive and well. Once these crabs are returned to the sea, they will grow a slightly smaller replacement claw, known as a "retread."

## CHOOSING HEALTHY SEAFOOD

Because crabs, like shrimp, are moderately high in cholesterol, they were once considered unhealthy for those on a cholesterol-restricted diet. It's now recognized, however, that very little dietary cholesterol is absorbed by the body; rather, saturated fats found in the diet are the greater source of blood cholesterol. Crab contains very little saturated fat and, like other fish and shellfish, provides omega-3 fatty acids, which improve the blood lipid profile by lowering triglycerides and modestly raising HDL cholesterol.

Current advice from the American Heart Association warns people with heart disease to limit their cholesterol intake to no more than 200 mg per day. If followed, that restriction should not unduly constrain even those with heart disease from occasionally eating crab—especially if it's not dipped in butter. Eating a balanced diet low in saturated fats is the best way to maintain good heart health.

What is generally referred to as "crab butter" is actually a gland (see Hepatopancreas, page 414) that functions as both liver and pancreas, filtering toxins and producing digestive enzymes. This organ may accumulate pollutants, as the liver of any animal does, or naturally-occurring marine toxins (see "Red Tide" Marine Toxins, page 415), and should be eaten only occasionally by healthy adults and not at all by pregnant women and young children.

## IN THE KITCHEN

There are as many recipes for crab as there are crabs. The succulent meat and rich juices are probably most satisfying when you just pick and eat from a freshly cooked crab. Crabs, crab legs, and even leftover shells make a great addition to fish stock. The "crab butter" (see page 109), can be used to enrich vinaigrettes or other dipping sauces.

### "LIVEBACKING" CRABS OR CLEANING AND CRACKING COOKED CRABS

The process is the same for preparing a live crab for cooking—"livebacking"—or for cleaning and cracking a cooked crab, except for initially killing the live crab.

1. Place a live crab on its back and hold it in place with a large cleaver or French chef's knife positioned on the center line of the crab, between the two sets of legs (see photo A). Strike the cleaver a sharp blow with the heel of your hand or a rubber mallet, chopping the crab in half and killing it instantly.

2. Pull off the triangular-shaped apron from the underside of the crab. Turn the crab over and pull off the top shell, exposing the gills (clear feathery fingers situated just above the legs). Remove the gills and the beaklike mandibles, or mouth parts, at the front of the crab (see photo B).

3. To remove the viscera, grasp all the legs of half the crab in one hand and give a single sharp shake with a snap of the wrist. A quick

A. A CHEF'S KNIFE, POSITIONED ON THE CENTER LINE OF THE CRAB, IS STRUCK WITH A RUBBER MALLET, CHOPPING THE CRAB IN HALF AND KILLING IT INSTANTLY.

B. THE ARROW AT THE TOP INDICATES THE MOUTH PARTS TO BE REMOVED; THE ARROW AT THE BOTTOM LEFT POINTS TO THE CLEAR, FEATHERY GILLS, WHICH ARE SITUATED ON BOTH SIDES OF THE CRAB, ABOVE THE LEGS.

rinse may be in order but is not necessary. Repeat with the other half of the crab. At this point, you have two crab sections that can be boiled in salted water (see "Boiling Whole Dungeness Crabs" on page 111). For other cooking methods, proceed to the next step.

C. SLICING THE CRAB INTO EASY-TO-EAT SECTIONS BY CUTTING THROUGH THE BODY JOINT BETWEEN EACH LEG.

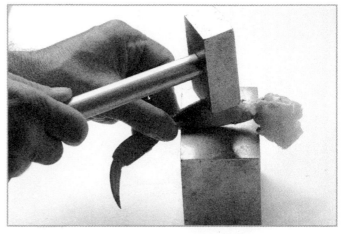

E. CRACKING THE LEGS WITH A CRAB HAMMER AND BLOCK.

D. HALF A CRAB CUT INTO SECTIONS, READY TO BE CRACKED.

4.  Slice each half of the crab into five sections by cutting through the body between each leg (see photos C and D). Now you have ten legs with a body section connected to each piece. This is where a crab hammer and block come in handy (see page 40).

5.  Crack each section of each leg (see photo E). If the crab is cooked, it is ready to serve; otherwise, it is now ready to cook. If your recipe calls for fresh-picked crabmeat, the meat can now be easily removed from the shell of a cooked crab.

### BOILING WHOLE DUNGENESS CRABS

Start with at least a gallon of water in the largest pot you have. For every gallon of water, add a half cup kosher salt or a quarter cup sea salt (although this may seem like a lot of salt, it is only 2 percent, considerably less than the 3½ percent of normal seawater). Remember, by volume, table salt and sea salt are twice as salty as kosher salt. The point is not to season the crab but to create a balance between the density of the crab and the cooking water so that the crab's essential flavors are not drawn out into the water in the pot. This proportion of salt will give you a lightly salted flavorful crab.

CRAB

111

A. SNIP OFF ABOUT HALF AN INCH OF THE FRONT PART OF THE CRAB'S SHELL, QUICKLY KILLING IT.

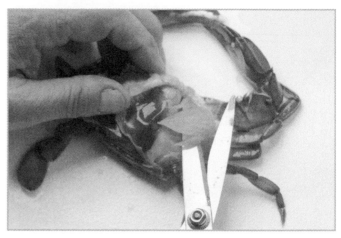

B. PULL OFF THE SOFT AND PLIABLE SHELL ASIDE AND SNIP AWAY THE FEATHERY GILLS SITUATED JUST ABOVE THE LEGS.

Bring the water to a boil, add the crab to the pot, and return the water to a boil; at this point begin timing. A one and a half- to two-pound crab takes about fifteen minutes to cook; a two and a half- to three-pound crab, about eighteen minutes.

### COOKING LIVEBACKED CRABS

Livebacked crabs—those that have been cleaned of the carapace and all viscera before cooking—cook more quickly and evenly than whole crabs and absorb seasoning and flavors better when charcoal-grilled, sautéed, pan-roasted, steamed, or boiled. When added to soups or stews, they contribute more flavor to the dish than when cooked crabs are used. When crabs are simply boiled without being cleaned, bile found in the viscera may impart a bitter flavor and discolor the body meat.

The final benefit of livebacked crabs: You probably already own a pot in which you can cook enough precleaned crabs for six or eight people.

To boil livebacked crabs, use four tablespoons of coarse kosher or two tablespoons of sea salt for every gallon of water, or use a court bouillon, (page 30). Bring the water to a boil, add the crab to the pot, and return the water or court bouillon to a boil; at this point begin timing and cook for five minutes at a slow rolling boil.

### CLEANING SOFT-SHELL CRABS

1. With a pair of scissors, snip off about a half inch of the front part of a crab's shell, which removes the mouth parts, eyes, and brain and quickly kills the crab (see photo A above).

vinegar over the crabs until you have an inch of liquid in the bottom of the steamer pan, and sprinkle the seasoning mix over the crabs. Bring the liquid to a brisk simmer over medium heat; cover and steam for twenty minutes.

**C.** CUT THE APRONLIKE FLAP FROM THE UNDERSIDE OF THE BODY AND THE CRAB IS READY TO COOK.

2. Lift the sides of the papery shell and cut away the fingerlike feathery gills situated just above the legs (see photo B on page 112).
3. Turn the crab over and cut the apronlike flap from the underside of the body (see photo C above); now the crab is ready to cook.

### STEAMING BLUE CRABS

Maryland blue crabs are most often steamed after being liberally seasoned with equal amounts of coarse salt and Old Bay seasoning, a spice mix whose list of ingredients are similar to that of the Indian spice mix garam masala. You can create your own recipe or use one of the many commercial brands on the market. Use a quarter cup kosher or an eighth cup coarse sea salt mixed with a quarter cup seasoning for every dozen crabs. Put the crabs in a steamer basket, pour equal amounts of water and cider

# CRISPY PANFRIED SOFT-SHELL CRABS
# WITH GREEN PAPAYA SALAD

SERVES 4 AS A MAIN COURSE

While traveling in Thailand, I noticed that green papaya salad is often prepared by first mashing a tiny pickled crab in a mortar to make the dressing. This got me thinking about how nicely the flavors of Green Papaya Salad would complement soft-shell crab. Green papaya can be found in Asian markets nearly year-round. Unripe green mangoes may be substituted for green papaya, but don't dress the salad until the last minute or the salad and flavors will fade.

The crabs may be breaded and panfried, which gives them a nice crunchy crust to soak up the dressing. But because soft-shell crabs are so rich on their own, I prefer them simply dredged in seasoned flour and sautéed.

4 soft-shell crabs, cleaned (see page 112)

Seasoned flour: ½ cup all-purpose flour mixed with 2 teaspoons fine kosher salt and ½ teaspoon freshly ground black pepper

4 tablespoons unsalted butter

4 tablespoons refined peanut or another high-heat oil for frying

Green Papaya Salad (recipe follows)

Lime wedges for garnish

Steamed rice for serving

Heat a large sauté pan or skillet over medium-high heat. Dredge the crabs in the seasoned flour. Add the butter and oil to the pan. As soon as the butter finishes foaming, put the crabs in the pan, back-side down, and cook for 3 or 4 minutes on each side, or until golden. Using tongs, transfer the crabs to paper towels to drain. Place some Green Papaya Salad on each plate and arrange a fried crab on top. Garnish with lime wedges and serve with steamed rice.

# GREEN PAPAYA SALAD

2 red Thai bird or serrano chiles, seeded
and minced

1 tablespoon minced garlic

Pinch of coarse sea salt

½ teaspoon sugar

4 cherry tomatoes, quartered

1 tablespoon tamarind water (see page 39)

2 tablespoons fish sauce

3 tablespoons freshly squeezed lime juice
with pulp

2 tablespoons water

1 cup coarsely shredded green papaya

1 cup shredded firm inner napa cabbage
leaves

½ cup shredded carrot

½ cup fresh cilantro leaves, coarsely
chopped

Using a mortar and pestle, pound the chiles,
garlic, salt, and sugar into a coarse paste. Add
the cherry tomatoes and crush. Stir in the
tamarind water, fish sauce, lime juice, and half
the water, tasting for flavor before adding
more water. In a medium bowl, combine the
papaya, cabbage, carrot, and cilantro. Add the
dressing and toss to coat.

NOTE: To shred the green papaya, use the coarse
shredding blade of a mandoline. If you don't
have a mandoline, you may use the large holes
of a box grater, but the texture will suffer.

# CHARCOAL-GRILLED DUNGENESS CRABS

SERVES 4 AS A MAIN COURSE

Charcoal-grilling is the most delicious way imaginable to cook crab, but it does require a full-fledged commitment to getting dirty. Fingers and teeth are required for prying and digging, but believe me, it's well worth the effort. The intense flavor of the grilled crab makes any other method pale by comparison.

For an accompaniment: Slowly cook lots of minced garlic and thinly sliced scallions in peanut oil. Add some baby bok choy, spinach, or another kind of quick-cooking greens, and cook for another minute. Add a splash of vinegar. Toss with cooked Chinese egg noodles or another fresh pasta.

¼ cup refined peanut or another mild-
    flavored oil

2 tablespoons minced garlic

1-inch piece fresh ginger, grated (about
    2 tablespoons)

4 scallions, including light green parts,
    finely chopped

1 or 2 jalapeño or serrano chiles, seeded
    and minced

Grated zest and juice of 1 lemon

2 live Dungeness crabs, cleaned and cracked
    (see page 110)

1 teaspoon sea salt

Coarsely chopped fresh cilantro for garnish

1. In a large bowl, combine the oil, garlic, ginger, scallions, jalapeño, and lemon. Add the crab sections, tossing to coat, then marinate for 1 or 2 hours, tossing occasionally.

2. Prepare a medium-hot fire in a charcoal grill. Remove the crab from the marinade and season with the salt. Grill the crab pieces for 4 or 5 minutes on each side. Garnish with chopped cilantro and serve.

# CRAB CAKES

Crab cakes were born for experimentation. Substitute crème fraîche or sour cream for the Mayonnaise; jalapeño and cooked corn for that Latin flavor, or fresh ginger and lemongrass for an Asian touch. Just remember to cook and cool any vegetables before adding them to the mix.

Chesapeake Bay crab cake purists will scoff at the amount of bread crumbs I use, saying crab cakes should be 99 percent crabmeat, but I find that fresh bread crumbs make a light, tender, and flavorful crab cake.

2 tablespoons unsalted butter

½ onion, finely chopped (about ¼ cup)

2 stalks celery with tops, finely chopped (about ¼ cup)

1 pound fresh crabmeat, picked over for shell

2 tablespoons Mayonnaise (page 37)

1 large egg, beaten

1 cup fresh bread crumbs, plus ½ cup for coating

Sea salt to taste

½ cup clarified butter (see page 34)

Red Pepper–Saffron Aïoli (see page 401) or Red Pepper Mayonnaise (recipe follows)

**1.** In a medium sauté pan or skillet, melt the 2 tablespoons butter over medium heat and sauté the onion and celery until translucent, 2 to 3 minutes; transfer to a bowl and let cool completely. In a large bowl, combine the crabmeat, celery, onion, Mayonnaise, beaten egg, and the 1 cup bread crumbs. Gently mix. Taste for salt and season if necessary. Depending on the moisture of the crabmeat, you may also need to add a little more Mayonnaise at this point to help bind the cakes.

**2.** Form the mixture into 8 patties, each 2 inches in diameter and ¾ inch thick. Lightly press more bread crumbs onto each side. In a large cast-iron pan, heat the clarified butter over medium heat and cook the crab cakes for 3 to 4 minutes on each side, or until golden.

**3.** Serve with Red Pepper–Saffron Aïoli or Red Pepper Mayonnaise.

VARIATION: Smaller-sized crab cakes, one inch in diameter and about ⅓ inch thick, can be baked on a greased baking sheet with a pea-sized spot of butter on top. Bake in a preheated 350°F oven for fifteen minutes, turning once halfway through cooking. It takes longer, but there's less attention required and less mess—which makes it a good method for parties. Makes about twenty-four.

## RED PEPPER MAYONNAISE

MAKES ½ CUP

1 red bell pepper

Squeeze of fresh lemon juice

Pinch of cayenne pepper

½ cup Mayonnaise (page 37)

Cut the sides off a red bell pepper and shred the inner flesh side on the large holes of a box grater; discard the skin. Drain the flesh in a sieve, reserving the juice. Mix the shredded bell pepper, lemon juice, and cayenne pepper with the Mayonnaise. Stir in the reserved red pepper juice to the desired consistency.

## PAN-FLASHED VIETNAMESE NOODLES WITH CRABMEAT

SERVES 4 AS AN APPETIZER

The Slanted Door restaurant is only about a quarter of a mile down the Embarcadero from Pier 33 and Monterey Fish. It's a quick stop for our daily early-morning deliveries, as well as a convenient spot for a cold beer and lunch on the way home. One of my favorite dishes is chef Charles Phan's glass noodles with crabmeat.

Glass noodles are used in Chinese, Japanese, and Southeast Asian cuisines. Because the noodles are made from mung bean flour, they don't need to be boiled, so they're quick and convenient. Simply soften them for five or ten minutes in warm water until "glassy" and soft.

Well-seasoned restaurant woks and high heat give Charles's noodles a rich, smoky flavor that is impossible to replicate at home. Even so, pan-searing just the noodles, scallions, and crabmeat in a smoking-hot wok or cast-iron skillet, and then seasoning the mixture on the plate yields a delicious and quick first course.

1 package (3½ ounces) glass (cellophane) noodles

8 ounces fresh crabmeat, picked over for shell

½ cup chopped scallions, white and light green parts only

1 garlic clove

1-inch piece fresh ginger, peeled and minced

2 tablespoons fish sauce

2 tablespoons freshly squeezed lime juice

1½ teaspoons black peppercorns, cracked
in a mortar with a pestle

2 tablespoons refined peanut oil or another
high-heat oil for frying

Chopped fresh cilantro

Lime wedges

1. Put the glass noodles in a bowl, add warm water to cover, and let stand until they start to soften but are still quite crunchy, about 5 minutes. Drain and pat dry. In another bowl, combine the noodles, crabmeat, and scallions and toss to blend.

2. Using a mortar and pestle, mash the garlic and ginger to a paste. Stir in the fish sauce, lime juice, and black pepper.

3. Heat a wok or large cast-iron skillet over high heat until searing hot, about 5 minutes for a wok and 10 minutes for a cast-iron skillet. Add the oil, which will start to smoke, and immediately toss in the noodles, crabmeat, and scallion mixture. Stir-fry for 20 seconds. Divide among 4 plates and spoon the seasoning mixture over the steeping hot noodles. Garnish with the cilantro and lime wedges.

## Do Crabs and Lobsters Feel Pain?

Anyone who has listened to a lobster scrambling around in the bottom of a pot of boiling water or watched a crab continue to flail about many minutes after being chopped up into a pile of sections and briskly sautéed has faced the question: Do crabs and lobsters feel pain? It is one of the most oft–asked questions of fishmongers, fishermen, chefs, and food writers. Representatives of the Maine Lobster Council say that they are asked this question more than a thousand times a year.

Many food journalists, cookbook writers, and cooks assume that because we humans feel pain when scalded or cut, it's only natural that a crab or a lobster is in agony when boiled or broiled. PETA (People for Ethical Treatment of Animals) members, in particular, feel crustacean pain, going so far as to publish a pamphlet that includes instructions on how to kidnap lobsters from supermarket live-tanks and set them free.

This entrenched belief in crustacean pain has begat a wealth of "humane" techniques designed to lessen the pain and suffering of lobsters and crabs on their way to the dinner table. Hypnosis, freezing, death by drunkenness, lobotomy, and placing the animal in cool water before surreptitiously turning on the heat are just a few of the techniques touted as painless.

What these "solutions" all have in common is that they take for granted that crabs and lobsters feel pain in the same way that we do, a highly unlikely phenomenon. The awareness of pain in higher animals is derived from specific regions of the cerebral cortex, parts of anatomy that crabs, lobsters, shrimp, and crayfish simply do not possess. In fact, it is only very loosely that crustaceans, which are classified as insects, and their very close relatives—ticks, cockroaches, spiders, and scorpions—could even be said to have a brain.

The lobster's decentralized nervous system, nearly identical to that of a grasshopper's, has been well studied because it is so simple, an uncomplicated collection of nerve bundles tied together at various points throughout the animal's body. While the nervous system is designed to respond to basic stimuli and to control the animal's actions, it lacks a cerebral cortex to register the conscious perception of pain.

The behavior of an animal also provides clues about pain. Crabs and lobsters will leave a still-moving limb behind as a decoy when being pursued by a predator. They discard their entire exoskeleton many times during their life, and when subjected to massive injuries continue to go about the business of migrating, feeding, and mating in a normal manner. To many scientists, this indicates that these animals simply do not feel pain like humans.

In today's world, we're often insulated from the reality of our food's origins. We're able to walk by the fast-food hamburger joint whose sign crows "Five Billion Served" without giving it a second thought, yet we cringe at the idea of becoming personally involved in the death of a crab or lobster. In truth, those five billion hamburgers come from animals that are far more intelligent, aware, and responsive to pain than the "sea bugs" we call lobsters.

All living things deserve respect. It is healthy to be aware of where our food comes from and the impact that we, as the planet's top predators, have on the animals we eat. But it is also important to keep things in perspective. Lobsters and crabs die very quickly, and likely without pain, whether dropped in a pot of boiling water or deftly cut through the midline with a large knife. The animal may continue to move from reflex action, but that is no indication that the animal is aware or even alive.

# CRAYFISH

O f the more than five hundred species of crayfish found worldwide, 70 percent are indigenous to the United States. The United States may be home to the richest diversity of crayfish, but the largest crayfish are found in Australia, where the Tasmanian crayfish grows to two and a half feet in length and may weigh as much as twelve pounds.

Nearly seventy-five thousand tons of crayfish are farmed or trapped each year in the United States; the majority of these are **red swamp crayfish** (*Procambarus clarkia*), native to the wetlands of the Mississippi basin. Crayfish aquacultured in the rice fields, ponds, and wetlands of Louisiana, the "crawfish" capital of the world, are not only enjoyed throughout the United States but also exported to Sweden, France, and other crayfish-loving countries.

The Pacific Northwest is home to the **Pacific**, or **signal**, **crayfish** (*Pacifastacus leniusculus*), which is harvested from the rivers and slow-moving tributaries that meander amid the agricultural farmlands of Washington, Oregon, and California. The red swamp crayfish is also found in the Pacific Northwest, having successfully invaded rice fields and wetlands there, but it does not compete with the Pacific crayfish—they prefer a different habitat. Both the red swamp crayfish and the larger indigenous green Pacific crayfish are commercially harvested from the wild throughout the Pacific Northwest.

Wild crayfish emerge from winter hibernation in April, and the fishery begins in earnest, lasting through the summertime. The harvesting of farmed crayfish is usually timed to take place during the winter, when wild crayfish are scarce.

Crayfish are most often sold alive in the United States, though in local areas of production you may find whole cooked crayfish. Crayfish ship quite well and will remain alive for several days in the refrigerator if kept covered with a damp towel. Cooked and shelled crayfish tails produced domestically are of the highest quality but difficult to find; those processed in China are common, inexpensive, and of indeterminate quality.

## CHOOSING SUSTAINABLE SEAFOOD

Crayfish aquacultured in the nutrient-rich waters of flooded rice fields eat leftover plant material, which in turn promotes decomposition and delivers nutrients into the food web, a symbiosis of sorts. Crayfish grown in this way do not need to be fed any additional fish-meal-based feed, which makes them an ecologically sound choice.

Crayfish flourish in clean water, making them important indicators of water quality and environmental health.

## HEALTH BENEFITS AND CONCERN

Although crayfish are moderately high in cholesterol, it's now recognized that very little dietary cholesterol is absorbed by the body; rather, saturated fats found in the diet are the greater source of blood cholesterol. Crayfish contain very little saturated fat and, like other fish and shellfish, provide omega-3 fatty acids, which improve the blood lipid profile by lowering triglycerides and modestly raising HDL cholesterol.

The orange fat of the crayfish, found inside the head and also attached to the tail after peeling, is actually a gland (see page 414) that functions as both liver and pancreas, filtering toxins and producing digestive enzymes. Although eating the "crayfish fat" is no more of a concern than eating the liver of any animal, discretion should be exercised by pregnant women and young children.

## IN THE KITCHEN

The French incorporate crayfish into a number of dishes, including maybe the most famous of all, sauce Nantua (a cream sauce enriched with crayfish butter). The Swedes love crayfish and hold a nationwide festival every August celebrating the pairing of crayfish and aquavit. But it is the bayous of Louisiana (where crayfish is most often referred to as "crawfish" or "crawdads") that are more closely associated with this crustacean than any other place in the world. Crayfish gumbo, etouffée, Cajun popcorn, jambalaya, crayfish bisque, and a simple crayfish boil are just a few popular local ways to eat this shellfish.

The tail and claws of the crayfish contain sweet white lean meat, but aficionados, particularly Cajuns, take great delight in sucking the heads of any leftover "fat" (see page 122). The flavorful bright orange–colored fat is considered an integral part of many traditionally prepared Cajun dishes.

# CREOLE CRAYFISH RISOTTO

Risotto can be as simple or as complicated as you like. The key feature in a good risotto is well-cooked rice; each grain should be separate, al dente, and surrounded by a savory warm sauce. It needs to be cooked just before serving and stirred occasionally, but it doesn't need to be constantly tended—there is plenty of time to do other things such as make a salad or have a glass of wine.

Cooked crabmeat, cooked lobster meat, or shelled raw shrimp can easily be substituted for the crayfish in this recipe. If using clams or mussels in risotto, it is easier to steam them separately; use the cooking liquor in the risotto, then add the shellfish back at the end. When adding scallops, salmon, or other fish to a risotto, I usually sear the raw fish for a minute in a hot sauté pan or skillet before adding it to the rice near the end to finish.

You may substitute cooked and peeled crayfish tails and four cups chicken stock for the whole crayfish and crayfish stock, but a risotto made with freshly cooked crayfish and a stock made from their shells will shine.

■ ■ ■ ■ ■ ■ ■ ■ ■ ■ ■ ■ ■ ■ ■ ■ ■ ■ ■ ■ ■ ■ ■ ■

4 pounds live crayfish or 1 pound cooked
   and peeled crayfish tails

4 cups Quick Crayfish Stock (recipe follows)

4 tablespoons unsalted butter

½ cup diced onion

½ cup diced carrot

½ cup diced celery

1½ cups arborio, canaroli, or other
   risotto rice

1 teaspoon cayenne pepper

1 large ripe tomato

½ cup dry white wine

¼ cup heavy cream

½ cup freshly grated Parmesan cheese
   (optional)

GARNISHES

2 tablespoons olive oil

¼ cup finely chopped tasso (see Note)
   or smoked ham

¼ cup finely chopped green bell pepper

1 large lemon, scrubbed, plus lemon wedges

**1.** In a large pot of salted boiling water, cook the crayfish until they are bright red, 3 or 4 minutes; drain and let cool. Shell the tails, just as you would peel a shrimp, and reserve the shells and heads for making the stock. If the intestinal vein is dark and visible, you may want to remove it: Make a cut down the back of each crayfish tail with a small, sharp knife and remove the vein.

2. In a large saucepan, bring the stock to a simmer and keep it hot over low heat. In a large, heavy saucepan, melt the butter over medium heat and sauté the onion, carrot, and celery for 2 or 3 minutes, or until the onion is translucent. Add the rice and stir for 3 minutes, or until the grains turn white and opaque. Stir in the cayenne.

3. Cut the tomato in half horizontally, squeeze out the seeds, and grate the flesh side on the largest holes of a box grater. Add the tomato flesh to the rice and discard the skin. Add the wine and stir; it will be quickly absorbed by the rice. Add 1 cup of the hot stock; stir well one or two times while it is being absorbed—it doesn't require constant attention. Add each remaining cup of stock one at a time, stirring once or twice and allowing it to be absorbed before adding the next. Each cup should be absorbed in about 4 minutes, for a total cooking time of 15 to 18 minutes.

4. When the risotto is just about done (almost al dente), add the crayfish tails and cream for the final 2 or 3 minutes of cooking.

5. Stir in the cheese if you like; the Italians would say no to this and I'd be inclined to agree, particularly if using lobster or shrimp, but I like Parmesan with the crayfish and feel it adds to this particular dish.

6. Cover, turn off the heat, and let the risotto stand for 3 minutes while you prepare the garnishes.

7. For the garnishes: In a medium sauté pan or skillet, heat the oil over high heat and quickly fry the ham and bell pepper until just crisp, about 1 minute. Serve the risotto in 4 bowls, garnished with the ham and bell pepper, a quick grating of lemon zest, and lemon wedges.

NOTE: Tasso is a highly seasoned, intensely flavored smoked pork favored in Louisiana Cajun cookery. In other locales, it can be found in specialty foods stores, and always online.

# QUICK CRAYFISH STOCK

2 tablespoons unsalted butter

Reserved crayfish shells

1 onion, chopped

1 carrot, chopped

1 stalk celery, chopped

½ cup chopped tomato

4 cups water

2 cups dry white wine

Salt to taste

Lemon juice to taste

1. In a nonreactive stockpot, melt the butter over medium heat and sauté the reserved crayfish shells for 5 minutes. Add the onion, carrot, and celery and cook until they begin to soften, about 5 minutes. Add the tomato and cook for 5 minutes.

2. Cover with the water and wine and bring to a simmer over medium heat, skimming off any foam that rises to the top. Simmer, uncovered, for 30 minutes. Strain the stock through a fine-meshed sieve and season with salt and lemon juice.

# CROAKER, ATLANTIC

The **Atlantic croaker** (*Micropogonias undulatus*) spends the winter in warm offshore waters. In the spring, it migrates to inshore waters, and from spring through fall it is one of the most abundant fish found in the environs of the Chesapeake Bay, the Carolinas, and the northern Gulf of Mexico.

The croaker, a member of the noisy drum family, is the noisiest of them all. It's sometimes called the "talking fish" for the croaking, grumbling, and drumming sounds it makes during courtship and spawning.

In Virginia and the Carolinas, fishing for croaker is one of the most popular summer pastimes for children and adults alike. This important recreational fish is a popular regional specialty enjoyed fresh at the shore, usually simply dressed, dusted with cornmeal, and panfried. When fresh, the croaker is tender, with a mild, sweet flavor.

There is steady demand for croaker in the Southeast and Gulf states, where it is easily found in supermarkets and fish stores. Croakers are sold as whole fish, dressed fish, or fillets. The fillets are pure white but may have a pinkish tinge, which is fine. Be sure the fish has no bruising or discoloration of the flesh. Pan-dressed fish should look and smell fresh; cuts at the belly and nape should appear fresh, with no brown or yellow discoloration.

Outside of these traditional areas of availability, croaker is also carried in Chinese and other Asian markets. Always buy whole fish at these markets—counter fillets in Asian markets may have been cut from fish that is no longer fresh enough to be displayed as whole fish—and be sure to check for all the typical signs of freshness: clear eyes, red gills, firm flesh, and the smell of the sea. The market will gladly clean or fillet your fish. Fresh whole croaker usually average one to two pounds each and display bright silver and gold coloration, with luminescent pink overtones.

Croaker has never gained widespread popularity in other regions of the country. A large percentage of the commercial landings of croaker are exported to China as inexpensive frozen fish. As one observer says, "The box is worth more than the fish." On the other hand, a small amount of top-quality croaker is shipped to Korea, where, once dried and properly packaged, it is transformed into one of the most highly esteemed and expensive fish on the market.

Croakers caught by pound net or seine in the fall when the fish are fat and the water temperatures have cooled are top-quality delicious fish capable of pleasing the most discerning diner. An abundant fish that grows quickly and reproduces at an early age, the croaker is a great environmental choice and a far more interesting dining choice than many aquacultured fish. It's definitely worth a try.

## CHOOSING SUSTAINABLE SEAFOOD

The Atlantic croaker matures early and is short-lived and very abundant. Populations vary greatly, in large part because the croaker is highly dependent on just the right environmental conditions. Currently, we are in a favorable cycle, with croakers thriving and large in number.

In the past, many millions of croaker were caught in shrimp nets and discarded. Today, mandatory bycatch reduction devices used by shrimpers have greatly reduced the number caught, in all likelihood another contributing factor in the current abundance of croakers.

Unknown but probably very large numbers of croakers are taken in the southeast Atlantic fishery that targets menhaden to be used as feed for poultry, pigs, and farmed fish, as pet food, and for industrial purposes (see Fishing Down the Food Chain, page 48 ).

## CHOOSING HEALTHY SEAFOOD

The croaker is a low-fat source of protein that provides some B vitamins and minerals and

small amounts of the omega-3 fatty acids said to lower blood cholesterol, reduce inflammatory response, and enhance brain function.

Croakers are short lived, so they don't usually bio-accumulate pollutants, but because they are often caught in inshore waters, it's recommended that recreational fishermen check with local authorities for any regional pollution advisories (see Persistent Organic Pollutants, page 417).

### IN THE KITCHEN

Croaker is a very lean fish that is full of flavor and sweetness. The skin is edible. Croaker fillet is most often dredged in cornmeal or breaded and panfried; whole croaker may be baked, charcoal-grilled, or steamed (as is popular in Asian restaurants). The full flavor of croaker will stand up to Asian sauces and marinades: Sauces that include miso, soy sauce, fresh ginger, garlic, and even fermented black beans and

Asian sesame oil enhance the fish without overwhelming it. Fillets can be broiled or cooked in aluminum foil (see page 130).

A common complaint about croaker? Bones. In truth, croakers have the same amount of bones as any other fish. It's just that because of their small size, every serving seems to have bones. One way to avoid bones is to cook croaker by the Mediterranean technique used to make fish soup from small whole bony fish: Simmer the cleaned fish in wine, water, and vegetables until almost opaque throughout, then pick the meat from the bones and set it aside. Pound and grind the remaining carcasses and vegetables through a heavy strainer, colander, or China cap to create a stock that is thick with tiny pieces of vegetable and fish. Cook fresh vegetables and seasonings in the stock, then add the reserved fish at the last minute for a hearty fish soup.

# GRILLED SWEET-AND-SOUR CROAKER
## IN ALUMINUM FOIL

Any time I come up with a meal that doesn't make a mess in the kitchen, my wife heartily approves. Cooking in aluminum foil on the grill is perfect for those hot summer nights when you don't want to heat up the kitchen or have to worry about cleanup.

Croakers are inexpensive and underutilized but tasty, a good fish to try as an alternative to Atlantic cod or Pacific rockfish. A regional specialty that is seldom cooked any way other than panfried with a cornmeal crust, the croaker is quite good when cooked in this sweet-and-sour sauce.

Brochettes of tomato, squash, onion, and mushrooms, brushed with a little oil and seasoned with salt and pepper, should take the same amount of time as the fish. Sliced potatoes wrapped in a foil packet with a tablespoon or two of butter will take about twenty minutes, so start them on the grill earlier.

**Four 5-ounce croaker fillets**

**1 onion, thinly sliced**

**2 organic lemons, scrubbed and thinly**
**sliced**

**Kosher salt and freshly ground black**
**pepper to taste**

**¼ cup chopped celery heart with leaves**

**¼ cup golden raisins, soaked in**
**2 tablespoons white wine to plump**

**2 tablespoons white wine vinegar**

**¼ cup olive oil**

**16 fresh mint leaves**

**1.** Prepare a medium-hot fire in a charcoal grill, or preheat a gas grill to 375°F. Cut 4 pieces of aluminum foil large enough to hold the croaker fillets, with a 4-inch border all around so the fish can be enclosed in the foil. Place a quarter of the onion slices on the center of each piece of foil, then a few lemon slices and a croaker fillet on top. Season with salt and pepper and place the rest of the lemon slices on top of each fillet. Mix the celery, the raisins, and the wine they soaked in with the vinegar and oil. Spoon over the top of each fillet and place 4 mint leaves on top.

**2.** Fold the sides of the foil up and bind them together to form a sealed packet. Place the foil packets on a hot grill and cook for 8 minutes over charcoal, 10 minutes on a gas grill.

## Accidental Hero

My friend Howell is a shrimper. Growing up as a kid in coastal Georgia, he spent many years shrimping with his dad, Sinkey. They fished the briny saltwater inlets just north of the creek in the spring and then moved farther south and offshore through the summer. Most of the time, they fished over hard mud bottom, rarely dipping into the eelgrass, and shrimp was the main catch. If they started coming up with too many small fish—young king mackerels, croakers, weaks, or flounders—Howell's dad would invariably pull up their nets and move to another site. "Let's leave those fellas to get big for your Uncle Ted next year," Sinkey would say to his son; "they'll be your cousin Timmy's tuition upstate in the fall."

### GOOD FOR SHRIMP'IN

In fact, nothing interfered with good shrimping more than all the *other* stuff that came up in the nets. Sometimes it was logs or trash that tore up the nets—one year they even caught two washing machines. The occasional shark or stingray could be a problem just because they were so big and mean, but most ended up going back over the side. Porgies and snails were part of almost every tow—the porgies they sold or ate; the snails they kicked out through the scuppers with the trash and weeds.

Back then, if a turtle happened to come up in the net, well, that meant "pork chops" (turtle) for Sunday night. But when the horseshoe crabs started moving inshore to spawn, so many would get tangled up in the net that shrimping became impossible. You might whack a crab or two with a club in the hopes that fewer of them would show up next year, but that never made a difference. Same thing with the jelly balls: When the cabbage-head jellyfish got thick, the net would come up so full of jelly balls that there was room for little else.

Nothing made Howell's dad madder than all those jelly balls and horseshoe crabs messing with his shrimping. So he tried to come up with a way to fix it. He knew the jelly balls tended to float up, so he decided to put a gate at the top of the net's "bag" to let them out. The more he thought about it, the more he liked the idea. Sinkey built his gate and sewed it into his net and went fishing. It turned out that not only did the jelly balls float out of the net, but so did the horseshoe crabs, sharks, stingrays, and trash. An oversize Kenmore washing machine might even fit through.

CONTINUED

The fishermen at the docks saw that Sinkey's gate allowed him to keep fishing even when the jelly balls and horseshoe crabs were at their thickest. Before you knew it, everybody in southeast Georgia wanted one of Sinkey's gates, and he was happy to sell them. He called his invention the Georgia Jumper, because you could see it jump open when something big like a shark went through.

## GOOD FOR TURTLES

After a few years of using the Georgia Jumper, Sinkey and the others realized they weren't catching turtles anymore. "When we first started using the Georgia Jumper, there were hardly any turtles at all," Howell recounts. "But now they're popping up everywhere. We've even got loggerheads and giant leatherbacks, which aren't supposed to be here, all over the place."

But the turtle population was faring poorly in other shrimping hot spots. By the 1980s, the National Marine Fishery Service (NMFS) found itself under intense pressure from environmental groups to do something about all the dead sea turtles washing up on Gulf of Mexico beaches during shrimp season. In response, NMFS developed an unwieldy cagelike device with a metal-framed trap door and promoted its voluntary use. Fishermen complained that the device was dangerous and dumped too much shrimp along with the turtles; less than 2 percent of the shrimp fleet even tried it out.

The Georgia Jumper had been designed and perfected over the years by a fisherman who understood how to install it so that the handling of the boat was unaffected and shrimp were not lost. Recognizing that his device may be the answer to their problems, the fishery service turned to Sinkey for help. The Georgia Jumper was more readily accepted by the shrimp community, and other fishermen who learned from Sinkey's design created similar gates. The fishery service designated these traps Turtle Excluder Devices (TEDs), and since 1990 all U.S. shrimp boats have been required to use them.

## GOOD FOR THE FUTURE

Because of the use of TEDs, turtle mortality has been greatly reduced. Under industry pressure, the fishery service initially reduced the size of Sinkey's device to make it easier to tow, which was fine for the endangered Kemp's ridley and green turtles but less so for larger turtles. In 2003, fishery service regulations increased TED size to match Sinkey's original design in an effort to further protect the giant leatherback and loggerhead turtles and hopefully reduce turtle mortality in the U.S. shrimp fishery to near 0 percent.

In coming up with a simple but ingenious method to rid his nets of jelly balls and horseshoe crabs that were spoiling his shrimping, Sinkey became an accidental hero. He has saved the lives of countless turtles. Today, he travels the world preaching the gospel of conservation and teaching other fishermen and governments how to properly use the Georgia Jumper.

Howell still fishes for shrimp in the same waters where he and his father dropped their nets years ago, sending us fresh, sweet "Georgia whites" two or three times a week. He keeps the snails now, sending them to the Fulton Fish Market, where they're sold as *scungilli*.

And the jelly balls? Well, they haven't been a problem since somebody found out that the Chinese love jelly balls. "I can't believe people would want to eat those things," Howell says. "They dry 'em and put 'em in soup. We've even got a full-time buyer right here on the dock who'll buy as many jelly balls as we can catch, but most everybody would still rather go shrimping."

That's because the shrimping in Darien is still thriving, thanks to Sinkey and his Georgia jumper. And it may even get better: The fishermen at the Darien co-op recently asked the Georgia Department of Natural Resources to consider opening the shrimp season later to give the shrimp more time to spawn. It will cost them a few fishing days, but they know it will be nothing but good for the future.

# DORY, JOHN

The olive-green **John Dory** (*Zeus faber*), with golden highlights and a distinctive silver dollar–sized black spot on its side, is found in a number of the world's waters. In Europe, it's known as Saint-Pierre, or "Saint Peter's fish," so named for the "thumbprint" on its side, supposedly left by St. Peter when he grasped the fish to remove a coin from its mouth to pay the temple tax collectors. Its common name, John Dory, is the subject of debate. Some believe it derives from the French *jaune d'oree* ("with a yellow edge"), in reference to the fish's coloring.

Ten large dorsal spines rising up from its back give the John Dory the angry look of a skinny, rebellious teenage boy with an outsized Mohawk. Its fierce appearance belies its wonderful eating qualities. The fish is firm-textured, with a mild, sweet flavor; when filleted, it can easily be mistaken for a particularly fine sole in both appearance and flavor.

The John Dory most often seen in the American market is imported from New Zealand. Though available year-round, it is most readily available during our winter, when it's summer in the southern hemisphere.

While John Dory is more likely to be seen on restaurant menus, it can also be found in upscale seafood markets. If it's not a regular item in your fish market, it's common enough that you should be able to special-order it. Markets that already sell such New Zealand staples as tai snapper, bluenose, and New Zealand grouper are a good source.

Whole John Dory should have lustrous skin, bulging eyes, firm flesh, and a pleasant sea smell. The fillets should be lustrous and moist looking, with no discoloration or drying along the edges. Reject any fillets with a musty or yeasty smell, the first sign of deterioration.

A similar species, the **silver Dory** (*Zenopsis conchifera*), is found along the U.S. Atlantic Coast from Canada to North Carolina, and comes to market on the East Coast during the summer. Its appearance is very similar to the John Dory but for its mirrorlike silvery skin—hence its name. Though not as highly regarded as the John Dory, the silver Dory is still quite good.

## CHOOSING SUSTAINABLE SEAFOOD

New Zealand fisheries policies are generally precautionary, and most species are well managed. Still, it is difficult to judge the exact status of New Zealand John Dory, which is taken mainly in multispecies trawl and seine fisheries. East Coast silver Dory is not a heavily targeted species and could even be considered underutilized.

## CHOOSING HEALTHY SEAFOOD

The John Dory is a low-fat, high-protein source of B vitamins and minerals. Most fats are of the heart-healthy polyunsaturated variety.

## IN THE KITCHEN

The John Dory's scales are very fine and need not be removed. The skin is often removed before cooking, but if you're cooking the whole fish, you can leave it on. Simply chopped into chunks with the bone left in, it makes a fine addition to stews. The bones make a rich and flavorful stock.

John Dory can be eaten raw as sashimi, pickled in vinegar or fruit juice. When cooking, steam, poach, or gently sauté for best results.

# JOHN DORY WITH LEMONGRASS, GINGER, AND TOMATO–MUSSEL BROTH AÏOLI

Substitute sole, haddock, halibut, lingcod, or any other mild-flavored white fish for the John Dory, or try this recipe with salmon or white sea bass. Serve with asparagus roasted with olive oil and sea salt.

⅓ cup dry white wine

2 dozen mussels, scrubbed and debearded

3 to 4 stalks lemongrass, white part only,
  peeled and minced

½-inch piece fresh ginger, peeled and
  minced

1 tomato, peeled, seeded (see page 39),
  and finely diced (about ¼ cup)

1 tablespoon refined peanut oil or another
  high-heat oil for frying

Four 5-ounce skinless John Dory fillets

Kosher salt and freshly ground black
  pepper

⅓ cup Aïoli (recipe follows)

2 tablespoons minced fresh chives or
  flat-leaf parsley

1. In a large saucepan, bring the wine to a boil over high heat. Add the mussels, cover, and cook, shaking the pan a few times, until the mussels open, about 3 minutes. Transfer to a large bowl. Shell the mussels and reserve. Rinse out the pan and pour the mussel liquid back into the pan, stopping before you reach the grit.

2. Over medium heat, bring the mussel liquid to a simmer; add the lemongrass and ginger and simmer for 3 or 4 minutes. Add the tomato and simmer for 1 minute, then reduce the heat to low.

3. In a large sauté pan or skillet, heat the oil over medium-high heat. Season the John Dory fillets with salt and pepper and cook until golden, about 3 minutes per side.

4. Whisk the Aïoli into the mussel broth and add the reserved mussels. Transfer the John Dory fillets to shallow bowls and spoon the mussels and sauce around it. Garnish with the minced chives or parsley and serve.

## Aïoli

Note that all the ingredients for this sauce should be at room temperature.

2 or 3 garlic cloves
¼ teaspoon coarse sea salt, plus salt to taste
Pinch of cayenne pepper or hot paprika
1 large egg yolk
1 teaspoon warm water
¾ cup olive oil
1 tablespoon freshly squeezed lemon juice
1 tablespoon white wine vinegar

Using a mortar and pestle, grind the garlic, the ¼ teaspoon salt, and the cayenne or paprika to a smooth paste. You may continue in the mortar or transfer the mixture to a larger bowl or a food processor. Add the egg yolk and water and whisk or process until smooth. While constantly whisking or with the machine running, gradually pour in the oil, starting with just a few drops at a time; as the sauce begins to thicken, add the remaining oil in a slow, fine stream. If the aïoli becomes too thick, thin with a bit of warm water. Whisk the lemon juice and vinegar into the aïoli and season with salt to taste. The sauce can be stored for several days in a clean jar in the refrigerator.

# GROUPER

Groupers are members of the prized Serranidae, or true sea-bass, family of fishes, and have long been a mainstay of both commercial and recreational fisheries and among the most sought-after fish in the home kitchen and restaurants alike. The versatile, easy-to-cook, and delicious groupers are to the southeast Atlantic and Gulf states as rockfish are to the West and cod to the Northeast.

South Atlantic and Gulf waters are rich with grouper. Florida accounts for around 90 percent of the nation's annual grouper catch, about half of which is the mildly sweet-flavored **red grouper** (*Epinephelus morio*). **Gag grouper** (*Mycteroperca microlepis*), often referred to as black grouper in the market, is the second most common grouper. It is highly prized for its firm flesh, shellfishlike flavor, and high meat yield. **Yellowedge groupers** bring up the rear in availability and perceived quality at the table.

Of the dozen or so other groupers caught in South Atlantic and Gulf waters, most are eaten only locally. **Warsaw**, **scamp**, and **black groupers** are some of the most highly esteemed.

South Atlantic and Gulf groupers are rarely sold in markets on the West Coast, but you will see the occasional offering of **red Baqueta grouper**, **broomtail grouper**, and **spotted cabrilla** from Pacific coast Mexican waters. The **hapu'upu'u** of Hawaii is a very popular and important species in Hawaiian markets and is occasionally sold on the mainland Pacific Coast. The New Zealand grouper, popular on the Pacific Coast, is not a true grouper but rather a member of the closely related temperate bass family (see Wreckfish, page 399).

Fresh grouper fillets should have a clean, fresh ocean smell with no mustiness. They should be translucent white to pale pink in color and appear firm, with a satiny, lustrous sheen. There should be no visible bruising, tears, or gaps. Avoid fillets that are discolored or feel soft. Imported grouper is usually sold with the skin removed, while domestic grouper is likely to have the skin on for identification.

Whole groupers should have a clear, viscous, naturally occurring protective coating of slime; the complete absence of slime may indicate repeated washing to hide its age. Groupers come in a variety of sizes: the strawberry grouper averages one to two pounds while the giant black sea bass (a true grouper) may easily top three hundred pounds; most market-sized fish in the United States average between three and fifteen pounds. Larger fish are usually filleted. U.S. Atlantic and Gulf coast–caught groupers are not available during the February 15 through March 15 spawning closure and are scarce in November and December. During this time, most grouper on the market is imported from Mexico or South America. In many cases, these fisheries are unregulated and the quality is often inferior to U.S.-caught grouper. This is a great time to try sustainably managed wreckfish of North Carolina waters (see page 400) as an alternative to grouper.

### CHOOSING SUSTAINABLE SEAFOOD

The grouper had been so common and plentiful for so long that it never occurred to us to pay attention to its welfare until drastic action was needed. A number of factors have led to the depletion of many grouper species in U.S. waters. The fish are long lived, slow to mature, and gather in large groups to spawn. Fishing vessels often target spawning aggregations, a practice that removes large numbers of reproducing individuals from the water.

In response, marine preserves meant to protect grouper spawning aggregations have been established on both the Atlantic and Gulf coasts of Florida. Longlines are being restricted to deeper water, and trap fisheries responsible for excess bycatch of immature groupers are being phased out. Quotas for red grouper were established in 2005, which should help return this fish to former abundance.

A positive note has been the rebuilding of Atlantic Coast gag grouper stocks (often sold as black grouper) and the cessation of overfishing and reduced quotas on gag grouper in the Gulf. Gag groupers mature earlier than most groupers, so have responded well to conservation efforts; other grouper populations will require many more years of concerted effort to fully recover.

The Hawaiian hapu'upu'u, well regulated and relatively abundant in the Northwest Islands, is listed as a "good alternative" choice by the Monterey Bay Aquarium's Seafood Watch Program (www.mbayaq.org).

The establishment of the Northwestern Hawaiian Islands Marine National Monument in 2007 will ensure a healthy future for the hapu'upu'u. But as all fishing will be halted in this area by 2011—an area that has been responsible for producing 50 percent of all Hawaiian bottom fish—concerns have been raised that Hawaii will now import these fish from other areas of the Pacific, which do not have the resources to manage and monitor their fisheries effectively.

## CHOOSING HEALTHY SEAFOOD

The grouper is an excellent low-fat, high-protein source of antistress B vitamins and minerals, particularly potassium and selenium, which may help reduce mercury absorption. It is also a source of omega-3 fatty acids, said to improve blood lipid profile, reduce inflammatory response, and ensure good brain function among other health benefits.

Reef-dwelling fish from tropical waters may accumulate naturally-occurring marine toxins. While almost unheard of in U.S. waters, imported grouper, particularly larger fish of over ten pounds, have been reported to cause ciguatera (see page 411).

The very oldest and largest groupers may accumulate higher mercury levels. Young children, women considering pregnancy, and pregnant and nursing mothers should avoid eating large groupers. Ultimately, it's best to eat a variety of different kinds of seafood that come from different places.

## IN THE KITCHEN

Grouper has traditionally been the workhorse of local cuisines throughout its range. Florida has its ubiquitous grouper sandwich; Louisiana has blackened grouper; the Atlantic its fish chowder. Hawaiians prefer their hapu'upu'u as sashimi or cooked Chinese style in rice porridge (*jook*). It's no wonder that grouper is beloved by all: This mild-mannered fish has a complex shellfishlike flavor and a forgiving nature that keeps it moist.

The lean, firm-fleshed, and muscular grouper has a wonderfully toothsome texture—but it also means that larger grouper can be very tough, particularly when cooked by high-heat methods. Fillets of grouper thicker than about two inches should be cut into thin slices or scallops about a quarter inch thick. This reduces cooking time and shortens the muscle fibers, preventing toughening and curling when cooking.

Grouper bones are among the best bones for stock. The skin of most large fish is too tough to eat, but for smaller specimens, which are delicious braised, baked, or grilled whole, the skin is thin and tender enough to be enjoyed.

Grouper is a favorite in the Nuevo Latino recipes of south Florida, where it is often paired with locally grown tropical fruits and vegetables. For a simple, fragrant, and delicious sauce for this fish, push cooked guavas through a strainer, then thin the puree with olive oil and Key lime juice. Sauté or grill grouper and serve with a sweet-sour sauce of caramelized onions, grapefruit juice, and sherry wine vinegar, or make a mango–Scotch bonnet chile salsa. Braised grouper prepared with bell peppers and onions is delicious, as is grouper baked with chayote squash (*mirliton*), sour orange juice, and oregano.

# PAN-ROASTED GROUPER WITH CARIBBEAN SOFRITO

Sofrito is a seasoning mix used in just about all Puerto Rican recipes. Two of its ingredients, culantro, an herb whose flavor is similar to that of cilantro, and aji dulce peppers, a mild Scotch bonnet–style chile, are difficult to find if you don't shop in New York City or Miami. If you can find authentic culantro and aji dulce peppers, by all means use them, but I've substituted the easier-to-find cilantro and a combination of hot Scotch bonnet and sweet red peppers for the aji dulce in this recipe. Serve with rice and steamed chayote squash (*mirliton*) and Tostones, which are twice-fried slices of plantain (recipe follows).

- - - - - - - - - - - - - - - - - - - - - - - - - - - - - - - -

**8 thin slices prosciutto or serrano ham**

**Four 5-ounce grouper fillets**

**CARIBBEAN SOFRITO**

**¼ onion**

**1 sweet green Italian pepper or Anaheim chile, seeded**

**1 Scotch bonnet or habanero chile, seeded**

**1 thin-skinned sweet red pepper, such as gypsy, or ½ red bell pepper, seeded**

**1 garlic clove, minced**

**6 tablespoons olive oil**

**½ cup dry white wine**

**½ cup freshly squeezed orange juice**

**Juice of 1 lime**

**2 tablespoons minced fresh cilantro**

**1 orange, segmented (see page 35), for garnish**

1. Preheat the oven to 375°F. Wrap 2 slices of the prosciutto or serrano around the middle of each grouper fillet, leaving the ends uncovered.

2. To start the sofrito: Using a chef's knife or a food processor, finely chop the onion, chile, red pepper, and garlic. Set aside.

3. In a large, heavy ovenproof sauté pan or cast-iron skillet, heat 3 tablespoons of the oil over medium-high heat. As soon as it is shimmering hot, carefully lay the grouper fillets in the pan. Cook the grouper over medium-high heat for 2 to 3 minutes, or until the ham and exposed fish are crispy and brown. Turn the fillets over. Add the chopped sofrito vegetables to the pan and when it begins to sizzle, after about a minute, add the white wine, orange juice, and lime juice. Place the pan in the oven and roast the fish for about 5 minutes per inch, or until almost opaque throughout.

**4.** Remove the pan from the oven and transfer the fish to 4 plates. On the stove top, cook the pan juices over high heat to reduce to about ⅓ cup. Remove from the heat and quickly whisk in the cilantro to finish the sofrito and the remaining 3 tablespoons olive oil to thicken the sauce. Garnish with the orange segments and spoon the sauce over each fillet.

### ▪ ▪ ▪ TOSTONES ▪ ▪ ▪

Peel and cut plantains that have ripened to yellow with a few black specks into 1-inch-thick coins. Panfry on each side in hot peanut oil until firm, about 3 minutes. Remove and press flat between sheets of aluminum foil or wax paper. Re-fry the flattened coins of plantain until crunchy and golden.

# HALIBUT, CALIFORNIA

The **California halibut** (*Paralichthys californicus*) is found from Baja California to British Columbia, with the greatest concentrations taken in California (hence its name). It is not a true halibut but rather a giant flounder—the California halibut can reach weights in excess of forty pounds. While there's been an unverified report of a seventy-two-pound fish, the accepted record for a commercial catch stands at sixty-one pounds—a fish that was nearly five feet long. Most fish are much smaller, however.

The California halibut, like all newborn flatfish, begins life near the surface, swimming upright, with an eye on either side of its head. As the fish matures, a dramatic change takes place: One eye migrates across the top of the fish's skull to a position next to the eye on the other side of the body. During this transition, the young halibut swims with an ever-increasing sideways tilt. When the change is complete, both eyes are on one side of its head and the halibut is oriented to the horizontal. The adult California halibut then takes up residence on the bottom, where it lies in ambush to feed on passing squid, sardines, and anchovies.

The highest-quality California halibut are taken by hook and line from early spring through late fall, when they migrate offshore. California halibut are sold in markets up and down the West Coast. Though California halibut is not as highly regarded as the closely related East Coast summer flounder (fluke), Japanese markets often carry it for sashimi. In some years, California halibut is shipped to Japan for the sashimi trade.

Sashimi-quality hook-and-line–caught California halibut are a rich olive-green on one side and pure white on the other, with no red bruising or discoloration of the skin. The fillets are often a translucent sea-green, while trawler-caught fish tend to be an opaque white.

## CHOOSING SUSTAINABLE SEAFOOD
Gill-netting for California halibut was banned in 1994, which helped reduce the number of immature fish taken and ameliorated the fisheries' impact on seabirds. In response to the banning of gill nets, many fishermen turned to rod-and-reel gear, vastly improving the overall quality of the catch. As a result, there has been a dramatic increase in the average size and number of halibut landed throughout the 1990s, indicating a healthy, growing population.

## CHOOSING HEALTHY SEAFOOD
Because some wild fish may be susceptible to infective parasites, care should be exercised when eating raw halibut (see Raw Seafood: How to Stay Safe, page 408).

## IN THE KITCHEN
The roe, liver, and cheeks of the halibut are edible, and the bones make a very nice stock. The skin is tough and must be removed before cooking.

The flesh of the California halibut is firm, with a mild-sweet flavor. Due to its low fat content, however, it can easily become very dry. Gentle cooking and moist-heat methods such as steaming or poaching seem to work best; cooking times should be kept to a minimum.

Cooking California halibut in parchment is almost foolproof, but wrapping the fish in grape leaves, cabbage, or any other vegetable leaf and then steaming or braising also works well. Raw fish preparations such as sashimi, tartar, ceviche, or poke are excellent.

# HOT-PLATE HALIBUT
# WITH WARM HERB VINAIGRETTE

Judy Rodgers, now the owner of the Zuni Café in San Francisco, was the lunch cook early on at Chez Panisse. At that time, I would drag wooden crates laden with a colorful mélange of fish to the back door of Chez Panisse for inspection. Among the rockfish, sea bass, and halibut slotted for dinner service were evil-tempered wolf eels that refused to die even hours out of the water. Because the cooks were expected to find a use for everything, the task of using those wolf eels often fell to Judy.

Judy was greatly relieved when I found a market in Chinatown for wolf eels and she was able to move on to more elevated fare. California halibut, prepared in this way, became one of her favorites. It is the perfect cooking technique for California halibut, guaranteeing a moist and flavorful piece of fish. Serve with salad greens and fresh corn kernels dry-roasted in a hot cast-iron pan for six to eight minutes, or until just cooked crisp-tender. Season with butter, salt, and pepper.

1 tablespoon white wine vinegar

2 tablespoons freshly squeezed lemon juice

Grated zest of 1 lemon (about ½ teaspoon)

2 tablespoons minced mixed fresh herbs,
   such as flat-leaf parsley, chives, and
   chervil

½ cup mild olive oil

Four 4-ounce slices California halibut,
   no thicker than ¼ inch

Coarse kosher or sea salt and fresh-cracked
   black pepper to taste

**1.** Preheat the oven to 200°F and place 4 oven-proof plates inside.

**2.** In a small bowl, combine the vinegar, lemon juice, lemon zest, parsley, chives, and chervil. Whisk in the olive oil to make a vinaigrette. In a small saucepan, heat the vinaigrette until warm to the touch.

**3.** Put the fish slices between sheets of oiled plastic wrap or parchment paper and gently pound them with a mallet until they are ⅛ inch thick. Gently roll a rolling pin over them to make them even.

**4.** Remove the plates from the oven and preheat the broiler. The plates should be hot, but not too hot to handle quickly without an oven mitt. Spoon a little of the vinaigrette onto each plate and follow with a slice of halibut. Spoon a little more vinaigrette over the top and season with salt and pepper.

**5.** Place the plates under the broiler, 4 to 5 inches from the heat source, for 1 to 2 minutes, or until the halibut slices start to turn opaque. The halibut will continue to cook gently while being served on the hot plates.

# HALIBUT, PACIFIC

The **Pacific halibut** (*Hippoglossus stenolepis*) is one of the great success stories in recent fishery conservation and management—and good thing, too, because it's the kind of delicious, versatile fish that makes every cook look good.

The range of the Pacific halibut covers the entire North Pacific and Bering Sea from Canada to Russia, but the inshore fishing grounds of Southeast Alaska always seem to produce the freshest and best-handled fish. Thanks to direct air-freight connections from ports such as Juneau, Sitka, and Ketchikan to the lower forty-eight, these fish are quick to market as well. Alaskan halibut season opens on March 1, and excellent-quality fish are readily available until fall, when quality and availability begin to erode just before the season's end on November 15.

The fish's East Coast counterpart, the **Atlantic halibut** (*H. hippoglossus*), has not fared as well. Although it is available year-round from Canada, it is now commercially extinct in U.S. waters (trawlers fishing for other species are permitted to land two fish per trip, however). Longline fishermen still actively pursue halibut from ports in the Maritimes of Canada, but Canadian stocks are highly stressed from overfishing.

Pacific halibut is an environmentally sound and healthy seafood choice that is available in all parts of the country eight months of the year. I see little point in eating Atlantic halibut when we have an abundance of sustainably fished Pacific halibut. Ask your fishmonger for Pacific halibut when it's in season; move on down the counter when it's not.

Halibut is readily available throughout the season, so it should always be fresh if you shop at a busy quality fish store or upscale market. I don't recommend buying halibut in Chinese or other ethnic markets; it is not particularly favored in Asian cuisine so is less likely to sell quickly and be fresh.

Whole Pacific halibut may reach three hundred to four hundred pounds, and Atlantic halibut grow even larger. Years ago I bought a 780-pound halibut from Nova Scotia and had to call on two burly fishermen friends to help me fillet it. While I knelt on the ground, sweating and slicing away with a nine-inch fillet knife, my arm buried inside the halibut to the shoulder, my two fishermen friends struggled to support the weight of the fillet as it came off the bone. Halibut today are marketed at much smaller sizes; ten to twenty pounds each, twenty to forty, forty to sixty, sixty to eighty, and eighty pounds up are the common size designations in the wholesale market; fish over 150 pounds are rare.

A healthy, fresh-from-the-sea halibut has a firm, lively-looking tautness. It should be sparkling white, with no sign of red or yellow discoloration on the bottom side and a rich black or gray-green on the top. Check for the presence of fresh red blood in the belly cavity and look at the edge of any cuts made for cleaning to ensure that they are fresh.

Fresh halibut fillets and steaks have a glassy, translucent appearance and a clear to light-green-colored flesh. Super-fresh halibut will show a rainbow sheen of color where the meat has been sliced across the grain. The fat on the backside of fresh halibut fillets ranges from silver or white to various shades of blonde and copper—any of which is acceptable. Avoid fish with green or yellow discoloration of the fat; chalky, dull flesh lacking in translucency; or yeasty odors.

## Good Management Makes the Pacific Halibut Sustainable

The Pacific halibut is a recent fishery conservation and management success story. The creation of the International Pacific Halibut Commission led to the successful rebuilding of Pacific halibut stocks and a new type of fishery management.

For many years prior to 1970, an unlimited number of boats were allowed to fish for as much halibut as they could catch. By 1970, as more fishermen entered the fishery and the fleet became more sophisticated, Pacific halibut became overfished and the halibut commission was forced to shorten the season. Year after year, things got worse, until by 1990 the same amount of halibut that had been caught in a year was now being caught in an insanely dangerous and supremely wasteful two-day derby.

When the two-day season opened, fishermen would go out in any weather and refuse to quit fishing until it closed. Once gear was set in a specific locale, there was no time to move, even if too many small fish were being taken. If gear became tangled, it was simply cut loose and allowed to "ghost fish." The desire to catch as much fish as possible in the two-day season often led to disaster; boats were known to sink from being overloaded with halibut. The captain of a boat loaded to the gunwales with flopping monster halibut might call the Coast Guard in distress, yet continue to haul fish until help arrived.

In some high-volume ports, five or six days were needed to unload all the fish caught in one day, most of which arrived frozen and often of mixed quality.

In 1995, the halibut fishery was changed to an Individual Fishery Quota system (IFQ), whereby a restricted number of fishermen who had historically been involved in the fishery were given partial ownership of it. Fishermen could buy or sell their quota and were allowed to fish at any time within an eight-month season. If the halibut resource did well, so did a fisherman's quota. The fishermen, in other words, had a vested interest in seeing that the fishery remained healthy.

The very first year of the new system, ghost fishing and bycatch were reduced by 80 percent, fewer undersized halibut were taken, and overfishing ended. The result has been a sustainable fishery that delivers an abundance of top-quality fresh Pacific halibut to the market from March through November every year. This is good for the fish, the fishermen, and the market.

Many other fisheries, including Gulf red snapper and Atlantic cod, are being considered for fishery quota management plans in hopes that they, too, can be returned to a healthy state.

## CHOOSING SUSTAINABLE SEAFOOD

The Pacific halibut was severely overfished prior to 1960, and was in much the same shape that we find the Atlantic halibut today. The creation of the International Pacific Halibut Commission led to the successful rebuilding of halibut stocks, however, and the fishery is now a model of sustainability and good management. (North Pacific halibut has been certified a sustainable well-managed fishery by the Marine Stewardship Council; see www.msc.org.)

Pacific halibut fishermen take their reputation as an environmentally friendly fishery seriously. They recently helped develop and now voluntarily use bird-scaring lines when deploying their hooks, to prevent seabirds from getting tangled in their gear.

Atlantic halibut, on the other hand, is on the International Union for Conservation of Nature and Natural Resources' Red List of endangered or threatened species (www.iucn.org). Any halibut now landed in U.S. waters are bycatch, associated with trawl vessels fishing for other species. There is as yet no rebuilding plan for the Atlantic halibut, and managers and fishermen should be ashamed of the state of this fishery.

## CHOOSING HEALTHY SEAFOOD

Halibut is a very good low-fat, high-protein source of antistress B vitamins, minerals (particularly potassium and selenium) and a moderate source of omega-3 fatty acids, which have been shown to lower blood cholesterol, reduce inflammatory response, and enhance brain function, among other health benefits. Because halibut is drawn from the clean north Pacific waters, it is generally free of organic pollutants, although mercury may reach moderate levels in larger, older fish.

Halibut are susceptible to two conditions that, while not of concern to human health, do adversely affect the texture and appearance of the fish, causing the flesh to become bland and watery when cooked. The first, "chalky fish," is brought on by an excessive buildup of lactic acid in the flesh of a struggling halibut. This creates a condition in which the flesh appears very white and chalky rather than translucent. The second, known as soft spot syndrome (see Kudoa, page 412), shows up as small, suppurating spots in the flesh. These conditions are usually obvious to the naked eye and fish that have them should be intercepted by a knowledgeable retailer before the point of sale. Consider changing fish markets if you see this type of fish on the counter.

While some fish may be susceptible to infective parasites, halibut that are cleaned as soon as they are captured are affected less often. Care should always be exercised when eating raw seafood (see Raw Seafood: How to Stay Safe, page 408).

## IN THE KITCHEN

Halibut is mild flavored, with a forgiving nature that keeps it moist even if left on the heat too long. It is a versatile fish that is adaptable to any cooking method and accepts pairing with most ingredients, making it the perfect palette for any sauce or cooking style. Halibut can be cold-smoked, as it often is in northern Europe, and is delicious when cured with salt and sugar in the style of gravlax, using black pepper, juniper berries, and gin for seasoning. Raw halibut slices can be dressed with olive oil and lemon or marinated in lime juice and garnished with chopped green olives. Halibut fillets can be steamed in napa cabbage leaves, then drizzled with chile oil, or grilled over charcoal with wild mushrooms.

Halibut cheeks are considered a delicacy; firm and sweet flavored, they resemble a large scallop and can be used in the same way. Remove any silvery skin from the cheeks before sautéing, grilling, or frying, then serve with a pungent Romesco Sauce (page 346). The liver can be poached and used to enrich a soup or sauce, making a fine substitute for the traditional monkfish liver when added to a rouille.

Halibut bones make an excellent-flavored stock and, as an extra benefit, seldom need more than a perfunctory cleaning, having been thoroughly cleaned on the boat. Although the skin can successfully be tanned for leather, it is too tough to eat and is usually removed before cooking; if left on, as it is with halibut steaks, it is discarded after cooking.

# HALIBUT BAKED
# IN PUMPKIN SEED MOLE

Pumpkin seed mole is a popular sauce in central and eastern Mexico, where it often accompanies tamales or shrimp. It's a versatile sauce; Diana Kennedy in *The Essential Cuisines of Mexico* braises duck in pumpkin seed mole.

At first glance, this recipe may appear complicated, but the technique is simple: the Sauce is made in a blender, and the ingredients are surprisingly easy to find. Sharply tart tomatillos are smoothed and tempered by the toasted pumpkin seeds, creating a mole, or sauce, that marries perfectly with seafood. Shrimp, grouper, wreckfish, or just about any white-fleshed fish work fine in this recipe; the more flavorful amberjack, yellowtail, or mahimahi are good options as well. Serve with rice and a simply steamed vegetable such as squash.

**PUMPKIN SEED MOLE**

¾ cup unsalted hulled pumpkin seeds
(see Note)

½ teaspoon coriander seeds

1 pound tomatillos

Pinch of ground cumin

2 serrano chiles

1 small white onion, diced

2 garlic cloves

½ cup chopped fresh cilantro

2 or 3 large romaine lettuce leaves, torn into
pieces (about 1 cup)

1½ teaspoons kosher salt

½ cup water

Four 5-ounce halibut fillets

**GARNISHES**

1 bunch red radishes, cut into thin slices

Cilantro sprigs

1. Preheat the oven to 350°F.

2. For the mole: In a dry medium sauté pan or skillet, lightly toast the pumpkin seeds over medium heat for 4 to 5 minutes, or until they start to pop; cook for just another minute or two while gently shaking the pan. Do not let them overbrown, or they will taste bitter. Pour the pumpkin seeds into a bowl. In the same pan, toast the coriander seeds until fragrant, about 3 or 4 minutes. Crush the coriander seeds in a mortar. Let both kinds of seeds cool.

3. Remove the papery husks from the tomatillos. In a medium saucepan of boiling water, cook the tomatillos for 3 to 4 minutes, or until they change color from bright green to yellow-green.

4. In a blender or food processor, combine all the mole ingredients and blend to a slightly textured puree, adding the water as needed to keep the sauce moving freely.

**5.** Pour half the mole into an ovenproof baking dish; place the halibut fillets in the dish and cover with the remaining mole. Bake, uncovered, for 15 to 20 minutes, or until the sauce is bubbling and the fish is almost opaque throughout.

**6.** Serve garnished with radishes and cilantro sprigs.

N O T E : Pumpkin seeds are available in natural foods or Latin grocery stores (where they are known as *pepitas*).

## HALIBUT BAKED IN PARCHMENT WITH TOMATOES AND CORN

SERVES 4 AS A MAIN COURSE

Cooking in parchment is absolutely my favorite way of cooking fish. It is healthful, needing little or no fat, and always delicious. Even delicate fish never seems to be overcooked or dry when cooked in parchment, and it comes to the table with style.

Halibut, tomatoes, and sweet corn are all at their peak and in good supply during summer. Use a juicy tomato such as an Early Girl or beefsteak for this recipe; the tomato and fish juices mingle to create a surprising amount of light, summery broth. Prepare the packets an hour or two in advance when having company, then just preheat the oven and pop them in at your convenience. Serve with an avocado, jícama, and grapefruit salad.

Four 5-ounce halibut fillets

1½ cups fresh corn kernels (about 2 ears)

1 pound tomatoes, diced (2 cups)

½ cup diced scallions, including light green parts

2 stalks celery with tops, finely diced

1-inch piece fresh ginger, minced

1 serrano chile, seeded and minced

2 tablespoons olive oil

Juice of 1 lime

Kosher salt and cayenne pepper to taste

**1.** Preheat the oven to 400°F. Tear off four 18-inch sheets of parchment paper. Fold each parchment sheet in half, then spread it back open. Place 1 halibut fillet on half of each sheet of paper two inches above the fold.

**2.** Mix the remaining ingredients together in a bowl. Place a quarter of the mixture on top of each piece of halibut.

**3.** Fold the sheet of parchment paper over to enclose the ingredients. Starting with the corner near the folded edge, make overlapping folds, one on top of the other, about 10 folds, until the opposite corner of the folded edge is reached. Twist the last fold at the end of the package several times to make a tight seal, and tuck it under the packet.

4. Place the packets on a baking sheet and bake until the paper turns brown around the edge and puffs up, 10 to 12 minutes.

5. Place each packet on a plate. Carefully cut an X in the top of each to allow steam to escape. For the full visual and aromatic effect, cut them open at the table.

NOTE: Parchment paper is found in the baking section of grocery stores and gourmet food shops. Folding parchment paper is a simple technique that makes perfect sense once you try it.

# JACK

The jacks are a large family of more than two hundred fish. Many are familiar to anyone with a love for seafood; two examples are the incredibly delicious hamachi, or Japanese **yellowtail** (*Seriola quinqueradiata*), popular in sushi bars, and the **Florida pompano** (*Trachinotus carolinus*). But a number of other excellent-eating jacks can be found in U.S. waters. The **greater amberjack** (*Seriola dumerili*) of Atlantic and Gulf Coast waters; the **almaco jack** (*S. rivoliana*), found both in Gulf and Hawaiian waters; and the **yellowtail jack** (*Seriola lalandei*) of Southern California and Mexico are all of note.

The greater amberjack, almaco, and yellowtail jack are all closely related and similar looking. In the United States, these jacks are often more appreciated for their fighting ability than their eating qualities. But in the world of Japanese sushi, they are nearly as important as tuna.

Cultivated Japanese yellowtail has been cultured and sold in Japan as hamachi sushi for many, many years. At about a year old and weighing from fifteen to twenty pounds, the fish are harvested at the peak of their flavor and fatty richness. More than ten years ago, American chefs began following the example of Japanese chefs by using hamachi in both raw and cooked dishes in the United States. Since then, the rich, flavor-packed hamachi has become so popular that it's available not only in Japanese markets but in American specialty supermarkets and fish markets as well.

More revered in Japan than hamachi and gaining popularity in the United States is the cultured kampachi, our very own common **greater amberjack**. The closely related **almaco jack**, known as *kahala* in the Hawaii dialect, is being cultured on the Big Island of Hawaii by an environmentally sensitive company, Kona Blue Water Farms, and marketed as "Kona kampachi." Kona Blue Water Farms (www.konakampachi.com) is leading the way toward sustainable aquaculture. Because they hatch their own fish so as not to adversely impact wild stocks, and use feed manufactured from the sustainable Peruvian anchovetta fishery, their kampachi is very high in omega-3s and tests at nondetectable levels for mercury, good fish from a good company.

Aquacultured jacks from farms in Japan and Hawaii are available in specialty supermarkets, fish markets, and Japanese markets year-round. Less expensive and far more widely available than cultured fish, wild jacks are less fatty but equally as complex and delicious in flavor. Wild California yellowtail is one of my favorite fish.

Jacks of less than twenty pounds are the best choice, and are at their firmest and best flavored during the winter months.

## CHOOSING SUSTAINABLE SEAFOOD

The jacks—much like mahimahi—spawn many times in a season, producing prodigious numbers of offspring. Nevertheless, years ago the California yellowtail was overfished by purse seiners fishing for the canneries. Today, California yellowtail is taken only by hook and line, and the California Department of Fish and Game has deemed the variety healthy.

Under a new federal management plan for the Gulf of Mexico, amberjack quotas have been reduced, size regulation has been instituted, and commercial fishing is no longer allowed from March through May during spawning season.

Pompano grow rapidly and are very resilient, but their popularity keeps them on the edge of sustainability. A ban on commercial gill nets in Florida waters did little to ease pressure on the pompano: Commercial gill-netters simply moved offshore, and recreational fishermen increased their take tenfold in inshore waters. Better management is needed before the pompano suffers as well.

## CHOOSING HEALTHY SEAFOOD

Jacks are high in the omega-3 fatty acids that help prevent chronic heart disease, reduce inflammatory response, and enhance brain function, among other health benefits. They are an easily digestible high-protein source of B vitamins and minerals.

Wild amberjack and almaco jack seem to be particularly susceptible to infective parasites (see page 412), so I suggest leaving raw preparations of these wild jacks to professionals. Aquacultured fish such as hamachi and kampachi are always completely parasite free, and wild California yellowtail is seldom parasitized.

Reef-dwelling fish from tropical waters may accumulate naturally-occurring marine toxins. Jacks in Hawaii have been reported to cause ciguatera (see page 411). Commercial fishermen in Hawaii understand ciguatera, are knowledgeable of local waters, and do not take fish from reefs that are under suspicion.

Members of the jack family that have not been quickly and properly chilled after capture may, similar to tuna, produce histamines in their flesh (see Scombroid, page 413).

## IN THE KITCHEN

Jacks are extraordinarily delicious when impeccably fresh—and they must be impeccably fresh. Moderately fatty, with firm cream to beige-colored flesh, they are moist with a long tender flake when cooked. The best way to describe the flavor of jacks? Intensely sweet. Like all fish, jacks have both light and dark muscle. The light beige meat is mild flavored, while the powerful, darker myoglobin-rich red muscle tissue is much stronger flavored, particularly in large, mature fish. The dark meat may be trimmed away for a milder taste.

Aquacultured hamachi is fed an extremely rich diet until their fat content reaches an almost unheard-of-in-nature 30 percent—making it, you could say, the foie gras of the sea. Its creamy-smooth fatty texture is reminiscent of tuna belly. Kampachi and its close cousin Kona kampachi are rich tasting but leaner than hamachi, more like the leaner cuts of tuna.

Cultured hamachi and kampachi are usually sliced thick, like tuna, to be served raw, but are also excellent when coated with sesame seeds, quickly broiled or grilled, and served with a simple squeeze of lemon. Japanese restaurants, after removing the fillets for sashimi, marinate the collarbones in miso paste and mirin before broiling. Diners then nibble and pick fatty bits of meat off the bone.

All the jacks are excellent broiled or grilled and take well to mixing with acidic ingredients such as vinegar, citrus, tomatillos, and tamarind. Grilled amberjack served with a green tomatillo salsa is delicious; try pairing grilled, broiled, or baked amberjack with a tamarind-rich curry, a citrus and chile marinade, or a Yucatecan achiote and sour-orange recado.

Although California yellowtail is not aquacultured, it is popular both raw and cooked. Its mild, delicate flavor is best raw in the Italian style of *crudo*: just a sprinkling of lemon, coarse salt, a touch of olive oil, and maybe a little minced parsley or chives.

Pompano has the same rich, full flavor as that of other jacks and can be prepared either in whole fish preparations or as fillets. It can be used in mackerel, black sea bass, or butterfish recipes, but is probably most often simply sautéed.

## GRILLED AMBERJACK WITH GAZPACHO VINAIGRETTE

SERVES 4 AS A MAIN COURSE

Most of the work in making this versatile and easy sauce is done by the blender. The acidity of the vinaigrette complements full-flavored oily fish, such as the jacks, mahimahi, and sardines, yet the bright flavors also make a perfect match for steamed shrimp, scallops, or any white-fleshed fish. It's best made in the summer when tomatoes are at their peak. (Uncooked, the vinaigrette makes a nice gazpacho: Simply blend all the ingredients and chill. Add cooked lobster or shrimp as a garnish for a cold summer soup.)

Populations of many wild jacks are well managed and healthy, including the Gulf of Mexico amberjack and the California yellowtail; either would be a perfect choice for this recipe. This dish pairs nicely with couscous and grilled okra that can be cooked alongside the fish.

Olive oil for brushing
Four 5-ounce amberjack slices
Kosher salt and freshly ground black
    pepper to taste

GARNISHES

3 tablespoons olive oil
1 tablespoon red wine vinegar
2 tablespoons diced peeled cucumber
2 tablespoons diced red or green
    bell pepper
2 tablespoons chopped scallion
Minced fresh flat-leaf parsley to taste
Kosher salt and freshly ground black
    pepper to taste

Gazpacho Vinaigrette (recipe follows)

1. Prepare a medium fire in a charcoal grill, or preheat a gas grill to 350°F.
2. Oil the grill rack well, brush the fillets lightly with oil, and season with salt and pepper. Grill, turning the fish once halfway through cooking, for a total of 10 minutes per inch of thickness, or until almost opaque throughout.
3. For the garnishes: Whisk the olive oil into the vinegar and mix in all the vegetables and parsley; season with salt and pepper.
4. Ladle some Gazpacho Vinaigrette onto each of 4 plates, place the fish on top, and garnish with the vegetable mixture.

## Gazpacho Vinaigrette

MAKES ABOUT 2 CUPS

½ slice country-style bread, crust removed

4 tablespoons olive oil

¼ cup chopped onion

1 green or red bell pepper, seeded and
   chopped

2 garlic cloves, minced

1 pound ripe tomatoes, peeled and seeded

2 to 3 tablespoons sherry vinegar or
   red wine vinegar

Kosher salt to taste

1. Tear up the bread, put it in a small bowl with cold water to cover, and soak for 10 minutes.

2. In a medium saucepan, heat 1 tablespoon of the olive oil over medium-high heat and sauté the onion and bell pepper for 2 minutes. Add the garlic and cook 1 minute more. Add the tomatoes and cook until bubbling and just heated through, 2 or 3 minutes.

3. Squeeze all the water out of the bread. In a blender, puree the tomato mixture with the remaining 3 tablespoons olive oil and the vinegar, adding enough of the bread as needed to thicken the sauce. Season with salt and keep warm on the stove.

# GRILLED HAMACHI
# WITH THAI GREEN CURRY AND MELON RELISH

Good-quality green Thai curry pastes that contains difficult-to-find ingredients such as kaffir lime leaves and galangal (a gingerlike rhizome) are available in most Asian markets and many supermarkets. Even many Thai restaurants use these commercially prepared pastes, but I prefer the fresh flavors of a simpler homemade Thai Green Curry Paste.

The hamachi in this recipe can be charcoal grilled or broiled while the Thai green curry sauce is made separately. Any fatty, distinctively flavored fish, such as one of the other jacks, mackerel, mahimahi, or even swordfish, would also work well. Serve with steamed rice.

2 tablespoons refined peanut oil or another
   high-heat oil for frying

5 tablespoons Thai Green Curry Paste
   (recipe follows)

½ cup dry fruity wine such as a dry Riesling

1 tablespoon cornstarch mixed with
   1 tablespoon water

1 teaspoon kosher salt, plus more to taste

½ cup coconut cream (see Note)

Four 5-ounce slices hamachi

Freshly ground black pepper
   to taste

Melon Relish (page 162)

1. Prepare a medium-hot fire in a charcoal grill or preheat a gas grill to 375°F.

2. In a large sauté pan or skillet, heat the oil and the Thai Green Curry Paste over medium heat until bubbling. Add the wine and simmer for 10 minutes. Drizzle the cornstarch mixture into the simmering sauce while stirring. Stir in the 1 teaspoon salt and coconut cream and turn off the heat. The sauce should be just thick enough to coat the back of a spoon.

3. Oil the fish and season with salt and pepper. Grill for 3½ to 5 minutes on each side, for a total of about 10 minutes per inch of thickness, or until almost opaque throughout.

4. Ladle some of the curry sauce on each plate and place the grilled hamachi on top of the sauce. Serve with the Melon Relish on top or alongside.

NOTE: Since I don't live in Tahiti where fresh coconut milk is sold in the market, I take the easy way and use the best quality canned or frozen coconut milk I can find. To make coconut cream, separate the cream in canned coconut milk by leaving the can in the refrigerator undisturbed for several days; the cream will separate and float to the top. The longer the cream is left undisturbed, the thicker it will be. Turn the can over, open the bottom, and pour off the thin, watery milk. A 13½-

ounce can of coconut milk will have about 1 cup of cream on top. The same can be achieved with frozen coconut milk by thawing it, pouring it into a glass, and allowing it to separate in the refrigerator.

## THAI GREEN CURRY PASTE

MAKES 1 CUP

1 cup packed fresh cilantro leaves

2 stalks lemongrass, white part only, peeled

2-inch piece fresh ginger or galangal, peeled

4 Thai bird or serrano chiles, minced

1-inch strip lime zest, or 2 fresh kaffir
    lime leaves

2 shallots

2 garlic cloves

1 tablespoon fish sauce

Juice of 1 lime

2 tablespoons refined peanut or another
    mild-flavored oil

In a blender or food processor, combine all the ingredients and puree until smooth; add a bit of water if necessary to help puree the ingredients.

NOTE: The curry paste can be stored in the refrigerator for weeks and used to make a number of different Thai seafood curries. Typically, Thai curries are a combination of seafood and vegetables simmered in curry paste, coconut milk, and stock. Shrimp and small round Thai eggplants; halibut, green beans, and Thai basil; or mixed fish and shellfish with cauliflower all make wonderful Thai curries.

# MELON RELISH

**1 teaspoon coriander seeds**

**1 cup finely diced cantaloupe**

**2 tablespoons fruity dry wine such as a**
   **Riesling**

In a small dry sauté pan or skillet, toast the coriander seeds over medium heat for 2 or 3 minutes, or until fragrant, then pound with a pestle in a mortar. In a small bowl, combine the crushed coriander with the cantaloupe and wine; stir well. Cover and refrigerate for at least 1 hour or up to several hours.

# LOBSTER

Lobsters are separated into two general categories: those with claws and those without. While there are only two species of clawed lobsters—the American lobster and the Northern Europe lobster—some four dozen species of clawless, or spiny, lobster can be found throughout the world's waters.

## AMERICAN LOBSTER

The **American lobster** (*Homarus americanus*), commonly called the Maine lobster, has become a national icon in more ways than one, representing both the rugged individualism of the Maine fisherman and the very best of American cuisine. Maine lobster is popular from the shoreside lobster shack to the finest white-tablecloth restaurant. But this wasn't always so: The first Down East Yankees weren't averse to using the amazingly abundant American lobster as fertilizer or fish bait, and it wasn't until well into the twentieth century that most Americans came to consider lobster as anything more than a low-priced staple in a can. Only in recent times has the lobster been elevated to its current exalted place at the table.

Although many of our favorite seafoods are undergoing tough times, the American lobster seems to be bucking the trend. Nowhere in the world are lobsters more abundant than in the Gulf of Maine. It is estimated that the waters off Maine's coast contain some 100 million lobsters and 3 million lobster pots. Last year's catch was an unheard-of 63 million pounds—about 20 million pounds above the one-hundred-year average—and these numbers continue to grow.

No one truly knows why the American lobster is flourishing as never before—it's the subject of as much speculation in the halls of science as in Maine's waterfront bars. Some scientists think that a shift in the Gulf Stream has been responsible for delivering more lobster larvae to their nursery habitat; others believe the overfishing of cod, a prime lobster predator, is allowing more lobsters to reach adulthood. Yet another theory, held by Carl J. Wilson, chief lobster biologist for the state of Maine, is that "lobsters may be thriving because they are effectively being farmed. With nearly 3 million baited traps in the water, young lobsters can stop into a trap for a snack and then leave through the escape vents designed to let undersize lobsters escape."

The real answer may be a combination of all these theories—or, as many lobster fishermen believe, none of the above. The fishermen are of the opinion that their own stewardship is what's responsible for the American lobster's success. A number of years ago, a conservation ethic took hold among a handful of lobstermen, then gradually spread throughout the entire Maine lobster-fishing community. State regulations provide that all small lobsters, really big lobsters (which are prime breeders), and "berried" lobsters (those carrying eggs) must be returned to the sea. But Maine lobstermen have taken conservation one step further: Fishermen cut a V-notch in the tail of all berried lobsters so that other lobstermen know they are brood stock, even if they're not carrying eggs when they're caught. Virtually every one of the nearly seven thousand lobstermen in Maine return the V-notched brood lobsters to the water—and the really positive note is that fishermen elsewhere, seeing the results, are beginning to follow suit.

The best season for American lobster is from May through November, when the weather is good and the lobsters are active. During this period, most lobsters are "new caught," meaning they're fresh off the boat. Many lobsters sold during the winter are "pounded" lobsters, that is, they were caught during the summer and kept in artificial impoundments until the winter. Not surprisingly, the stress of crowding, unnatural conditions, and artificial feed makes for a poorer-flavored lobster.

For the best bargains on American lobster, wait for September and October: More lobsters are caught during these months than at any other time of the year; correspondingly, this is when prices are at their lowest.

## SPINY LOBSTER

The beautiful, rust-colored shell of the **spiny**, or **rock**, **lobster** is dappled in reds, blues, greens, and yellows. Large-spiked, whiplike antennae and a powerful tail can be used either in defense or for a quick escape, while sharp, formidable-looking spines emanating from its head not only discourage predators, but also give the spiny lobster its name.

Unlike American lobsters, spiny lobsters do not fare well out of the water, so most are sold as frozen raw tails. "Cold-water" tails, which come from western Australia, New Zealand, and South Africa, are considered the highest-quality spiny lobsters and are the most expensive. "Warm-water" tails from Brazil, Mexico, and the Caribbean are considerably cheaper and aren't as well regarded, though I suspect that may be due more to a lack of quality control in processing than to the innate characteristics of the lobster itself. In my opinion, fresh spiny lobster is far superior to frozen, regardless of provenance. Some of the best spiny lobsters I've ever eaten have been "warm-water" Caribbean and Mexican lobsters. I can recall with great fondness every one of the two dozen or more fresh lobsters I consumed when I last vacationed in St. Martin—but I can't remember a single frozen lobster tail I've eaten.

Although American lobsters are found in the live tanks of restaurants and markets across the nation, spiny lobsters are far more sensitive to the stress of travel. Usually, live spiny lobster is only found near where it is caught, which in the United States is coastal California from Monterey southward (*Panulirus interruptus*) and Florida (*Panulirus argus*).

A live spiny lobster should have a hard shell and seem heavy for its size. Be careful when handling spiny lobster, for even a sedentary-looking one will kick like a mule if it senses an opportunity for escape. This can not only hurt but result in a very nasty cut.

Live spiny lobster is available from September through March in both California and Florida, with the heart of the season occurring in the fall. In many parts of the Caribbean, spiny lobster season lasts year-round.

### CHOOSING SUSTAINABLE SEAFOOD

The greatest concern with the American lobster resource is that it is heavily represented by only a few year classes. Lobsters born in the same year tend to have similar biological strengths and weaknesses, so a change in ocean conditions can be devastating to a year class, and disease can easily become pandemic.

Just such a thing happened in 1997, when a virulent bacterial disease known as black spot began attacking lobsters in Long Island Sound, affecting molting cycles, breeding behavior, and lobster flavor. Science has failed to find a cure as yet, and the disease is steadily marching northward. Thirty percent of the lobster population in Connecticut and Rhode Island has been infected to date—and in 2004, the disease was first detected in southern Massachusetts.

The harvesting of California and Florida spiny lobsters is regulated by size and season. Florida has been steadily reducing the number of traps and boats on the water since 1992, in an attempt to stabilize the fishery and reduce damage to coral reefs. Both the Florida and southern California spiny lobster fisheries are well managed and are considered sustainable. The red spiny lobster of Baja, Mexico, and the Western Australia rock lobster fisheries have been certified as sustainable fisheries by the Marine Stewardship Council.

### CHOOSING HEALTHY SEAFOOD

Lobster, which is moderately high in cholesterol, was once considered unhealthy for people on a cholesterol-restricted diet, but it is now recognized that very little dietary cholesterol is absorbed by the body; rather, it's the saturated fats in our diets that are converted by the body into blood cholesterol. Because lobster contains very little saturated fat, it is no longer excluded from typical low-cholesterol diets and is even considered a heart-healthy source of protein. Like other fish and shellfish, lobster contains omega-3 fatty acids, which improve the blood lipid profile by lowering triglycerides and raising HDL ("good") cholesterol. Lobster is also an excellent source of zinc, copper, phosphorus, selenium, and vitamin B$_{12}$.

Lobster is a common cause of shellfish allergies (see page 414); those who are allergic to shrimp and crab are also often allergic to lobster.

The lobster's liver, called tomalley (see Hepatopancreas, page 414), which acts as a filter for toxins, should be eaten only occasionally and not at all by pregnant or nursing women and young children.

### IN THE KITCHEN

A cooked lobster yields only 25 to 30 percent meat, but the meat is so rich that a one and a quarter-pound lobster (containing six ounces of meat) is sufficient for most people. Although it's a commonly accepted belief that small lobsters taste better than large ones, I have never noticed a difference in texture or flavor. Spiny lobster is much more coarsely textured than American lobster, but the flavor is equally delicious.

American lobster can be cooked by rapid-heat methods such as boiling, steaming, or grilling. It also is good in stews, braised, or baked. Spiny lobster can be boiled or steamed, but it tastes much better grilled, broiled, or braised, and is excellent served as sashimi. Although many Japanese restaurants serve American lobster sashimi, it pales in comparison to the firm, crunchy texture and delicious flavor of sashimi made from spiny lobster.

Leftover lobster shells are great for making stock or bisque. The strongly flavored tomalley is also edible, though not recommended on a regular basis (see Choosing Healthy Seafood, page 166). The red coral, or unripe roe, of female lobsters can be used as an enrichment for lobster sauces.

Although there are thousands of elaborate lobster recipes, the beautiful flavor and firm texture of lobster is well suited to the simplest methods of cooking. I particularly like it grilled over charcoal. No matter how a lobster is cooked, however, you'll find many better accompaniments than melted butter. A simple vinaigrette of olive oil, lemon, mashed garlic, and parsley is delicious and healthy. Alternatively, a Mexican salsa, Italian salsa verde, Harissa (page 323), Charmoula Marinade (page 396), ponzu, a dashi and citrus-based sauce used in Japanese cooking, or yogurty Raita (page 71) are all relatively simple to make and provide a refreshing counterpoint to the buttery richness of lobster.

### CHOOSING AMERICAN LOBSTERS

Lobsters are wild, so many factors affect their flavor. But the one objective quality the average consumer can consistently use in choosing good-tasting lobsters is the relative hardness and appearance of the shell. When choosing lobsters, look for those that have undergone their yearly shed. New-shell lobsters will have a bright, clean appearance; the body section right behind the head and in front of the tail, the thorax, will give under pressure when squeezed. A lobster that has shed very recently will have a very soft paper-thin shell with very little meat inside, although the flavor is sweet. The perfect lobster is one that shed several months ago; the shell will feel hard but still give somewhat when squeezed. The meat in these lobsters will be full and sweet.

Avoid old-shell lobsters with rock-hard shells that resist like steel, particularly those with barnacles, seaweed, or any other growth on their shells. Lobsters that have a mossy or slimy feel to their shell have been in a lobster pound or tank too long and will not have good flavor. Also to be avoided are lobsters that show evidence of black shell rot, a bacterial disease that eats away at the shell and taints the flavor of the meat. A little bit of black discoloration of the shell where a lobster has lost part of a claw is acceptable, but if there are black spots larger than a dime on more than one part of the shell, the flavor will be bitter and unpalatable.

### BOILING LOBSTERS

We want the water to come back to the boil as quickly as possible after adding the lobsters, so start with the largest pot you have and add as much water as possible while still leaving room for the lobsters. For every gallon of water, add a half cup kosher salt or a quarter cup sea salt (although this may seem like a lot of salt, it is only 2 percent, considerably less than the 3½ percent of normal seawater). The point is not to season the lobster, but to create a balance between the density of the lobster and the cooking water so that the lobster's essential flavors are not drawn out into the water in the pot. This proportion of salt will give you a lightly salted flavorful lobster.

Bring the water to a boil, then slide the lobsters into the boiling water headfirst. If they won't all fit, cook the lobsters in batches, adding more water between cooks if needed. After the water returns to the boil, begin timing: Boil the lobster eight minutes for the first pound, then add another four minutes for each additional pound. If the lobster has a very soft shell, reduce the cooking time by two minutes per pound.

### STEAMING LOBSTERS

In the bottom of a steamer pan, bring an inch or two of liquid to a brisk simmer over medium heat. Place the lobsters in a steamer basket and put the basket in the steamer pan. Cover and steam for ten minutes for the first pound and add four minutes per additional pound.

The timing formulas given for both boiling and steaming lobsters is applied the same whether cooking one or six lobsters in a pot; just be sure they are all the same size. If the lobster has a very soft shell, reduce the cooking time by two minutes per pound.

### GRILLING, BROILING, STEWING, OR STIR-FRYING LOBSTERS

To prepare either a spiny lobster or an American lobster for cooking in any of these ways, the lobster must first be split in half and cleaned. This can be done an hour or two in advance; refrigerate the prepared lobster until ready to cook. The same procedure is used for cleaning a cooked lobster.

If you are right-handed, grasp the live lobster by the thorax with your left hand. Position the lobster perpendicular to yourself with its head facing toward your right, or cutting hand. Firmly press the lobster to the cutting board. There's a naturally-occurring cross-hatch mark in the center of the shell, approximately one inch behind the eyes. Using a sharp chef's knife, insert the tip of the knife into this mark (see photo A) and press the knife straight down through the head between the eyes, pressing down into the cutting board. Rotate the now-dead lobster 180 degrees and repeat the procedure, splitting the lobster completely in half.

### CLEANING LOBSTERS

Remove the gritty sand sac (gullet) from behind the eye (see photo B, arrow No. 1 on page 169) (where you would think the brain ought to be) and the attached dark-colored intestinal vein, running the length of the lobster tail close to the shell. In the thoracic cavity behind the sand

A. TECHNIQUE FOR KILLING A LIVE LOBSTER: WITH ONE CONTINUOUS MOTION, INSERT THE TIP OF A SHARP KNIFE INTO THE CROSS-HATCH MARK IN THE MIDDLE OF THE THORAX AND SLICE THROUGH THE HEAD.

B. TECHNIQUE FOR CLEANING A LOBSTER: ARROW NO. 1 SHOWS THE GRITTY SAND SAC, OR GULLET, IN THE HEAD AREA. ARROW NO. 2 SHOWS THE DARK-COLORED ROE, OR CORAL, OF THE FEMALE LOBSTER. ARROW NO. 3 POINTS TO THE LIGHT GREEN–COLORED TOMALLEY (HEPATOPANCREAS).

sac we sometimes find the very dark green roe of female lobsters (photo B, arrow No. 2 above); it will turn bright red when cooked. Remove any roe. The remainder of the cavity will be filled with a large light green gland (hepatopancreas) known as the tomalley (photo B, arrow No. 3 above); remove it as well.

At this point, the lobster is ready for broiling or grilling. If using in stew or stir-fry, the lobster can be chopped into smaller pieces.

# CHAR-GRILLED LOBSTER SALAD
# WITH SALSA VERDE

Grilled lobster is delicious on its own and is also excellent used in other preparations. Grilling intensifies the sweetness of lobster and adds complexity. Pasta, risotto, bread salad, or any other dish made with grilled rather than boiled or steamed lobster always tastes better to me.

I like to grill any of the chicories—escarole, curly endive, loose-headed radicchio, or Belgian endive—to serve alongside this lobster salad. The salsa verde is excellent with nearly any seafood; the tomato used in this recipe is an optional addition.

**SALSA VERDE**

1 small tomato

1 cup packed fresh flat-leaf parsley leaves

¼ cup packed fresh mint leaves

2 or 3 scallions, white part only

2 tablespoons capers, rinsed

1 garlic clove, minced

2 anchovy fillets, rinsed

½ slice coarse bread, crust removed

2 tablespoons red wine vinegar

½ cup olive oil

Grated zest and juice of 1 lemon

Salt and freshly ground pepper to taste

Two 1¼-pound Maine lobsters, split in half and cleaned (see page 168)

Olive oil for brushing

¾ cup finely diced English or Japanese cucumber

Mixed lettuce leaves for serving

Grilled Chicory (optional; recipe follows)

1. Prepare a medium-hot fire in a charcoal grill, or preheat a gas grill to 375°F.

2. For the salsa verde: This sauce is best simply chopped with a chef's knife, although it can be made in a blender or food processor. Char the tomato on the grill until lightly charred and soft. On a cutting board, chop the parsley well. Add the mint, scallions, capers, garlic, and anchovy fillets; continue to chop until everything is well mixed and finely diced. Remove the skin and core from the charred tomato, put the tomato in a bowl, and crush with a fork or pestle. Add the parsley mixture to the bowl.

3. Let the bread soak in the wine vinegar for 10 minutes. Squeeze out most of the vinegar and crumble the bread into the parsley mixture. Whisk in the olive oil, lemon zest, and lemon juice; season with salt and pepper.

4. Brush the meat side of the lobsters lightly with olive oil and grill for 5 minutes on each side. Transfer to a cutting board and let cool to the

touch. Remove the meat from the shell, chop it coarsely, and while still warm mix with the salsa verde. Gently mix in the cucumber and serve on a bed of mixed lettuces.

## GRILLED CHICORY

Half or quarter the chicory, depending on size. Dip the pieces in water to wash and allow them to drain. Do not thoroughly dry them; some water left in the leaves prevents burning. Brush them with olive oil and red wine vinegar and season with salt and pepper. Grill until lightly browned and crispy on the outside and soft in the center, turning them often. They may take a little longer to cook than the lobster.

# SWEET CORN AND LOBSTER BISQUE

This recipe has plenty of flavor when it's made with water alone, but if you use a lobster stock, the rich flavor of lobster really stands out.

Note that the cooking method in step 1 makes it easy to remove the lobster meat from the shell while still leaving the lobster slightly undercooked.

Two 1¼-pound Maine lobsters

2 tablespoons unsalted butter

1 small yellow onion, diced

2 stalks celery with tops, diced

½-inch piece fresh ginger, peeled
   and minced

1 tomato, chopped

1 cup dry white wine

2 tablespoons white wine vinegar

2 cups water, Shellfish Stock made with
   lobster shells (page 27), or Quick Lobster
   Stock made with lobster shells
   (page 28)

2 cups corn kernels (about 3 ears)

Kosher salt to taste

Freshly squeezed lime juice to taste

**GARNISHES**

2 tablespoons unsalted butter

2 tablespoons minced green bell pepper

2 tablespoons minced red bell pepper

2 tablespoons minced scallion

1 teaspoon ground mild New Mexico chile
   or sweet Hungarian paprika

Splash of dry white wine

¼ cup heavy cream

Chopped fresh chervil, flat-leaf parsley,
   or basil

1. Fill a pot large enough for both lobsters with salted water (½ cup kosher salt or ¼ cup sea salt per gallon) and bring to a boil. Add the lobsters to the pot headfirst, return the water to a rolling boil, and cook for 1 minute. Turn off the heat, cover the pot with a tight-fitting lid, and leave the lobsters to steep in the water for 5 minutes. Remove the lobsters from the water and quickly rinse under cold water. Twist off the tails and claws; clean the lobster (see page 168), remove the meat, and reserve the shells for the stock. Chop the lobster meat coarsely and put aside. Make the stock using the reserved shells if desired.

2. In a medium saucepan, melt the butter over low heat. Sauté the onion and celery until translucent, 3 to 4 minutes; add the ginger, tomato, white wine, and vinegar. Increase the heat to medium and cook until the liquid is reduced by half, then add the water or stock and the corn. Bring to a simmer, reduce the heat, and cook for 10 minutes. Pour into a blender and puree until smooth. Season with

salt and lime juice, then return to a pot on the stove over low heat.

3. For the garnishes: In a large sauté pan or skillet, melt the butter over high heat and quickly sauté the lobster meat with the peppers and scallion for 1 or 2 minutes, or until the lobster is sizzling hot and the vegetables are just crisp-tender. Turn off the heat, stir in the chile or paprika, and cook in the residual heat for 30 seconds. Deglaze the pan with a splash of white wine, stirring and scraping the bottom of the pan with a wooden spoon. Add the cream. Spoon the hot bisque into 4 bowls, stir a quarter of the lobster garnish into each, and sprinkle with some of the chopped herb.

## CHARCOAL-GRILLED SPINY LOBSTER WITH PERSILLADE

SERVES 4 AS A MAIN COURSE

The Caribbean island of St. Martin is half French and half Dutch. The Dutch side is full of high-rise casinos and glitz; the French side is known for its laid-back ways and good food—especially spiny lobster. While vacationing there, my wife Joan, my daughter Kelley, and I ate spiny lobster just about every day, almost always charcoal-grilled. The local lobster shack on the beach where we stayed grilled their lobster with a persillade: minced parsley and garlic mixed with olive oil and butter, then ladled over the lobster while it cooked. The wonderful aroma that wafted across the beach was the only advertisement our lobster shack needed.

When minced together, parsley and garlic become a powerful mixture that brings wonderful flavor to a dish. A persillade can be used as a sauce for grilled fish or as a topping for broiled clams, mussels, or bay scallops on the half shell. Sauté shell-on shrimp, razor clams, scallops, or squid in a lightly oiled hot pan for several minutes, then add the persillade at the last minute to season. Or add half a cup of fresh bread crumbs to the mixture to make a persillade topping for baked fish.

At our little lobster shack on the beach, sliced oranges and rice pilaf were served on the side, and the table always held the most basic of hot sauces: minced Scotch bonnet chiles in vinegar.

CONTINUED

**PERSILLADE**

3 garlic cloves

½ teaspoon coarse sea salt

1 cup packed fresh flat-leaf parsley leaves

¼ cup olive oil

4 tablespoons unsalted butter, melted

Grated zest of ½ organic orange

Freshly ground pepper to taste

4 spiny lobsters, split in half and cleaned

Lemon wedges for garnish

1. Prepare a hot fire in a charcoal grill.

2. For the persillade: On a cutting board, crush the garlic one clove at a time into a paste with the side of a chef's knife. Add the salt and chop, then add the parsley and continue chopping until the garlic and parsley are well minced. Put the mixture in a bowl and add the olive oil and butter; season with orange zest and pepper.

3. Brush a little of the persillade on the meat side of the lobsters and grill, meat-side down, for 4 to 5 minutes, or until the edges of the shell begin to blacken lightly and the flesh is grill marked. Turn the lobsters over and ladle the persillade into the shell and over the lobster. Cook for 4 to 5 minutes on the second side, or until the persillade is bubbling and the smell of cooked lobster wafts off the grill. Serve garnished with lemon wedges.

## Why Do Lobsters Taste Better at the Shore?

Ever wonder why that lobster on the beach of some picturesque shoreside New England town is so sweet and delicious, while lobster at home or even in the fanciest restaurant is often just okay?

I know of a lobster shack out in Deer Island, Maine, nestled among the fishing piers jutting into the bay, which to this day sells a boiled lobster dinner for $8.99. The yellow linoleum tables feel greasy and the mismatched chairs are rickety; the air is filled with steam and funky smells coming off the water. Loud conversation and laughter are punctuated by the crackle of lobster shells and the pop of beer can tops, and the lobsters are always sweet and delicious.

Mike Brito, a third-generation lobster fisherman whose grandfather came from the Azores, owns Mike's Lobster and supplies all the lobsters from his own boats. The lobsters he culls out for the restaurant are those that all the lobstermen know to have the best flavor, the "new-shells."

But flavor is not the reason Mike keeps those new-shells at home; it's economics. When lobsters come off the boat, they are graded as new-shell, hard-shell, or old-shell lobsters. New-shell lobsters that have recently shed their shells have papery-thin shells that crackle and give a bit when squeezed; they have less meat-to-shell ratio, but the flavor is sweeter, cleaner, and just better than that of other lobsters. The new-shells served at Mike's are usually so soft they crackle and make you wince in sympathy when the body is squeezed. The only tools needed to crack them open are fingers and teeth, though the ladies usually get a *lobstah crackah*.

New-shell lobsters that have recently shed their shells always have wonderfully sweet flavor but are weak when taken out of the water. If Mike puts them on the truck for the drive to Boston, they're all half dead and worthless by the time they get there. So the market for new-shells is local, and the prices stay cheap.

Hard-shell lobsters that have not shed recently have a firm shell with just a little give to the thorax when squeezed. They have a better meat-to-shell ratio than new-shells and a good, ocean-fresh flavor, but don't always have that extra-sweet oomph of flavor that makes you think you're on summer vacation. The sturdier hard-shell lobsters can be shipped to Boston or New York or even Los Angeles and expected to arrive alive, so hard-shell lobsters command a higher price.

Old-shell lobsters that have not shed since the previous season have a shell like a rock and are very hardy out of the water. They tend to be coarser flavored and more prone to funkiness, but can successfully be air-shipped anywhere in the world. They command the very highest prices in the international markets of Paris and Tokyo.

So, as you can see, there is an inverse relationship between price and flavor with lobsters. The eight-dollar lobster found at Mike's in Maine is always delicious, while chances are the eighty-dollar lobster in a three-star Paris restaurant is apt to be as much about presentation as flavor. To me, somehow, this is how it ought to be.

# MACKEREL

For culinary purposes, mackerel can be separated into two groups: the small, oily, full-flavored mackerels and the larger, milder-flavored members of the mackerel family. The first group includes the highly regarded **Boston mackerel** (*Scomber scombrus*), found in Atlantic waters from the Gulf of Saint Lawrence to North Carolina, and the closely related Pacific Coast **American mackerel** (*S. japonicus*). Nearly indistinguishable from one another, both are sharply dressed in iridescent blue-green coats. Silvery highlights along the sides are broken with black, wavy bands, and the belly is pure white.

The larger mackerels are equally as rich in oils but have a milder taste and are not nearly as perishable as the smaller mackerels. This group includes some of the most delicious fish in the sea, the Pacific **Sierra mackerel** (*Scomberomorus sierra*) and the **Spanish**

(*S. regalis*) and **king** (*S. cavalla*) **mackerels** of southern Atlantic and Gulf of Mexico waters. Similar in appearance to one another, these three mackerels have highly streamlined, torpedo-shaped bodies. They are blue-green with silver highlights, their backs and sides punctuated with golden-yellow spots. Sierra and Spanish mackerel usually range between one and five pounds, while it's not unusual to see king mackerels of twenty pounds or more.

Mackerel are at their best during fall and winter, when their fat content can reach as high as 30 percent, but they are most readily available during the spring when stocks aggregate to spawn and are easiest to catch. Fresh mackerel is easy to recognize: Its iridescence fades soon after the fish dies, but the eyes should appear bright and clear, almost alive. The gills should be clean and the skin moist, with small, smooth, tightly-adhering scales that have a velvety feel. The very freshest mackerel should be stiff with rigor and not bend when held by its head or tail.

Boston and American mackerel are sold as whole fish in Asian, Latin, and other ethnic markets where consumers are comfortable buying whole fish. Boston mackerel is very popular in Japanese cuisine (where it is known as *saba*), so expect to find quality Boston mackerel in Japanese markets, if not fresh, then frozen from Norway. The larger species of Sierra, Spanish, and king mackerel are usually sold as fillets in fish markets and grocery stores, particularly in the southern Atlantic and Gulf coast states, but also in large northern cities. All mackerel fillets should be firm and moist looking. Most important, the dark hemoglobin-rich muscle tissue close to the skin should be bright red.

## CHOOSING SUSTAINABLE SEAFOOD

Mackerel populations mature quickly and spawn prolifically, making them resilient to fishing pressure. Mackerels are taken predominantly by seine, trap, gill net, and hook, all of which are responsible for little bycatch or habitat impact. Nearly all mackerel stocks are healthy and abundant. The one exception, the Gulf of Mexico king mackerel, is recovering from past overfishing.

## CHOOSING HEALTHY SEAFOOD

Health professionals recommend that we eat more small, fatty fish rich in heart-healthy omega-3 fatty acids, such as anchovies, mackerel, and sardines, as a way to avoid chronic heart disease. All mackerel are a very good, high-protein source of B vitamins and minerals, particularly selenium, which may help reduce mercury absorption, and are an excellent source of omega-3-rich unsaturated fats.

While most mackerels are a healthy choice, king mackerel (see mercury chart, page 405) may contain high levels of mercury and should not be eaten by pregnant women, nursing mothers, and very young children.

Although some wild fish are susceptible to infective parasites, mackerel are seldom affected, though care should always be exercised when eating raw seafood (see Raw Seafood: How to Stay Safe, page 408).

### IN THE KITCHEN

Fresh mackerel is one of the tastiest, cheapest, most healthful fish available. It is deliciously rich-flavored and moist. In the kitchen, it is a versatile fish, taking readily to just about any method of cooking, including smoking, curing, and using in raw preparations. It is an excellent fish to charcoal-grill: Smeared with chile paste and lime, grilled sierra mackerel is a favorite on the beaches of Mexico.

Lightly vinegared mackerel is standard fare in sushi bars. The mackerel's high fat content and assertive flavor make it an excellent choice for pickling (as in an escabeche), marinating, or cooking with such favored acidic ingredients as tomatoes, vinegar, or fruit juices, or in more adventurous preparations with rhubarb, tamarind, pomegranate, or verjus.

The bones of mackerel are too oily to make a stock, but can be marinated in soy, fresh ginger, and garlic and then grilled until crisp. The meat between the bones is delicious and the bones themselves where crisp and crunchy can be eaten as well. The roe and milt may be eaten, and the skin as well.

Mackerel has long been on the menu at the best Japanese restaurants. But it's now showing up in the kitchens of the country's most celebrated non-Asian chefs, too, and customers love it. This portends well for the mackerel's future—for where the star chefs go, the public is sure to follow.

# BROILED BOSTON MACKEREL
# WITH MINT-YOGURT MARINADE

Yogurt and mint balance the rich flavor of Boston mackerel and are equally good with other rich, fatty fish such as the other mackerels, sardines, shad, tuna, or even late-season salmon. Reserve half the marinade for a table sauce. I like a little Harissa (page 323) or prepared hot sauce as counterpoint to the cool mint and yogurt. Serve with couscous and carrots braised with cumin or ginger.

4 to 6 garlic cloves, minced

2 teaspoons coarse sea salt

¼ cup freshly squeezed lemon juice

¼ cup olive oil

Grated zest of 2 organic lemons

½ teaspoon cayenne pepper

2 cups thick (Greek-style) whole yogurt
   (see Note)

1 cup finely chopped fresh mint, about
   2 bunches

Four 5-ounce Boston mackerel fillets

1. In a small wooden bowl or a mortar, mash the garlic and salt together with a pestle. Add the lemon juice and whisk in the olive oil, lemon zest, and cayenne pepper. Whisk the yogurt until it is smooth and somewhat light. Whisk the yogurt and mint into the olive oil. Reserve half of the marinade to serve as a sauce with the fish.

2. Put the mackerel fillets in a baking dish, completely cover with half the yogurt mixture, and marinate at room temperature for 30 minutes or in the refrigerator for up to 2 hours.

3. Preheat the broiler. Remove the fillets from the marinade, leaving a thin coating of yogurt on the fish. Place the fish on a cast-iron griddle pan or broiler pan, 5 or 6 inches from the heat source, and broil for 5 minutes on one side only. The marinade partially cooks the fillets, so there is no need to turn them while cooking; they will cook nicely through from one side only. Serve with the reserved yogurt sauce.

NOTE: Thin American-style yogurt can be drained for an hour or two in a coffee filter or cheesecloth-lined sieve until thick.

# CRISPY-SKIN SPANISH MACKEREL
# WITH QUICK PICKLED ONION AND FENNEL

Spanish mackerel may be the mildest and sweetest-flavored mackerel you'll ever encounter, but it can still stand up to strong flavors. Crispy-skin Spanish mackerel is started on the stove top and finished under the broiler. Use an edgeless flat steel pan such as a Mexican *comal* or a cast-iron griddle pan. Note that the technique used in this recipe will ensure crisp-skinned results with any skin-on fillet, from salmon to black sea bass, whether grilled, sautéed, or baked.

Serve this with Yukon gold potatoes mashed with yogurt, or rice pilaf seasoned with Indian spices, such as a mixture of whole coriander, cumin, and cardamom, and steamed spinach.

**Four 5-ounce fillets Spanish mackerel,**
   **skin on**
**3 or 4 tablespoons kosher or coarse sea salt**
**3 tablespoons curry powder or Curry Spice**
   **Mix No. 2 (page 36)**
**3 tablespoons olive oil**
**1 teaspoon freshly squeezed lemon juice**
**Quick Pickled Onion and Fennel**
   **(recipe follows)**
**1 pink grapefruit, segmented (see page 35),**
   **for garnish**

**1.** Salt the skin side only of the mackerel fillets. The skin should be almost entirely covered with salt. Refrigerate for 30 minutes to 1 hour.

**2.** Place a mackerel fillet on a cutting board, skin-side up. Hold the fillet in place by a corner of the skin. Using the sharp edge of a chef's knife, held at a 90-degree angle to the skin, push the knife away from you across the surface of the skin, keeping the sharp edge of the knife perpendicular to the skin. Stroke the blade across the surface of the skin 8 or 10 times while applying light pressure. This scrapes away the salt and draws moisture to the surface, where it can be wiped away. Dry the fish well. Repeat with the remaining fillets.

**3.** Mix the curry powder or Curry Spice Mix No. 2 with 1 tablespoon of the olive oil and the lemon juice to make a paste. Spread the paste on the flesh side of the mackerel fillets and set aside.

**4.** Preheat the broiler. Heat the *comal* or griddle pan over high heat on the stove top until very hot. Add the remaining 2 tablespoons oil to the pan and add the mackerel, skin-side down; give the pan a quick shake to be sure the skin doesn't stick. Cook for about 5 minutes, giving the pan an occasional shake to be sure the skin is not sticking to the pan. Place under the broiler 3 to 4 inches from the heat source for another 3 to 4 minutes, or until the fish is almost opaque throughout. The skin will continue to crisp on the hot pan while the top broils.

**5.** Top with a crunchy cold tangle of Quick Pickled Onion and Fennel, then garnish with grapefruit segments.

## QUICK PICKLED ONION AND FENNEL

**1 white onion, very thinly sliced**

**1 small bulb fennel, trimmed, cored, and very thinly sliced**

**½ cup freshly squeezed grapefruit juice**

**½ cup cider vinegar or white wine vinegar**

**1 tablespoon sugar**

**1 teaspoon minced fresh cilantro**

**Pinch of kosher salt**

**½ cup ice cubes**

Put the onion and fennel in a bowl and add boiling water to cover; let stand for 1 minute. Drain, return to the bowl, and add the grapefruit juice, vinegar, sugar, cilantro, and salt. Toss to coat and let stand until cool. Add the ice cubes and refrigerate for at least 1 hour or up to 2 days. To keep for up to 1 week, omit the cilantro and add just before serving.

## Dem Bones

Most of us simply discard fish bones after cleaning our fish, and with those bones goes a good portion of the meat we've paid for, right into the garbage can. Probably 10 percent of the edible flesh of most fish is usually discarded with the bones. There is more than enough meat left on the skeleton of most large fish such as salmon or sea bass after filleting to make a meal. And as the saying goes, "The closer the bone, the sweeter the meat."

Chinese fish markets and restaurants have little interest in salmon fillets, but the bones and heads are highly prized—a popular dish in Chinese restaurants is steamed salmon bones in black bean sauce. There is a restaurant in San Francisco's Chinatown that has made its reputation on bones: A flounder is filleted, the flesh is steamed, and the bones are deep-fried to a deliciously toasty crunch—a wonderful juxtaposition. Barbecued sablefish, salmon, or hamachi bones, first marinated in soy and ginger, then barbecued, are popular with my Japanese and Korean friends, and an Italian fisherman I know deep-fries the bones left from cleaning salted anchovies. Sardine and mackerel bones, when panfried to a crisp, can be eaten nearly in their entirety. Crispy, crunchy fish bones are delicious when nibbled for a snack, which is also a great way to get your MDR of calcium. Any cooked fish bone can be eaten, and when compared to fish eyes and throats and gonads and tongues, I'd say they're pretty tame and very tasty.

Large bones can be chopped into manageable pieces and cooked any way you like: steamed, grilled, broiled, or panfried. Sauce them if you like, then chew and suck the meat from the bones. It's just like eating baby back ribs, but a lot less expensive. Smaller bones from anchovies, mackerel, sardines, or herring are best fried or barbecued until really well done, as crispy and crunchy as a fish-flavored potato chip.

CRISPY BREAD CRUMB–
COATED FRESH SARDINE
SALAD WITH HERBED
MUSTARD DRESSING
(PAGE 259)

■ ■ ■

SQUID AND SARDINES AT
THE DOCK, MONTEREY,
CALIFORNIA

Peruvian Tiradito of White Sea Bass with Soy Dipping Sauce (page 398)

■ ■ ■

Coriander–Crusted Tuna with Hot and Sweet Mango Salsa (page 373)

Spot prawns and
anchovies,
Monterey Fish
Market

■ ■ ■

Red grouper,
silk snappers,
and lane snap-
pers for sale at
the old Fulton
Fish Market

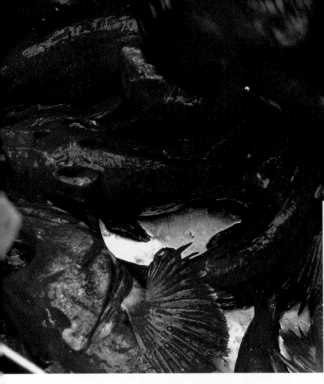

UNLOADING LIVE CHANNEL ROCKFISH,
ALSO KNOWN AS SCORPION FISH OR
IDIOTS, MOSS LANDING, CALIFORNIA

■ ■ ■

Panfried Flounder
Fillets with Tomato-
Parsley Vinaigrette
(page 315)

*This page, left to right clockwise:* FISHING FOR DUNGENESS CRAB, HALF MOON BAY, CALIFORNIA

CAPTAIN DONNIE PEMBERTON, HEADING BACK TO PORT

THE AUTHOR, PAUL JOHNSON

■ ■ ■

PORTUGUESE CLAM BOIL WITH CHOURIÇO AND KALE (PAGE 91)

First of the
season king
salmon

Fair Fish Co.,
Fulton Fish
Market

· · ·

Grilled Hamachi
with Thai Green
Curry and Melon
Relish (page 160)

OYSTERS AT HOG ISLAND
OYSTER FARM, TOMALES
BAY, CALIFORNIA

■ ■ ■

"RACK AND BAG" OYSTER
BEDS, TOMALES BAY,
CALIFORNIA

Dusk on the water,
Monterey, California

Black Sea Bass Fillets Braised with
Lemon, Olives, and Artichokes (page 53)

Fish and Shellfish Minestrone
with Pesto (page 100)

■ ■ ■

Setting out on the crab
vessel *Stacy-Joanne*, Half
Moon Bay, California

HARVESTING AND SORTING
CRABS—FEMALES AND SHORTS
GO BACK OVER THE SIDE

■ ■ ■

SOPA DE FIDEO WITH MUSSELS
AND AÏOLI (PAGE 198)

4:00 A.M. AT THE FULTON
FISH MARKET

SHAD IN A LIGHT BROTH
WITH SORREL, PEAS, AND
MINT (PAGE 280)

■ ■ ■

HALIBUT BAKED IN
PARCHMENT WITH
TOMATOES AND CORN
(PAGE 153)

ALBACORE CONFIT
(PAGE 380)

▪ ▪ ▪

CHARCOAL-GRILLED
WILD KING SALMON
WITH CHERRY TOMATO–
BASIL RELISH (PAGE 246)

TAPATIO SHRIMP
COCKTAIL (PAGE 292)

■ ■ ■

FULTON FISH MARKET

*Small picture, bottom left:*
BLUEFISH AND SCUP, FRESH
FROM THE POINT JUDITH
FISH TRAP

*Small picture, bottom right:*
HOOK-CAUGHT PACIFIC LING-
COD ON ICE, MONTEREY FISH
MARKET, SAN FRANCISCO

Tuna being prepared
for market

Working the crab pots

■ ■ ■

Escarole-Wrapped Monkfish
in a Tomato-Olive Sauce
(page 192)

FRIED SQUID WITH SWEET
PEPPERS, HOT CHILES,
AND SHREDDED GINGER
(PAGE 324)

∎ ∎ ∎

FULTON FISH MARKET

THE WORK DECK
ON THE *Stacy-
Joanne*, HALF
MOON BAY,
CALIFORNIA

Red grouper at the
Fulton Fish Market

Braised Wreckfish with
a Golden Pan Sauce and
Red Pepper–Saffron
Aïoli (page 400)

■ ■ ■

Anchovies, fresh from
San Francisco Bay

SARDINES IN A JAPANESE IRON BOWL

■ ■ ■

# MAHIMAHI

Also known as dolphinfish or dorado, the mahimahi (*Coryphaena hippurus*) is a swift-swimming deepwater species found in all the tropical and subtropical waters of the world. A freshly caught mahimahi displays an astonishing array of bright and vibrant colors. Indeed, mahimahi is easily one of the most stunningly beautiful fish in the ocean, its upper body a brilliant green with streaks of cobalt blue and lavender. Rising from its back, the dorsal fin is electric blue with green and yellow spots. Flashy yellow sides fade to cream on the belly.

Young mahimahi of from two to five pounds frequent inshore waters in search of food to fuel their prodigious growth (as much as five pounds a month). As they grow larger, they range farther offshore, often congregating around floating objects such as logs, buoys, or even boats.

The deepwater islands of Hawaii, Fiji, and Tahiti consistently produce the freshest and best-quality mahimahi, because the fishing grounds are close to shore. Excellent-quality mahimahi is also taken during the spring and summer months in the Caribbean, the Gulf of Mexico, and the Pacific waters of Mexico when the ocean is calm and small artisanal boats are able to reach offshore fishing grounds. A closely related species, the **pompano mahimahi** (*Coryphaena equiselis*), often referred to as dolphinfish, is taken in southeast Atlantic waters from North Carolina to Florida and into the Gulf of Mexico. There is an active dolphinfish commercial fishery, and many recreationally caught fish find their way into restaurants and markets.

In the fall and winter, much of the commercial catch of fresh mahimahi is flown in from Ecuador, Panama, and Costa Rica. The quality of these fish must be more closely monitored than domestically caught fish. Mahimahi fillets should appear moist and translucent, exhibiting a tightly formed bright red blood line and consistently colored pink or beige flesh. Often, darker coffee-colored fillets are stronger flavored. Green discoloration along the belly can be the first sign of age or improper handling.

Although the United States imports thousands of pounds of frozen mahimahi from China, most of it is testament to the fact that mahimahi simply doesn't freeze well. Upscale markets that specialize in local fish, or markets that regularly sell exotic species from the Caribbean or Hawaii are the best places to buy mahimahi. Ethnic markets do not usually carry quality mahimahi. Very inexpensive mahimahi with a brown blood line has probably been frozen and should be avoided.

Dressed mahimahi should show signs of red blood in the belly cavity and around the nape where cuts have been made for cleaning. Brown or yellow discoloration of cuts indicate exposure to air and age.

### CHOOSING SUSTAINABLE SEAFOOD

The mahimahi has a life span of only five years, yet can quickly reach ninety pounds in weight. This short-lived species achieves maturity by five months of age and breeds prolifically. The female mahimahi may spawn three to four times per year, often producing more than a million eggs each time. The fish's rapid growth and fecundity allow it to withstand heavy catch efforts with little fear of overfishing.

Mahimahi is commercially targeted by trolling with hooks and is often taken as by-catch in longline fisheries directed at tuna or swordfish. Although Pacific mahimahi is not actively managed, a fishery management plan was instituted in 2004 for the Gulf of Mexico and south Atlantic. Mahimahi is not considered overfished, but the goal is to maintain the status quo of the fishery.

## CHOOSING HEALTHY SEAFOOD

Mahimahi provides low to moderate amounts of omega-3 fatty acids and is a good low-fat, high-protein source of B vitamins and minerals. The open ocean–loving mahimahi is seldom parasitized and, because of its short life span, doesn't accumulate organic pollutants, although it may accumulate low amounts of mercury.

Old or poorly handled mahimahi has been known to produce allergy-provoking histamines (see Scombroid, page 413). Fresh, well-handled mahimahi does not have this problem.

### IN THE KITCHEN

One of the very best pieces of mahimahi I've ever eaten was at a small Indian restaurant near my house called Ajanta. Rubbed with spices, the fish was cooked perfectly in the 700°F Indian tandoor oven. The tender, juicy, large-flaked flesh was sweet and delicious. But I'm sorry to say this is more the exception than the rule. Mahimahi is the type of fish that can go from being cooked just right to overcooked in no time. It should be watched carefully, particularly when using dry-heat methods such as grilling or roasting.

For the most consistent results, I recommend gently sautéing or simmering mahimahi in a sauce such as an Indian curry or a spicy Thai coconut-basil sauce. Frying in the Chickpea and Rice Flour Batter (page 275) seals in the moisture. For a milder flavor, cut away the dark lateral blood line that runs down the center of the fillet before cooking.

If cured, marinated, or used for ceviche, the fish should be eaten the same day, because the fats quickly oxidize. Mahimahi lends itself well to hot-smoking.

Mahimahi not only goes well with tart, acidic sauces such as the Green Chutney (page 71), Tomato-Parsley Vinaigrette (page 316) or Soy Dipping Sauce (page 398), but matches up equally well with rich sauces such as Romesco Sauce (page 346) or Aïoli (page 137).

The skin of the fish is too tough to be eaten, and the bones are generally too oily for clean-tasting stock. The ever-present edible roe of the female can be used in any recipe for shad roe, or pressed and salt-cured as are mullet and tuna roes (*bottarga*) in Italy.

# MAHIMAHI WITH RHUBARB-GINGER CHUTNEY

I remember being introduced to rhubarb as a child by my old neighbor, Mrs. Hinkley. She gave us neighborhood kids a bowl of sugar and a knife and directed us to a patch of rhubarb in the weeds behind her chicken coop. After fending off Donald, her "watch-duck" who noisily attacked anyone who came too near the chicken coop, we sat in the weeds through the afternoon dipping stalks of rhubarb in sugar until we'd eaten our fill.

Rhubarb has recently undergone a culinary renaissance and can be found in savory as well as sweet dishes. Its astringency is a perfect foil for fatty fish such as sardines, mackerel, shad, or salmon. Spring and early summer is the best time to find tender, new-growth rhubarb. Spring is also the time when the best-quality domestic mahimahi begins to come on the market.

Rhubarb makes a beautiful garnet-colored, sweet-tart chutney that goes well with any white-fleshed fish. Serve this dish with steamed spinach and a rice pilaf seasoned with coriander seeds and lemon zest.

**RHUBARB-GINGER CHUTNEY**

3 stalks rhubarb

¼ cup water

1 tablespoon sugar

1 tablespoon refined peanut or another
     mild-flavored oil

1 teaspoon minced fresh ginger

1 tablespoon freshly squeezed lemon juice

2 tablespoons freshly squeezed orange juice

Grated zest of 1 lime

Kosher salt to taste

Four 5-ounce mahimahi fillets

Seasoned flour: ¼ cup all-purpose flour
     mixed with 1½ teaspoons kosher salt and
     ¼ teaspoon freshly ground pepper

3 tablespoons refined peanut oil or another
     high-heat oil for frying

¼ cup shredded fresh mint for garnish

1. For the chutney: Cut the most tender center section of the rhubarb into ⅓-inch dice (about ½ cup) and reserve. Coarsely chop the rest of the rhubarb. In a medium nonreactive pan, combine the coarsely chopped rhubarb, water, and sugar. Bring to a boil, reduce the heat to a simmer, and cook for 10 minutes, or until tender. Strain through a sieve, pressing well with the back of a large spoon to extract all the juice.

2. In a medium saucepan, heat the oil over medium heat and sauté the ginger for 1 minute, then add the lemon juice, orange juice, reserved diced rhubarb, and strained rhubarb juice. Simmer for just a minute or so until the rhubarb is crisp-tender. Add the lime zest and

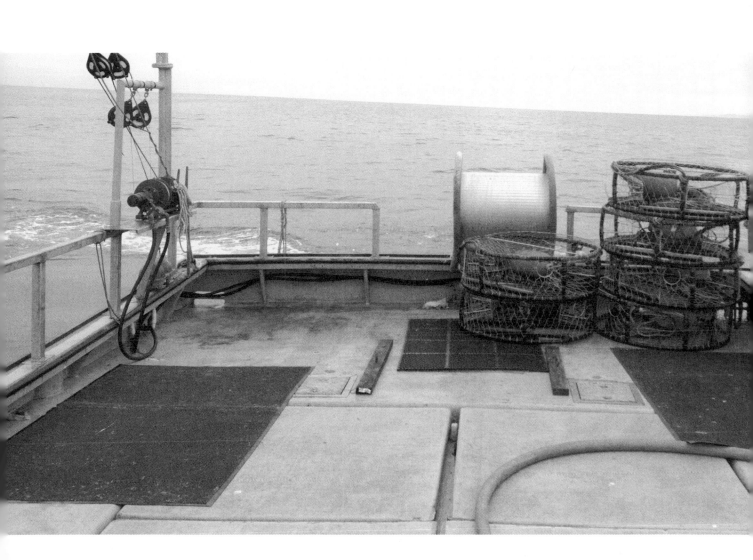

season with salt. Remove from the heat and let cool while you cook the mahimahi.

3. Preheat a large sauté pan or cast-iron skillet until hot. Dredge the mahimahi fillets in the seasoned flour. Add the oil to the pan and as soon as it begins to shimmer, add the fillets and cook over medium-high heat for 3 or 4 minutes on each side, or until golden on the outside and almost opaque throughout.

4. Put the mahimahi fillets on individual plates, spoon some of the rhubarb chutney over, and garnish with the mint.

# MONKFISH

Flattened on the ocean bottom, waiting in camouflaged ambush, the **monkfish** (*Lophius americanus*) entices unsuspecting prey by waving a wormlike appendage attached to its head. Leaping out on short, stubby front fins, it snatches its prey in its grotesquely large mouth filled with needle-sharp teeth. The monkfish is known as "angler" because it fishes for its food in this dramatic fashion along the Atlantic seaboard from North Carolina to Newfoundland.

Monkfish is marketed as the "poor man's lobster," and has become a consumer favorite in the United States. It can be found on the menu of restaurants nationwide and in many grocery stores and markets. For years, the monkfish was considered little more than a trash fish and was often discarded by trawl and scallop fishermen—that is, until the 1980s, when Julia Child herself sang its praises on her cooking show.

In a classic Julia Child moment, she wrestled a slippery and slimy giant fifty-pound monkfish with head still attached around her work table, trying desperately to prevent it from sliding onto the floor. Today, monkfish seldom grow larger than ten or fifteen pounds, but landings are significant, bringing more money to East Coast fishermen than cod and haddock combined.

Monkfish is almost always sold as whole tails, which average from one to five pounds, or fillets, which weigh between a half pound and two pounds each, but whole head-on monkfish are available. Fresh monkfish tails should have bright, shiny chocolate-brown-to-black skin with no yellow discoloration at the nape where the head has been removed. Fillets should be snowy white with pink hues; the gray membrane that clings to one side of the fillet should be pure gray, with no red bruising.

Monkfish are caught year-round, but landings are highest in spring when the weather is good and fishery quotas are renewed. The best-quality monkfish are caught during the fall and winter, however. Most monkfish are caught by trawl, but gill net fisheries, which are less detrimental to habitat, have emerged to fill a growing demand for top-quality monkfish. The large-mesh gill nets work to keep monkfish alive until landed. Encourage your fishmonger to search out high-quality gill net–caught monkfish, which has less impact on the environment.

## CHOOSING SUSTAINABLE SEAFOOD

Demand for U.S. monkfish in Europe and Asia in the 1980s led to rapid growth in the fishery and ultimately to overfishing of the stock. In response, a ten-year recovery plan was implemented in 1999. Based on recent indices, stocks are no longer being overfished and monkfish populations from Cape Cod north are considered healthy; the recovery of mid-Atlantic stocks still lags behind. A minimum size regulation has recently been added to the regulatory plan. Demand for American monkfish from Asia and Europe has sent prices ever higher and recently reduced fishing quotas will keep them there.

## CHOOSING HEALTHY SEAFOOD

Monkfish is a very good high-protein source of B vitamins and minerals, and a low to moderate source of omega-3s.

Monkfish liver, popular in Japanese, Korean, and French cuisine, may contain pollutants that have been filtered from the fish's bloodstream. Although this is no more of a concern than eating the liver of any animal, the same discretion should be exercised when eating monkfish liver.

NOTE: Monkfish have no scales, so should be avoided by those with religious-based dietary restrictions.

## IN THE KITCHEN

The monkfish's appearance may be what nightmares are made of, but fine flavor and versatility in the kitchen make it a dream to work with. Its dense, firm texture is adaptable to a broad range of cooking methods, and its mild, sweet flavor pairs nicely with almost any ingredient.

The monkfish liver, full and fat, is at its prime in the winter. It is highly prized by Koreans, Japanese, and the French as an addition to soups. In sushi bars, where it is known as *ankimo*, it is often poached in sake and served with scallions, grated daikon, and ponzu sauce.

Monkfish cheeks are edible and, though smaller than halibut cheeks, can be used in much the same way. The large central cartilaginous bone and any trimmings make an excellent mild-flavored stock.

Monkfish is a favorite in the Mediterranean kitchen; its gelatinous flesh creates a rich stock, making it an excellent addition to fish stews. A traditional bouillabaisse ingredient, it can also be used in any of the classic fish stews of the region, from bourride to zarzuela. Monkfish is excellent in paella, tagine, or gumbo, or served with Romesco Sauce (page 346). Slices of monkfish can be braised with potatoes and onions in saffron-tinged cream, or with tomatoes, savory, and fava beans.

Many chefs use monkfish to create rich, "meaty" dishes inspired by such traditional meat recipes as saltimbocca, osso buco, or choucroute garni.

# PAELLA OF MONKFISH, CLAMS, AND CHORIZO

SERVES 4 AS A MAIN COURSE

In southeastern Spain, paella is not only a regional food but a diet staple adapted to whatever seasonal ingredients are available. Well-cooked rice is more important to paella than the number of ingredients, and short-grain Spanish Callasparra or Bomba is the rice of choice. Italian risotto rice can be substituted.

A shallow paella pan is the standard, a spun-steel sauté pan is nearly as good, and a well-seasoned cast-iron skillet will work if the cooking time is reduced a couple of minutes. To serve more people, paella grows in diameter rather than in height, and the cooked rice should be no more than an inch thick. A ten-inch pan makes paella for just four people.

The secret to paella is to stir while sautéing the rice and while adding the stock at the start of cooking time; after that, the rice should never be stirred again. Paella should be cooked over medium heat so that the liquid is absorbed rapidly, the rice remains al dente, and a crispy crust, called a *socarrat*, forms on the bottom. It's often cooked completely on the stove top or over an open flame, but large paellas can be finished in the oven to ensure even cooking.

¼ cup olive oil

4 ounces chorizo sausage, preferably dried Spanish chorizo

1 small onion, finely diced

1½ cups paella rice

2 garlic cloves, minced

2 teaspoons bittersweet (mildly hot) Spanish paprika (pimentón)

10 to 12 saffron threads

1 ripe tomato

3 cups Quick Clam or Mussel Stock (page 28), Fish Stock (page 26), or chicken stock

¾ cup green peas

20 Manila clams, scrubbed

12 ounces monkfish fillets, cleaned and cut into 1½-inch cubes

1 red bell pepper, roasted, peeled (see page 38), and sliced

GARNISHES

Lemon wedges

Chopped fresh flat-leaf parsley

1. Preheat the oven to 450°F. In a 10-inch paella pan, sauté pan, or cast-iron skillet, heat the oil over medium heat. Add the sausages and cook, turning, for 3 or 4 minutes, or until browned on all sides. Set aside and allow to cool, then slice into ¾-inch coins.

MONKFISH

191

2. In the same pan, sauté the onion for a minute and then add the rice. Cook, stirring, until it turns white and opaque, 3 to 5 minutes. Add the garlic, paprika, and saffron and cook for another minute or two. Cut the tomato in half, squeeze out the seeds, and shred the flesh side on the largest holes of a box grater into the rice; discard the skin.

3. In a small saucepan, bring the stock to a simmer. Taste and season the stock—it should be mildly salty. Pour the hot stock over the rice and let it come to a boil, then stir the rice once well; don't stir it again. Cook the paella, uncovered, for 6 to 8 minutes, or until the stock has been absorbed almost to the level of the top of the rice. It may be necessary to move the pan around on the burner so the rice on the edge of the pan cooks evenly. Arrange the peas, clams, monkfish, and sausage on top of the rice. Press everything lightly into the rice. Scatter the sliced peppers over all. Continue to cook on the stove top, or place the pan in a preheated 450°F oven for 10 minutes until all the stock is absorbed and the rice begins to fry and forms a well-done crust (a *socarrat*) on the bottom of the pan.

4. Remove the pan from the heat, cover with aluminum foil or a cloth, and let rest for about 5 minutes. Serve the paella from the pan, garnished with lemon wedges and parsley.

## ESCAROLE-WRAPPED MONKFISH IN A TOMATO-OLIVE SAUCE

SERVES 4 AS A MAIN COURSE

Cooking fish wrapped in leaves is a popular culinary technique. Not only does it help keep the fish moist, but the flavor and fragrance of the leaves beautifully season the fish. Latin Americans wrap fish in corn husks or *oja santa* leaves before cooking on a griddle until charred. Banana and ti leaves are used by Hawaiians and Southeast Asians, and in the Caribbean for roasting fish in the coals or steaming. Salmon wrapped in fig leaves and charcoal-grilled, deliciously sweet and smoky, is one of my favorites. But everyday easier-to-find leaves such as cabbage, lettuce, or chard can also be used to create tasty and good-looking little fish parcels that can be steamed, sautéed, or braised.

Wrapping fish in leaves sounds involved, but this recipe is actually quite easy and quick. Rockfish, halibut, sea robin, grouper, or any mild-flavored fish may be substituted for the monkfish. This dish is great eaten on its own with bread and a salad, but it is also nice served over pasta or couscous.

Leaves from 1 head escarole

One 1½-pound monkfish fillet

Kosher salt and freshly ground black
pepper to taste

½ cup oil-cured black olives, such as
kalamata or niçoise

4 tablespoons olive oil, plus more
for drizzling

1 yellow onion, finely sliced

1 red bell pepper, seeded and julienned

2 garlic cloves, minced

1 cup dry white wine

1 pound tomatoes, peeled, seeded (see page
39), and finely chopped (about 2 cups)

2 tablespoons capers, rinsed and drained

1 teaspoon minced fresh oregano (optional)

Juice of 1 lemon

1. Blanch 16 of the largest escarole leaves in boiling salted water for just a minute; rinse under cold water and drain well. Spread the escarole leaves out on a flat surface. Coarsely chop the rest of the escarole, about 1 cup, and set aside.

2. Cut the monkfish fillet into 16 equal-sized pieces and season with salt and pepper. Place each piece of fish on one of the escarole leaves, roll once or twice the long way, fold the sides in, and continue rolling.

3. Place the olives between a clean kitchen towel, and pound lightly with a mallet or saucepan. Pick out the pits and discard. Chop the olive meat coarsely and set aside.

4. In a large sauté pan or skillet, heat 2 tablespoons of the olive oil over medium heat and sauté the onion and bell pepper for 3 or 4 minutes, or until the onion is translucent. Add the garlic and cook for 1 minute. Add the white wine, tomatoes, capers, and oregano and bring to a simmer. Taste and adjust the seasoning.

5. In a large sauté pan or skillet, heat the remaining 2 tablespoons oil over high heat and sauté the fish packets for about 1 minute on each side, or until they begin to brown lightly, then add them to the simmering sauce. Add the reserved chopped escarole to the hot pan and stir to wilt. Add the wilted escarole, chopped olives, and lemon juice to the simmering sauce and cook gently for 5 or 6 minutes, or until the monkfish packets feel firm when pressed. Serve in shallow bowls with a drizzle of olive oil added at the last moment.

# MUSSEL

**P**rior to the introduction of myticulture (mussel farming) to North America in the 1970s, mussels were mostly thought of as bait—which is what they were. Large, barnacle-encrusted mussels with impossible-to-remove beards were dredged up from the bottom of the sea or wrested from rocks. Full of mud and tough as an old shoe, mussels were eaten by no one, with the possible exception of Euell Gibbons.

After European methods of mussel culture were adopted, however, tender, plump young mussels without a trace of grit became an instant success in America. Today, the United States consumes more than 50 million pounds of mussels a year, much of it imported from Prince Edward Island in Canada. Anywhere you come across mussels in America, they're likely to be from P.E.I.

In fact, mussel-growing cooperatives on Prince Edward Island ship so many mussels to the U.S. market that the very term "P.E.I." is often used to mean any cultivated mussels.

The best time to eat mussels is September through April, when the water is chilly and the mussels are fat. During the warm summer months, mussels turn their attention to sexual reproduction; expending all their energies to produce sexual gametes, they become flabby and weak.

The common advice, which is to choose mussels that smell clean like the ocean and remain tightly closed, still holds true—but with one caveat: Farmed mussels are grown on ropes suspended from rafts, leaving them submerged underwater twenty-four hours a day. This provides for a quick growing season and a tender, grit-free mussel, but mussels raised by this method tend to gape when out of the water. Check open mussels to see if they are alive by squeezing the shells together; a live mussel will react by trying to hold the closed position.

Some mussel growers are beginning to experiment with the French method of myticulture, in which mussels are grown on wooden posts known as *bouchots*. Exposure to tidal fluctuations creates a stronger, longer-lasting, and superior-flavored mussel that does not gape.

More than any other shellfish, the mussel must be gotten to the table quickly. Although mussels may live as long as a week after harvest,

they quickly lose their sweetness and are prone to off flavors once they're out of the water more than two or three days. P.E.I. mussels can often be quite good, but locally grown mussels that get to the table quickly are always the best flavored.

The common **blue mussel** (*Mytilus edulis*), indigenous to the U.S. Atlantic seaboard, is the most popular mussel grown today. Numerous mussel farms, both small and large, can be found in the waters stretching from the Maritimes of Canada to the mid-Atlantic states, where conditions are ideal for growing mussels.

The **Baltic mussel** (*M. trossolus*) of northern Europe is grown at Penn Cove Mussel Farms in Puget Sound, Washington, and several other farms in the Pacific Northwest. An intriguing story credits Sir Francis Drake's ship, the *Golden Hinde*, with carrying the first Baltic mussels to Pacific shores. According to this account, mussels attached to the ship's hull seeded the bays wherever Drake visited.

The **Mediterranean mussel** (*M. galloprovincialis*) is a broader-shelled, softer-fleshed mussel with a good, though pronounced flavor. Grown by a number of small producers on the Pacific Coast, the winter-spawning Mediterranean mussel was first introduced as an alternative to blue mussels, which are often of poor quality during the summer.

The **green-lip mussel** (*Perna canaliculus*), first grown in Asia as a source of food for flocks of muscovy ducks, is now aquacultured in New Zealand and air-shipped from there to the

United States for human consumption. Its distinctively beautiful iridescent green shell can be seen year-round in Asian markets and restaurants, but this mussel is at its best during our summer, when it's winter in the southern hemisphere.

## CHOOSING SUSTAINABLE SEAFOOD

Mussels today are farmed almost exclusively by off-bottom methods, which not only produce a clean mussel but also have little impact on their sea floor habitat. Mussels and other filter-feeding shellfish improve the water quality where they are grown, by removing excess nutrients from the water.

## CHOOSING HEALTHY SEAFOOD

Mussels contain twice the amount of iron as beef, and very high levels of vitamin $B_{12}$ and selenium, which may help reduce mercury absorption. They are also high in beneficial omega-3 fatty acids.

Mussels were once thought to contain high levels of cholesterol. It is now understood that mollusks that filter plant-based phytoplankton from the water for food contain very little cholesterol or saturated fat. Rather, they contain cholesterol-like plant-based sterols, which actually interfere with the uptake of cholesterol. As a result, mussels are no longer excluded from a typical low-cholesterol diet and are considered a heart-healthy, low-fat source of protein.

Naturally-occurring algal blooms (see "Red Tide" Marine Toxins, page 415), which create toxins, may occasionally affect the safety of mussels. Commercially harvested mussels are tested by local health departments and monitored under the auspices of the National Shellfish Sanitation Program (NSSP), which certifies the safety of commercially harvested mussels. Mussels should be displayed with their NSSP harvest tag.

Growers are familiar with local waters and vigilant to the appearance of these algal blooms.

## IN THE KITCHEN
### SHUCKING MUSSELS

Mussels are much easier to open than either clams or oysters: Approaching the mussel from the concave curved inner side, push the tip of a thin-bladed knife between the shells. Pull the knife through the single abductor muscle located near the rounded front end of the mussel (see photo on page 197). Ease back the top shell and run the knife across the inside of the shell to cut the abductor muscle from the top shell. Run the tip of the knife around the inside edge of the shell to release any meat that has come away with the top shell. Twist off and discard the top shell. Run the knife across the inside of the bottom shell to cut the abductor muscle free. Run the tip of the knife around the inside edge of the bottom shell to completely free the meat.

Mussels can be eaten raw or cooked. Most often, they're simply steamed or used in mixed

TECHNIQUE FOR SHUCKING A MUSSEL: PUSH THE TIP OF A THIN-BLADED KNIFE BETWEEN THE SHELLS, THEN PULL THE KNIFE THROUGH THE ABDUCTOR MUSCLE IN THE DIRECTION OF THE ARROW.

seafood stews, but they can be prepared in a number of more versatile ways. Cooked mussels can be removed from the shell and used in seafood salads, or returned to the shell topped with a ravigote or other sauce and passed around as finger food. They make a nice first course when topped with seasoned bread crumbs and baked or broiled. Mussels and their liquor can be used to make a tomato-based or garlic and oil–based pasta sauce, just as you would with clams.

Mussels steamed with shallots and white wine are standard, but other seasonings also work well in the steamer: tomato, saffron, and fennel; dried chiles with a bit of orange juice; or Thai basil and lemongrass all add a delicious flavor. The addition of a few mussels to fish stocks or soups greatly enriches the flavor.

Blue mussels are usually harvested at between fifteen and twenty per pound, while green-lip and Mediterranean mussels run eight to ten per pound. Most cultured mussels are washed and cleaned of most of their beard before shipment, which makes them very easy to prepare but lessens their shelf life. Simply scrub the shell with a stiff brush just before cooking to remove any remaining beard or dirt. Discard any mussels that have broken shells or that refuse to react when squeezed shut. If there is any obvious beard left attached to the mussel, it should be removed as described below.

Wild mussels, or those from small artisanal growers, will need to be debearded: While firmly grasping the mussel in one hand, pointed end down and concave side toward the other hand, grasp the beard and yank sharply, ripping the beard from the mussel. Scrub the shell with a stiff brush to remove any dirt. Debearding should be done right before cooking.

# SOPA DE FIDEO
# WITH MUSSELS AND AÏOLI

Pasta takes on a wonderful toasty flavor when roasted in the oven or gently sautéed before cooking. Sardinian fregola, a small, round semolina pasta similar to Israeli couscous, is sold already toasted in Italian markets and specialty stores—and it's most often cooked with clams. Toasted pasta is popular in the Middle East, and *sopa de fideo*, toasted vermicelli soup, is found throughout Spain, Mexico, and Cuba in many variations.

Mix seafood and meat together in this dish as you would for paella, or mix fish and shellfish to turn it into a *sopa de mariscos*. Stir in a spoonful of Aïoli at the end for a delicious finish if you like, but it isn't needed. Cappellini, angel hair, spaghettini, or vermicelli pasta broken into 1-inch pieces all work well for this dish. Serve with green beans or summer squash cooked with tomatoes and basil.

**3 pounds mussels, scrubbed and debearded**

**4 cups water**

**3 tablespoons olive oil**

**12 ounces spaghettini or other thin pasta, broken into 1- to 2-inch lengths**

**2 garlic cloves, minced**

**Red pepper flakes to taste**

**2 tablespoons minced fresh flat-leaf parsley**

**Aïoli (recipe follows)**

1. Cook the mussels and make a mussel stock as per the directions for Quick Mussel Stock (page 28), using 3 pounds of mussels and 4 cups of water rather than the 2 pounds of mussels and 2 cups of water called for in the stock recipe. After adding the mussels, cook them just until the shells open so they do not overcook. Strain the stock through a fine-meshed sieve and season. Remove most of the mussels from their shells and reserve; leave a few in the shell for garnish.

2. In a large sauté pan or skillet, heat the olive oil over medium heat until shimmering. Add the pasta and cook, stirring constantly, until golden, about 3 minutes. Add the garlic and a sprinkle of red pepper flakes and cook until fragrant, about 1 minute.

3. Add the mussel stock and bring to a boil. Reduce the heat to a simmer, cover, and cook until the pasta is just al dente, about 10 minutes. Nestle the reserved mussels in the pasta, stir in the parsley, and heat through. There should be a bit of liquid left in the pan; add a little water if the pasta is too dry. Serve with Aïoli alongside to stir in at the table.

# A ÏOLI

A traditional aïoli is made with just olive oil, but if you wish to lighten the flavor you may substitute refined peanut oil for half the olive oil in this recipe. Note that all the ingredients should be at room temperature.

3 or 4 garlic cloves
¼ teaspoon coarse sea salt, plus more
　　to taste
1 large egg yolk
1 teaspoon warm water, plus more
　　as needed
¾ cup olive oil
Juice of 1 lemon

Using a mortar and pestle, combine the garlic and the ¼ teaspoon salt and grind to a smooth paste. You may continue using the mortar and pestle in the traditional manner or transfer the garlic paste to a bowl or food processor. Add the egg yolk and 1 teaspoon water and whisk or process until smooth. While whisking constantly, or with the machine running, slowly pour in the oil. Start with just a few drops at a time and, as the sauce begins to thicken, add the rest of the oil in a slow, fine stream. If the aïoli becomes too thick, thin with a bit of warm water. Stir in the lemon juice and salt to taste. Use now, or cover and store in the refrigerator for up to 2 days.

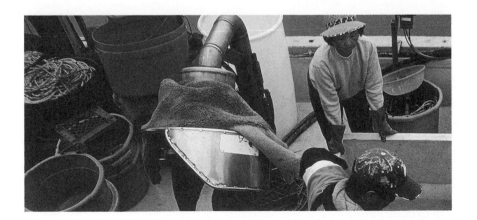

# MEDITERRANEAN MUSSELS BAKED
# WITH BREAD CRUMB TOPPING

SERVES 4 AS FIRST COURSE

Unlike the more common blue mussel, Mediterranean mussels are at their peak of quality from June through September, making them the perfect choice for a summertime shellfish. The distinct flavor of Mediterranean mussels works really well with assertive flavors, like the rosemary and sausage in this dish.

The mussels can be steamed open in a little white wine before baking, but the dish is best when they're shucked with a thin-bladed knife. You'll need rock salt for this recipe, to make a bed for baking the mussels so they don't tip over.

Common blue mussels, bay scallops, or littleneck or razor clams are all delicious when baked with a bread crumb topping. For these, however, I usually make a milder-flavored topping with sautéed onion, parsley, and prosciutto mixed with fresh bread crumbs.

**BREAD CRUMB TOPPING**

1 tablespoon olive oil

1 hot Italian sausage, removed from the
    casing and finely minced

2 pickled Italian cherry peppers, minced
    (available in grocery stores)

½ cup fresh bread crumbs

1 teaspoon minced rosemary

16 large Mediterranean mussels,
    shucked (see page 196)

Lemon wedges for garnish

**1.** For the topping: Preheat the oven to 425°F. In a small sauté pan or skillet, heat the oil over medium-high heat and sauté the sausage for 2 minutes, or until cooked. Add the minced peppers and the bread crumbs and cook until the crumbs absorb all the fat and juices and begin to brown a little, about 2 or 3 minutes. Mix in the rosemary. Remove from the heat and set aside.

**2.** Pack about 1 tablespoonful of the bread crumb mixture on top of each mussel. Place the stuffed mussel on a baking sheet that has been lined with rock salt. Bake for 10 to 12 minutes, or until the juices are bubbling and the topping is brown and crispy. Serve garnished with lemon wedges.

## Aquaculture: The Good, the Bad, and the Ugly

A group of chefs and seafood wholesalers have gathered for a weekend at Taylor Shellfish Farms in Washington state. The first thing that comes to mind when I enter the crowded cement building on the shores of Hood Canal is the old Charlton Heston movie *Soylent Green*. Tanks of every size and shape bubble merrily away, growing nutrients to feed a population of billions. The liquid in the tanks varies in color from lime green to black-tea brown. In the movie, a surprise ending reveals the unsavory contents of the tanks, but the Hood Canal shellfish hatchery has few surprises and is far less frightening. The color of the tanks reflects one of the thirty-seven varieties of phytoplankton being grown to feed the billions of baby shellfish starting life here.

At the company's hatchery in Quilcene, the algae-laden tanks produce food for tiny oysters, geoducks, Manila clams, and Mediterranean mussels. Students on apprenticeship from the University of Washington are examining plates under a microscope in a back room. Often, when university or government grant money is available for research, Ph.D.s from around the world come here to observe. As in *Soylent Green*, this is high-tech science driving a low-tech world. Once the shellfish being nurtured here reach a certain size, they are simply scattered on the beach to fend for themselves until they reach harvestable size.

By starting shellfish in a hatchery, the most dangerous period of a shellfish's life in the wild is avoided. The statistics bear this out: About 2,000 out of 10,000 of the geoducks that begin life at Taylor Shellfish Farms will reach maturity (20 percent), while in the wild only 1 in 10,000 (.0001 percent) are lucky enough to survive.

### THE BOUNTY OF A HEALTHY ECOSYSTEM

Later in the day, the group strolled on one of the nearby beaches. Armed only with knives, we took on an impressive list of prey, which we devoured on the spot. Greg Higgins from Portland found the biggest Kumamoto oyster I'd ever seen in my life—until he found a bigger one. Jon Rowley, the leader of the tour, took only a minute to locate a dozen eastern Virginia oysters that were equal in flavor to any I'd had from their native Atlantic waters. Olympias, Pacifics, European flats—nothing on the beach was safe from this group of hungry seafood lovers. Tiny snails were pried from their shells, Mediterranean mussels were served up on the half shell, and even the tiny green crabs that scuttled about were eaten, shell and all. I'd never encountered such a delicious and healthy-looking ecosystem.

## AQUACULTURE AT WORK

Much like a marine preserve, shellfish hatcheries and farms work to strengthen wild shellfish stocks. All the shellfish grown in the hatchery were originally derived from indigenous wild Puget Sound shellfish. So the shellfish scattered on local beaches adds to and encourages the natural set of wild shellfish.

Without a doubt, the growing of mollusks—clams, mussels, scallops, and oysters—represents all that is good in aquaculture. Shellfish farms take pressure off wild stocks, no wild animals are used for food, habitat is improved, and, just as important in my mind, mollusks are equally delicious whether from the farm or the wild.

Filter-feeding mollusks such as clams, mussels, scallops, and oysters are an important component of a healthy marine environment. Wherever these shellfish are grown, water quality improves. They clean bay and estuary waters by filtering algae and other microorganisms, providing a benefit to all the animals that live there. In Sweden, mussel farmers are being paid to clean nitrogen from local waters. In Chesapeake Bay, it's been recognized that the single most efficient way to restore the health of the bay is through the restoration of the Chesapeake Bay oyster.

Fish farms where landside tanks use filtered and recirculated water are also a good form of aquaculture, particularly when the fish are fed a grain-based diet that contains little or no wild fish. Tilapia, catfish, carp, and blackfish are perfect examples here. Trout, char, and sturgeon are not far behind; raised in land-based tanks, their diet is based on grain and wild fish, but farmers are constantly working to decrease the amount of wild fish used in their food.

## AQUACULTURE'S DOWNSIDE

The bad side of aquaculture—the proverbial escapees from Pandora's Box—is open-ocean net-pen aquaculture. Aquacultured salmon, cod, tuna, and halibut, for the most part, have followed the model of western industrialized agriculture where corporate expansion and profit override concerns for the environment. With only a few notable exceptions, open-ocean net-pen fish farms pollute; foul the sea with waste, chemicals, and drugs; and introduce disease into wild populations. Worst of all, growing predatory fish is inefficient and puts pressure on stocks of wild forage fish. It can take four to five pounds of wild fish to produce a pound of farmed fish. This can only end in the depletion of forage fish, putting further pressure on wild stocks.

Even as fears grow about the impact inshore net-pen fish farms have on the environment, the federal government is promoting net-pen aquaculture of tuna and other predatory species in offshore federal waters. Hoping to increase domestic aquaculture production fivefold in the next twenty years, the National Oceanic and Atmospheric Administration (NOAA) has drafted the National Offshore Aquaculture Act, which will open the door for virtually unregulated offshore aquaculture. In essence, federal agencies are promoting the same laissez-faire attitude that created the problems of near-shore aquaculture. This may help the global corporate aquaculture industry, but it only hurts the local fisherman, the fishing community, and responsible fish farmers.

Some in the marine fish aquaculture industry are working toward environmental responsibility: learning to grow disease-free fish without the use of antibiotics, preventing escape of fish into the wild, using less forage fish in feed, and improving water quality control. As one salmon farmer whose goal is the "sustainable production of healthy, happy fish" recently said to me: "It sure would be nice to find a sustainable way to feed the world without trashing the place." It is time for national regulatory standards to create environmentally sustainable aquaculture, and not to throw our oceans open to unregulated exploitation.

# OCTOPUS

The elusive octopus hides by day and hunts at night. It possesses an amazing ability to mimic other animals, and can also change shape and disappear like a phantom, shooting a confusing jet of ink to cover its retreat. It communicates by rapidly changing its skin color: black one moment, stark white the next, or quickly flashing neon orange to say, "I'm mad." With its eight legs, powerful beak, and three hearts that pump green blood through a body without bones, a stranger creature would be hard to find in the chronicles of science fiction.

The delicious and versatile octopus is far easier to prepare than its reputation asserts. It is particularly abundant throughout the Mediterranean, Latin America, and Asia, where it has long been a delicacy and even a staple. The recent influx of Asian and Latin American populations into the United States, which has been accompanied by a growing interest in their cuisines, has finally fueled American interest in the octopus.

The **common octopus** (*Octopus vulgaris*), found worldwide in tropical and semitropical waters, is the target of most of the world's commercial octopus fisheries. Portugal, Spain, and the West African countries of Morocco, Mauritania, and Senegal produce most of the world supply of this octopus species, 80 percent of which is consumed in Japan. South America and the Philippines are secondary producers. In the United States, the range of the common octopus extends from the waters off Virginia southward through Florida into the Gulf of Mexico. There is no directed U.S. fishery for octopuses, but those that are caught incidentally in trap and trawl fisheries are sold either to ethnic markets or to white-tablecloth restaurants—a strange dichotomy. They usually weigh between one and eight pounds.

The **old woman octopus** (*Cistopus indicus*), marketed as "**baby octopus**," is found in Southeast Asian and Indian waters. These small creatures are popular because they can be purchased in convenient amounts and don't require long cooking. "Baby octopuses" are usually sold at fifteen to twenty-five or twenty-five to forty to the pound.

The giant **Pacific octopus** (*O. dofleini*) enjoys the colder waters of the Pacific Coast from California to Alaska. As the name suggests, it may grow as large as thirty-two feet and six hundred pounds, though it's usually taken at much smaller sizes. There is a directed-diver fishery for giant Pacific octopus along the east coast of Canada's Vancouver Island (which is pretty incredible to imagine), as well as a pot (trap) fishery in Washington state. Still, most giant octopuses are taken as incidental catch in crab traps and trawls. Markets that sell giant octopus don't require you to purchase the entire animal; instead, a manageable-sized piece of tentacle or mantle will be cut off.

**Hawaiian octopus** (*Octopus cyanea*) is very popular in the islands, where there is a small commercial fishery. But a much greater amount is taken by subsistence and recreational fishermen using spears or snag hooks.

Octopuses are very perishable, so when you buy them they almost always have been cleaned. They should have very little odor. Raw octopus is covered with a beige or grayish-purple edible skin, and the flesh underneath is translucent.

When cooked, octopus skin turns red or maroon, and the underlying flesh turns milky white. Precooked common octopus can conveniently be purchased in Japanese markets, ready to be used in sushi or any other preparation. Those steamed in sake are deemed to be the highest quality. Raw octopus is considerably cheaper than the precooked variety and can be purchased in Latin American, Asian, and specialty stores.

## CHOOSING SUSTAINABLE SEAFOOD

Octopuses are very resilient. They seldom live more than a year before producing a large clutch of eggs, which they jealously guard until they hatch—after which the adult dies.

Traditional artisanal pot fisheries still exist in some countries such as Portugal and Senegal, but most of the octopus caught today is taken by trawl. Monterey Bay Aquarium lists the Hawaiian octopus as a "good alternative" because it is captured by spear and snag hooks. Other U.S.-caught octopuses are incidental catches and of low consequence from a resource perspective.

## CHOOSING HEALTHY SEAFOOD

Octopus, like squid, is a nutritionally ideal source of protein, containing all of the essential amino acids in perfect proportions. It is an excellent source of B vitamins and minerals.

Octopus is moderately high in cholesterol; however, it is now recognized that saturated fats in the diet are a much greater concern than dietary cholesterol. Since octopus contains very little saturated fat, it may be considered a heart-healthy source of protein.

Current advice from the American Heart Association warns people with heart disease to limit their dietary cholesterol intake to no more than 200 mg per day. This restriction should not unduly constrain anyone from occasionally eating octopus, especially if it's not battered or breaded and fried. Eating a balanced diet low in saturated fats is the best way to maintain good heart health.

## IN THE KITCHEN

Baby octopus does not have to be precooked. Simply treat as you would squid: deep-fry, charcoal-grill, or sauté very quickly over high heat, just until the flesh becomes opaque, or cook very slowly for a longer period of time as in stewing or braising.

Large octopus is usually precooked before further preparation (see Cooking Octopus, page 207), but raw octopus can simply be braised or roasted for a longer time instead.

Grilled, fried, braised, or prepared as sushi, octopus has long been popular in Greek and other Mediterranean restaurants and, of course, sushi bars. When simply simmered and served as part of an aïoli or salad, octopus has a simple, fresh sea flavor. Braised in red wine or tomatoes, however, it takes on more complexity, tasting almost like beef. Dress octopus while it is still warm when serving in salads.

Grilled octopus is the current favorite preparation in upscale American restaurants. Octopus poke, a popular Hawaiian marinated octopus salad, is available anywhere in Hawaii, including supermarkets.

Latin American and Southeast Asian immigrants, who view octopus as an everyday ingredient, have brought new excitement to octopus preparations. In spicy, red pepper–sauced cocktails or as an ingredient in seafood soups and stews, octopus is popular in the simplest of Mexican restaurants. Peruvian restaurants feature octopus ceviche, while Thais enjoy octopus curry, and then there is Korean barbecued octopus—now *that* sounds good.

## COOKING OCTOPUS

For the home cook, the most realistic way to tenderize an octopus is by long, slow cooking. If the octopus is not already cleaned, remove all the viscera. In a basin of cold water, wash the octopus well, massaging and rubbing it against itself vigorously to remove any slime. Change the water and repeat this process at least once. In a large pot, bring to a boil enough salted water (four tablespoons of kosher or two tablespoons sea salt per gallon) to cover the octopus. Slowly lower the octopus into the boiling water tentacles first, which will cause the tentacles to curl up attractively.

Gently simmer for thirty to forty-five minutes, skimming off and discarding any foam that rises to the surface. The octopus is ready when a thin wooden skewer will easily pierce the fattest part of a tentacle. Turn off the heat and leave the octopus in the pot to rest for thirty minutes; it will be tender and ready to quickly grill, sauté, add to soups, or dress for salad.

## CHAR-GRILLED OCTOPUS WITH PINEAPPLE SAMBAL

SERVES 4 AS AN APPETIZER

Baby octopus can be grilled over a hot fire for three or four minutes as you would for squid; small octopus of one pound or less can be grilled over a medium fire for ten to fifteen minutes until tender. Larger octopuses need to be boiled or steamed until tender before grilling. The sweet-and-sour note of the sambal provides the perfect counterpoint to the crispy charcoal flavor of the grill. It also makes a nice accompaniment to charcoal-grilled squid, shrimp, lobster, or just about any grilled fish.

▪ ▪ ▪ ▪ ▪ ▪ ▪ ▪ ▪ ▪ ▪ ▪ ▪ ▪ ▪ ▪ ▪ ▪ ▪ ▪ ▪ ▪

**PINEAPPLE SAMBAL**
2 garlic cloves
2 or more Thai bird or serrano chiles,
    seeded and chopped
Juice of 1 lime (shells reserved)
1 teaspoon packed brown sugar
2 tablespoons fish sauce
2 tablespoons rice vinegar

¼ cup water
Two 1-inch-thick slices pineapple, peeled

1 pound cleaned baby octopus
Olive oil for brushing
Kosher salt and freshly ground black
    pepper to taste
Frisée or other bitter lettuce for serving

1. Prepare a hot fire in a charcoal grill, or preheat a gas grill to 400°F. Soak wooden skewers in water for 30 minutes.

2. For the sambal: Using a mortar and pestle, mash the garlic and chiles to a paste. Add the lime juice, then scrape the pulp from the reserved lime shells with the tip of a knife and add. Stir in the sugar, fish sauce, rice vinegar, and water and mix until the sugar is completely dissolved. Transfer to a large bowl.

3. Grill the pineapple for 1 minute on either side, or until lightly browned in places. Core and finely chop the pineapple, adding the chopped flesh to the other ingredients in the bowl. Taste to be sure there is a balance of sweet, sour, and salty, and season with more sugar, vinegar, or fish sauce if needed.

4. Drain the skewers and thread the octopus on them so they can be more easily turned. Oil the grill rack well, lightly brush the octopus with oil, and season with salt and pepper. Grill the octopus, turning it repeatedly for about 3 or 4 minutes, or until it's charred at the edges and the tips of the tentacles but not burned. If using a gas grill, baste the octopus with some of the sambal for the last minute, to help it char. Serve on a bed of frisée, with the sambal spooned over.

## The Secret to Tender Octopus

A young Italian from the Amalfi Coast with a gift for storytelling and a penchant for red wine immigrated to New York. Anthony, as we'll call him, was a wonderful cook and soon found a job in a tiny Italian restaurant in Greenwich Village.

Anthony turned out extraordinary dishes he knew from home. The customers raved about his shrimp fra diavolo, scungilli marinara, and, most of all, his fork-tender octopus salad. The customers lined up at the door, and business was better than ever.

Anthony was a wonderful cook, but when he drank too much he became sloppy, dropping things everywhere, occasionally even in the food. Every now and then lost items turned up on diner's plates. The owner loved his new cook and the business he brought in, but he was also a man of temperate ways. He warned Anthony that he'd be without a job if he continued to drink at work.

## A CORK IN EVERY POT

One afternoon just before service, the owner passed through the kitchen and poked his head in the pots. There, in a pot of simmering octopus he spotted a wine cork bobbing across the surface—apparent evidence of Anthony's vice and the sloppiness that accompanied it.

When confronted, Anthony quickly swore that he hadn't been drinking at all; rather, a wine cork added to a pot of simmering octopus was his secret to tender octopus, a culinary tip passed down through the generations. Not wanting to lose the best cook he'd ever had, the owner accepted his explanation. The story spread, and wine corks soon appeared on the surface of simmering pots of octopus throughout the land.

Many a cook has been convinced that a simple cork added to the pot will tenderize the toughest octopus, but that isn't the only arcane practice being used to clean and tenderize octopus today. A well-known Japanese chef uses a large ridged Japanese mortar (suribachi), slapping the beast up and down over the washboardlike ridges to clean his octopus. He then laboriously pounds the octopus with a large daikon radish to tenderize it.

A Brooklyn wholesaler who specializes in octopus has taken his inspiration from stories of Greek and Italian fishermen pounding octopus on the rocks. He gives his octopus a good going-over in a large cement mixer, which, of course, he bought new just for the purpose. Octopus flown in from Spain or Portugal is cleaned and loaded into the mixer with rock salt and coarse ice for a ten-minute spin before being sold to the fanciest of Manhattan restaurants. He swears this process cleans the octopus of all slime and tenderizes it at the same time, creating a fast-cooking, clean-flavored octopus—and the chefs he sells his octopus to seem to agree.

While secret formulas for tenderizing octopus abound, the most reliable method I know of for the home cook is patience and long, gentle simmering (see Cooking Octopus, page 207).

# ONO

Fiji, Tahiti, Hawaii, and other Pacific islands are important sources of **ono** (*Acanthocybium solandri*). The fish is also the focus of major commercial and recreational fisheries in the Gulf of Mexico and south Atlantic, where it is called **wahoo**. When the first Europeans mapped the Hawaiian Islands, Oahu was often written as Wahoo, which is said to be the origin of ono's familiar mainland name.

Whether you know it as ono or wahoo; this largest member of the mackerel family is abundant worldwide in tropical and temperate seas. Solitary hunters that range the open ocean, ono quickly grow to seven feet and one hundred pounds, and are highly prized by sport fishers for their strong fighting abilities and deliciously sweet flavor.

Most of the ono that comes to market is very high quality. The deepwater fishing grounds of Hawaii, Fiji, and Tahiti are all relatively close to shore, while regulations in the Gulf and Atlantic encourage short fishing expeditions. Although ono is captured year-round, the greatest numbers of fish are caught from May through October.

Ono is also at times imported from South America. The same hook fishermen that target the mahimahi grounds of Ecuador and Costa Rica also occasionally catch ono. The quality of these fish must be monitored more closely than that of domestically caught fish.

Ono fillets are light sea green to steel gray in color, and should appear moist and translucent and be very firm. The myoglobin-rich dark meat of the blood line and on the back of the fillet should be bright red and well delineated from the lighter colored meat. There should be no green or yellow discoloration, either of the dark meat or along the belly of the lighter meat.

## CHOOSING SUSTAINABLE SEAFOOD

The ono, or wahoo, fish are abundant; they grow quickly and reproduce at an early age, making them a good sustainable choice. Ono is commercially targeted by trolling with hooks, and is also sometimes taken as bycatch in longline fisheries directed at tuna and swordfish.

A South Atlantic and Gulf fisheries management plan instituted for ono in 2004 prohibits longlining and allows only the more conscientious practice of troll fishery. Although ono is not considered overfished, the purpose of this action was to ensure the safety of sea turtles and reduce the bycatch of other species.

## CHOOSING HEALTHY SEAFOOD

Ono is an excellent low-fat, high-protein source of B vitamins and minerals, and also provides moderate amounts of omega-3 fatty acids.

## IN THE KITCHEN

Ono, or wahoo, is a member of the mackerel family, but its large size and firm, lean, mildly sweet flesh makes it an appropriate substitute in recipes for swordfish, or albacore and other tunas. The open ocean–loving ono is seldom parasitized, so is a perfect choice for soused and cured raw preparations. Its mild flavor is complemented by either citrus or soy-based marinades, such as Peruvian-style tiradito or Hawaiian poke. Firm-fleshed, it's very easy to slice for Italian-style crudo. After a short overnight cure in a Yucatán-style recado of achiote and sour orange, it can be sliced on the diagonal and charcoal-grilled, broiled, or sautéed for just a moment. Ono, or wahoo, should be cooked rare—much like tuna—to maintain moisture and good flavor. The lean flesh is also very good steamed.

The ono's scales are very fine and need not be removed; you may eat the skin, as well as the liver and roe. If cooked quickly, the bones make a good but distinctively flavored stock.

# TAHITIAN ONO FISH SALAD

Many years ago while vacationing in Tahiti, my wife Joan and I were introduced to the local specialty, *poisson cru*. Locally caught fish, usually albacore or ono, is soused in lime and then mixed with coconut cream; the result is smooth, crisply tart, and refreshing.

Sousing fish in seawater and then mixing it with coconut cream has long been a popular method of preparing fish in the South Pacific islands. After the introduction of citrus in the nineteenth century, lime juice replaced the seawater in this preparation. I always temper the overly acidic flavor of the green Persian limes available in this country with a touch of sweet orange juice.

Pacific Islanders make their own coconut cream, but if you have neither the time nor the inclination, coconut cream skimmed off the top of a can of coconut milk works fine.

1 pound skinless ono fillet

¼ cup freshly squeezed lime juice

¼ cup freshly squeezed orange juice

½ cup coconut cream (see Note, page 160)

1 teaspoon minced fresh ginger

1 to 2 serrano, Fresno, or other chiles, seeded and minced

1 small cucumber, peeled, seeded, and sliced

½ small onion, finely sliced

1 small tomato, sliced

1 teaspoon salt

Lettuce leaves for serving

With a sharp knife, remove the dark blood line that runs down the center lateral line of the ono fillet. Discard the dark flesh. Cut the rest of the fillet into ⅓-inch dice. Put the fish in a stainless-steel or glass bowl, add the lime and orange juices, and refrigerate for 1 or 2 hours. Drain off and discard the citrus juice. Add the coconut cream, ginger, chile, cucumber, onion, and tomato. Toss well and season with salt. Refrigerate for at least 2 hours to chill. Serve on lettuce leaves.

# OPAH

The beautiful **opah** (*Lampris guttatus*) would appear at home in a tropical aquarium: rich blue on the back, hot pink on the belly, with highlights of rose and gold, all covered with a sheen of purple and reflections of silver. White spots dapple the body, while the fins jump with fiery crimson. An adult opah can weigh over 150 pounds—oval shaped, and six feet long by four feet high, it is a startlingly beautiful fish.

From Jane Grigson's *Fish Cookery* comes this description: "A large fish of curves and perfect beauty of color. The huge, plump body, a taut oval up to six feet long, is softly spotted with white. The sickle tail has reminded people of the moon's shape; the ribs of its fins have seemed like the scarlet rays of the sun."

The opah is a widely distributed and, seemingly, rather abundant species—though little is known of its life history or population structure.

A pelagic wandering species, it is often found in the company of tunas and billfish. Though never directly targeted, the opah is caught incidentally in swordfish and tuna fisheries all over the world. An important part of the catch in Hawaii's longline tuna fishery, the opah is also frequently taken in other swordfish and tuna fisheries in the Pacific, the Gulf of Mexico, and the Atlantic.

The flesh of the opah is highly esteemed, said to be somewhat like a cross between tuna and swordfish. But that's too simple a description. The top loin is the most attractive part of the fish: A beautiful, deep red-orange, it is sweet and lean, with a texture similar to tuna. The belly loin is a light pink color; high in fat like tuna belly, it's best for slicing into thin scallops. Because of its large, oval shape, the opah also has a third type of meat that comes from its unusually large breastplate—meat that likely would be considered the throat piece or tongue on a smaller, perch-shaped fish. It is dark—nearly the color of liver—rich, and a little tough. My friend Sus Kato, who worked in fishery research and management for years, tells me that this cut is excellent for sashimi, provided the fish is very fresh.

Opah is available year-round; its availability coincides with that of tuna and swordfish. Fillets should appear moist; some clarity and a nice red color distinguish the top loin, and a fine, lighter-colored marbling of fat gives the belly a pink color. Neither cut should be varie-gated in color or brown. Opah should never smell musty or sour, or smell of oxidized fats like an old mackerel.

### CHOOSING SUSTAINABLE SEAFOOD

There is considerable concern about the bycatch associated with longlining, but opah is bycatch that is utilized, and therefore good. While U.S. fishermen have made great strides in reducing and documenting bycatch in their longline fisheries, some international fisheries are less conscientious in their methods.

### CHOOSING HEALTHY SEAFOOD

Opah belongs to the group of cold-water, fatty fish that are very rich in the beneficial omega-3 fatty acids, which have been shown to lower blood cholesterol and have an anti-inflammmatory effect, among other health benefits. It is also an easily digestible, high-protein source of antistress B vitamins and minerals, particularly selenium, which may neutralize mercury toxicity.

Care should always be exercised when eating raw seafoods (see Raw Seafood: How to Stay Safe, page 408).

### IN THE KITCHEN

The opah's flesh is rich, fatty, and versatile. The top loin is usually cut into nearly rectangular-shaped slices that are quite easy to handle. Any preparation of this cut works well: charcoal-grilling, steaming, gently simmering in Dashi (page 370) with vegetables and noodles, or cooking in a curry (see page 216), as is popular in Indonesia. The entire top loin fillet is sometimes smoked.

The lighter, salmon pink–colored flesh of the opah belly is sliced thinly and used for quick cooking or raw preparations. The fatty texture of opah belly is very similar to that of tuna belly.

Panfry the belly quickly and serve with a fresh tomato coulis that's been enlivened with oil and vinegar. The dark breastplate is sliced thinly; it can be steamed or sautéed, and then sprinkled with soy, peanut oil, and scallions.

The skin is thin and can be eaten; the bones, however, are too distinctive in flavor to make a good stock. The cheeks are large and tasty.

# CURRIED OPAH
# WITH GREEN MANGO AND TOMATO

This recipe works well with just about any type of fish, from fillet of sole to salmon.

Semiripe green mangoes are easy to get in this country, simply because that is the state in which most mangoes are imported. They have a very nice mildly sour flavor that really perks up this simple curry. Choose the firmest, hardest mangoes you can find. I see them in Chinatown, in Mexican markets, and even in my corner upscale grocery store. Firm-fleshed tart apples such as Granny Smith or pippin may be substituted for the mango. Serve with steamed rice and a chutney of your choice.

1½ pounds opah fillets, cut into
   1½-inch dice
2 tablespoons Curry Spice Mix No. 2
   (page 36), or commercial curry
   powder
4 tablespoons refined peanut oil or
   another high-heat oil for frying
1 small yellow onion, finely diced
1-inch piece fresh ginger, peeled and
   minced
3 garlic cloves, minced
½ cup dry white wine
2 tomatoes, peeled, seeded (see page 39),
   and diced (about 1 cup)
1 or 2 semiripe green mangoes, peeled,
   pitted, and diced (about 1 cup), or
   1 cup chopped tart apple
¼ cup heavy cream
Cilantro sprigs for garnish

1. Put the opah and the Curry Spice Mix No. 2 in a paper bag and shake well; reserve the mix or powder that doesn't stick to the fish.

2. In a large sauté pan or skillet, heat the oil over high heat until shimmering hot. Quickly sauté the opah pieces until brown and fragrant, about 30 seconds on each side. Using a slotted metal spatula, transfer to a plate.

3. Reduce the heat to medium, add the onion to the pan, and sauté until starting to turn golden, about 4 or 5 minutes. Add the ginger and garlic, sauté for 1 minute, then add the reserved curry powder and stir for 30 seconds. Add the white wine and stir to scrape any curry powder that may have stuck to the bottom of the pan. Add the tomatoes and mangoes and bring to a boil.

4. Reduce the heat to low and cook at a low simmer for 2 or 3 minutes. Return the opah chunks to the pan, add the cream, and heat through. Serve garnished with cilantro sprigs.

# OYSTER

Most of the oysters that make it to the oyster bar today are grown under the watchful eye of a commercial oyster farmer. Oyster farmers are a well-educated lot. It's not unusual to find a trained marine biologist working the mudflats, and it's common for growers to have studied the subject at the university level. Yet ostreaculture, the cultivation of oysters, is not just a science but also an art. The best growers understand the nuances of seasonal change, water composition, and tidal action and the effect these have on the oysters.

The diversity of oysters today is astonishing—not only is the variety greater than ever before, but the flavors are more wide ranging and the quality more consistent. And the ease with which aquaculture can be monitored has made oysters cleaner and safer than ever.

The Pacific Coast is a world leader in innovative aquaculture techniques and produces many of the country's most sought-after half-shell oysters. In fact, more oysters now come from Washington state than any other place in the country. Oyster farmers in New England and the mid-Atlantic states—having seen the success of Western growers—are now using many of the same techniques. Farmers on the Gulf Coast are more apt to tend natural-set oysters, culling and tending natural oyster beds until they can be harvested at the perfect size and readiness.

Oysters are best during the "r" months, from early fall through spring, when waters are cold. During this time, oysters store the fats, sugars, and starches that are responsible for their wonderful flavor. Depending on how much food is available to the oyster, it may vary from full and fat to slightly thin. A nice, fat oyster will have depth and variety of flavor, with suggestions of melon, cucumber, or butter. A thinner oyster is crisp in texture and allows mineral and seawater flavors to shine through.

As summer approaches and water temperatures warm, oysters turn their attentions to reproduction. Fats and sugars responsible for the oyster's fine flavor and texture are turned into sexual gametes, and the oyster becomes disagreeably soft, chalky, and unpalatable. All oysters do not spawn at the same time, nor does this condition usually last for longer than several weeks, so while one oyster may be spawning, the oyster just down the beach may still be fine.

To really appreciate the good flavors that nature has worked so hard to develop, choose the freshest oysters possible. Oysters should be displayed on ice and separated from oysters grown in different locations. A copy of the National Shellfish Sanitation tag showing origin and harvest date should be displayed with the oysters. Locally grown oysters are often the best choice. Store oysters in the refrigerator, cup-side down, covered with a damp towel; place several ice cubes on top.

Shucked oysters sold in glass jars should be surrounded by clear liquid and should have a pull date; these oysters are usually quite large and are only recommended for cooked oyster dishes such as oyster stew or oysters in black bean sauce.

There are five species of oyster grown in the United States today. Although provenance is responsible for much of an oyster's flavor, some general characteristics can be used to describe each species.

## AMERICAN OYSTER

The **American oyster** (*Crassostrea virginica*) is native to the U.S. Atlantic and Gulf coasts, where nutrient-bearing streams and rivers feed shallow coastal waters, thus creating the ideal oyster habitat. Often described as mild yet complex in flavor, in its more southerly range the oyster seems to pick up sweet musky or grassy flavors. In its northern range, it tends more toward crisp, salty, and mineral flavors.

## EUROPEAN FLAT OYSTER

The indigenous **European flat oyster** (*O. edulis*) is often described as coppery, metallic, or bitter-lettucelike in flavor. Slow growing, this oyster is intolerably expensive in Europe but can be enjoyed here for a reasonable price; they are grown in Maine, California, and Washington state.

## KUMAMOTO

Named for the southern Japanese prefecture where it originated, the **Kumamoto** (*C. sikamea*) was previously thought to be a subspecies of the Pacific oyster (*C. gigas)* but has recently been designated a separate species. The Kumamoto's small size, deep cup, and delicious flavor—often described as mildly briny, with hints of butter and cream—have made it a big hit in the half-shell trade. Kumamotos are grown exclusively on the U.S. Pacific Coast, with most production in Washington state and California. Only tiny remnant populations still exist in Japan.

## OLYMPIA OYSTER

The tiny, slow-growing **Olympia oyster** (*Ostrea concaphilia*) is the native Pacific Coast oyster. It is closely related to the European flat oyster, both taxonomically and from the stand-point of flavor. Often described as having a coppery, metallic, or bitter-lettucelike flavor, the Olympia is a good, strong-flavored oyster with a pleasant aftertaste. It's available commercially from Puget Sound in Washington state.

## PACIFIC OYSTER

Introduced to the Pacific Coast from Japan in the 1930s, the **Pacific oyster** (*C. gigas*) was long considered inferior to the American oyster and was grown mainly for shucking. In the 1980s, an innovative generation of oyster farmers adapted new growing techniques that elevated the Pacific oyster to star status at the oyster bar. The Pacific oyster is often grown in greater concentration and in more saline waters than Atlantic Coast American oysters. This creates a thin, clean, crisp, briny-flavored oyster—although Pacific oysters grown in the nutrient-rich reaches of Hood Canal can be every bit as fat and complex in flavor as an eastern oyster. The famed "Portugaise" oyster of Europe, once though to be a separate species, is now recognized as *C. gigas*.

## OTHER VARIETIES

Available during our summer months are **New Zealand coromandel** and **Rilan Bay oysters** and **Chiloe Island oysters** from Chile (all *C. gigas*), and occasionally the native **Chilean oysters** (*O. chilensis*).

## CHOOSING SUSTAINABLE SEAFOOD

Healthy oyster populations are essential to the well-being of many marine ecosystems. Filter-feeding oysters and other bivalves improve water quality wherever they are grown. The declining health of the Chesapeake Bay, for example, can be attributed to nutrient pollution from farms and encroaching development, combined with the demise of wild oyster shoals. At one time, wild oysters could filter the entire volume of water in the Chesapeake Bay in a week, removing light-blocking algae and other nutrients. It is estimated that today it takes over a year for the depleted oyster populations to filter the bay's waters.

## CHOOSING HEALTHY SEAFOOD

Oysters contain incredibly high amounts of vitamins D and $B_{12}$. They are nature's most concentrated package of zinc—giving rise to the idea that they are effective as a sexual enhancer—and an excellent source of iron, copper, and selenium.

Oysters were once thought to contain high levels of cholesterol. It is now understood that mollusks that filter plant-based phytoplankton from the water for food contain very little cholesterol or saturated fat. Rather, they contain cholesterol-like plant-based sterols, which actually interfere with the uptake of cholesterol. As a result, oysters are no longer excluded from a typical low-cholesterol diet and are considered a heart-healthy source of protein.

Oysters also contain very high levels of omega-3s, which improve the blood lipid profile by lowering triglycerides and raising HDL ("good") cholesterol.

Oysters may harbor potentially harmful pollution-related or naturally-occurring pathogens. Commercial shellfish beds are monitored and tested for pathogens by state and federal authorities under the auspices of the National Shellfish Sanitation Program, and oysters from those beds should be displayed with their NSSP harvest tag. To be completely safe, pregnant women, young children, and those with compromised immune systems should refrain from eating raw oysters at any time (see Raw Seafood: How to Stay Safe, page 408).

## IN THE KITCHEN

Oysters go particularly well with licorice-like seasonings, such as fennel, anise, chervil, and tarragon, or the anise-flavored liqueur Pernod. A simple oyster stew of onions, fennel, cream, and oysters is delicious. Whole oysters can be barbecued or baked in their shell with a sauce or seasoned topping. Fried oysters are popular in the form of two regional sandwiches: the "peacemaker" of Maryland and the "po-boy" of Louisiana. Out west, a few fried Olympias may be used to garnish a Caesar salad. Oysters and pork seem to have a particular affinity for one another: Holiday stuffing for birds, seafood gumbo, and Chinese braised oysters and pork all combine the two with success.

## The Oyster Century

It is doubtful that any other country has ever been as enamored with the oyster as was the United States during the nineteenth century. Wild oysters from the Atlantic and Gulf coasts were harvested from shoals of oysters so massive that they were said to be a navigational hazard. Every town of any note had numerous "oyster cellars," where the public could enjoy oysters in a friendly atmosphere. Large cities such as Philadelphia and New York had oyster saloons, and oysters were sold on every block by street peddlers whose signs advertised "All the Oysters You Can Eat for Six Cents." Oyster-express wagons heavily loaded with fresh oysters from the Chesapeake Bay thundered across the Alleghenies, frequently shifting to fresh horses. They delivered oysters so far inland that Abraham Lincoln, then living in Springfield, Illinois, was able to give oyster parties at which incredible quantities of the bivalve were devoured. When the speedy new transcontinental railroad was finished, new markets as far away as the gold fields of California were opened; heavily iced barrels of oysters were shipped from Cape Cod all the way to San Francisco.

Today, the era of the wild American oyster is coming to a close. Few wild oyster beds remain in the Northeast, and Chesapeake Bay oysters are a shadow of their former selves. Although wild Gulf of Mexico oysters are faring somewhat better, they, too, are under pressure: Overharvesting and pollution are partly to blame, but the major culprits seem to be two oyster diseases, Dermo and MSX, accidentally introduced into Atlantic Coast waters some forty years ago.

### SHUCKING OYSTERS

Place the oyster, cup-side down and flat-side up, on a folded towel or pot holder. Fold the towel or pot holder over the round end of the

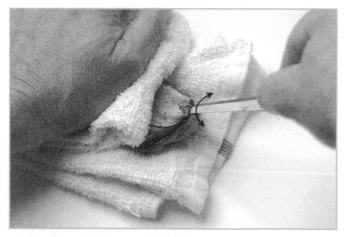

WHILE HOLDING THE OYSTER FIRMLY IN PLACE, PUSH THE TIP OF AN OYSTER KNIFE INTO THE HINGE, THEN ROCK AND TWIST AS INDICATED BY THE ARROW.

oyster, leaving only the narrow hinged end exposed. Hold the oyster in place with the heel of your left hand—and be sure the pot holder or towel is protecting your hand in case the knife slips. Insert the tip of an oyster knife into the hinge; push, twist, and pry (see photo)—the shell will release with a pop.

Pry open the top shell and run the knife across the inside of the shell to cut the single abductor muscle, located near the front, rounded end of the shell. Run the tip of the knife around the inside edge of the shell to release any meat that has come away with the top shell. Discard the top shell. Run the knife across the inside of the bottom shell to cut the abductor muscle free. Run the tip of the knife around the inside edge of the bottom shell to completely free the meat.

# OYSTERS ON THE HALF SHELL
## WITH POMEGRANATE GRANITA

Oysters on the half shell straight from the sea are perfect on their own, but this pomegranate granita adds spice and citrus flavor without being overwhelming. Its royal red color adds festivity to fall holiday gatherings, a time of the year when both pomegranates and oysters are at their peak.

You'll need seaweed, rock salt, or raw rice to make a bed for the oysters when serving.

½ cup pomegranate juice (1 pomegranate)

½ cup freshly squeezed orange or tangerine juice

½ teaspoon ancho chile powder, available at Latin markets

¼ teaspoon hot chile powder or cayenne pepper

24 oysters, shucked (see page 222)

1. Place a small serving bowl in the freezer. Roll the pomegranate on a countertop, then gently massage the fruit with your fingers until all the seeds seem to be broken. Poke a hole in the pomegranate and squeeze the juice into a bowl. Add the orange or tangerine juice and season with the chile powders.

2. Pour the ingredients into an 8-inch glass baking dish and freeze for 20 minutes, or until the mixture is slushy. Stir with a fork and return to the freezer. Repeat every 20 minutes until the granita is well frozen into separate ice crystals that are light and fluffy, about 1 hour in all. Scrape the pomegranate granita into the frozen serving bowl and return it to the freezer until just before serving the oysters.

3. Arrange the oysters on a platter of seaweed, rock salt, or raw rice. Serve the granita alongside for guests to top their oysters.

# OYSTER SAUCE BOK CHOY

Cantonese oyster sauce, made from dried oysters and soy sauce, is used in a wide range of steamed and stir-fried Asian dishes. If you've never tried oyster sauce, this is a good recipe to see if you like it. It works equally well with any greens that can be quickly blanched or steamed, from mustard to romaine lettuce.

12 ounces baby bok choy

1 tablespoon Asian-style unrefined peanut oil

3 scallions, including light green parts, diagonally sliced

3 tablespoons oyster sauce

1 tablespoon soy sauce

1. In a pot of salted boiling water, blanch the bok choy for 1 minute, or until slightly wilted. (Or steam over briskly simmering water in a covered pot for 1 or 2 minutes.) Remove and drain well. Arrange in a warmed serving dish.

2. In a small sauté pan or skillet, heat the oil over medium-high heat and sauté the scallions for 1 minute. Remove from the heat and add the oyster sauce and soy sauce. Pour over the bok choy and serve immediately.

## Salt Pond Oysters

Uncle Emil and I were sitting on the front porch watching a Boston whaler being tossed about on the wake of the Block Island ferry when Harold slogged up the front walk. Graying and grizzled, his black boots making a squishing sound with every step, he carried a dripping-wet burlap sack slung over his shoulder. He called out a *Hey!* and stepped up on the porch, letting the burlap sack drop on the old wooden plank table we sat around. Tipping the bag over, he poured out a wet pile of sparkling oysters, no bigger than a couple of inches across. Gleaming-bright bits of seaweed, sand, grit, and periwinkles were part of the mix; a few tiny crabs scuttled across the pile trying to hide. Seawater dripped on the floor. Harold, oblivious to the mess, asked, "Got a knife?" My uncle looked at the pile, looked back at us, and stood up to go inside. He came back with an oyster knife, a box of saltine crackers, and three cans of beer from the icebox. "It's a good thing your Aunt Esther isn't here," he said, shaking his head.

### A FISHERMAN'S GARDEN

Harold, a retired fisherman who lived on the far side of Charleston Pond, had decided to go into the oyster business. The sandy flats in front of his house were like a fisherman's garden; he tended and culled, raked and harvested, then scattered the old shells back in the water to attract a new crop for next year. With oysters, the more you work a bed and the more old shells you throw back in the water, the more oysters you get the following year. This was the third year in a row that his salt pond had produced more oysters than he could eat or give away to all his friends. And that's what gave him the idea to go into the oyster business. He'd brought some by the house to get Uncle Emil's opinion—not that Uncle Emil hadn't given him his opinion many times before.

Harold sat down at the table and deftly popped the top off one briny little oyster after another. Uncle Emil and Harold talked about oysters and how to sell them while the three of us popped open shells and slurped. Oysters had never held that much interest for me; in fact, I was still young and if pressed I would probably admit to not really liking oysters. But these little salt pond oysters were a delicious revelation: Their flavor was as briny and fresh as they looked, bright and crisp followed by layers of sweetness and musk.

CONTINUED

Harold's salt pond oysters were like no other oyster I had ever eaten, and there is a reason for that. No two oyster beds enjoy exactly the same conditions; therefore, no two oyster beds produce an oyster that tastes the same. The ideal habitat for an oyster is the mouth of an estuary, creek, or salt pond where nutrient-rich freshwater mixes with mineral-rich saltwater. The ensuing mixture and variety of trace minerals, nutrients, salinity, and water temperature encourage the growth of marine plants (microalgae) that give an oyster its flavor.

During the fifteenth century, the oyster growers of Marenne, France, noticed that the delicious oysters fattened in the local salt marshes developed a unique green tinge to their meat. Growers insisted, and a law was passed, that only the oysters grown in the surrounding salt marshes could be marketed as Marenne oysters. This not only distinguished them from other, less-prized oysters, but inspired the French viticultural system of *appellation d'origine contrôlée* (AOC). Just as the world-famous *vertes de Marennes* acquire their color and fine flavor from a particular type of chlorophyll-bearing marine algae, *Navicula ostrearia*, Harold's salt pond oysters acquired their unique sweet and musky flavor from the marine algae on which they grazed.

If you've sampled the variety of oysters offered in one of the country's well-stocked oyster bars, you may find it hard to believe that most of the oysters grown in the United States are one of only two species. The flavor of a briny, crisp Pacific oyster grown in the saline waters of Tomales Bay is vastly different from a mild and fruity Eagle Creek oyster grown in the nutrient-rich waters of Hood Canal, yet they are the same oyster. An Apalachicola oyster tastes nothing like a Chincoteague, and Harold's Charleston Pond oysters are vastly different from the bluepoints, Wellfleets, and Cotuits I had eaten before, yet they are all the same species. There is a very good reason why it seems as if you have a different oyster for every creek, beach, shoal, and point in the country: When an oyster grazes on the marine plants or algae that flourish in the waters where it is grown, it absorbs the very signature of the place.

## HEALTHY CHOICE

The same marine plants that are responsible for an oyster's flavor are also the source of plant sterols that make oysters so healthful for us. Mollusks that filter plant-based algae from the water for food contain very little cholesterol or saturated fat; rather, they contain cholesterol-like plant-based sterols that interfere with the uptake of cholesterol, making oysters one of the healthiest as well as tastiest foods we can eat.

# ROCKFISH

**R**ockfish (genus *Sebastes*) have defined the western U.S. fish market from the earliest days of commercial fishing on the Pacific coast. The name refers to a fantastic array of closely related fish, all sporting ferocious-looking spines, bony plates, brilliant colors, and a wide variety of markings. The rockfish's striking appearance inspired its genus name, *Sebastes*, which means "magnificent." In 1854, William Ayres, the first ichthyologist at the newly formed California Academy of Sciences, had only to wander over to the docks of San Francisco's Barbary Coast to identify and assign scientific names to the different species of this new grouping—an unbelievable sixty-five of which still roam the waters between the Gulf of California and Alaska.

These various rockfish might have been newly discovered from science's point of view, but

the Portuguese and Italian fishermen who worked the waters of central California had already given colloquial names to each of the species that roamed coastal waters: European-influenced names like Santa Maria, Boccacio, Barriaga, Viuva, Becafico, Garrupa, and Gallo. As time went by, the language of designation switched to English, but the new names were no less colorful or diverse—including turkeys, gophers, canaries, chuckleheads, widows, and thorny spine idiots, among others.

The late food authority and seafood expert Alan Davidson once told me that one of the most impressive sights to a European coming to the West Coast for the first time was the vast array of rockfish in the local fish markets. "They're absolutely stunning—real eye-openers," he marveled. "It's hard to believe that so many diverse-looking fish could all be so closely related."

It's impossible for anyone but the seafood professional or fishery scientist to keep the various rockfish species separate. For the casual observer and cook, it is most important to understand the general characteristics of the various rockfish categories. Although rockfish are generally similar in flavor and texture, some are more suited to particular cooking methods than others. Over the years, rockfish have evolved into three general categories: Category 1 are the small, spiny, firm-fleshed varieties that are used for whole-fish preparations; Category 2 are the meaty, deep-bodied, fine-flavored varieties that are similar to grouper or French

rascasse at the table; and Category 3 comprises the smoother, elongated varieties that are most often sold as common "Pacific red snapper" fillets.

## CATEGORY 1

These territorial and solitary loners generally live near the shore in rocky crevices. They are small fish (under two pounds) with numerous long spines, similar in looks to the closely related lionfish, with horny projections and bony plates about the head, thick skin, and heavy scales. They are most often sold in Asian fish markets, either live in tanks or as whole fish on the counter. Their small size and coarse, firm texture make these varieties ideal candidates for steamed or fried whole rockfish. These fish are as much about presentation and appearance as flavor, which tends to be mild, even neutral. This is the most expensive rockfish group; live fish may sell for as much as twelve dollars a pound. **Gopher**, **China**, **black and yellow**, **copper**, **kelp bass**, and **quillback** are typical varieties.

## CATEGORY 2

These deep-bodied, hearty-looking fish sport less pronounced but still formidable spines and horny projections. The skin is thick and scales moderately heavy. These fish tend to live in deeper water around reefs and rock piles, areas that are traditionally difficult for trawlers to go into, and are often targeted by hook-and-line fishermen. These are the best-flavored and -textured rockfish, meaty and thick fleshed and reminiscent of grouper. A firm texture, a moderately coarse flake, and sweet sea flavor make these fish the most versatile rockfish in the kitchen. Sold as whole fish, steaks, or higher-priced fillets, this category includes **golden eye**, **vermillion**, **cow cod**, **turkey rockfish**, **redbanded**, and **canary amongst others**.

## CATEGORY 3

These fish are also found around rocky reefs, but because they school for protection they are less in need of protective armor. These rockfish are slender and elongated, with weak spines and no horny projections about the head. These varieties make up the vast majority of fish sold as **"Pacific red snapper"** and **"ocean perch"** fillets in fish markets and supermarkets throughout the country. Soft-fleshed and mild flavored, they're good sautéed, baked, braised, or cooked in stews. Included here are the **Boccacio**, **yellowtail**, **chilipepper**, **widow**, and **black** and **blue rockfishes**. **Blackgill** and **shortraker rockfish** have recently become important commercial species because they reside outside newly created rockfish conservation zones. Two deepwater species, the **North Atlantic redfish** and its probable ancestor, the **Pacific Ocean perch**, are sold as ocean perch fillets.

### CHOOSING SUSTAINABLE SEAFOOD

The major commercial rockfish species in Washington, Oregon, and California have seen a widespread decline. The collapse of rockfish stocks can be traced to mismanagement and overfishing in the 1970s and '80s. Poor ocean conditions related to recent El Niño weather patterns and the extremely slow growth rate of rockfish have hampered their comeback. Although some populations remain healthy, seven species have been declared overfished in Pacific coastal waters. Huge swaths of the Pacific Coast, designated as "rockfish conservation areas," have been closed to fishing in an attempt to rebuild stocks.

Because rockfish often intermingle, one species with another, fishing for all rockfish has been heavily restricted. For example, chilipepper rockfish are abundant, but they are not fishable because they may mingle with Boccacio rockfish, an overfished species. As a result, all species of rockfish are available much less often than in the past and at times not at all.

Alaskan, and to a lesser extent Canadian, rockfish fisheries are still healthy, but managers, learning from the mistakes of Washington, Oregon, and California, have severely restricted quotas.

The Pacific Coast rockfish fishery represents the epitome of the good fisherman in a bad fishery dilemma (see Good Fisherman in a Bad Fishery, page 102).

In the last five years, the hook-and-line rockfish fisherman has all but disappeared from the Pacific Coast. It is important to search out and buy from what hook-and-line fisheries remain, for without the small-boat sustainable fisherman there'll be no choice at the market. Monterey Bay Aquarium recommends the inshore black rockfish fishery of Washington state, but there are other hook-and-line fishermen working local waters. Contact the Pacific Coast Federation of Fishermen's Association at www. pcffa.org, an organization that represents most of the hook-and-line fishermen on the Pacific Coast, or press your seafood supplier or retailer to source hook-and-line rockfish. Though you will pay extra for the fish, the quality will be worth it.

### CHOOSING HEALTHY SEAFOOD

Rockfish is a good, low-fat, high-protein source of antistress B vitamins and minerals, particularly selenium, and provides moderate amounts of omega-3 fatty acids, which have been shown to improve the blood lipid profile, reduce inflammatory response, and enhance brain function.

Rockfish and other saltwater fish may be susceptible to the infective parasites known as cod worms. Immediately cleaning fish after it is caught removes most parasites. Rockfish that are caught by small boats that fish sustainably and clean each fish as it comes onboard rarely contain cod worms. Care should be exercised when eating raw or undercooked seafood (see Raw Seafood: How to Stay Safe, page 408).

### IN THE KITCHEN

Until recently, rockfish could be found on every menu and in every market on the West Coast. Although small rockfish are often cooked as a whole fish, usually in the Chinese style, most rockfish, or Pacific red snapper, is simply looked upon as everyday white-fleshed fish, seldom inspiring any truly unusual or distinctive dishes.

Mild-flavored and coarse-flaked rockfish absorb the flavors of other ingredients well, are an excellent addition to soups and stews, and are very good braised. The bones make a fine stock, particularly those of the Category 2 species (page 228). The skin is very good when cooked crisp.

# ROCKFISH VERACRUZ STYLE

Many years ago, on a sweltering evening in a Gulf-side cafe in Vera Cruz, Mexico, I first tried *huachin-ango a la veracruzana*, red snapper baked in a spicy and tart tomato sauce. Since then, I've made it many times with West Coast rockfish. The way I like it best is simple. Rather than prepare a tomato sauce, I dice everything as if I were making a salsa—it couldn't be easier: Dice the tomatoes, onion, and chile, add pimiento, green olives, and capers; then bake everything with the fish. The liquid is thinner than an actual sauce, but the flavors are fresher. When served with steamed rice, the juices are absorbed and season the rice perfectly. This dish is best made during tomato season. Serve it with rice, steamed chayote squash, and warm corn tortillas.

Use any of the hook-caught rockfish that are still abundant, Pacific Coast lingcod (which has made a strong comeback recently), the abundant yellowtail snapper of Atlantic and Gulf waters, or even haddock.

Four 5-ounce rockfish fillets

¼ cup freshly squeezed lime juice

1 teaspoon kosher salt

1 pound tomatoes, seeded (see page 39) and
    chopped (about 2 cups)

½ cup diced white onion

2 or 3 jalapeño or serrano chiles, seeded
    and minced (see Note)

1 pimiento or red bell pepper, roasted,
    peeled (see page 38), and diced

1 tablespoon minced garlic

¼ cup olive oil

½ teaspoon dried Mexican oregano,
    toasted in a pan

6 to 8 coriander seeds, toasted and crushed
    in a mortar

1 cup green olives, pitted (see Note)

2 tablespoons capers

GARNISHES

Cilantro sprigs

Lime wedges

1. In an ovenproof casserole that will hold all the fish in one layer, marinate the rockfish fillets in the lime and salt for 1 hour at room temperature.

2. Preheat the oven to 350°F. In a medium bowl, mix together all the rest of the ingredients except the cilantro and lime wedges. Mix well and pour over the fish. Taste and adjust the seasoning.

3. Cover the dish with a lid or aluminum foil and bake for 20 to 25 minutes, or until the sauce begins to bubble and steam. Remove from the oven and let rest for 5 minutes. Garnish with cilantro sprigs and lime wedges to serve.

CONTINUED

ROCKFISH

231

NOTE: Two fresh Anaheim chiles, roasted and peeled (see page 38), can be used in place of the serrano chiles.

NOTE: To pit the olives, place them between clean kitchen towels and pound lightly with a mallet or saucepan. Pick out the pits and discard.

## The Rockfish Crash of 2002

Commercial fishing for rockfish in California first began on San Francisco's Barbary Coast during the Gold Rush. Fish of every hue and color, with colloquial names as varied as their appearance, were caught by hook-and-line fishermen. On a good day when all the fishermen had been working, it was not unusual to see twenty-five or thirty varieties of rockfish come across the dock, including Turkey reds, gophers, chinacods, chilipeppers, cowcods, quillbacks, Boccacios, canaries, goldeneyes, idiots, rougheyes, and vermillions.

As a child growing up in my native New England, I listened to family members and friends complain about the foreign trawlers and how they ruined the fishing for cod. Twenty years later in San Francisco, I watched American fishermen do the same thing with rockfish. Vietnamese immigrants introduced gill nets to the fishery, and trawlers began using "roller" gear to access rock- and coral-laden reef areas that had previously been a refuge for immature and spawning fish. An Oregon fisherman discovered that rockfish leave the rocks to congregate and spawn at night. Midwater trawlers entered the virtually unregulated fishery and trained their sights on huge schools of widow rockfish gathering to spawn.

An unbelievable array and abundance of rockfish fueled an *abbondanza* during the 1980s, which I unwittingly took part in. Every market sold eight or ten varieties of rockfish, Chinese markets even more; live fish, whole fish, steaks, and fillets—this fish was our bread and butter, providing wealth and stability to the West Coast seafood industry.

I vividly remember the first time I realized that the vast amount of fish coming across the dock might have an ominous side. I was watching a midwater trawler unload widow rockfish at the dock. Two more boats were queued up behind her waiting to unload. From the scuppers, a yellow discharge of billions of fish eggs ran down the sides into the sea. Behind me were stacked so many bins of widow rockfish that they couldn't possibly be cut for two days, and three times as many fish were about to come across the dock. Beneath my feet the same constant yellow discharge of fish eggs leaked from the bins down into the gutters.

Prices of rockfish fell so low that *no one* benefited—least of all the fisherman and the fish. Buyers bought too much fish that went bad, fishermen caught too many fish they couldn't sell, and fishery managers watched and did nothing. The final blow was dealt by Mother Nature: The strong El Niño years of 1988–89 had a devastating impact on the spawning success of rockfish stocks. In a very short period of time, new gear, greed, and a flawed system of fisheries management brought about the crash of what was once considered an inexhaustible resource.

In the year 2002, the strongest restrictions ever placed on West Coast fishing were instituted. In order to halt the bycatch of seven endangered species of rockfish, a moratorium on all groundfish fishing was implemented on the Pacific Coast, and the National Marine Fisheries went to work reorganizing its management policies. Nonetheless, the near-total closure of fishing on the Pacific Coast has really hit the fishing community hard.

The following is an excerpt from a story by Dan Bacher (published in the *Anderson Valley Advertiser*, July 2002) about the mismanagement of Pacific Coast rockfish by the Pacific Coast Management Council, one of the eight regional councils responsible for managing U.S. fisheries—the sentiment was held by many:

> It's not hard to see why the rockfish fishery has been totally mismanaged, when you consider that the Council's composition is a classic example of the "fox guarding the hen house." The council is made up mostly of "men in suits," including federal and state wildlife and fisheries agency representatives, commercial fishing industry interests and seafood processors. Recreational anglers, divers, conservation groups, Indian tribes and grassroots commercial fishermen have little or no representation.
>
> Paul Battsford, a purple-haired commercial salmon troller out of Fisherman's Wharf in San Francisco, summed up the gut level feeling of many fishermen when he told the council during the "public comment" session, "You should all be put in prison!"

Today, the Pacific council has become one of the more conservation-minded of the eight regional fishery management councils. Vast swaths of the Pacific have been designated rockfish conservation areas in an attempt to re-establish historic rockfish populations.

# SABLEFISH

The sleek coal-black **sablefish** (*Anoplopoma fimbria*) is found in the chill, deep waters of the North Pacific. The fish's codlike appearance is responsible for its common name, "black cod." Sablefish are found from California north through British Columbia and into the Bering Sea of Alaska, but the most highly prized and environmentally sound sablefish come from the icy-cold waters of Alaska and British Columbia. The Alaskan sablefish season runs concurrently with the Alaskan halibut season, March 1 through November 15.

Alaskan sablefish has been fished for many years, but until recently was only sold frozen for export to Japan or as smoked black cod in the Pacific Northwest and New York's Lower East Side delis. In the 1980s, fresh sablefish prepared in two traditional Japanese recipes, kasu black cod and miso black cod, became very popular in the Pacific Northwest cities of Seattle and Vancouver. Over time, these recipes helped vault fresh sablefish to popularity throughout the United States.

Sablefish fillets can range in color from ivory to a café au lait hue. The raw flesh will feel soft, almost gelatinous, but there is an underlying resiliency to its texture. The dusky black skin is often left on to facilitate handling but should be removed before cooking. Fillets should be consistent in color, with no reddish bruising or blood spotting. Green or yellow discoloration along the belly indicates improper cleaning. Of course, any fish with off odors should be avoided.

Whole sablefish, after heading and gutting, are graded by size (three to five, five to seven, and seven pounds and up). The largest fish have the most fat and flavor, so they bring the highest price. Fresh sablefish should have a full, firm tautness and a deep-rich coal-black color to its skin. The tiny scales should be firmly attached. Check for the presence of fresh red blood in the belly cavity and make sure that any cuts made for cleaning are fresh-edged. The eyes of sablefish caught at great depths (hundreds of fathoms) may be cloudy due to decompression, so they are not always a good indicator of freshness.

Sablefish should be readily available when in season (see page 234). If your local seafood market does not regularly carry sablefish, ask your fishmonger to order some from his Alaskan halibut supplier. Japanese fish markets often carry sable-fish as well as all the ingredients needed to make the traditional Japanese kasu black cod and miso black cod.

## CHOOSING SUSTAINABLE SEAFOOD

Sablefish is an environmentally sound and healthy seafood choice and highly recommended as an alternative to Chilean sea bass (see page 237). It's a resilient species that reaches maturity in three to five years, yet lives a very long time—in fact, the oldest sablefish to date was 113 years old. Alaskan sablefish is currently under assessment by the Marine Stewardship Council for certification as a sustainably managed fishery.

The sustainably managed Alaskan and British Columbia sablefish are predominately trap caught. Less well managed are those West Coast fisheries where fish are more likely to be trawl caught.

Despite the objections of fishermen and environmentalists, the U.S. and Canadian governments are both preparing to license open ocean sablefish aquaculture projects. The threat of environmental degradation and damage to wild fisheries is being overridden by political maneuverings.

## CHOOSING HEALTHY SEAFOOD

Cold-water sablefish are one of the richest of all fish in omega-3 fatty acids, shown to prevent chronic heart disease, reduce inflammatory response, and enhance brain function, among other health benefits. They are an easily digestible, high-protein source of B vitamins and minerals.

## IN THE KITCHEN

Its pearly-white flesh, large velvety flakes, and sweet, rich flavor make sablefish a favorite with just about anyone who tries it. The skin of the sablefish is edible, and when well crisped provides a nice crunchy contrast to the delicate flesh. The bones are too distinctively flavored and oily to make a good stock, but are quite tasty if barbecued to a well-done crunch as is popular in both Japanese and Korean cuisines.

Although it's often associated with Japanese cuisine, sablefish is never used in raw preparations; its tender flesh is best suited to cooking.

It is delicious braised in a saffron-vegetable broth and served with Harissa (page 323), stir-fried with black bean sauce, or steamed with soy and fresh ginger. A favorite of the late James Beard was smoked Oregon sablefish steamed with new potatoes and dill.

Sablefish can be very soft at certain times of the year; this can be easily remedied with a salt cure to firm the flesh. Traditional Japanese recipes call for marinating in a sweet-salty Japanese-style kasu or miso marinade (see recipe, page 238), and smoked black cod is cured in a brine of kosher salt, garlic, and paprika. Cover sablefish fillets in kosher salt or a gravlax-style salt and sugar cure (two parts kosher salt to one part sugar) and refrigerate for several hours before cooking to ensure good texture. Rinse off the salt cure before cooking.

## Take a Pass on Chilean Sea Bass

The rich, velvety-textured Chilean sea bass, or Patagonian toothfish, made a splash when it debuted in the world seafood markets only a few years ago. With a texture as satisfying as Atlantic cod, the richness of mackerel, and a flavor as delicate as sole, it quickly became one of the most sought-after fish in the ocean. The deep, chill waters of Antarctica seemed to hold a vast wealth of this wonderful new fish, and the future seemed bright for fishermen and consumers alike.

That is, until the reality of trying to manage a fishery deep in the Antarctic Ocean sank home. Hundreds of millions of pounds of Chilean sea bass were caught, both legally and illegally, and as prices rose and stories of disappearing stocks began to surface, poaching and piracy ran rampant. The *Viarsa*, an infamous pirate ship caught poaching in Australian waters, led authorities on a 4,000-mile chase through building-size waves, densely packed ice, and an obstacle course of icebergs until the captain and crew were finally arrested and brought back to Australia for trial. The story of this chase, of the "discovery" of Chilean sea bass, and of the efforts to save the fish are told in *Wall Street Journal* reporter Bruce Knecht's book *Hooked: Pirates, Poaching, and the Perfect Fish*.

The slow-growing, slow-to-reproduce Chilean sea bass could not keep up with demand and quickly went from gloriously plentiful to near commercial extinction. In response, The National Environmental Trust began a consumer education campaign entitled "Take a pass on Chilean sea bass," designed to educate the public about the crisis. Many concerned chefs promised to quit serving Chilean sea bass until proper regulations were in place.

It has become more difficult to import illegally caught Chilean sea bass into U.S. ports; the international management and monitoring of fishing grounds has become better. However, the Southern Ocean is vast, and illegal fishing for Chilean sea bass continues.

To find a sustainably managed fish that is just as delicious and versatile as Chilean sea bass, we only need to look in our own backyard, the U.S. Pacific Coast, to find the well-managed sablefish.

# MISO-GLAZED SABLEFISH

Sablefish marinated in sake and miso—a salty paste made from fermented soybeans—and then broiled is popular in restaurants from Manhattan to Seattle. It's as sweet as it is savory, but delicious all the same.

This is also a popular way to cook salmon (kids love it), but any fish such as bluefish, weakfish, or California sea bass can be used in this recipe. Serve with a crunchy salad of sliced radishes and cucumbers sprinkled with a little rice vinegar or lemon juice, and steamed short-grain rice.

½ **cup mirin**

½ **cup sake**

¼ **cup sugar (traditional recipes double or triple this amount)**

1 **cup white miso paste**

**Four 5-ounce sablefish fillets**

1. In a medium saucepan, bring the mirin and sake to a boil to evaporate the alcohol. Add the sugar and stir until it dissolves. Remove from the heat and whisk in the miso paste until smooth. Set aside and let cool completely.

2. Put the sablefish fillets in a nonreactive dish and slather them with the cooled marinade. Cover tightly and refrigerate for at least 6 hours or up to 3 days. (Note: Sablefish does well with the long marinade time, but salmon and other fish should only be marinated for an hour or two.)

3. Preheat the broiler and set the rack as far from the heat source as possible so that the fish does not brown too quickly. Preheat the oven to 425°F in case it cooks too fast under the broiler.

4. Wipe off any excess miso clinging to the fillets. Place the fish on the broiler pan, 6 to 8 inches from the heat source and broil for 8 to 10 minutes, or until almost opaque throughout. If the fish browns too quickly and is in danger of burning, finish cooking it in the preheated oven.

# SALMON, WILD

M y friend Kitty moved to San Francisco from New York just in time to experience the excitement that accompanies the opening of king salmon season in early May. "Explain this whole salmon thing to me," she said. "It's all anyone seems to talk about." I tried, with little success, to convey some sense of the role wild salmon has played in the history and culture of the West Coast. Realizing that I was attempting to condense volumes into sentences, I gave up and said, "It needs to be *experienced* to be best understood. Let's go to dinner." That Christmas I gave Kitty *Salmon Nation*, a book full of stories and insights into man's relationship to wild salmon, past and present.

Wild king salmon from the Copper River, beautiful ivory kings from the Fraser, and giant spring kings from the Columbia River are all awe-inspiring fish that have been enjoyed in markets and restaurants across the country for years. But wild salmon is much more than just flavor-rich king salmon drawn from a few celebrated rivers. Six species of Pacific salmon can be found in thousands of rivers throughout the Pacific Northwest. Each river may host as many as four genetically distinct races, or runs, of each species. A single river system may be home to ten or more runs of salmon, each one distinctly different from the others and equally delicious.

No question, king salmon is the most well known of the salmon species, yet less than 5 percent of the wild salmon captured in the United States are king. Twice as many coho salmon as kings are caught, and many people would be hard-pressed to detect the difference. Twenty times as many sockeyes as kings enter the Copper River, and they are every bit as healthy and delicious as kings; in fact, many people, including just about the entire nation of Japan, consider sockeye salmon to be the best tasting of all salmon. Mild-flavored chum salmon, another favorite in the Japanese market, is reasonably priced but underappreciated and underutilized in the United States.

Salmon in Washington, Oregon, and California are fished in months-long open ocean troll fisheries (trolling is a form of hook and line). These fish are tender, lean, and delicate early in the spring but become firm, fatty, and more assertively flavored by late summer and fall. Most Alaskan and Canadian salmon are caught with gill nets and purse seines in short-but-intense fisheries that focus on specific runs as they prepare to enter their river of birth. These fish are fat, delicious, and at their peak of edibility as soon as the season starts, but as the season progresses and the fish begin to head upriver they become less desirable. As a rule, the farther upriver a salmon is caught, the poorer the quality.

The best-tasting salmon are caught in the open ocean; they are sleek, streamlined creatures with flawlessly bright and silvery skin. When they prepare to enter their natal streams, their skin color begins to "blush" a light rosy pink. Once a salmon commits to its final, arduous journey upriver, it quickly turns into a snaggle-toothed, hook-nosed old hag or crank, its skin tattered and black, or marked calico with red and black. Though river fish can be quite beautiful, they are often soft-fleshed and insipid, or worse: They taste of mud, moss, and mildew from river algae.

Wild salmon must be completely eviscerated as soon as they are captured to remove all bacteria and digestive enzymes. The belly cavity of whole salmon should be free of all viscera and blood, including the blood line along the backbone. A breakdown, or jellying, of the fleshy lining in the belly cavity, referred to as "belly burn," indicates that the fish was not cleaned in a timely fashion. A properly cleaned and iced fish days out of water will taste fresher than an improperly cleaned fish hours out of the water.

Salmon fillets should appear moist and glis-

## Barrel Fish

Some salmon boats use a refrigerated seawater system (see High-Tech Isn't Always the Best Tech, page 351) to chill their fish. Referred to as "barrel fish" from times past when salmon were stored on deck in barrels of iced seawater, these fish may develop mushy texture and off flavors even though the whole fish looks fresh. Greenish discoloration of the fat on the backside of a salmon fillet is a clue that the fish has been in the refrigerated seawater too long. Salmon that has simply been packed in fresh ice always have better flavor and texture than "barrel fish."

ten with translucence; if the skin is removed the fat should be silver, with highlights of gray. Salmon that has been frozen will appear dull and flat, but good-quality frozen salmon is always preferable to river fish or farmed salmon.

As the demand for wild salmon continues to grow among consumers, the marketplace is sure to become more democratic, with the less popular species finding a market niche. Although a salmon's flavor and fat content is dependent on diet and season, certain general characteristics can be used to describe each species.

### CHUM (KETA)

**Chum salmon** (*O. keta*), a mild-flavored fish with a low fat content, is most often sold in supermarkets and is also becoming popular in the rapidly expanding "value-added market" as salmon burgers, sausages, and the like. At one time, the featured fresh salmon found in supermarkets across much of the United States was chum, but the rising tide of farmed salmon changed that.

Chum salmon generally spawn in streams very close to the ocean so don't store large amounts of fat. As a result, the quality of chum salmon drops precipitously soon after it enters freshwater, more so than any other salmon. Chum salmon should have bright, silvery, unblemished skin. Quality chums are marketed as "silver bright." Chums are the last of the five wild species to enter freshwater, generally spawning in late fall.

Chum salmon eggs are prized in Japan, where they are known as *ikura*.

## COHO (SILVER)

Cohos (*O. kisutch*) are generally leaner and smaller than kings, seldom topping twelve pounds, but their flavor, appearance, and meat color are similar to that of kings. Cohos are fished from Oregon north to Alaska (they spawn in smaller streams closer to the ocean); most fish are available in late summer and fall, including a Copper River opening in September. Cohos will stand up to assertive ingredients and grilling, but like lean, early-season-troll kings, are often best when poached, steamed, or baked.

## KING (CHINOOK)

King salmon (*Oncorhynchus tschawytscha*) stay at sea longer than any other salmon, which allows them to grow larger than other salmon as well—some reach well over one hundred pounds. The omega-3–packed fat of a king salmon often exceeds 20 percent—higher than that of any other wild fish. Yukon River King salmon that swim two thousand miles to reach their spawning grounds may accumulate an unbelievable 35 percent fat content.

The first ocean-troll king salmon fishery of note begins in California in mid-April, with Oregon, Washington, and British Columbia following by June 1. These ocean-troll fisheries target fish that enter rivers in the fall, so they often last well into October. Ocean-troll salmon are lean, tender, and delicately flavored in the spring, becoming firm, fat, and full flavored in late summer and fall.

The Alaskan Copper River run begins May 15, shortly after other celebrated runs such as the Kenai and Yukon rivers begin. Alaskan fish are fat and at their best quality as soon as the season opens, but have usually peaked by mid-summer. A small fishery for ocean-troll king salmon takes place in southeast Alaska, with most fish landed in December and January.

King salmon are often graded by size (seven to eleven, eleven to eighteen, and eighteen pounds and up), with larger fish being the firmest, fattest, and best flavored, perfect for the charcoal grill.

## PINK

Pinks (*O. gorbuscha*) are the smallest and shortest-lived salmon, but they are also the most abundant. Great eating either fresh or hot smoked, the delicate, fine-textured pink flesh is similar to that of trout. Unfortunately, the largest pink salmon runs take place over a short time and often in the most remote areas, so nearly all pink salmon is canned. Some pinks are frozen for sale in supermarkets, but the fish's delicate texture and flavor suffers for it.

## SOCKEYE (RED)

The sockeye salmon (*O. nerka*) averages six pounds and seldom grows larger than ten. Its deep red–colored flesh has a particularly delicious flavor and high oil content and is very rich in omega-3s. The sockeye's diet is composed almost exclusively of small shrimplike krill that contain the carotenoids responsible for the rich red color of all salmon. It is well suited to any cooking technique including smoking, and is also used in raw preparations such as sashimi.

Most of the world's sockeyes are caught in Alaskan waters. The first sockeye runs enter the Copper River in May. By mid-July, the huge Bristol Bay, Alaska, runs are underway, where during a few short weeks in July, 40 percent of the world's sockeye are captured. The Togiak River, which is part of the Bristol Bay watershed, is noted for its particularly large, fat fish. The Fraser River in British Columbia is noted for its late-summer run of sockeye.

## STEELHEAD

**Steelhead** (*O. mykiss*) is a highly revered sport fish that is reserved for recreational fishermen in California and Oregon, and still promoted as a commercial fishery in Washington state. In the 1970s, the Quinault Indian tribe on the Olympic Peninsula began a hatchery program using native steelhead stocks. Since then, a combined total of 8 million salmon and steelhead have been released annually into the Quinault River. They are now under review for Marine Stewardship Council certification as a sustainable fishery. These fish—harvested in December and January when they return from the sea—average ten to fifteen pounds and are moderately fatty, with red flesh and the same fine texture as their stay-at-home freshwater version, the rainbow trout. At Monterey Fish, we encourage our customers to use winter-run steelhead as an alternative to farmed fish.

### CHOOSING SUSTAINABLE SEAFOOD

Although many salmon runs on the Pacific Coast are threatened or endangered, others remain healthy. The management of wild Alaskan stocks has been particularly successful. All wild Alaskan salmon fisheries have been certified as sustainable by the Marine Stewardship Council (MSC). The wild salmon fisheries of British Columbia and California are undergoing review for MSC assessment.

Dams, water issues, private property rights, timber, cattle and agriculture, and overfishing have all played a role in damaging salmon stocks. In several notable instances, farmers, fishermen, and landowners have been able to work together for the good of the fish. But many problems still exist. The greatest threats to healthy wild salmon stocks today are destructive logging and stream management practices; federal water policies that favor politically powerful industrial agriculture over independent fishermen and salmon; and the lack of political will to take down obsolete dams that have little value.

Fortunately, salmon are resilient fish. If we protect the watershed and let the rivers run, the salmon will return.

### CHOOSING HEALTHY SEAFOOD

Salmon's benefits, both culinary and curative, have not been lost on Americans, who are eating more of this fish than ever before. Wild salmon are very high in heart-healthy omega-3s, proven to reduce heart disease and purported to be involved in everything from healthy brain development and intelligence in children to preventing Alzheimer's in adults. Dr. Nicholas Perricone, a popular dermatologist and author who promotes wild salmon as the perfect food for skin care, is said to carry daily servings of wild salmon in his briefcase when he travels. Salmon is also an excellent source of B vitamins and minerals, particularly selenium.

Salmon and other saltwater fish may be susceptible to either cod worms or tapeworms. Care should always be exercised when eating raw or undercooked seafood (see Raw Seafood: How to Stay Safe, page 408).

## IN THE KITCHEN

The legendary French chef Auguste Escoffier insisted that "salmon should be served as plainly as possible," and I have to agree. Nothing is better than a simple piece of salmon fresh from the sea, grilled over charcoal and dressed with little more than a pinch of sea salt and a squeeze of lemon. But then Escoffier didn't live on the Pacific Coast, the land of salmon, where the fish is considered one of the most versatile in the sea.

Salmon's luxuriant qualities can be heightened with a rich sauce such as a beurre blanc. But bright, acidic sauces—those made with lemon, tomatoes, vinegars, or capers, for example—also work well, for the opposite reason: They cut through some of the richness. Its character helps salmon stand up to the strongest of flavors. Any fish that isn't overwhelmed by being cooked on a cedar plank or grilled over pine needles should have little problem standing up to Indian spices, red wine, or even Asian ingredients, such as miso, soy, sesame oil, and fermented black beans.

Salmon can be cooked by any method. Poach it in olive oil; give it a short gravlax cure and grill it; steam with black bean sauce; make a salmon tagine with Harissa (page 323); bake it in parchment; smoke it, pickle it, or just serve it raw. It's all good.

Salmon is a favorite served raw; for Italian-style crudo, slice it as thinly as possible on the diagonal, drizzle it with fresh lemon juice and extra-virgin olive oil, then sprinkle it with sea salt, freshly ground black pepper, and minced fresh chives and chervil. For salmon tartare, minced raw salmon is seasoned with olive oil, lemon, mustard, shallots, capers, and parsley.

Leave salmon skin on to be broiled, grilled, or pan-roasted to crispness. Salmon bones can be used as the basis for salmon chowder; simmer them for a very short time and be aware the stock will have a very distinct salmon flavor; leaner species will make a less distinctively flavored stock. In Chinatown, salmon bones and heads are more highly regarded than fillets; a favored preparation is to make a simple, clear broth with salmon bones and heads and pick the meat from the bone; steamed salmon head with black bean sauce is popular as well. A Japanese friend marinates salmon bones in teriyaki sauce before charcoal grilling. Fresh chum salmon roe, available in Japanese markets, and steelhead roe make a salmon caviar far superior to any you can buy in a jar (see Homemade Salmon or Steelhead Caviar, page 347). Or the eggs can be placed between layers of cheesecloth and marinated in miso paste like Miso-Glazed Sablefish (page 238), then used as a garnish on rice or mixed with julienned daikon radish to make a salad.

## CHARCOAL-GRILLED WILD KING SALMON WITH CHERRY TOMATO–BASIL RELISH

SERVES 4 AS A MAIN COURSE

The flavor of fresh wild salmon grilled over charcoal, the tang of cherry tomatoes, and the aroma of fresh basil are incomparable. If I could make every recipe in this book as simple and tasty as this, I would. It's nothing but simple fresh ingredients that complement one another perfectly. Serve with corn on the cob and green salad. The relish is great on the corn and as a dressing for the salad as well.

**Four 6-ounce wild king salmon fillets
   or steaks
Sea salt and freshly ground pepper to taste
Olive oil
Cherry Tomato–Basil Relish
   (recipe follows)**

Prepare a hot fire in a charcoal grill. Season the fish with sea salt and freshly ground pepper. Oil the grill rack well and lightly brush the fish with oil. Grill the fish, turning halfway through the cooking process, for a total of 8 to 10 minutes per inch of thickness, or until slightly charred on the edges and still slightly translucent in the center. Serve with Cherry Tomato–Basil Relish alongside.

# Cherry Tomato–Basil Relish

Cherry tomatoes are usually more sharply acidic than many of today's tomatoes, a good thing in my mind. A little balsamic vinegar, olive oil, fragrant basil leaves, and a sprinkling of salt are all that's needed to balance their flavor. Use only the best-quality oil and vinegar.

1 basket cherry tomatoes

1 garlic clove

1 teaspoon coarse sea salt

1 tablespoon balsamic vinegar

¼ cup olive oil

1 cup firmly packed fresh basil leaves, coarsely chopped

Cut the cherry tomatoes in half if they're small or in quarters if they're large. In a wooden bowl, mash the garlic and salt to a paste with a pestle, then stir in the vinegar. Whisk in the oil, then add the tomatoes and basil, gently tossing everything together. Serve immediately.

# SAKE-SIMMERED SILVER SALMON

Sake-simmering is one of the classic ways of cooking fish in Japan. The result: a luscious, tender fish and a richly flavored sauce. In Japan, small whole flounders or tai snappers are often cooked this way.

For this recipe, I like to use delicate salmon varieties such as chum, pink, or any lean, early-season salmon. To turn this dish into a delicious soup, add more Dashi, cooked udon noodles, and spinach (see Variation).

½ cup sake

¼ cup mirin

1 tablespoon rice wine vinegar

1-inch piece fresh ginger, peeled and
　grated

¼ cup soy sauce

1 tablespoon sugar

1 cup instant homemade Dashi (page 370)

Four 5-ounce silver (coho) salmon fillets

Steamed short-grain rice for serving

1. In a small saucepan, combine all the ingredients except the salmon and rice. Bring to a boil, reduce the heat to a simmer, and cook for 5 minutes.

2. Place the salmon fillets in a large sauté pan or skillet. Pour the simmering sauce over the fish. While repeatedly spooning the hot liquid over the fillets and without turning, gently cook the fillets over medium-low heat for 8 to 10 minutes to the inch, or until still slightly translucent in the center.

3. Serve with steamed rice and spoon the stock over the fish and rice.

NOTE: The ingredients called for in this recipe are available at any Japanese market and even many supermarkets.

VARIATION: To turn the simmering sauce into a soup, add 2 more cups Dashi, 2 cups packed spinach leaves, blanched, and 12 ounces udon noodles cooked according to the package directions. Serve in 4 shallow bowls with the salmon fillets nestled among the spinach, noodles, and broth.

# SLOW-ROASTED SALMON SALAD
# WITH NEW POTATOES, FENNEL, AND AVOCADO

Of all the ways to cook salmon, slow-roasting has to be the simplest. A large piece or even an entire side of salmon is baked in a low, humidified oven, giving moist and tender results. The salmon requires almost no preparation, and very little attention needs to be paid to it while cooking, leaving plenty of time to do other things while it roasts. Slow cooking is the perfect way to cook an entire side of salmon to serve at a buffet or picnic and serve with Chimichurri Sauce (page 64) or Charmoula Marinade (page 396).

One 1½-pound center-cut salmon fillet

Olive oil for coating

Grated zest of 1 orange

2 tablespoons coriander seeds, toasted
    in a dry pan and ground

Kosher salt and freshly ground black
    pepper to taste

DRESSING

1 tablespoon minced shallot

1 tablespoon Dijon mustard

2 tablespoons freshly squeezed lemon juice

2 tablespoons white wine vinegar or
    Champagne vinegar

7 tablespoons mild olive oil

Salt and freshly ground black pepper
    to taste

5 to 6 unpeeled small new potatoes

4 slices thick-cut, good-quality apple-
    smoked bacon, cut into ½-inch pieces

8 cups mixed salad greens

1 avocado, peeled, pitted, and cut into
    ¼-inch-thick slices

1 fennel bulb, trimmed, cored, and cut
    into paper-thin slices

1. Preheat the oven to 225°F. Bring some water to a boil and pour it into a shallow pan placed on the floor of the oven. (The humid environment helps to keep the salmon moist while cooking.)

2. Coat the salmon fillet well with olive oil and place it in a baking pan. Sprinkle the orange zest, coriander, salt, and pepper over the salmon. Bake for about 40 minutes, or until the salmon is firm to the touch and white coagulated juices are beginning to collect on top. Remove the salmon from the oven and set it aside at room temperature until ready to serve.

3. Meanwhile, make the dressing: In a small bowl, whisk the shallot, mustard, lemon juice, and vinegar together. Gradually whisk in the oil until emulsified. Add salt and pepper. Set aside.

4. In a small saucepan, boil or steam the potatoes until cooked, allow them to cool, then slice and set aside.

5. In a small sauté pan or skillet, fry the bacon over medium heat until just crisp; using a slotted spoon, transfer to paper towels to drain.

6. Put the greens in a large bowl. Skin the salmon and break the flesh into bite-sized chunks, removing any pinbones as you go. Add the salmon and bacon to the bowl. Pour all but 2 tablespoons of the dressing over and toss gently. Divide the greens, salmon, and bacon evenly among 4 plates or arrange on a large platter.

7. Arrange the potato slices and avocado around the plates and top with the fennel. Drizzle the reserved dressing over all and grind some pepper to taste on top.

## Salmon from the Farm

Four or five times a summer, I head out the back door of my house and tramp up the hill to a place I know well. Sheltered in a clearing of bay trees on a hillside is my favorite blackberry patch. I push through the briars and brambles until I find a spot where the berries are ripe enough that I can just pick and eat. Early in the season, it's hard to find many that are ripe, and sour is often the flavor of the day, yet even then

the taste is always surprisingly interesting and good. By midsummer, the patch produces so many ripe berries that I can eat my fill and take some home. By the end of the summer, only a few berries linger, but they're perfect: juicy and sun warmed, tasting of herbs and sweet fruit. Put one of those perfect berries in your mouth and your tongue lets you know that *this is a blackberry*.

Store-bought blackberries that are carefully raised on a farm are always nicely formed and pleasant. They are almost always available. But it is hard to believe that they are related to my wild berries in any way other than name. And that's pretty much how I feel about farmed salmon.

Farmed salmon comes in uniform shapes and sizes. The flavor and texture are always agreeable, and the fish is always available. It's perfect for portion control and cost analysis, and it's easy to cook, but the flavor never sings. Wild salmon, like my wild blackberries, changes with the weather and the season. It's not always perfect, but when it is, you sit up straight and take notice. A fat, fresh piece of salmon pulled from the sea, passed over the coals and into your mouth, will light your senses and let you know that *this is real salmon.*

## THE FEEDLOT

The heart of the farmed-salmon controversy as presented in the media is the environmental effect of pollution and disease from overcrowded farms, the escape of fish into the wild, the use of antibiotics, colorants, and other chemicals, and the inefficient use of wild fish for food. These are all real threats to the environment, but they are problems that can be cured, and will be once public outcry demands it. Some farms are already reducing density levels in pens, taking steps to prevent escape, reducing the amount of wild fish used in the feed, and better managing the way fish are fed so there is less waste. There are good small artisanal salmon farmers who have instituted these "best practices," and they should be supported and encouraged, but for the most part the industry is made up of giants.

## INDUSTRIALIZED AQUACULTURE

It's estimated that more than half of the fresh salmon consumed in the world today is Atlantic farm-raised salmon, and nearly all that salmon comes from the farms of a few giant multinational aquaculture corporations. Multinationals control the industry from "boat to throat"—they are involved in everything from catching and manufacturing the feed to marketing the fish. Farmed salmon are a product of industrialized aquaculture and have little to do with fishing as it has been defined in the past. The problems associated with salmon farming are the same as those involved with industrial agriculture.

Large corporations attempting to tame and industrialize the last major source of wild food on the planet have created problems that are far more insidious than salmon farming's immediate effect on the environment.

First, the year-round availability—or I should say glut—of farmed fish works to alter our perception of the environment. The apparent ease with which we can replace wild fish with salmon from farms gives the impression that we have come up with a viable solution for the real problems of wild fisheries. Farmed salmon is always available. Simply unfurl another net pen, paint it with an antifouling agent, and start broadcasting dried food pellets. Wild salmon, on the other hand, is part of the natural order of things, and its future is dependent on the much more difficult task of good stewardship of our rivers and forests.

There are also social consequences: Competition from artificially low-priced farmed salmon has driven wild salmon prices to the lowest levels in thirty years, forcing thousands of wild-salmon fishermen off the water. In effect, this turns small independent fishermen and their support community into low-paid factory workers at the local salmon farm, or worse, puts them on the dole.

## CORPORATE WELFARE

The reason that farmed salmon can be sold at rock-bottom prices is because corporate farmers have not taken full economic responsibility for the cost of raising these fish in open ocean net pens. The cost of environmental and social damage caused by raising salmon in open ocean net pens is absorbed by governments and paid for with our tax dollars. It's a great economic model for corporate salmon farmers, but not so great for wild salmon fishermen or the taxpayer. Tax dollars would be better spent protecting the watershed and improving the rivers.

I just don't see the point in creating an environmentally expensive, artificial system to raise greasy salmon with innocuous flavor when a natural system is already in place, one that produces more fine-flavored wild salmon than we could ever possibly want. If we just take care of the natural system, it will produce all the delicious wild salmon we need in a perfectly efficient manner.

From *Salmon Nation*, the book that I gave to my friend Kitty last Christmas, comes this: "The key to healthy wild salmon populations lies in strengthening our ties to the land, and that—deliciously—includes eating them." Eat wild salmon—in season—and when it's not in season, eat one of the other thousands of species of fish that are.

# SAND DAB, PACIFIC

Seldom is the **sand dab** discussed in cookbooks, and rarely is it seen in seafood markets. This is a shame, because it's easily one of the most delicious fish in the sea. Sand dab, besides being one of my favorite fish, is a perfect example of the type of underutilized fish we should be promoting to replace some of the more depleted standard species.

Until recently, the sand dab was about as regional a seafood as you could find. It has long been a staple of the San Francisco–style grill restaurant, and only in the last few years has this delicate little fish been found anywhere other than San Francisco proper. Available year-round, the sand dab is now fished in Oregon and Washington as well as California and is becoming more popular.

The sand dab is plentiful, healthy, cheap, and delicious, so how can it be one of the most rarely used fish from the Pacific Ocean? In a word, bones. The sand dab is so small, about eight ounces each, and delicate that it is seldom sold any way other than trimmed and pan-ready. Most chefs agree that cooking fish with the bones left in greatly improves flavor, but we Americans are confirmed "ichthyoanginaphobics" (a cool word for someone afraid of choking on a fishbone). One of the reasons for this, I'm convinced, is that the fish are seldom properly prepared for cooking with the bones in. Done the right way, the bones can be removed with ease, but done the wrong way the result is too often an impossible-to-eat, bony nightmare. I say, lose your fear of bones: See page 33 to learn the right way to prepare a whole flatfish.

### CHOOSING SUSTAINABLE SEAFOOD

Dense schools of sand dabs are easily targeted over a sandy ocean bottom. Bycatch is minimal when sand dabs are caught by trawl or Danish seine because they school as a single species.

At Monterey Fish, we buy sand dabs from Steve Fitz on the *Morgan*, a Danish seine boat that works the waters of Half Moon Bay. Danish seine produces the best-quality sand dabs with little or no impact on habitat.

### CHOOSING HEALTHY SEAFOOD

The sand dab is a very good low-fat, high-protein source of B vitamins and minerals.

Sand dabs may be susceptible to soft-spot syndrome (see Kudoa, page 412); though of no concern to human health, it does adversely affect the texture of the fish, which becomes soft and mushy when cooked. Sand dabs with this condition are obvious to the knowledgeable retailer and should be intercepted before the point of sale.

### IN THE KITCHEN

Sand dabs are best cooked with simple, unfussy preparations. At home, I seldom do more than dust the fish with a little seasoned flour and quickly sauté, serving them with only a squeeze of lemon. The Hayes Street Grill in San Francisco is popular for its classic mesquite-grilled sand dabs with beurre blanc.

# SAND DABS WITH FRIED CAPERS, PARSLEY, AND LEMON

Capers fried for just a minute have a crispy exterior with a little softness in the center. This gives them a nice texture and takes some of the edge off so they don't overwhelm the delicate flavor of the sand dabs. Serve this dish with boiled new potatoes and wilted escarole: Chop, wash, and sauté the escarole in olive oil, covered, for two or three minutes, then season with salt and pepper. This recipe can be used for any flounder, pan-ready or fillet.

¼ cup mild olive oil

2 tablespoons capers, rinsed, drained, and patted dry

8 pan-ready sand dabs (see Note)

Seasoned flour: ¼ cup all-purpose flour mixed with 1½ teaspoons kosher salt and ¼ teaspoon freshly ground pepper

½ cup dry white wine

Juice of 1 lemon

2 tablespoons minced fresh flat-leaf parsley

2 tablespoons cold unsalted butter, cut into bits

1. In a large cast-iron skillet, heat the olive oil over medium heat until it shimmers.

2. Add the capers and fry until slightly crisp and a shade darker, about 1 minute. Using a slotted spoon, transfer to paper towels to drain.

3. Dredge the sand dabs in the seasoned flour and carefully add them to the hot pan. Cook for 3 or 4 minutes on each side, or until golden brown. Transfer to a plate and keep warm.

4. Pour off any oil remaining in the pan. Add the white wine and lemon juice, stirring to scrape up the browned bits from the bottom of the pan. Cook to reduce the liquid by two thirds. Turn off the heat and add the parsley. Whisk in the cold butter, a bit at a time, until the pan juices become silky and thick. Pour the sauce over the sand dabs and garnish with the fried capers.

NOTE: Sand dabs are most often sold pan-ready; if not, follow the directions on page 33 for preparing whole flatfish for cooking.

# S A R D I N E

**P**acific sardines (*Sardinops sagax*) first appear
in southern California waters in early spring.
They then migrate north, following the
plankton-rich upwelling of the continental shelf.
After a summer of feeding, the fattest and best-quality
sardines of fall enter coastal waters from Monterey
Bay north.

The Pacific sardine has been available in West
Coast markets for several years, and its popularity is
on the rise in other parts of the country. The long-
established center of sardine fishing is Monterey,
California, but because of booming consumer interest
in fresh sardines, fishermen in ports throughout
Oregon, Washington, and British Columbia have
returned to fishing for Pacific sardines.

The **European sardine** (*Sardina pilchardus*),
very similar to the Pacific sardine in both appearance
and flavor, is the sardine most commonly enjoyed fresh

on the East Coast and in many other parts of the country European sardines flown in fresh from the Azores, Spain, and the Mediterranean are excellent during the midsummer-through-fall season. Portuguese and Spanish sardines that have been frozen are available year-round.

About 12 million pounds a year of **Spanish sardines** (*Sardinela aurita*) are taken from the waters of Florida and the Gulf of Mexico. This is strictly a bait fishery, but with today's surging interest in the heart-healthy sardine, the Spanish sardine is a welcome addition to the table.

Sardines fresh from the sea will have a rainbow sheen of iridescent color along the back and still be stiff with rigor. Any sardines with broken or ripped bellies should be discarded, as they have gotten too warm at some point.

### CHOOSING SUSTAINABLE SEAFOOD

Sardines are highly resilient and fertile when conditions are favorable. The Pacific sardine is a recent success story, making an explosive recovery in the wake of favorable ocean conditions and a forty-year moratorium on fishing.

A faultless, well-managed fishery puts sardines on everyone's highly recommended list. Purse seine and midwater trawls (see pages 420 and 421), used to target dense schools of sardines in the upper-water column, are responsible for very little habitat destruction or bycatch. Both Pacific and European sardines are well managed and sustainably fished, while Spanish sardines from the Gulf of Mexico can be considered underutilized.

Sardines and other small pelagic fish are of utmost importance to the health of the ocean's food web. Although human consumption of sardines currently has a negligible effect on populations, industrial fishing fleets that fish down the food chain for animal and fish feed are the greatest threat to this critical part of the marine food web (see Fishing Down the Food Chain, page 48).

### CHOOSING HEALTHY SEAFOOD

Doctors today recommend that we eat more sardines and other small, fatty fish such as anchovies and mackerel and less of the "apex predators" such as tuna and swordfish. Sardines are without a doubt one of the healthiest choices in the sea; living in clean offshore waters where they filter plankton for food, they are very rich in heart-healthy omega-3s, and are an excellent source of B vitamins, phosphorus, potassium and iron, and a valuable source of calcium when tinned. DMAE (dimethylaminoethanol), a compound sold in natural foods stores to "boost brain power," is particularly abundant in sardines and anchovies.

Sardines seldom come in contact with shore-based pollutants and do not live long enough to bio-accumulate mercury or other pollutants.

Much like shellfish, filter-feeding fish such as sardines may accumulate naturally-occurring marine toxins during algal blooms (see "Red

## Tinned Sardines

The word *sardine* derives from the island of Sardinia, where the canning of pilchards, now called sardines, was first popularized. Canned sardines can be any one of a number of different small fish closely related to the herring family. Brislings, pilchards, and silds are the most common, with brislings considered the best quality. Stretching the definition of sardine, immature Atlantic herring, which are harvested in the coastal waters of Maine, are canned and sold as sardines. Top-quality canned sardines should have some of the flavor attributes of a good cheese or cured olive, without any overt fishiness.

The French produce tinned sardines under various labels that connote quality, the best are packed under the label "Millésimé," meaning "vintage." Sardines captured at peak fattiness are charcoal-grilled, then hand-packed in iron tins (not aluminum) with extra-virgin olive oil and dated. The tins are placed in aging cellars, where they are turned every six months to aid in even aging, ultimately developing the exquisite flavor, and high price, of a fine, well-aged blue cheese.

As Do Mar of Portugal produces a top-quality, more reasonably priced tinned sardine (pilchard) easily found in this country. Napoleon Scottish brand produces both large pilchards and my personal favorite, the tiny brisling sardine. Maybe one day in our own country we'll see a renaissance of Monterey's Cannery Row once-thriving sardine canning industry.

Tide" Marine Toxins, page 415). Commercial fisheries are carefully monitored.

### IN THE KITCHEN

Sardines should be quickly scaled before cooking by scraping toward the head with the edge of a paring knife while rinsing under running water. The skin can be left on for cooking. The entire sardine, including the bones when well cooked or tinned, is edible, but sardines of 3 inches or larger should be gilled and gutted or filleted.

### PREPARING SARDINES

Small whole sardines can be cleaned of head, guts, and bones by the same technique as used for fresh anchovies (see page 45). Remove the scales by rinsing the fish under running water while gently scraping away the scales with a fingernail. While grasping the head of the fish firmly with the fingers of your right hand, use the fingers of your left hand to pinch through the flesh just below the collar, then gently and evenly pull toward the tail. With a little gentle persuasion and some practice, two boneless fillets will strip away from the backbone. Discard the head with attached backbone and entrails.

Larger sardines must be cleaned by cutting the belly open with a sharp knife, then removing the entrails by scraping them out with a spoon; be sure to remove the blood line, which runs along either side of the backbone. Rinse and pat dry.

If you see really fresh sardines in the market but have other plans for dinner, simply fillet or gut them, cover with a generous coating of kosher salt, and refrigerate. They'll keep for several days and will be as good as fresh after rinsing off the salt.

Sardines can be simply chopped and served raw as a tartare, or salt-cured in the manner of anchovies. They are delicious charcoal-grilled, fried, baked, braised, smoked, or pickled.

We most often take our cues for cooking sardines from the countries of southern Europe, which have a long tradition of sardine cookery. In Sicily, fresh sardine pasta is enjoyed on the day of San Giuseppe; in Spain, a classic empanada of sardines is a favorite; while in Portugal, grilled sardines are part of the country's heritage. The natural sweetness of fresh sardines provides a wonderful counterpoint to acidic or bitter ingredients. Pair fresh sardines with pickled vegetables, bitter greens, or sauces and marinades containing mustard and vinegar. An Italian salsa verde, Moroccan charmoula, or Mexican mint recado are examples of bright, acidic sauces that are excellent with sardines.

# CRISPY BREAD CRUMB–COATED FRESH SARDINE SALAD WITH HERBED MUSTARD DRESSING

SERVES 4 AS AN APPETIZER

I like to make this dish in the spring when the first sardines of the year hit the market and the cool-weather-loving frisée is at its best. Early-season sardines are leaner than they will be in the fall but are still delicious. Bitter frisée lettuce and smoky paprika are the perfect foils for sweet, succulent sardines. First-of-the-season asparagus, drizzled with a little olive oil and a sprinkle of kosher salt, will roast in about the same amount of time as the sardines. Add Quick Pickled Onion and Fennel (page 181), a well-chilled bottle of rosé, and country-style bread for a perfect spring lunch.

### VINAIGRETTE

½ cup olive oil

2 tablespoons Dijon mustard

1 tablespoon freshly squeezed lemon juice

½ tablespoon minced fresh flat-leaf parsley

½ tablespoon minced fresh mint

Kosher salt and freshly ground pepper
   to taste

8 sardines (about 2 pounds total), scaled
   and dressed or filleted

½ cup fresh bread crumbs

1 tablespoon sweet Spanish paprika
   (pimentón)

Generous pinch of salt

Frisée or other bitter lettuce leaves

Lemon wedges for garnish

1. Preheat the oven to 450°F. Coat a baking sheet with olive oil.

2. For the vinaigrette: In a glass bowl, whisk the olive oil into the mustard and lemon juice; add the parsley and mint, then season with salt and pepper. Remove and reserve half of the vinaigrette to dress the frisée.

3. Add the sardines to the bowl with the remaining vinaigrette and marinate at room temperature for 30 minutes.

4. In a shallow bowl, combine the bread crumbs, paprika, and salt. Stir to blend. Remove the sardines from the marinade and roll them in the bread crumb mixture until they are thoroughly coated.

5. Bake the sardines on the prepared pan without turning until golden brown, about 15 minutes for dressed fish, 10 minutes for fillets. Toss the frisée with the reserved vinaigrette and place the sardines on a bed of greens, along with the lemon wedges, to serve.

# SARDINE PASTA WITH FENNEL, TOMATO, AND BREAD CRUMBS

This is a great dish for late summer and early fall. The sardines are fat, the first of the tender young fennel is coming to market, and the late-summer tomatoes are packed with flavor. It's best to fillet the sardines for this dish to avoid the bones.

3 tablespoons olive oil

1 bulb fennel, trimmed, cored, and
    finely sliced

½ onion, finely diced

3 garlic cloves, minced

1 cup finely diced tomato

2 tablespoons golden raisins, soaked
    in ½ cup dry white wine

Juice of ½ lemon

1 teaspoon kosher salt

1 teaspoon coarsely cracked pepper

2 pounds sardines, filleted (see page 258)

1 pound perciatelli, bucatini, or
    spaghetti pasta

2 tablespoons pine nuts, toasted
    (see page 37)

**BREAD CRUMB TOPPING**

2 tablespoons olive oil

1 cup coarse fresh bread crumbs

1 tablespoon grated lemon zest

¼ cup chopped fresh flat-leaf parsley

**1.** In a large sauté pan or skillet, heat the olive oil over medium-high heat. Add the fennel slices and sauté until golden, about 5 minutes. Add the onion and sauté for 1 minute, then add the garlic and sauté until just starting to color. Add the tomato and golden raisins, along with their soaking wine. Add the lemon juice, salt, and pepper. Reduce the heat to a simmer and cook for 10 minutes. Add the sardines and cook for 1 minute, or until almost cooked throughout. Using a slotted metal spatula, transfer the sardines to a warmed plate.

**2.** Meanwhile, cook the pasta in a large pot of boiling salted water until al dente, about 10 minutes. Drain the pasta, reserving some of the water. Add the pasta to the simmering sauce and cook for 1 minute, thinning the sauce to the desired consistency with some of the reserved pasta cooking water.

**3.** While the pasta is cooking, make the topping: In a medium sauté pan or skillet, heat the olive oil over medium-low heat and stir in the bread crumbs. Cook until golden brown, 3 or 4 minutes, and stir in the lemon zest and parsley. Set aside. Add the toasted pine nuts and the cooked sardines to the pasta and gently toss. Divide the pasta among 4 warmed pasta bowls and sprinkle with the bread crumb topping.

## Cannery Row

During the 1930s, Monterey, California, was a bustling and lively working port. The Pacific sardine supported the largest commercial fishery in the western hemisphere, accounting for one fourth of all the fish landed in the United States. Canneries and shoreside support industries employed thousands.

Fishery scientists at the time estimated that sardine populations would remain stable if fished at 250 million pounds of sardines a year. Yet between 1930 and 1936, almost two billion pounds of sardines a year were landed at Monterey, California's Cannery Row. Shortsighted greed on the part of a few, coupled with inhospitable ocean conditions, started a cycle that led to the complete and abrupt collapse of the Pacific sardine. Canneries shut down, fishermen went bankrupt, shoreside support industries collapsed, and a colorful gallery of characters as chronicled in Steinbeck's *Cannery Row* disappeared.

While working on an oral history project, my friend Ed Ueber interviewed an old-timer who claimed to have fished during the final glory days of the sardine fishery. He told of setting his seine net over a monster school of sardines, hauling in well over fifty tons of sardines by day's end. Then the industry came crashing down. In the ensuing forty years, he saw only the occasional sardine. "We thought we had caught a lot that day," the old-timer lamented, "but we'd caught them all." He had set his nets over what was probably the last big school of sardines on the Pacific Coast.

If discretion and forethought had prevailed, Monterey's Cannery Row would still be a working wharf rather than a tourist destination. In a story that has become all too familiar, a long-term healthy economy was sacrificed for short-term gain. The economic benefit to the area from forty years of a sustainable sardine fishery is inestimable. Two hundred fifty million pounds of sardines year after year for four decades represents economic wealth, jobs, and community that can now never be regained.

It would seem that Cannery Row would provide a lesson easily learned. But as recently as 1994, the story repeated itself on the Grand Banks of eastern Canada. Warnings by Canadian fishery scientists of overfishing and habitat destruction by factory trawlers were repeatedly ignored for political reasons. The heretofore seemingly inexhaustible cod stocks of the north Atlantic that had been sustainably fished for hundreds of years crashed. All fishing was halted, processing plants were closed, forty thousand people were put out of work, billions of dollars were lost, and a multigenerational way of life came to an end. Today, despite a fifteen-year fishing moratorium, cod stocks on the Grand Banks are showing no convincing signs of recovery.

Sustainable management is often perceived as being economically punitive to the fishing industry, but the opposite is true. Sustainable fisheries are the only economically viable fisheries for the future.

# SCALLOP

Scallops—unlike clams, which never stray from their sandy bed, or mussels, which hold fast to rocky sea walls for life—are free to move about whenever they please. It skitters erratically across the sea bottom in search of a new home or to avoid starfish, propelling itself through the water by clapping its shells together. Driving the scallop through the water is a single powerful oversized abductor muscle, the meat of the mollusk and the focus of our culinary attentions.

## BAY SCALLOPS

Wild **bay scallops** (*Argopecten irradians*) from their native habitat, the estuaries and salt ponds of the Atlantic Coast from southern New England to the mid-Atlantic, are available from October to January. The eelgrass habitat of the bay scallop is currently under great pressure from nutrient pollution and associated algal blooms (see Too Much of a Good Thing, page 268). Fortunately, however, many communities have become aware of the need for wetlands restoration if the bay scallop is to return to its former importance.

Fresh bay scallops are one of the best-flavored ingredients in the sea's larder. The intensely delicious bay scallop is full of sweet natural sugar neatly balanced with brininess. Fresh bay scallops have very little odor other than a mild ocean-fresh smell, and the color of the meat should be a uniform creamy white or coral.

Aquacultured bay scallops are available from Nova Scotia and Nantucket, Massachusetts. Bill Taylor of Taylor Bay Farms in Nantucket sells beautifully variegated purple, pink, and tan scallops live in the shell. Equal in flavor to wild bay scallops, aquacultured bay scallops may be shucked for their meat or simply eaten in their entirety on the half shell. Grown and harvested in an environmentally friendly manner, aquacultured bay scallops are available from fall through spring.

China aquacultures some 200,000 tons of bay scallops a year, many of which are frozen and sold in the United States. Although they are the same species—the original brood stock from Nantucket—you would never know it from eating them: They are bland and insipid when compared to bay scallops from their native waters.

## CALICO SCALLOPS

The calico scallop is about the size of a pencil eraser, and is dredged in deep waters off the eastern seaboard of Florida and in the Gulf of Mexico from December to May. Calico scallops are closely related to the bay scallop. I'm sure the flavor is excellent when they are freshly hand-shucked, but the way in which they are processed results in a scallop that is largely undistinguished: A jet of steam blasts the abductor meat from the shell and removes the viscera at the same time. Further washing, rinsing, and soaking in STP-laced water removes much of the flavor as well.

## SEA SCALLOPS

The most important scallop in the U.S. market is without a doubt the **Atlantic Coast sea scallop** (*Placopecten magellanicus*), which is found in great profusion along the Atlantic continental shelf from Newfoundland to North Carolina.

In 1994, prime scalloping grounds on New England's Georges Bank were closed out of concern for bycatch of cod, flounder, and monkfish by scallop boats. The ongoing recovery of these species on the Bank and improved fishing methods led to the reopening of the scallop grounds in 2000. The temporary moratorium on fishing, along with favorable ocean conditions, conspired to create an embarrassment of riches when the grounds were reopened. In fact, recent scallop catches have been higher than ever recorded and anecdotal evidence points to more of the same for the future. Most satisfying is that new regulations have encouraged small trawl, day-boat scallopers that produce top-quality scallops with less environmental impact.

Like other shellfish, scallops are at their best from late summer through winter.

Only the large abductor mussel of the scallop is usually sold in the United States. Live, whole sea scallops and scallops with the roe attached may occasionally be available through specialty dealers, but archaic U.S. health laws have made it difficult for U.S. seafood dealers to develop a market for live or roe scallops such as there is in Europe.

A fresh sea scallop is dry or slightly sticky to the touch, opaque and creamy white to coral in color. The sweet odor of the scallop may seem strong, but is inoffensive and nothing to be concerned with; a scallop with no odor may well have been soaked in sodium tripolyphosphate, or STP (see Modern Chemistry, page 265). Old scallops, however, will smell fishy or sour.

Marketing terms for scallops such as "diver," which means they were caught by a commercial diver, and "day-boat," which implies the boat was only at sea for one day, have been thoroughly diluted by overuse, so much so that the terms are now meaningless. Maine is noted for its fall day-boat scallop fishery, a very tiny portion of which is taken by divers, and new regu-

lations have encouraged small day-boat scallopers to enter the southern New England–Long Island fishery, but these are niche fisheries. In truth, whether a scallop boat has been out one or three days has less to do with quality than if the scallop was shucked immediately, quickly iced, and whether or not it has been treated with sodium tripolyphosphate (see Modern Chemistry at right).

Other scallop fisheries that are of minor commercial importance include the **spiny pink scallop** taken by commercial divers in the Straits of Georgia, British Columbia. These are only sold live in the shell during the fall and winter. Both the giant **lion's paw scallop** of Baja California, Mexico, and the Mexican bay scallop of the Pacific Coast are sold throughout California. The **southern bay scallop** of the southeast Atlantic and Gulf Coast, equal in flavor to the **northern bay scallop**, is enjoyed locally. From the remote Kodiak Islands of Alaska comes the **weathervane scallop**, a large and excellent-flavored sea scallop, but because of the remoteness of the fishing grounds it is almost always sold frozen.

CHOOSING SUSTAINABLE SEAFOOD
Great improvements have been made in the sea scallop fishery and should be recognized as such. The number of boats allowed to fish is limited, and each is required to carry a vessel-monitoring device and an onboard observer to ensure that all regulations are followed. Gear has been lightened to mitigate bottom damage,

## Modern Chemistry

The persistent story of the nefarious scallop dealer fashioning "scallops" from skate wings or shark meat is pure urban myth. Why resort to such labor-intensive subterfuge when we have modern chemistry? It is common practice to soak, also known as "dip" or "treat," sea scallops in a sodium tripolyphosphate (STP) solution, the same chemical used to preserve and retain moisture in ham. Soaking or treating

scallops in STP-laced water is a legal practice but one that is often used to obfuscate quality issues and to misrepresent weight. Treated scallops gain as much as 25 percent in water weight—and of course lose 25 percent of their flavor in the process. When cooked, they invariably weep water, are impossible to brown or sear, and usually end up stewing to toughness. By federal law, treated scallops must be labeled as such, and at a certain point, when more than 20 percent of their weight is added water, they become "scallop product"—but this information seldom, if ever, reaches the consumer.

My only advice is to learn to recognize the signs of STP abuse. Scallops that have been soaked in an STP solution will feel slippery or soapy, appear glassy and translucent, and have either no odor or a mild chemical smell. The most common telltale sign—scallops displayed in a pool of milky white liquid—indicates that they have undoubtedly been processed with sodium tripolyphosphate and should be avoided. Better yet, simply find a knowledgeable, trustworthy fishmonger who believes that a satisfied customer is a return customer—and you'll discover plenty of wonderful fresh scallops out on the market today.

escape routes for fish have been enlarged, and scallop fishermen allow nets to lay fallow for several minutes at the end of a tow in order to facilitate escape by groundfish.

Sea scallop populations are healthy and management is excellent, but many environmental groups see the method of fishing as the weak link in the fishery. Although repeated scallop dredging and trawling stirs up the feed that contributes to a healthy scallop population, it also homogenizes the bottom, discouraging biodiversity.

The bay scallop is short lived and very fecund but also very sensitive to ocean conditions, resulting in wide population swings from year to year. The scallop's inshore estuarine habitat is subject to pollution-related damage, which has adversely impacted populations.

## CHOOSING HEALTHY SEAFOOD

Clams, mussels, oysters, and scallops were once thought to contain high levels of cholesterol. It is now understood that mollusks that filter predominantly plant-based phytoplankton from the water for food contain very little cholesterol; rather, they contain cholesterol-like plant-based sterols that actually interfere with the uptake of cholesterol. Therefore, they are no longer excluded from typical low-cholesterol diets and are even considered a heart-healthy low-fat source of protein.

The scallop's abductor muscle, the meat typically eaten in the United States, is always completely safe, but the viscera and gonads (roe and milt) of scallops may contain natural marine toxins at certain times (see "Red Tide" Marine Toxins, page 415). Live scallops, both aquacultured bay scallops and wild pink scallops, are monitored and tested for pathogens by state and federal authorities under the auspices of the National Shellfish Sanitation Program and should be displayed with their NSSP harvest tag. Although scallop meats are completely safe, pregnant women, young children, and those with compromised immune systems should refrain from eating whole raw scallops containing the viscera or roe (see Raw Seafood: How to Stay Safe, page 408).

## IN THE KITCHEN

Aquacultured bay scallops or Pacific Coast pink scallops, which are sold live in the shell, can be eaten in their entirety either raw or cooked. Scallop meat can be eaten completely raw (as in tartare and sashimi), or marinated as in ceviche, or cooked in various ways.

The standard refrain not to overcook scallops lest they become tough and dry is good advice. At the same time, however, scallops need to be thoroughly cooked to develop full flavor. When cooking scallops, the proteins must be sufficiently broken down to allow adequate intermingling of the fats, amino acids, and sugars needed to create full flavor. To my taste, scallops come to the table best when cooked medium rare—that is, the center is still slightly translucent but the ambient temperature of the surrounding flesh allows continued cooking to the point of doneness.

Smoked or salt-dried scallops have a concentrated flavor and taste and are often used as a seasoning ingredient in Asian recipes. XO sauce, a popular Hong Kong condiment similar to oyster sauce, is based on dried scallops.

## SEARING SCALLOPS

Although scallops can be seared in a nonstick pan over medium-high heat, I prefer the texture and flavor created in cast iron over high heat. Preheat a large cast-iron skillet over high heat until it is smoking hot. Clean the scallops by removing the small hard muscle attached to the side of the meat and quickly rinsing away any sand or attached viscera. Dry the scallops thoroughly before adding them to the pan. Dab a paper towel in oil and quickly wipe the bottom of the pan with a thin film of oil. Add the scallops to the pan but do not crowd them; leave an inch of space around each one (it may be necessary to cook them in batches). If the scallops are more than three fourths of an inch thick, cut them in half horizontally so you have two thinner coins of scallop.

If at any time the scallops begin to weep juices, remove the scallops from the pan, wipe out any moisture, and allow the pan to come back up to high heat. Dab any moisture from the scallops with a paper towel and return them to the pan to continue searing.

## PAN-SEARED SEA SCALLOPS WITH CHIPOTLE MAYONNAISE

SERVES 4 AS A MAIN COURSE

This spicy mayonnaise is also very good with Florida stone crab claws, shrimp, salmon, or even chilled lobster. Serve this dish with Mexican-style *arroz verde*: rice pilaf cooked with lots of minced cilantro, parsley, and onion, in chicken stock.

**CHIPOTLE MAYONNAISE**
¾ cup Mayonnaise (page 37)
¼ cup Mexican crema or crème fraîche
 (page 34)
1 garlic clove, minced
Juice of 1 lime
1 chipotle chile in adobo sauce, minced to
 a paste, plus 1 teaspoon adobo sauce

Refined peanut oil or another high-heat
 oil for frying
1 pound sea scallops, cleaned
Coarse sea salt or kosher salt

1. For the chipotle mayonnaise: In a small bowl, combine all the ingredients and stir to blend. Set aside.

2. Heat a large cast-iron skillet over high heat until smoking hot. With a paper towel dipped in oil, wipe the bottom of the pan so it is lightly coated with oil. Pat the scallops dry and season with salt. Add them to the pan without crowding, and sear for 2 or 3 minutes on a side without moving (turning only once). They should be sweetly caramelized and brown on the exterior and still slightly translucent in the center. Serve with the chipotle mayonnaise.

## Too Much of a Good Thing

The 450-mile shoreline and waters of the Peconic Bay estuary on the East End of Long Island is one of the most idyllic and productive ecosystems on earth. The Montauk band of Algonquin Indians were dependent on the estuary for most of their food when Europeans first set foot in America. Long Island Bay fishermen have depended on the waters of the estuary since. Not that many years ago, 40 percent of all the bay scallops captured in the United States came from Peconic Bay. Some years, the fishing was so good bay scallops would dip down to a few dollars a pound.

Those times are gone. Today the price of Peconic Bay scallops is closer to twenty-five dollars a pound; bay men are restricted to bringing in a bushel a day, and recreational fishermen even less. A couple of weeks after the season opening, it's not even worth fishing. Most commercial fishermen go back to harvesting clams and lobster or striped bass.

Long an icon of the area, the bay scallop has nearly disappeared. Not because of overfishing, mind you, but because the East End is such an idyllic spot. Attracted by the natural beauty of the area, people built summer cottages and golf courses everywhere. Today some 200,000 summer homes, thirty-four golf courses, and uncounted parking lots line the shores of Peconic Bay.

Under normal conditions, nutrient-rich waters enter the bay at a steady rate, nurturing the ecosystem, but the houses and parking lots that now front the bay create flood conditions every time it rains. An excess of fertilizer-laden storm water runs off the land, flooding the bay with nutrients. All these nutrients in the water encourage explosive algal growth. Summer blooms of algae can be so thick that the waters of the estuary are stained brown. These algal blooms deplete the bay of oxygen and light, killing thousands of acres of the rich eelgrass beds that are the habitat of the bay scallop. As a result, the once-booming scallop population has been reduced to a few lucky survivors.

Nutrient pollution, mostly nitrogen from human activities, is the greatest threat to world fisheries today, according to the United Nations Environment Programme. Estuarine nursery areas, so integral to the future of our fisheries, are being threatened by too much of a good thing, too many nutrients. Uncontrolled nutrient runoff from livestock and farms threatens the Chesapeake Bay, Florida Keys coral reefs are near collapse from algal blooms, and everywhere along the Gulf of Mexico the sea is encroaching on dead and dying wetlands. Louisiana alone has lost fifteen hundred square miles of wetlands. A so-called dead zone located off the mouth of the Mississippi River in most years is larger than the state of Massachusetts. Its annual summer incarnation suffocates any life too slow to escape and chases fish to deeper water.

The good news in Long Island these days is that people have become motivated and organized, eel-grass is being replanted, bay scallops are being seeded, and, most important, the Peconic Estuary Program, a partnership of government, business, and citizens, is working with the community to stop the excess runoff of nutrients into the estuary. Homeowners and businesses can control runoff from roofs so it runs into the ground rather than be diverted to city streets. New parking lot construction must provide for runoff sinks to the same purpose. And golf courses in the area have made a difference by agreeing to the more efficient and timely use of fertilizer, all simple but effective things we can do. The success of grassroots programs on the local level shows that nutrient pollution can be controlled, but it remains an issue that needs to be addressed on a national level.

The 1972 Clean Water Act went a long way toward cleaning up America's waters. It turned off the toxic sludge pouring out of industry pipes, but it failed to address the issue of "non-point pollution"—runoff from the land—which the EPA has identified as today's greatest threat to America's waterways.

# SEA ROBIN

The **northern sea robin** is not a popular food fish in the United States. It is taken as bycatch by commercial trawls and inshore recreational anglers and often discarded as too ugly to eat. It's a shame, really: Few people are aware that the sea robin is closely related in both flavor and family to the celebrated gurnard, or grondin, of bouillabaisse fame. Even the red gurnard of New Zealand, a striking orange-colored sea robin, is found in U.S. markets more easily than our own sea robin, and always at a much higher price.

Found from Nova Scotia to Cape Hatteras, the northern sea robin is reddish brown above and pale yellow below. Its large, winglike orange pectoral fins are used in sexual or defensive display and to crawl along the bottom, where it picks, probes, and overturns stones in search of food. A noisy fish that croaks and grunts, the sea robin has a large, ugly head covered with bony plates and spines. This small fish averages only one to two pounds each.

## CHOOSING SUSTAINABLE SEAFOOD

The underutilized northern sea robin is a good-tasting fish that is often simply discarded. The fish that are caught can and should be put to better use. Full-retention trawl fisheries, which call for everything caught to be landed, would help discourage waste and be a great step forward for science, management, and our palates. As it stands today, one out of every three fish caught in trawl nets is discarded, often dead or dying, because of arcane regulations, or simply because low-value fish are more trouble to deal with than they are worth.

## CHOOSING HEALTHY SEAFOOD

Sea robins are a low-fat high-protein source of B vitamins and minerals; most of their fat is of the heart-healthy polyunsaturated variety.

## IN THE KITCHEN

The sea robin is mostly head but makes a good addition to soups or stews. Mild-flavored and moderately firm-fleshed, it has a flavor that has been compared to monkfish but in my estimation is more like sculpin or Pacific rockfish. The fish can be filleted before cooking, but is best cut into chunks, leaving the tailbone in. The skin can be easily stripped or left on; cooked, it becomes soft and edible. The eggs can be salt cured to make a "caviar."

## BATTERS AND DIPS FOR DEEP-FRYING SEAFOOD

For many years, the Foc'sle, a dingy little fishermen's bar across the street from the Point Judith fishermen's co-op, has featured a Friday-afternoon Fisherman's Special. Sea robin tails are skinned, battered, and deep-fried to be given away at the bar. They look just like chicken legs and can be eaten in the same way—as finger food. The Fisherman's Special encourages brisk sales during cocktail hour, as much for the tasty sea robin meat as the hot, greasy batter seasoned with salt and cayenne.

Here are three tried-and-true recipes for battered and fried seafood. A useful tip: To reuse any of the recipes' oil for deep-frying other seafood, strain it through a fine-meshed sieve, let cool, and refrigerate.

# BEER-BATTERED SEAFOOD

This is a traditional beer batter like the kind used for fish and chips. Try it with any white fish such as sea robin, cod, pollock, or rockfish. It's also great for shrimp.

**BEER BATTER**

¾ cup all-purpose flour

1 teaspoon salt

½ teaspoon freshly ground black pepper

2 large eggs, separated

2 tablespoons refined peanut oil or
    another mild-flavored oil

¾ cup beer

Refined peanut oil or another high-heat
    oil for frying

1 pound white fish fillets or shelled shrimp

All-purpose flour or cornstarch for
    dredging

Tartar Sauce (recipe follows) or Rémoulade
    Sauce (page 79)

**1.** For the batter: In a medium bowl, combine the flour, salt, and pepper. In a small bowl, beat the egg yolks with the oil and add them to the flour. Add the beer and stir the batter about 25 times, or until thoroughly mixed but not overworked. Cover the bowl with plastic wrap and refrigerate for 1 hour. In a large bowl, beat the egg whites to soft peaks; gently fold the egg whites into the batter.

**2.** In a Dutch oven or deep fryer, heat 3 to 4 inches oil to 350°F for large pieces of seafood, 400°F for small. Dredge the seafood in the flour or cornstarch, then the batter. Drain the excess batter and slip into the hot oil. Fry in batches, not crowding the pan, for 3 or 4 minutes, or until golden brown on all sides. Let the oil return to the correct temperature between batches. Using a wire skimmer, transfer the seafood to a wire rack to drain. Use the skimmer to remove any excess batter or crumbs from the oil between batches. Serve with Tartar Sauce or Rémoulade Sauce.

## TARTAR SAUCE

Tartar sauce is everyone's favorite with fried fish, but it also goes great with sautéed, grilled, or even poached fish. It's the perfect spread for a fish sandwich, whether it's griddled Florida grouper, fried haddock, grilled mahimahi, or a BLT: bacon, lettuce, and crisp panfried trout.

¾ cup Mayonnaise (page 37)

1 teaspoon Dijon-style mustard

2 teaspoons grated onion, or 2 tablespoons chopped scallion, white part only

1 tablespoon chopped sweet pickle

1 teaspoon sweet pickle juice

1 tablespoon capers, chopped

2 to 3 drops hot pepper sauce

Juice of 1 lemon and grated zest to taste

1 tablespoon chopped celery leaves

1 tablespoon minced fresh flat-leaf parsley

1 hard-cooked egg, chopped (optional)

1 tablespoon minced fresh dill

In a small bowl, combine all the ingredients and stir well to blend. Cover and allow the flavors to blend for an hour or two in the refrigerator.

## TEMPURA-BATTERED SEAFOOD

This light batter has a bit of crunch, and is nice for shelled shrimp, squid, or any quick-cooking finfish such as fillet of sole or John Dory. Sushi bars will often deep-fry the head of a spot shrimp in this batter to be served alongside sashimi made from the tail of the shrimp.

Refined peanut oil or another high-heat oil for frying

**TEMPURA BATTER**

1 large egg

1 cup ice water

1 cup cake flour or all-purpose flour

1 pound shrimp, shelled, or cleaned squid, or thin fillets of sole or John Dory

Cornstarch for dredging

Tempura Dipping Sauce (recipe follows)

1. In a Dutch oven or deep fryer, heat 3 to 4 inches oil to 350°F. While the oil is heating, make the batter: In a medium bowl, beat the egg and ice water together and stir in the flour just until smooth.

2. Dredge the seafood very lightly in the cornstarch, then the batter. Drain the excess batter and slip the seafood into the hot oil. Fry in batches, not crowding the pan, for 2 or 3 minutes, or until golden brown on all sides. Let the oil return to the correct temperature between batches. Using a wire skimmer, transfer the seafood to a wire rack to drain. Use the skimmer to remove any excess batter or crumbs from the oil between batches. Serve with Tempura Dipping Sauce alongside.

VARIATION: In place of Tempura Dipping Sauce, use Soy Dipping Sauce (page 398).

## ▪ ▪ ▪ TEMPURA DIPPING SAUCE ▪ ▪ ▪

MAKES 1½ CUPS

1 cup instant or homemade Dashi (page 370)
¼ cup mirin
¼ cup soy sauce
¼ cup grated daikon for serving
2 tablespoons grated fresh ginger
  for serving

In a small bowl, combine the Dashi, mirin, and soy sauce. Serve the daikon and ginger alongside in separate bowls and add to the dipping sauce to taste.

# CHICKPEA AND
# RICE FLOUR–BATTERED SEAFOOD

This gluten-free batter is airy-light and crispy but has more of its own distinct flavor than either of the other two batters. It goes well with Indian sauces and spices. Anchovies, sardines, mackerel, or one of the jacks would be nice, but don't be afraid to use this batter with other seafood as well.

Refined peanut oil or another high-heat
   oil for frying

**CHICKPEA AND RICE FLOUR BATTER**
½ cup chickpea flour
½ cup rice flour
½ teaspoon salt
¼ teaspoon baking powder
½ teaspoon cayenne pepper
¼ teaspoon ground cumin
¾ cup ice water

1 pound jack fillets or other rich-flavored
   fish fillets
All-purpose flour or cornstarch
   for dredging
Green Chutney (page 71) for serving

1. In a Dutch oven or deep fryer, heat 3 to 4 inches oil to 350°F for large pieces of seafood, 400°F for small.

2. While the oil is heating, make the batter: In a medium bowl, stir all the dry ingredients together well. Quickly whisk the ice water into the flour; stir a few times lightly.

3. Dredge the fish in the flour or cornstarch, then the batter. Drain the excess batter and slip the fish into the hot oil. Fry in batches, not crowding the pan, for 3 or 4 minutes, or until golden brown on all sides. Let the oil return to the correct temperature between batches. Using a wire skimmer, transfer the fish to a wire rack to drain. Use the skimmer to remove any excess batter or crumbs from the oil between batches.

4. Serve with Green Chutney alongside.

NOTE: Chickpea flour, also called besan, is available in Indian markets.

# SHAD

From Florida to New England, the star-shaped blooms of the shad bush are the first smattering of white to brighten the countryside after winter. The shad bush is so named because the appearance of its blooms is always closely followed by the return of the shad to local rivers. Triggered by warming water temperatures, these fish begin their upstream spawning trek in early spring when the shad bush is in abundant full bloom.

The **American shad** (*Alosa sapidissima*) is an excellent-flavored fish that has been thoroughly enjoyed from pre-Colonial times to the present. Ever since Native Americans introduced European settlers to it during their spring shad feasts, European Americans have happily dined on this fish. Along the way, shad and shad roe cookery have become an integral part of American cuisine. But in recent years, the shad has fallen out of favor. Blame it, some say, on the bones.

Page through any cookbook or field guide to the entry on shad, and without fail you will read, "The shad has a peculiar bone structure, which makes it very difficult to remove all of the bones," usually followed by a parable relating how an ever-complaining porcupine was turned inside out by a devious deity, creating the shad. This constant harping seems to have convinced the American public that shad is virtually inedible.

Sure, it may take a certain amount of skill and a bit of work to bone a shad, but that's why you go to the fish market and not the stream. Few people cut their own lamb chops or butcher their own steaks or even bone out a chicken breast, so, I ask, what is the big deal about shad? Buy it cleaned.

Visit a high-quality, service-oriented fish market like Charley Russo's in Savannah, Georgia, around the beginning of March and you'll find some nice, tasty, well-cleaned shad. For about a month, all Charley does is clean the shad that local fishermen bring to his back door. Charley says: "Every one of my customers buys shad and shad roe two or three times; it's delicious and they love it. By the time the local run is finished I'm sick of cleaning shad and everyone has pretty much had their fill, then that's enough until next year." As spring progresses, shad enter coastal rivers progressively farther north; the last runs in New England begin in May.

Shad roe is graded for quality by the fish house where it is packed. It must be fully developed but not overripe. The outer membrane is removed and all traces of blood, slime, and veins are removed. The inner membrane should not be torn but is left intact, connecting the two individual lobes, or skein. But don't worry: When you purchase shad roe in a fish market, they will prepare it properly for you. All that is required of you is a simple rinse to remove any residual blood.

The shad was introduced to the Sacramento River delta in 1871 and later Oregon's Columbia, Snake, and Willamette rivers and successfully spread throughout the Pacific Northwest. Spawning runs on the West Coast begin in the early summer, delayed by the cold-water Japanese current that brushes the coast.

## CHOOSING SUSTAINABLE SEAFOOD

The shad is anadromous, meaning it lives in the ocean but spawns in coastal rivers. It is susceptible to the degradation of river systems but has proven to be more resilient than the Atlantic salmon in similar conditions. Although far more abundant in the past, shad fish can be considered underutilized because much of what comes to the market is used only for its roe, with the fish being used for crab bait or animal food.

## CHOOSING HEALTHY SEAFOOD

Shad are even richer in heart-healthy omega-3s than salmon and are a good source of vitamins and minerals. Shad enjoy a particularly healthy diet, eating mostly plankton and some small fish at the bottom of the food chain. Although shad do enter rivers to spawn, they do not eat in the rivers, so are not exposed to any organic pollutants that may be found in urban areas.

## IN THE KITCHEN

Like its close relative the herring, the shad is white, sweet, moist, and distinctly flavored. Its high fat content and assertive flavor pairs well with acidic sauces. It is at its best pickled, smoked, charcoal-grilled, baked, or fried. In Bordeaux, France, where a similar species resides, the most popular way to cook this fish is with sorrel sauce.

Shad roe skeins come in pairs, and the two attached sacs of tissue that hold the eggs should be carefully separated before cooking. They may be gently poached for a minute or two in gently simmering water to facilitate handling. To cook, simply dredge the skeins in all-purpose flour and sauté in clarified butter over low heat for five minutes on each side, or until browned. Add a little crumbled cooked bacon and garnish with fried onions and parsley; or deglaze the pan with browned butter, lemon juice, and dry white wine, then toss in some minced fresh tarragon, fennel, or chervil for extra flavor. Fresh shad roe can also be baked or broiled.

# SAUTÉED SHAD ROE
# WITH MEYER LEMON RELISH

SERVES 4 AS AN APPETIZER

Meyer lemons are sweeter than other lemons; they have a tender, mild thin skin and a wonderful perfume. From the time I first encountered them in Berkeley, I was enamored. So many of these delicious lemons grow in Berkeley backyards that for years I thought they were a localized hybrid and referred to them as Berkeley lemons. Meyer lemons are now being cultivated in Texas and Florida as well as in California, and as a result are becoming more widely available.

Chef Jean-Pierre Moullé and the cooks at Chez Panisse have helped popularize Meyer lemons by using them in every possible guise from ice cream to this Meyer Lemon Relish, which is delicious with any simply cooked fatty fish and rich shad roe; for lean fish, increase the oil to a half cup. Always use enough herbs to create a relishlike consistency.

Serve this dish with boiled new potatoes and a peppery arugula salad for a nice lunch or light supper.

2 pairs shad roe skeins

3 tablespoons unsalted butter

3 tablespoons olive oil

Seasoned flour: (¼ cup all-purpose flour
mixed with 1½ teaspoons kosher salt and
¼ teaspoon freshly ground pepper)

Meyer Lemon Relish (recipe follows)

1. Preheat the oven to 350°F. Carefully separate the 2 lobes of roe by cutting the membrane that joins them, being careful not to tear the sac containing the eggs. Gently rinse each lobe and pat dry.

2. In a large ovenproof sauté pan or skillet, melt the butter with the oil over medium heat. Dredge the roes in the seasoned flour and lay them in the butter and oil as soon as the butter is melted. (If you put the roe in a very hot pan, the eggs will pop and splatter.) Cook for 5 to 7 minutes on one side, or until sizzling and nicely browned. Turn the roe over and place the pan in the preheated oven for another 5 to 7 minutes, or until the roe are firm to the touch.

3. Remove from the oven and let rest for a minute or two, then cut into 1-inch-thick slices. Dress with Meyer Lemon Relish.

## ▪ ▪ ▪ MEYER LEMON RELISH ▪ ▪ ▪

MAKES ¾ CUP

1 shallot, finely diced

1 tablespoon Champagne or good white
wine vinegar

Pinch of salt, plus more to taste

Juice of 2 large Meyer lemons
(2 tablespoons), plus 1 large organic
Meyer lemon

2 tablespoons minced fresh flat-leaf parsley

1 tablespoon each minced fresh chives and
chervil or basil

¼ cup olive oil

Cayenne pepper to taste

In a small bowl, combine the shallot, vinegar, lemon juice, and salt. Let stand for 10 minutes. Cut the ends off the organic lemon and slice it into ¼-inch-wide wedges. Remove the central core and any seeds; slice the wedges crosswise into thin slivers. Combine the slivered lemon and herbs and add to the shallot mixture. Stir in the olive oil and season with cayenne and salt to taste. This relish can be made several hours ahead but will not store well overnight.

# SHAD IN A LIGHT BROTH
# WITH SORREL, PEAS, AND MINT

The clean, acidic bite of sorrel, which is only just beginning to regain some of its former popularity, is a welcome addition to recipes for fatty fish. Salmon is an excellent substitute for shad in this recipe.

2 cups Vegetable Stock (page 29) or
    chicken stock

½ cup fresh green peas

Salt and freshly ground black pepper
    to taste

2 cups sorrel, cut into thin ribbons

2 or 3 tablespoons olive oil

Four 5-ounce shad fillets

Seasoned flour: ¼ cup all-purpose flour
    mixed with 1½ teaspoons kosher salt
    and ¼ teaspoon freshly ground
    black pepper

Small handful of fresh mint leaves, cut into
    thin ribbons, for garnish

**1.** In a small saucepan over medium heat, bring the stock to a simmer. Add the peas and simmer until softened but still bright green, about 2 minutes. Turn off the heat and season with salt and pepper. Add the sorrel to the broth and allow it to wilt while cooking the fish.

**2.** In a large, heavy sauté pan or skillet, heat the olive oil over medium-high heat. Dredge the shad fillets in the seasoned flour and sauté for 3 or 4 minutes on each side, or until brown and crisp, a total of about 8 minutes per inch of thickness.

**3.** Divide the fillets among 4 shallow bowls and pour ½ cup broth over each fillet. Garnish with the mint. Grind a little fresh pepper over each dish.

# SHRIMP*, COLD-WATER

The tiny but abundant cold-water shrimp, commonly called "bay" shrimp, are found in chilly northern temperate seas of both the Atlantic and Pacific oceans. They are particularly appreciated for their clean, sweet flavor. Unlike warm-water shrimp, which feed close to the bottom and sometimes ingest sand with their food, cold-water shrimp feed higher in the water column so are not gritty or sandy and never need to be cleaned.

**North Atlantic cold-water shrimp** (*Pandalus borealis*), found from the Gulf of Maine north, and **Pacific cold-water shrimp** (*P. jordani*), which inhabits Pacific waters from California to Alaska, are most often sold as cooked and shelled meat. The ubiquitous previously frozen, cooked "bay," or "cocktail,"

*While there are no rules as to what can be marketed as a prawn or a shrimp, there are very slight taxonomic differences between the two. All the "shrimp" in this section are actually prawns, but I refer to each of them by their common market name.*

shrimp found in nearly every grocery store and fish market across the nation is the common cold-water shrimp.

As consumers begin to appreciate the superior flavor of *fresh* bay shrimp meat, demand is creating availability. On the Pacific Coast, packers have been promoting fresh—never frozen—bay shrimp meat during the April to October season. First-of-the-season shrimp meat from Morro Bay, California, are noted for their large size (one hundred per pound) and excellent flavor.

Since the 1930s, there has been a small artisanal fishery for fresh cold-water shrimp in the Gulf of Maine. These shrimp, almost always sold fresh, are usually simply referred to as "Maine shrimp." Most boats work out of the Portland area from December to February. A few head-on fresh shrimp are quickly shipped to appreciative restaurants and markets on the East Coast, but most of these shrimp are sold as shelled fresh *raw* shrimp meat.

Fresh or frozen cooked bay shrimp meat should have very little odor and there should be no yellow discoloration near the head. Shrimp that smells of sulfur or feels slimy to the touch should be rejected. The heads of whole raw Maine shrimp quickly turn black and loosen with age; they must be used within a day or two. Uncooked meats should be bright pink in color and sticky to the touch, with little odor of any kind.

## CHOOSING SUSTAINABLE SEAFOOD

Cold-water bay shrimp mature relatively quickly and breed prolifically, making them resilient to fishing pressure.

Thanks to regulations that restrict fishing access away from the more sensitive reef habitat, the required use of a fish-excluder device called the Nordmore grate that limits bycatch, and the absence of endangered sea turtles in cold northern waters, northern cold-water shrimp are a sound ecological choice.

Pacific Coast spot prawns and two other closely related cold-water shrimp, the **side-stripe** and **coon-stripe** shrimp, are fished exclusively by trap, making them an excellent choice.

## CHOOSING HEALTHY SEAFOOD

All the same health considerations for southern shrimp hold true for northern cold-water bay shrimp and spot prawns. Sodium tripolyphosphate, the same chemical used to preserve and retain moisture in ham (see Modern Chemistry, page 265), may occasionally be used in processing cold-water bay shrimp meat. Its use imparts a slimy feel to the meat. Fresh spot, side-stripe, and coon-stripe prawns are never treated with chemicals of any kind.

## Spot Prawn

I've eaten lobster in Brittany, hairy crab in Hong Kong, and langoustine on the shores of the Mediterranean, but for my taste none compare to the flavor of fresh **spot prawn** (*P. platyceros*), a larger cold-water cousin to the bay shrimp. Spot prawns, so named for the white spot on either side of their bright pink tails, run about six to ten per pound at maturity. Sweet and packed with sea-fresh flavor, spot prawns are delicious charcoal-grilled, sautéed, deep-fried, or even baked in rock salt.

Spot prawns begin life as male, then change to female later in life, a process called protogynous hermaphroditism, not uncommon among creatures of the sea. Many of the largest spot prawns will be carrying a clutch of beautiful red eggs attached to their underside. These eggs are crunchy and delicious when used to make "caviar," enrich a sauce, or flavor pasta, or simply when cooked and sucked from the shell. Spot prawns are the shrimp most often found in sushi bars, and are referred to as *ama-ebi* (sweet shrimp); the body is served as sushi while the head is deep-fried in tempura batter to be presented alongside.

Not long ago, spot prawns were widely available on the West Coast, but because of a changing marketplace and regulatory constraint, today they're found nearly exclusively in the live tanks of Chinese fish markets or in sushi bars.

Spot prawns, which are caught in traps, are considered the most ecologically sound and well-managed shrimp fishery in the United States. The two largest spot prawn fisheries take place in British Columbia from May to July and southeast Alaska in October. Fresh head-off prawns are occasionally available during these times, and prices are at their best.

Live spot prawns are available year-round in Asian markets and restaurants on the Pacific Coast, and occasionally in other metropolitan areas, but be sure they are alive or at the very least still twitching when purchased. Like crabs or lobsters, prawns with their heads on remain firm for only hours after death. Powerful digestive juices found in the head attack the prawn's own flesh—resulting in a mushy-textured prawn.

While often touted as a good environmental alternative to other shrimp, in reality spot prawns are a very small niche fishery and a delicacy that most of us can ill afford to enjoy more than occasionally. Spot prawns are well worth seeking out when possible, but they are far from being a realistic alternative to the 1.5 billion pounds of shrimp Americans eat every year. A more affordable and practical environmental choice: Choose wild American shrimp (see Buy American, page 294) over foreign farmed shrimp.

## IN THE KITCHEN

Fresh whole "Maine shrimp" in the shell can be simply boiled, steamed, or sautéed and eaten as finger food. Peeled raw Maine shrimp meat is excellent for stuffing ravioli, or as an addition to seafood sausage or quenelles. It can also be quickly sautéed and used in any dish that calls for warm-water shrimp.

Cooked bay shrimp meat is delicious in salads and may be used in cooked dishes if simply added at the last minute to be warmed. During the bay shrimp season my friend and floor boss at Monterey Fish, Carlos, makes my absolute favorite wharfside breakfast. He chops his wife Tita's hot, crispy pork carnitas from home and folds in an equal amount of fresh bay shrimp. After adding a relish of cilantro, green chile, and onion, he then folds the delicious mélange into warm tortillas.

---

# PANZANELLA WITH BAY SHRIMP AND FETA CHEESE

SERVES 4 AS A MAIN COURSE

This is a great one-dish meal for a summer evening. You may substitute any cooked seafood, from the Albacore Confit (page 380) to grilled lobster, for the bay shrimp. The recipe begins with the same ingredients as a classic panzanella, or Tuscan bread salad, but then strays elsewhere with the addition of shrimp and feta cheese. Olives, grilled fennel, artichokes, arugula, green beans, or corn kernels are all welcome additions to this salad.

**DRESSING**

1 garlic clove

½ teaspoon kosher salt

1 small ripe tomato, peeled (see page 39) and chopped

3 tablespoons red wine vinegar

½ cup olive oil

1 pound day-old country-style bread, torn into pieces

2 tablespoons olive oil

1 pound ripe tomatoes, cut into bite-sized wedges

1 small red onion, thinly sliced

1 English cucumber, quartered and cut into ½-inch pieces

½ cup packed fresh basil leaves, torn

1 pound bay shrimp

½ cup crumbled feta cheese

Extra-virgin olive oil and red wine vinegar as needed (optional)

1. For the dressing: In a large wooden salad bowl, mash the garlic and salt together with a pestle, then add the tomato and mash to a pulp. Whisk in the vinegar and olive oil.

2. In a large cast-iron skillet, combine the torn bread and olive oil and toss to coat. Toast over medium heat, stirring frequently, until golden and crusty in places but still soft inside, about 3 or 4 minutes.

3. Add the tomatoes, onion, cucumber, basil, and toasted bread to the bowl with the dressing. Gently toss so that the bread soaks up the dressing. Refrigerate for at least 1 hour for the flavors to meld. When you're ready to serve, toss in the shrimp and feta, and season again with oil and vinegar if needed.

## China Camp

Small sun-dried shrimp and shrimp paste are used in various dishes throughout the world in much the same way that anchovies are used in numerous Mediterranean cuisines. Cooks in Indonesia, China, Latin America, and Africa use dried shrimp in one form or another as a seasoning. Dried shrimp is a key ingredient in a dish many Thai restaurant fans know well: pad thai, a stir-fry of noodles seasoned with dried shrimp.

It's easier to judge the quality of whole dried shrimp than that of either paste or ground shrimp. Dried shrimp should be a deep salmon pink and yield slightly to the touch; they should not disintegrate when squeezed, smell strongly of ammonia, or show brown discoloration. Kept refrigerated, they should last for months.

Many of the Chinese immigrants who worked the gold fields of California and helped build the transcontinental railway were from Guangdong province, where fishing is a way of life. When the railroad was finished and the placer fields played out, many immigrants settled in the San Francisco Bay Area. Before long, fishing camps appeared along the shore of the north bay, where Chinese fishermen took to seining the tiny **grass shrimp** (*Crangon franciscorum*) from the bay. These were sold locally both live and cooked, but the great majority—hundreds of millions of pounds—were dried on the shores of the bay and shipped to China.

Today, only one fishing camp, China Camp, remains where there once were dozens. Frank Quan is the last Chinese shrimp fisherman in the last fishing camp on the bay. On weekends, he cooks grass shrimp in a big old-fashioned boiler and sells them to curious locals and tourists who visit the picnic grounds next door at China Camp State Park. During the week, he sells live shrimp mostly to bait shops, but a few pounds find their way into the kitchens of the more adventurous restaurants in the Bay Area. These fresh-from-the-bay shrimp are the ultimate sashimi and are excellent simply boiled or even sautéed. The only caveat: Be sure to cover the pan with a splatter screen or the shrimp will be jumping on the floor!

# SHRIMP, WARM-WATER

A search for shrimp recipes would surely yield more results than for any other seafood the world over. Among the world's shrimp populations, one of the tastiest is the sweet southern **warm-water shrimp**. The nursery grounds for these shrimp are found along the entire southeastern U.S. coast and throughout the vast inshore waters of the Gulf of Mexico. The three most important species of wild States-harvested warm-water shrimp are the closely related **white** (*Penaeus setiferus*), **brown** (*P. aztecus*), and **pink** (*P. aztecus*) shrimp, so named for the color of their shells when alive.

Shrimp begin life as tiny plankton drifting on the ocean currents. They instinctively move inshore to shallow estuarine waters, where they grow to maturity. Adult shrimp leave the brackish backwater bays and estuaries during spring and summer "runs" to

return to the saline waters of the ocean. Pink and brown shrimp move far offshore, while white shrimp take up residence on inshore coastal shoals. These migrations of shrimp may last several weeks, and are attended with great anticipation by commercial and recreational fishermen alike.

Wild shrimp caught in inshore waters are always the highest-quality and best-flavored shrimp. These shrimp are most often consumed locally, but they are also shipped to quality markets and restaurants around the country, where they bring a premium price.

Offshore shrimp grounds have traditionally been worked by large boats carrying ice. These iceboats stay out at sea for many days. Shrimp from these boats are sometimes sold as fresh but more often are frozen at shoreside facilities. More and more, traditional iceboats are being replaced by modern freezer boats that are capable of freezing shrimp onboard. Frozen-at-sea shrimp (designated as such on the package) are generally superior in quality to shrimp from iceboats. In addition, frozen-at-sea shrimp processed immediately after capture are less likely to be treated with sulfites (see Sulfites and Allergy, page 291).

Fresh shrimp should have a shiny appearance and a slippery, almost greasy feel. Colors are bright and distinct: The legs can be a pink or red, and the tail often reflects a rainbow sheen of blue and green. Markings such as stripes or spots should stand out in distinct contrast.

Quality frozen shrimp should retain some of the colorful qualities and slippery feel of fresh shrimp. If the head is left on, it should be firmly attached, with no blackening. Irregular black striping or spots on the shell and a musty or ammonia-like odor are indications that the shrimp is old or has been improperly handled. Shelled raw shrimp should smell sweet, with no off odors; the meat should be translucent gray-blue or pink.

**Rock shrimp** (*Sicyonia brevirostris*), a deep-sea shrimp that spends its entire life in offshore waters, has gained widespread popularity of late. Harvested by trawl over coral and rock-laden reef, an environmentally unsound practice, rock shrimp are almost always twice frozen; once at sea as whole shrimp, then again on shore after being thawed, so the shells can be removed. The meat of the rock shrimp is translucent gray-blue, with fine purple-pink stripes. Yellow striping, discoloration where the head was removed, or black spots on the flesh indicate improper handling and temperature abuse. Landings are highest in the late summer and fall.

Other wild shrimp occasionally found in U.S. markets include the **Pacific white shrimp** of Mexico, the **deepwater royal red shrimp** of the southeast Atlantic, **Hawaiian red shrimp**, and the **California ridgeback shrimp**, a rock shrimp.

## CHOOSING SUSTAINABLE SEAFOOD

Warm-water shrimp reach maturity early, spawn repeatedly, and live less than a year. Although stocks have been heavily exploited for decades, the shrimp's prolific nature has ensured the continued health of populations.

Trawling over hard-bottom rock and coral reef (as is done in the rock shrimp fishery) is highly destructive. Fisheries for white, brown, and pink shrimp in both the U.S. Gulf and south Atlantic take place over soft sedimentary bottom that is frequently subject to storm surge. In extensive studies on the effects of shrimp trawling on this habitat, little evidence of long-term adverse consequences has been found.

The wild shrimp fisheries in the United States are some of the cleanest in the world (see Buy American, page 294), but the bycatch of juvenile fish and crabs is still of great concern. Bycatch-reduction devices (BRDs) have been successful at releasing mature fish, but less so with weaker-swimming juveniles and crabs. Experts say that bycatch of juvenile red snapper in shrimp trawls is a major reason for the slow recovery of the red snapper.

Although shrimp are naturally prolific, human encroachment is taking its toll. One of the greatest threats to the southern shrimp industry comes in the form of nutrient pollution from farms, sewage plants, and development (see Too Much of a Good Thing, page 268). Of even greater consequence is the diversion and bulkheading of rivers. The diversion of the Mississippi River has caused the loss of more than 1 million acres of wetlands in Louisiana alone. These lost wetlands not only acted as nursery area for shrimps, oysters, and fish, but they buffered the destructive force of hurricanes and other storms.

## CHOOSING HEALTHY SEAFOOD

Shrimp was once considered unhealthy for those at risk for coronary heart disease because of its moderately high levels of cholesterol. It's now recognized, however, that very little dietary cholesterol is absorbed by the body; rather, saturated fats found in the diet are the greater source of blood cholesterol. Shrimp contain very little saturated fat and, like other shellfish and fish, provide omega-3 fatty acids, which improve the blood lipid profile by lowering triglycerides and modestly raising HDL cholesterol.

Current advice by the American Heart Association still warns that people with heart disease limit their cholesterol intake to no more than 200 mg per day. If followed, that restriction should not unduly constrain even those with heart disease from occasionally eating shrimp—especially if it's not battered, breaded, or fried. Eating a balanced diet low in saturated fats is the best way to maintain good health.

A good source of B vitamins, selenium, and tryptophan (which helps encourage DNA repair), shrimp is also rich in iodine and zinc. Shrimp shells, which may be eaten, are a rich source of naturally-occurring vitamin A–related carotenoids and glucosamine, reportedly beneficial for cartilage repair and relieving the pain of osteoarthritis.

## IN THE KITCHEN

The entire shrimp, head, tail, and shell, can be eaten, particularly when the shells are thin from shedding or if they are prepared by high-heat methods such as blistering in a wok or grilling over a very hot charcoal fire. When shelling shrimp, be sure to reserve the shells for use in seafood stock or shrimp bisque.

The dark vein that runs along the back of shrimp is the digestive tract. Whether you should remove this vein or not is as much based on personal preference as necessity. I seldom bother removing the vein myself, except when it's very large and very dark. But then I grew up eating steamer clams, which are often full of grit and sand. One exception is rock shrimp:

If it's not deveined, it will "polish your teeth" with the remains of the indigestibly hard chitinous-shelled diatoms it eats. Rock shrimp are usually sold raw, already shelled and deveined. To remove the vein from other shrimp: Peel away the shell, cut down the back of each shrimp with a small, sharp knife, and pull out the intestinal vein.

Shrimp takes to any method of preparation—it can be grilled, fried, sautéed, boiled, broiled, smothered, stewed, or steamed. It works well in nearly any incarnation, from blazing-hot Indian curries to a simple chilled shrimp cocktail. But like all seafood, one main rule should always be adhered to when preparing shrimp: Never overcook it. Shrimp should only be cooked for two or three minutes, or until they turn an opaque pink.

## Sulfites and Allergy

Tradition holds that shrimp should be free of any black striping or spots on the shell. It was once believed that this black discoloration, known as black spot or "shrimp melanosis," was a telltale sign of the presence of bacteria. It is now understood to be merely an enzymatic action similar to browning in fruits and vegetables. For my money an occasional shrimp with minor black discoloration on the shell is preferable to the traditional preventative, the application of sulfites.

Sulfites are used in many processed foods to retard spoilage. Dried fruit, frozen French fries, canned vegetables, frozen shrimp, and wine commonly contain sulfites—in fact, all wines, even untreated organic wines, contain some level of naturally-occurring sulfites.

Although the FDA classifies sulfites as food-grade additives, some asthmatics may suffer dramatically adverse allergic reactions to sulfites. Sodium bisulfite, used to prevent "black spotting" and retard spoilage in processed shrimp, is generally safe when added judiciously but is easily abused in an uncontrolled setting. The overuse of sulfites has been a greater problem in the past, when iceboats stayed at sea for long periods of time. Today's frozen-at-sea shrimp generally contain only small amounts of sulfites, and "day-caught" wild inshore shrimp often contain none.

The amount of sulfites in shrimp may vary, but by law, any food containing more than ten parts per million of sulfite, about the amount occurring naturally in untreated wines, must be labeled as containing sulfites. Most frozen shrimp are labeled as containing sulfites, but the amount may vary widely from brand to brand. Those who suspect they may be allergic to sulfites should be aware of the signs of sulfite abuse. Shrimp that are dry and sandy feeling, and that have white spots and pitting of the shells, have been burned by low pH, a characteristic of excessive sulfite use.

**Shrimp is a common culprit in shellfish allergies (see page 414); those allergic to lobster and crab are also often allergic to shrimp. Sulfites (see Sulfites and Allergy above), known allergens, and phosphates are often used in processing shrimp.**

# TAPATIO SHRIMP COCKTAIL

This is a favorite with everyone at the wharf, which is how it got its name. Many of the guys at the wharf are "Tapatios"—that is, they come from the state of Jalisco, Mexico, where the favored hot sauce is the Tapatio brand, which is added to everything with abandon, including this shrimp cocktail.

Make the cocktail sauce first, and then add the shrimp while it's still warm. Quick cooking followed by immersion in a flavorful dressing helps the shrimp soak up the flavors quickly without getting tough and dry from a long marinade.

COCKTAIL SAUCE

1 pound tomatoes

3 fresh green New Mexico or Anaheim
   chiles

½ cup freshly squeezed lime juice

1 onion, diced

½ cup chopped fresh cilantro

Sea salt to taste


1½ pounds medium to large shrimp

Refined peanut oil or another high-heat
   oil for frying

12 corn tortillas

Salt to taste

Avocado slices

Tapatio or other hot sauce

1. For the cocktail sauce: Char the tomatoes and chiles under a preheated broiler or over an open flame until well blistered. Put the chiles in a bowl and cover, allowing them to steam in their own heat for 5 minutes.

2. In a blender, puree the unpeeled charred tomatoes. Push the puree, which should be quite thin and liquid, through a sieve with the back of a large spoon to remove most of the seeds and skin. (The charred skin imparts a nice smoky flavor.) Add the lime juice, onion, and cilantro and season with salt. Peel, seed, and dice the chiles, then add to the tomato mixture.

3. Prepare a large pot of well-salted boiling water and add the shrimp. When the water returns to a boil, turn off the heat. Let stand for 1 minute, then drain. Shell and chop the warm shrimp into bite-sized pieces. Add them to the cocktail sauce. Cover and refrigerate for 2 to 3 hours before serving. Any leftover can be covered and kept refrigerated overnight.

4. In a large sauté pan or skillet, heat ½ inch oil over high heat until shimmering. Cut the tortillas into triangles and fry for 1 minute on each side, or until crisp. Using a wire skimmer, transfer to a wire rack or paper towels to drain. Immediately sprinkle with salt to taste.

5. Serve the cocktail with the warm tortilla chips, avocado slices, and Tapatio or your favorite hot sauce for more spice.

# GRILLED LEMONGRASS SHRIMP
# AND RICE NOODLE SALAD

This recipe takes the familiar ingredients of Vietnamese spring rolls and scatters them on a plate to make an easy but delicious main course. The shrimp is first marinated in Lemongrass Marinade and then charcoal-grilled, but you may prefer to cook them in a grill pan or do a quick stir-fry instead. The Vietnamese dipping sauce, Nuoc Cham, is the perfect accompaniment.

1½ pounds medium to large shrimp

Lemongrass Marinade (recipe follows)

8 ounces dried thin rice flour noodles
   (vermicelli)

Leaves from 2 small heads tender lettuce,
   chopped

2 cups fresh bean sprouts

1 cup julienned or shredded carrot

1 Japanese or European cucumber,
   thinly sliced

½ cup fresh mint leaves

½ cup fresh cilantro leaves

½ cup chopped roasted peanuts

Nuoc Cham (page 47)

1. With a pair of scissors, cut the shrimp up the back so that they can be easily removed from the shell after cooking. (You may shell the shrimp instead if you wish, but cooking them in the shell makes them much tastier.) Devein if desired. Toss the shrimp in the Lemongrass Marinade, massaging some of the marinade into the shell. Refrigerate for 1 hour.

2. Prepare a medium-hot fire in a charcoal grill, or preheat a gas grill to 375°F. Soak 6 wooden skewers in water for 30 minutes. Soak the rice vermicelli in cold water for 20 minutes, or until pliable. Blanch the vermicelli for 30 seconds in boiling water, then drain and rinse in cold water to stop the cooking. Drain well.

3. Arrange the chopped lettuce on 4 plates, followed by the rice vermicelli, bean sprouts, carrot, and cucumber.

4. If using a grill pan, heat it over high heat and oil the grids with a paper towel soaked with oil. Thread the shrimp on the skewers and cook, turning frequently, for 5 or 6 minutes, or until they turn evenly pink. The sugar in the marinade will quickly color, so be careful not to burn them. Arrange the grilled shrimp on top of the vermicelli, then scatter the mint, cilantro, and peanuts over all. Serve with the Nuoc Cham sauce alongside to be spooned over all as you like.

# LEMONGRASS MARINADE

MAKES ½ CUP

3 to 4 stalks lemongrass, white part only,
   peeled

2 garlic cloves, chopped

8 to 10 basil leaves, minced

2 tablespoons refined peanut or another
   mild-flavored oil

2 tablespoons fish sauce

2 tablespoons sugar

Using a mortar and pestle, pound and smash the lemongrass. Add the garlic and pound to a paste, then add the basil and pound to bruise. Whisk in the oil, fish sauce, and sugar until well combined.

## Buy American

Shrimp is the most popular seafood in the United States. More than 1.5 billion pounds of shrimp were consumed in this country last year, and with good reason: Shrimp are healthy, delicious—and most of all, cheap.

Shrimp may also be the most controversial seafood on the market. A virtual storm surge of aquacultured shrimp has arrived on U.S. shores in recent years, and three quarters of it comes from the high-impact intensive-culture shrimp ponds of Latin America and Southeast Asia. What was once considered a special treat in most parts of the country is now as inexpensive and common as chicken. The most prominent seafood on the menu of most Asian and Latin restaurants is shrimp, and grocery stores and fish markets sell four or five different sizes. Go to any national chain restaurant anywhere in the country—including those found in the shrimp-rich bayous of Louisiana—and the shrimp on the menu is almost guaranteed to have been aquacultured in a developing country.

Until recently, consumers had little way of knowing where the shrimp they were eating came from and how it arrived on their plate. Why does it matter where shrimp are grown? Years ago, traditional shrimp aquaculture utilized low-density ponds that exploited the natural tides and had little environmental impact. More recently the demand for shrimp in the United States Japan, and Europe led to the explosive growth of shrimp aquaculture anywhere labor and land were cheap. Environmental oversight and health concerns were often ignored in the rush to sell shrimp to the developed world, and thousands of acres of mangrove swamps that served as nurseries for wild fish were bulldozed and turned into intensive-culture shrimp ponds.

The environmental repercussions of these slapdash operations are legion. Wastewater release from the ponds pollutes drinking water and the surrounding seas with pesticides, disinfectants, and antibiotics. Antibiotics, both banned and legal, are used with abandon and are commonly detectable as residue in foreign aquacultured shrimp. Diseases endemic to the overcrowded conditions of the ponds are released into the wild.

There are great differences in how shrimp are captured and cultured around the world. U.S. shrimp fishermen and aquaculturists are held to higher ecological and health standards than those in any other nation in the world. Problems still exist, but the required use of turtle- and fish-excluder devices, coupled with oversight and enforcement far more conscientious than that found in developing countries, has essentially made the U.S. wild shrimp fishery one of the cleanest warm-water shrimp fisheries in the world. From a marine conservation perspective, it is essential to support wild fisheries that have made improvements, and that is most assuredly the U.S. shrimp fishery.

Although U.S. shrimp are the healthiest and most sustainably captured and cultured shrimp in the world, until recently it was impossible to know if you were buying American shrimp or shrimp aquacultured in an environmentally irresponsible operation thousands of miles away. Country-of-Origin (COOL) Labeling legislation implemented in 2005 requires that seafood labels indicate the country of origin and whether the fish is aquacultured or wild. This legislation now gives consumers the opportunity to buy wisely, and buy American.

# SKATE

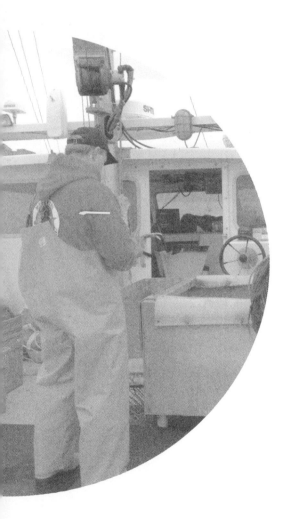

In the early 1990s, New England fishermen were encouraged to shift their efforts from cod and other troubled fisheries to skate, an underutilized species. The excellent-flavored **spotted**, or **winter, skate** (*Leucoraja ocellata*) quickly found a ready market in France. Today, much of the catch is still exported, but sophisticated diners on our own shores are fast recognizing how delicious skate can be.

Members of the skate family lay eggs that are enclosed in a hard, leathery protective case called a "mermaid's purse." The mermaid's purse is often seen washed up on the beach after being abandoned by a newly hatched skate.

The winter skate fishery of southern New England and the thorny skate (*Amblyraja radiate*) fishery of the Gulf of Maine are the two most important U.S. skate fisheries. A number of different skate species are taken on the Gulf and Pacific coasts, but most are caught as bycatch in bottom-trawl fisheries. Skates must be immediately bled and cleaned onboard to ensure a quality product (see Nature's Balance: Good Flavor in Skates, page 299). When purchasing skate, be particularly vigilant to the presence of any off ammonia-like smells, which indicates it has not been handled properly.

Available year-round, skate is sold as either a skinless triangular-shaped bone-in wing, consisting of a sheet of cartilage sandwiched between two fillets, or as a single boneless fillet. The flesh, which has been said to resemble thick corduroy or strands of bucatini pasta, should be creamy white to pale pearl pink.

Although skate has become quite popular in restaurants, it's often difficult to find in retail stores even in locations where it is caught. Placing a special order with a reputable fish market may be the best way to buy top-quality skate.

### CHOOSING SUSTAINABLE SEAFOOD

Skates are frequently taken as bycatch and discarded during other fishing operations. This is the most serious threat to skates. Large, low-fecund, late-maturing species are particularly susceptible. The Atlantic barndoor skate, never targeted in a directed fishery, is seriously depleted.

Full-retention trawl fisheries, which call for everything caught to be landed, would help discourage waste and be a great step forward for science and management. As it stands today, one out of every three fish caught in trawl nets is discarded, often dead or dying, because of arcane regulations, or simply because low-value fish are more trouble to deal with then they are worth.

Populations of winter skates are moderately healthy, while thorny skates from the Gulf of Maine are considered overfished. A management plan has been implemented to prevent further overfishing of commercially targeted skates.

### CHOOSING HEALTHY SEAFOOD

Skates are a low-fat, high-protein source of vitamins and minerals and provide moderate amounts of omega-3s. Skates test at very low levels for mercury and, like their close relation, the shark, are highly resistant to parasites.

### IN THE KITCHEN

The wings of the skate are the parts usually eaten, but the cheeks and the liver are edible as well. Traditional skate recipes call for sautéing or poaching in an acidic court bouillon, with a standard accompanying sauce of brown butter with lemon or capers.

Skate need not be relegated to the traditional, however: Small, firm cartilage-in skate wings can even be charcoal-grilled. Skate fillets can be rolled and stuffed with toasted bread crumbs, greens, prosciutto, and lemon, then roasted or braised. Cooked skate cut into individual strands to look like pasta can be served as a salad with a tomato, cucumber, and dill vinaigrette.

Even further from the traditional, I recently learned from Paul Canalis of Oliveto restaurant that skate could be served raw. Paul told me: "For a nice salad, first, salt the skate for one hour in a good sprinkling of kosher salt to firm the texture, then tear it into bucatini-like strips and marinate it for another hour in an olive oil–sherry vinaigrette with halved cherry tomatoes and julienned peppers and onions."

## SAUTÉED SKATE WITH ONION JAM

SERVES 4 AS A MAIN COURSE

Skate cooked this way is wonderful served immediately, and even better if allowed to marinate in the sauce for several hours and served at room temperature with a bitter green salad.

¾ cup dry white wine

2 tablespoons golden raisins

Four 5-ounce skate fillets

Seasoned flour: ½ cup all-purpose flour
    mixed with 1½ teaspoons salt and
    1 tablespoon hot paprika

8 tablespoons olive oil

2 yellow onions, halved and cut into
    julienne (about 1 cup)

1 tablespoon sugar

3 tablespoons white wine vinegar

½ teaspoon kosher salt

2 tablespoons minced fresh flat-leaf parsley

1. In a small saucepan, heat ½ cup of the wine over medium heat and pour it over the raisins in a small bowl to plump them.

2. Dredge the skate in the seasoned flour. In a sauté pan or cast-iron skillet, heat 4 tablespoons of the oil over medium-high heat until shimmering. Carefully lay the skate fillets in the pan and cook for 3 or 4 minutes on each side, or until golden brown. Using a slotted metal spatula, transfer the skate fillets to a plate and keep warm.

3. Pour off any oil that remains in the pan. Add 2 tablespoons olive oil to the pan. Add the onions and sauté, stirring constantly and scraping up the browned bits from the bottom of the pan, for 4 or 5 minutes, or until golden brown. Sprinkle the sugar over the onions, add the vinegar, white wine, and salt, and simmer for 1 minute. Turn off the heat; add the parsley and plumped raisins along with the wine they are soaking in. Whisk in the remaining 2 tablespoons olive oil and spoon the sauce over the skate.

## Nature's Balance: Good Flavor in Skates

Anyone who has purchased a beautiful pearl-pink, moist-looking skate wing, sparkling with apparent freshness, only to unwrap it at home and be staggered by the sharp smell of ammonia, has experienced one of the basic laws of nature: All things seek balance.

The animals that live in the sea are faced with a unique problem: Their blood and tissue are less dense than the seawater in which they live. Nature, seeking balance, encourages the less dense fluids found in a fish's living tissues to seek the denser seawater through the natural process of osmosis.

Marine fish, other than sharks and skates, use the organic compound trimethylamineoxide (TMAO) to osmotically balance their blood and tissue fluids with seawater. When these fish die, TMAO slowly breaks down into trimethylamine (TMA), which has the strong, fishy odor associated with low-quality fish.

Sharks and skates resist the natural process of osmosis in a different way. They make their body fluids as dense as the surrounding seawater by storing waste-related nitrogen compounds in their flesh. When skates and sharks are caught, these highly unstable nitrogen compounds start to break down into ammonia almost immediately. If not cleaned right away, skates may smell of ammonia after only a few hours out of the water—and this presents a problem from a culinary point of view.

Immediate cleaning of skates and sharks always ensures good, clean flavor. When sharks and skates (or any fish, for that matter) are properly cleaned immediately after death, involuntary squeezing (peristalsis) of the blood vessels continues to pump any remaining blood and waste products from the flesh. (Marine fish destined for the sushi bar are always bled and cleaned immediately after capture.)

It is best to buy skates from fisheries that target these fish, such as the Atlantic Coast spotted and thorny skate. Fishermen in these fisheries understand the importance of good handling technique and its relationship to good flavor and consumer acceptance.

Pacific and Gulf Coast skates that are captured as bycatch to other fisheries have a lower economic value than the targeted catch, so there is little incentive to properly care for them until the higher-economic-value targeted catch has been cleaned, iced, and put away. That is not to say that all skates caught as bycatch in other fisheries will be bad; it's just that they present a greater risk.

When you open up that package of beautiful-looking skate only to be confronted with the odor of ammonia, don't despair. A mild ammonia smell in skate can be neutralized by soaking the meat for thirty minutes in an acid-pH liquid such as a 10-percent-vinegar-to-water solution. Acidulated marinades that contain lemon juice, vinegar, buttermilk, yogurt, or even tomato juice also work well, performing the dual purpose of seasoning while neutralizing any base-pH ammonia products that may have remained in the tissue.

# SMELT

Run your fingers through a pile of fresh smelt, and a heady odor wafts upward—not a hint of the sea, as you might expect, but the fragrance of freshly cut violets. It's a powerful, delicious smell that makes you lean close and inhale deeply. But freeze smelt or allow them to be out of the water for a few days, and the wonderful smell disappears. This smell provides the best clue to freshness in the tiny fish.

The beautiful **rainbow smelt** (*Osmerus mordax*), olive-green on the back, silver on the sides, and overlain with a shimmering purple, pink, and blue iridescence, is the edible smelt of the Atlantic Coast. They may reach six to eight inches in the ocean, but lake smelt average closer to three to four inches. Rainbow smelt were introduced to the Great Lakes in 1912 as a forage fish for their close relatives, the also introduced landlocked salmon. They flourished to the point of becoming considered an overabundant nuisance.

Balance was restored once the local populace discovered their fine eating qualities, and smelt became the basis of important recreational and commercial fisheries.

The Pacific Coast is home to the **whitebait smelt** (*Allosmerus elongates*), which is very similar to the rainbow smelt and can be cooked in a similar manner—that is, in its entirety without being cleaned. They seldom grow larger than three inches. Several other species of Pacific Coast smelt that were historically very important, though less so today, are the **eulachon**, the **night smelt**, and the **surf smelt**. These large-size smelt may grow to eight or ten inches and must be eviscerated before cooking. They are usually treated like sardines in their preparation.

The first fresh Atlantic Coast rainbow smelt come to market just before Christmas. Great Lake and Pacific Coast smelt come to market later and are usually available through the spring.

### CHOOSING SUSTAINABLE SEAFOOD

Smelt are fast-growing and highly productive. It's estimated that smelt could be fished many times more intensively with little impact to the smelt population; however, they are important forage fish for larger fish.

Smelt spawn either along the shoreline near gravel beaches or in freshwater streams and rivers. This makes the smelt sensitive to shoreline development and stream degradation.

### CHOOSING HEALTHY SEAFOOD

Smelt, like other small, fatty fish, are high in the omega-3 fatty acids that help prevent chronic heart disease, reduce inflammatory response, and enhance brain function, among other health benefits. They are an easily digestible high-protein source of vitamin $B_{12}$ and minerals.

Although large predatory fish from the Great Lakes have been subject to consumption advisories for mercury and PCBs, the bio-accumulation of pollutants is not an issue for smelt, which are short lived.

### IN THE KITCHEN

The flesh of smelt is delicate and somewhat soft, with a rich flavor. Small rainbow and whitebait smelt can be cooked simply, without any preparation other than a simple rinse to remove sand or dirt. Larger rainbow, eulachon, night, and surf smelt must be cleaned before cooking, but there is no need to remove the bones or the very fine scales: The bones become soft enough to eat if well cooked.

Smelt are most often dusted with seasoned flour and panfried or deep-fried. They can also be breaded with bread crumbs or dipped in a thin flour or tempura batter. In the Pacific Northwest, large smelt are pickled, smoked, or charcoal-grilled. At a Great Lakes beach barbecue, a favorite way to cook smelt is to place a slice of bacon, a slice of onion, and several smelt on a piece of aluminum foil. This is then folded into a pouch and placed on the medium coals of a campfire for ten minutes.

Cut the head off with a pair of sharp scissors, then snip the belly open. With a spoon, remove the entrails by starting at the anus and scraping forward; be sure to remove the blood line, which runs along either side of the backbone. Rinse and pat dry.

## FRIED SMELT AND GREEN TOMATOES

SERVES 4 AS A MAIN COURSE

When I was eighteen, I spent a hot and dirty summer picking tomatoes on the shores of Lake Michigan. The incredibly low pay provided incentive to bring out the frying pan and search out the cheapest ingredients possible. Green tomatoes from the field were free, and smelt from the freezer case of the local supermarket were almost free, at twenty-nine cents a pound.

Serve this dish with a salad of equal parts chopped parsley, diced carrots, cucumbers, and celery dressed with a tart dressing of equal parts olive oil and lemon.

⅔ cup fresh bread crumbs

⅓ cup grated Parmesan cheese

1 pound green (unripe) salad tomatoes, sliced ⅜ inch thick

Seasoned flour: ½ cup all-purpose flour mixed with 1 tablespoon kosher salt and ½ teaspoon freshly ground black pepper

1 large egg beaten with ¼ cup milk

Refined peanut oil or another high-heat oil for frying

1½ pounds smelt, cleaned and rinsed well

1. Preheat the oven to its lowest setting. On a large plate, mix the bread crumbs and Parmesan together. Dredge the green tomatoes in the seasoned flour, then the egg mixture, and finally the bread crumb and Parmesan mixture. In a large skillet, heat ¼ inch oil over medium-high heat until shimmering and cook the tomatoes for 1 or 2 minutes on each side, or until brown and crispy. Using a slotted metal spatula, transfer to a wire rack to drain, then place in the oven to keep warm.

2. Put the remaining seasoned flour in a paper bag and add the smelt; shake vigorously to coat them with flour. In a large cast-iron skillet, heat about ¼ inch oil over medium heat until shimmering. Remove the smelt from the bag and shake off any excess flour. Carefully add them to the pan and cook for 3 or 4 minutes on each side, or until crispy and brown. Using a wire skimmer, transfer the smelt to a wire rack to drain.

# SNAPPER

rue snappers of the Lutjanidae genus are found worldwide in a variety of guises. But the **red snapper** (*Lutjanus campechanus*)—found from North Carolina south into the Caribbean and throughout the Gulf of Mexico, reaching as far south as Brazil—has the reputation of being the best eating snapper of all.

Six other snappers from the South Atlantic and Gulf waters also commonly enter our market, all of them delicious in their own right. Three of these, the **vermillion**, or **B-liner, snapper**, the **blackfin snapper**, and the **silk snapper**, have red skin and may occasionally be mislabeled as the pricier red snapper. Also making for excellent table fare are the **mangrove snapper** (one of the most common fish in Florida waters), the olive-green **mutton snapper**, and the abundant blue-and-yellow-spotted **yellowtail snapper**.

Hawaiian snappers include the highly prized **opakapaka** (pink snapper), the **onaga** (ruby snapper), **ehu** (red snapper), and **uku** (gray snapper). The onaga and ehu have always been highly valued fish in Hawaii. Their bright red color represents good luck in Asian culture, and the fish are often served on ceremonial occasions. All are fine eating fish and are enjoyed at home and in restaurants, both raw as sashimi and cooked. They are available less often in mainland Pacific Coast restaurants and fish markets.

Fishing for all of the above types of snapper is done almost exclusively by hook and line in the United States. Traditional hand lines are the only gear allowed in Hawaii, while rod and reel with anywhere from two to thirty hooks on each line are used in the Atlantic and Gulf fisheries. This and good handling practices means that domestically caught snappers, whether Hawaiian, Atlantic, or Gulf, are always of the best quality and command a deservedly high price.

Imported snapper account for the largest proportion of snapper sold in this country. These fish are often taken by more damaging methods of capture and must travel farther to market; consequently, they seldom match the quality of domestically caught fish.

Snappers are readily available in fish markets and grocery stores in areas where they are caught, but can be more difficult to find in other areas. Red snapper—the great majority of which is imported from Brazil or Mexico—is a

### Deceptively Red

Years ago I stopped by the fish counter of a well-known seafood retailer. It was midwinter and much of the country was experiencing bad weather, so there weren't many varieties of fresh fish around. To make his counter look better, the retailer had displayed the one kind of fresh fish he did have in a variety of poses; skin on, skin off, fat side up, fat side down, steaked, filleted, and whole, and each with a different label. He called them variously red snapper, rock cod, sea bass, lingcod, rockfish, and cod. It was deceptive marketing so over the top he had broken new ground.

Deceptive marketing has always been a problem in the seafood industry. Tight fishing restrictions create an incentive for seafood substitution: The consumer wants a particular well-known species but it isn't available, so a similar species takes its place. Or worse, there's economic fraud: A less valuable species is mislabeled and sold under the name of a more expensive one, such as shark for swordfish, farmed for wild salmon, anything and everything for sea bass. This is just one more reason to cultivate a good relationship with an honest fishmonger.

In 1995, an exposé by *American Journal* television producers discovered that more than 50 percent of the red snapper sold in restaurants was a substitute species. In 2004, University of North Carolina researchers published a report showing that 75 percent of all red snapper sold in markets was not red snapper at all.

While it is very difficult to tell the difference between various types of snapper fillets without relying on molecular-level tests, we can differentiate between similar-looking whole snappers.

Here's how to differentiate between similar-looking snappers with red skin: Real red snappers are scarlet to brick red, deep bodied, and most defining, have a red iris; silk snappers (which some consider equal to the red snapper at table) are very similar in appearance but can be distinguished by their yellow irises; vermillion snappers seldom exceed five pounds and are much more streamlined in appearance than the red snapper. They have a distinctly dark lateral line, and tend to have yellow and green highlights on their red skin. The final snapper commonly substituted for red snapper is the blackfin snapper. It has a prominent black spot the size of a quarter at the base of its pectoral fin.

The practice of labeling red-skinned Pacific rockfish (see page 229) as red snapper is so institutionalized that the FDA has simply given up trying to enforce deceptive labeling laws. They've compromised by allowing a dozen species of Pacific rockfish to be labeled as "Pacific red snapper."

West Coast markets and restaurants, particularly those in southern California, occasionally feature a variety of snappers from the Sea of Cortez and Mexican Pacific Coast; the most popular are the **yellowtail snapper** (*L. argentiventris*) and **Pacific red snapper** (*L. peru*). These *true* snappers sell for ten dollars per pound for whole fish and twenty dollars per pound for fillets, while the similar-in-name-only "Pacific red snapper" sells for six to eight dollars per pound for fillets.

favorite in white-tablecloth restaurants throughout the North and Midwest. Specialty supermarkets and some fish markets regularly carry red snapper; ethnic markets, particularly Chinese markets, carry a variety of whole snappers. Mangrove and yellowtail snappers average two to five pounds; most other snappers usually average less than ten pounds but some, including the Hawaiian snappers, may occasionally grow to thirty pounds.

Fresh snapper fillets should have a lustrous sheen and a dense, firm appearance; they should not appear soggy or waterlogged. There should be no visible bruising, tears, or gaps, and the flesh should be clear, with a translucent quality.

Whole fresh snappers should have tight, shiny scales, and their naturally-occurring protective coating of slime should be clear and viscous. The eyes should look bright and clear, and be convex in their sockets, not clouded or sunken. The gills should be clean and tinged with pink or red.

## CHOOSING SUSTAINABLE SEAFOOD

Red snapper has been actively managed in the United States since 1984. It was first declared overfished in 1989. These days, the red snapper is in no better shape than it was twenty years ago. Recreational and commercial fishermen point fingers at each other, but both groups point to the bycatch of juvenile red snapper in shrimp nets as a major cause of overfishing.

Shrimp fishermen are now required to use a device that allows fish to escape from their nets. Although it isn't a perfect solution, the problem is at least being addressed. In another promising turn, the red snapper fishery is about to switch from a wasteful, derby-style fishery to an individual fishing quota system that provides an incentive for fishermen to protect the fish population (see Good Management Makes the Pacific Halibut Sustainable, page 149).

Until their populations recover, give the overfished red and vermillion snappers a rest, and try one of the other delicious and more abundant yellowtail, mangrove, or mutton snappers instead.

Snapper conservation areas have recently been created around all of the main Hawaiian islands in hopes of establishing spawning preserves. Hawaiian snapper populations are stable in the distant northwest islands, while around the main islands opakapaka and uku are doing well, but onaga and ehu are overfished. The establishment of the Northwestern Hawaiian Islands Marine National Monument in 2007 will ensure a healthy future for all Hawaiian snappers.

## CHOOSING HEALTHY SEAFOOD

Snapper is an excellent low-fat, high-protein source of the antistress vitamins $B_6$ and $B_{12}$ and minerals, particularly selenium, which may act to reduce the effects of mercury. It is also a moderately good source of omega-3 fatty acids, which improve the blood lipid profile, reduce inflammatory response, and enhance brain function.

Reef-dwelling fish from tropical waters can accumulate naturally-occurring marine toxins (almost unheard of in domestic waters); see Ciguatera, page 411. Imported snappers, particularly large fish, are more apt to come under suspicion for such toxins. Commercial fishermen understand ciguatera, are knowledgeable of local waters, and try to avoid fish from reefs that are under suspicion.

### IN THE KITCHEN

Snappers are appreciated for their delicate, yet complex flavor and their fine texture. The skin is edible, as are the liver and any roe or milt. The bones make a delicious stock. Seldom parasitized, snapper can also safely be used in raw fish dishes, but eating raw or lightly cooked fish always carries some degree of risk.

Sautéing, baking, and grilling are all popular methods of preparing snapper fillets, but any method of cooking, including steaming, poaching, or braising, will produce a delicious dish. The skin-on fillets can be charcoal-grilled or sautéed; it crisps nicely under high heat (see Crispy-Skin Spanish Mackerel with Quick Pickled Onion and Fennel, page 180). Sauté skin-on fillets until crispy and nearly cooked through before turning over for only a minute, then present skin-side up. Small snappers, simply gutted and scaled, are moist and delicious when baked or charcoal-grilled.

Snappers are complemented by Latin flavors and citrus. In Mérida, yellowtail snapper is marinated in a Yucatán-style recado of achiote and sour orange, then baked or grilled. The classic *huachinango a la veracruzana* features snapper marinated in lime, then baked in a spicy tomato sauce of peppers, olives, and capers.

# SIMMERED YELLOWTAIL SNAPPER
## WITH TOMATO AND TARRAGON PAN SAUCE

Simmering is like poaching, but with less liquid. The fish is repeatedly basted while cooking, so it cooks evenly. Simmering fish in a small amount of liquid creates pan juices that are concentrated and flavorful, perfect for a delicious pan sauce. Pan sauces are a great enrichment to fish, bringing together all the seasoning ingredients that have complemented the fish while it cooks. Like fish, they are quick cooking and relatively simple to execute, and make a nice acidic counterpoint to the fish.

Yellowtail snapper is one of the more abundant and well-managed snappers in Florida waters. Summer flounder, petrale sole, haddock, or one of the more abundant Pacific rockfish such as chilipepper, black gill, or yellowtail will work well in this recipe. This is a quick and easy weeknight supper when served with couscous or steamed rice and some green beans or summer squash.

2 shallots, minced

1 tablespoon minced fresh tarragon

2 tablespoons white wine vinegar

1 tomato

1 cup dry white wine

Four 5-ounce yellowtail snapper fillets

Kosher salt and freshly ground black
   pepper

About ½ cup water

¼ cup olive oil

Freshly squeezed lemon juice to taste
   (optional)

Salt to taste (optional)

1. In a large sauté pan or skillet, combine the shallots, tarragon, and vinegar and cook over medium-high heat for 2 or 3 minutes, or until the vinegar has almost evaporated. Cut the tomato in half horizontally and squeeze out the seeds. Grate the flesh side of the tomato on the largest holes of a box grater directly into the pan; discard the skin.

2. Add the white wine to the pan and cook until reduced by half. Season the fish fillets with salt and pepper and place them on top of the tomato mixture; add enough water so the liquid covers the fish by three fourths. Gently cook the fillets, without turning, for 6 or 7 minutes per inch, while repeatedly spooning the hot liquid over the top of the fillets.

3. Using a slotted metal spatula, transfer the fillets to a warmed plate and cover. Over high heat, cook the liquid in the pan, adding any juices from the resting fish, until thick and syrupy, about ⅜ cup. Turn the heat off and whisk in the olive oil. The reduced acid and olive oil will emulsify into a thickened pan sauce. Taste and season with lemon juice and salt, if desired. Place each fillet on a plate and spoon some of the sauce over.

# SNAPPER CEVICHE

The flavor of ceviche is dependent on the acid used to souse the fish. The Key lime is probably the closest to the sweet-sour flavor of the *limón* most often used in Latin American ceviches. The addition of orange juice in this recipe imparts some sweetness to the tart acidity of the Persian limes typically available in U.S. stores. If you have access to Key limes, Seville oranges, yuzu, or any other interesting citrus with a good balance of acidity and sweetness, by all means give them a try.

This simple ceviche is almost a cliché, but it's still one of my favorites. On the West Coast, we often use local rockfish for this, but any firm-fleshed, mild-flavored white-fleshed fish works well; oily-fleshed fish such as Sierra mackerel or mahimahi are also good candidates, but ceviche made with oily-fleshed fish will not keep well overnight so should be eaten the same day.

1 pound snapper fillets, cut into ⅓-inch dice

¼ cup freshly squeezed lime juice, plus more as needed

2 tablespoons freshly squeezed orange juice, plus more as needed

½ teaspoon kosher salt, plus more for sprinkling

1 or 2 serrano or jalapeño chiles, seeded and minced

¼ cup diced white onion

½ cup diced tomato

2 tablespoons chopped fresh cilantro

12 corn tortillas

Refined peanut oil or another high-heat oil for frying

1. Put the diced fish in a small stainless-steel or glass bowl and cover with the ¼ cup lime juice and 2 tablespoons orange juice. Be sure the fish is completely covered; if more citrus juice is needed, add 1 part orange for every 2 parts lime juice. Stir in the salt. Cover and refrigerate for at least 1 hour and preferably 2 or 3. Thirty minutes before serving, stir in the chiles, onion, tomato, and cilantro.

2. Cut the tortillas into wedges and cook in hot oil until they puff up, turning once. Drain, sprinkle with salt, and serve while still warm, with the ceviche.

# SOLE:
## AMERICAN FLOUNDERS

All flatfish are masters of disguise and ambush, blending in perfectly with the color and texture of the sea bottom. Most burrow into sand or mud, leaping out in surprise to snatch their prey of crabs, shrimp, anchovies, or other passing fish. Swimming like a veil undulating in the wind, the flatfish then settles back to the bottom, where it flutters into its soft bed to await its next meal.

Of the thirty or so flatfish harvested in American waters, all are flounders, even if they're sometimes referred to as sole. True European "sole" may carry more cachet than mere flounder, but in truth there is very little difference between soles and flounders. European sole is excellent when eaten in view of the English Channel, but I can name four or five American flounders I consider its equal when they are pulled fresh from the sea.

The biggest fault with American flounder is the way it is processed and labeled by large-production fish-cutting houses. Flounder is too often sold as generic "fillet of sole," with little or no distinction made between one species and another. Standard practice for large-production cutting houses is to machine-cut "fillet of sole," and then package it with sodium tripolyphosphate (STP), the same chemical used in ham to retain moisture and preserve it; it is also used on scallops (see Modern Chemistry, page 265). The cooking qualities, texture, and flavor of flounder treated with STP are completely compromised by the use of this chemical. Flounder that has been "dipped," as they say, weeps water, is impossible to brown or sear, and usually ends up stewing in its own juices. Flounder treated with STP must be labeled on the packaging it is shipped in, but this information seldom, if ever, reaches the consumer.

To determine if flounder has been treated with STP, look for fish that feel slippery or soapy and appear glassy; fresh, untreated fillets should have a lustrous sheen, be dense and firm, and should not appear soggy or waterlogged. Buy whole fish or flounder fillets from a reputable retailer who cuts his own flounder or buys from a small-production house that does not use chemicals.

Freshness and good handling are often the most important factors in achieving good flavor and texture in seafood—and this above all holds true for flounder. American flounders are delicious, and each kind should be recognized for its own special attributes. Here are some of the best-flavored and most important American flounders.

## ATLANTIC FLOUNDERS

**Summer flounder**, or **fluke** (*Paralichthys dentatus*), of the same genus as California halibut, is one of a growing number of Atlantic species whose populations are being shepherded toward restored health by good management. Summer flounder are available year-round from southern New England and mid-Atlantic waters (the name "summer flounder" comes from the fish's habit of migrating to inshore areas during the summer months). The best-quality summer flounders are caught by trap or hook and line during the inshore summer season.

Summer flounder commonly marketed as fluke are large flounders that may grow to twenty pounds but are usually sold at between three and five pounds. Top-quality trap and hook-and-line fish are often sold whole. The flavor is excellent and the texture very firm; it's a favorite in sushi bars as *hirame* and excellent for any raw preparations, but is also very good cooked.

**Winter flounder** (*Pseudopleuronectes americanus*) is commonly called **blackback flounder** when small and **lemon sole** when large. Often sold as fillets but occasionally sold round, whole baby blackback flounders sautéed until crisp are delicious. Winter flounder has a rich, strong shellfish flavor that will stand up to stronger seasonings; the texture is softer than that of fluke but still very good. Winter flounder is most available in winter and during spring and fall migrations.

**Yellowtail flounder** (*Limanda ferruginea*) has a delicate flavor and a fine texture. Caught farther offshore at greater depths, yellowtails are usually sold as fillets.

**American plaice** (*Hippoglossoides platessoides*), or **dab sole**, was once very abundant but is now predominantly a Canadian fishery. These are usually sold as fillets.

**Witch flounder**, or **gray sole** (*Glyptocephalus cynoglossus*), is as fine a flatfish as is found, with an excellent, rich mineral flavor and fine, firm texture. This delicious fish, found in the Gulf of Maine and off Georges Bank, is excellent as fillets or pan-ready as whole fish. The witch flounder is slow growing, late maturing, and longer lived than other flounders.

## PACIFIC FLOUNDERS

The **petrale sole** (*Eopsetta jordani*) is the most sought after of all the Pacific Coast flounders, highly prized for its excellent flavor and firm, fine texture. Petrale is found from Baja California to Alaska, and is often sold as fillets, but small, pan-ready petrale, sold as "Catalina dabs" to distinguish them from sand dabs, are also popular.

The **rex sole** (*Errex zachirus*) and **sand dab** (*Citharichthys sordidus*) are small, abundant Pacific flounders that are sold only pan-ready or trimmed. The rex sole, an excellent eating fish, is very similar in flavor to Atlantic gray sole; the sand dab has its own delicious qualities (see page 252).

## OTHER FLOUNDERS

Other Pacific flounders include **starry flounder**, closely related and similar in flavor to Atlantic winter flounder; **English sole**, a good-flavored small sole, usually sold as fillets; and **Dover sole**, a large, commercially important sole of below-average flavor and texture.

Other Atlantic flounders include the small and thin but tasty **windowpane flounder**, a close relative of the European turbot; and **southern** and **Gulf flounder**, both closely related to summer flounder.

### CHOOSING SUSTAINABLE SEAFOOD

Most flounder are taken by trawl. Although trawling over hard-bottom rock and coral reef is highly destructive, trawling on sandy or muddy seafloor where flatfish live is far less damaging. There is some effect on habitat abundance and species diversity, but overall there is little evidence of long-term adverse effect to fishery habitat. However, repeated trawling of an area selects for smaller, faster-maturing fish. Smaller fish produce fewer eggs, adversely affecting the ability of the fish to replenish themselves.

The various flounders of the Atlantic Coast have been subject to overfishing for years and have undergone serious population declines throughout their range. Efforts to reduce bycatch of flounder in the scallop and other fisheries through improved fishing methods and gear have allowed stocks to begin to recover. Seasonal closures and regulations reducing days at sea have been tough on fishermen, but have had positive effects on sole populations. Flounders are inherently resilient to fishing pressure—they are relatively fast growing and reach maturity early—so the future should bring continued improvement. One of the most important things fishery management can do is continue to encourage the development of gear that reduces bycatch and the catch of immature fish. The government-funded and university-associated Sea Grant programs and conservation groups such as the Manomet Center for Conservation Sciences are working diligently toward this end. Many improved trawl gear designs are being tested.

Southern New England summer flounder has been restored to abundant levels. Georges Bank winter flounder and yellowtail flounder, once severely depleted, have made a comeback thanks to solid fisheries management. Gulf of Maine gray sole populations are in the process of rebuilding. All Pacific Coast flounder populations are healthy and abundant.

## CHOOSING HEALTHY SEAFOOD

Flounders are a very low-fat, high-protein source of B vitamins, vitamin D, and minerals, particularly potassium and selenium.

Wild fish may be susceptible to infective parasites, so care should always be exercised when eating them raw (see Raw Seafood: How to Stay Safe, page 408).

## IN THE KITCHEN

The skin of all flounders is edible and delicious. The bones are excellent for stock; the roe, cheeks, milt, and liver can all be eaten.

Although each flounder is distinctive in flavor, all are generally mild flavored. Because flounder fillets are so thin, they are best prepared quickly sautéed, broiled, steamed, or poached in a flavorful broth. Flounders are particularly rich in protein and neutral in flavor, making them perfect as the base for mousses, sausages, or quenelles.

Flounders are really at their best—moister and more full flavored—when cooked on the bone with the skin on. Any one of the above flounders may be simply trimmed pan-ready and sautéed, charcoal-grilled, or baked (see page 314).

# ROASTED WHOLE SOLE
# WITH BROWN BUTTER–FRIED SAGE

Any of the flounders can be trimmed and cooked whole. Small flounders, under one and a half pounds, are perfect for this dish, and because their small size makes them difficult to fillet they are usually much less expensive than larger fish. Serve with bowtie pasta (farfalle-butterfly) with diced prosciutto fried crisp in butter, fresh peas, and black pepper.

4 tablespoons clarified butter (see page 34)

Four 1-pound petrale sole or other flounders, prepared for cooking whole (see page 33)

Seasoned flour: ¼ cup all-purpose flour mixed with 1½ teaspoons kosher salt and ¼ teaspoon freshly ground black pepper

16 fresh sage leaves

2 tablespoons cold unsalted butter, cut into bits

Juice of 1 lemon

2 tablespoons dry white wine

1. Preheat the oven to 425°F. In a large oven-proof sauté pan or skillet, heat 2 tablespoons of the clarified butter over high heat until shimmering. Dredge the fish in the seasoned flour and sauté for 3 or 4 minutes, or until the fish is crisp and brown. Turn the fish over and put the pan, uncovered, in the hot oven for 6 or 7 minutes, or until the fish is almost opaque throughout.

2. Remove the pan from the oven and set the fish aside on a warmed platter. Add the remaining clarified butter to the pan. Over medium-high heat, fry the sage leaves until they become crisp and aromatic, 1 or 2 minutes. With a slotted spatula, remove them and arrange on top of the sole. Add the cold butter to the pan. When it starts to turn nut brown, add the lemon juice and white wine. Quickly stir to scrape up any browned bits on the bottom of the pan. Pour the browned butter over the sole.

# PANFRIED FLOUNDER FILLETS
# WITH TOMATO-PARSLEY VINAIGRETTE

Fresh bread crumbs toasted golden are what really make this dish stand out. They complement the fresh flavors of the fish and tomato perfectly. This is my daughter Kelley's favorite. Plain boiled potatoes and steamed green beans are perfect companions here; in summer, serve with fresh corn kernels sautéed with red onion, bacon, and basil. For a great sandwich, pair any leftovers with avocado and lettuce.

1 large egg

2 tablespoons milk

2 cups fresh bread crumbs

Four 5-ounce flounder fillets

Seasoned flour: ¼ cup all-purpose flour
    mixed with 1½ teaspoons kosher salt and
    ¼ teaspoon freshly ground black pepper

2 tablespoons unsalted butter

2 tablespoons refined peanut oil or another
    high-heat oil for frying

Tomato-Parsley Vinaigrette (recipe follows)

1. In a shallow bowl, beat the egg and milk until blended. Spread half the bread crumbs on a baking pan; reserve the other half. Dredge the flounder fillets in the seasoned flour, then pass them through the egg wash. Press the flounder fillets into the bread crumbs and sprinkle the reserved bread crumbs over them. Turn the fish over several times to ensure that they are completely coated.

2. In large sauté pan or skillet, melt the butter with the oil over medium-high heat. As soon as the butter stops foaming, lay the flounder fillets in the pan and cook for 3 or 4 minutes on each side, or until golden brown. Using a slotted metal spatula, transfer to a wire rack to drain.

3. Place the flounder fillets on a plate and nap with Tomato-Parsley Vinaigrette.

315

# TOMATO-PARSLEY VINAIGRETTE

MAKES 1 CUP

2 garlic cloves

Large pinch of kosher salt, plus more
   to taste

2 tablespoons minced fresh flat-leaf parsley

2 ripe tomatoes

2 tablespoons red wine vinegar

¼ cup olive oil

Freshly ground black pepper to taste

1. In a wooden bowl, use a pestle to mash the garlic cloves with the pinch of salt. Add the parsley.

2. Cut the tomatoes in half and squeeze out the seeds. Shred the flesh side of the tomato halves on the large holes of a box grater so that they fall into the bowl with the garlic mixture. Whisk the vinegar and olive oil into the tomato mixture to make a vinaigrette, then season with salt and pepper to taste.

# SQUID

To me, fresh squid epitomizes the rewards of searching out seasonal foods. Like many treasures worth making an effort to find, fresh squid is not easy to get your hands on; well-handled squid fresh from the sea is good for only about three days out of the water. Because fresh squid usually takes a day to reach the market, it really only has a two-day shelf life. It's no wonder that much of the squid found in markets today has been previously frozen. Texturally, squid stands up to freezing very well; some cooks even say the texture is improved, but the flavor of fresh squid is incomparable to frozen. It has that indefinable quality that makes a dish jump with flavor.

Three species of squid make up the majority of the U.S. domestic supply of squid. The **Atlantic long-finned squid** (*Loligo pealei*), commonly called **Boston squid**, is found from Massachusetts to

North Carolina. It is caught year-round, but fresh squid is most readily available in the market during spring and summer, when squid populations migrate close to shore. During the winter months, it is caught farther offshore and is more likely to be frozen. The larger and less desirable **short-finned squid** (*Illex illecebrosus*) is found from the Maritime Provinces of Canada to New Jersey. This squid was once harvested almost exclusively for use as bait, but is now accepted as food. The short-finned squid is harvested in summer and fall in deep offshore waters.

The **West Coast market squid** (*Loligo opalescens*), known as **California**, or **Monterey**, **squid**, is available year-round except for short periods in spring and fall when it becomes difficult for fishermen to find. Since 1993, squid has been the number one fishery in California, with landings of well over 100,000 tons yearly. California squid is captured during the winter months in southern California waters, and the fishery is centered in Monterey, California, during the rest of the year. California squid is exclusively an inshore variety, so it is available fresh year-round with little or no drop-off in quality or availability.

The best place to find fresh squid may be straight from dockside markets at the ports where squid is caught. On the East Coast, squid boats fishing the local waters land in ports from Cape May, New Jersey, to Portland, Maine, with the heaviest landings concentrated at Point Judith, Rhode Island. On the West Coast, most squid is captured in southern and central California but may occasionally be found as far north as Oregon.

For the rest of us, fresh squid can be found in Asian, Italian, and Spanish ethnic markets. With its rapidly increasing popularity, fresh squid may also now be found at busy fish markets and occasionally even the local supermarket. Japanese markets carry fresh or frozen Boston squid for sashimi; the West Coast market squid variety is usually too small for this use.

Squid are transparent immediately after capture; their skin is brown or gray and may show phosphorescent spots of color. They generally lose this transparency within a few hours, turning an opaque white by the time they get to market but retaining their brown to gray skin color and firm tubular shape. As squid ages, its natural tubular body begins to sag like a deflated balloon; after time out of the water, the skin turns pink, then red, and finally purple with time.

## CHOOSING SUSTAINABLE SEAFOOD

Squid plays an important role in the world's oceans, and the sound management of its fishery is needed to sustain the marine food web. Not only is squid eaten by numerous marine mammals, ocean birds, and fish, but it is a fierce predator in its own right, preying on fish, shrimp, and many other species.

In recent years, as the demand for California squid has grown, fishing crews from as far away as Washington, Oregon, and Alaska have flocked to California waters in search of it. Until recently, there were no state catch limits, permits, seasons, or boundaries, as other fisheries required. Fortunately, the California State Department of Fish and Game recently developed a sustainable management plan for the squid fishery in state-controlled waters. The plan sets fishing quotas, limits the number of boat permits, and recommends new research and oversight. The good news for many in the fishing community is that after several years of scientific study, a California Department of Fish and Game report found that squid populations on the West Coast appear stable and healthy despite heavy fishing.

To capture squid, boats shine powerful lights on the water at night to attract the squid, which are then encircled by purse-seine nets. This is a very clean fishery with no habitat impact and little bycatch. What bycatch there is—mostly sardines and mackerel—is utilized and accounted for.

On the U.S. Atlantic Coast, the inshore long-finned, or Boston, squid fishery consists of jigging with hooks, trapping, and trawling, while the short-finned squid is caught much farther out to sea by trawl. Squid fisheries are highly focused, so bycatch is minimal; jigging and trapping do not impact habitat. Atlantic Coast squid fisheries have been actively managed for well over a decade and are not considered over-fished.

## CHOOSING HEALTHY SEAFOOD

The squid ranks among the most healthful of seafood and is a nutritionally complete source of protein, containing all the essential amino acids in perfect proportions. This low-fat, high-protein creature contains higher levels of zinc, manganese, and copper than most other types of seafood.

Squid is moderately high in cholesterol, but it is now recognized that very little dietary cholesterol is absorbed by the body; rather, saturated fats found in the diet are the greater source of blood cholesterol. As squid contains very little saturated fat, it may be considered a heart-healthy source of protein. Like other fish and shellfish, squid also contains the omega-3 fatty acids said to improve the blood lipid profile, lower triglycerides, and modestly raise HDL cholesterol.

Current advice by the American Heart Association warns people with heart disease to limit their cholesterol intake to no more than 200 mg per day. If followed, that restriction should not unduly constrain anyone from eating squid, particularly if it's not battered, breaded, or fried. Eating a balanced diet low in saturated fats is the best way to maintain good heart health.

## IN THE KITCHEN

Cooking squid is simple if you understand one of its basic characteristics: Squid, lacking any internal skeletal support, have evolved a network of strong internal connective tissues intimately distributed throughout their muscle tissue to help support their bodies. The proteins

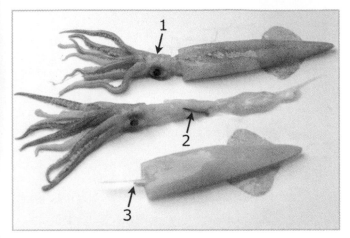

ARROW NO. 1 INDICATES WHERE TO CUT AWAY THE TENTACLES, ARROW NO. 2 POINTS TO THE INK SAC HIDDEN AMONG THE VISCERA, AND ARROW NO. 3 SHOWS THE CLEAR, QUILL-SHAPED BACKBONE PROTRUDING FROM THE BODY SAC.

in these connective tissues form very tough, elastic bonds if not cooked correctly. The rule for cooking squid is "Three minutes or thirty but nothing in between." In other words, squid should be cooked very quickly over high heat, as in deep-frying, charcoal-grilling, or parboiling; or very slowly for a long period of time, as in stewing or braising. The first method does not give the protein a chance to form bonds and become elastic; the second method allows these bonds to form but breaks them apart again by extended cooking.

It doesn't matter if you charcoal-grill squid and serve it with pineapple salsa, quickly sauté it with sweet and hot chiles, or stew it in red wine and leeks. If you follow the above rule, your squid will always be tender.

Squid ink can be used in making black pasta or Spanish *arroz negro*, which is seasoned with squid ink, or in making a sauce for squid in its own ink (*calamare en su tinta*). Although frozen

ink can be purchased in little packages, it is easy to save the silvery little ink sacs when cleaning squid. Easily recognized, they look like a drop of mercury that has escaped from a thermometer.

Some people always remove the skin from squid when cleaning it and other people never do. For reasons unknown even to me, I leave the skin on California squid but remove it from Boston squid.

Large Boston squid can be sliced for sashimi after a thirty-second dip in hot water to firm up the texture.

### CLEANING SQUID

Grasp the squid body in one hand and the head with tentacles in the other. Gently and evenly pull the head and body in opposite directions, separating the two parts. Most of the entrails will remain attached to the head and be pulled out of the body (see photo). Cut off the tentacles just above the eye (arrow No. 1 in photo) and squeeze out the garbanzo bean–shaped beak from the center of the tentacles. Reserve the small silver-blue ink sac (arrow No. 2 in photo) found among the entrails and discard the rest.

Pull the quill-shaped backbone (arrow No. 3 in photo) out of the body. Rinse the body cavity well with cold running water, using a finger to be sure all viscera is washed away. To remove the skin, scrape with a knife held at a ninety-degree angle to the body; the skin will easily detach in sheets. Cut the body into rings, if desired.

# THAI-STYLE SQUID SALAD

A healthy and delicious technique often used in Thai cooking is to quickly sear, char, or blanch squid, then immerse it in a dressing while it is still hot. The quick cooking causes the protein fibers to contract; after immersion in the dressing, the fibers relax and quickly absorb the flavorful liquid. The squid really soak up the flavor but don't get tough and dry from a long marinade. This technique also works well for octopus, shrimp, and lobster—all of which have similar muscle structure.

Serve this dish with steamed rice or rice noodles.

**DRESSING**

⅜ cup fish sauce

½ cup freshly squeezed lime juice

1 tablespoon toasted sesame oil

1 tablespoon sugar

2 garlic cloves, minced

1-inch piece ginger, peeled and minced

2 Thai bird or serrano chiles, seeded
    and minced

2 pounds squid, cleaned (see page 320)
    and cut into rings

1 small sweet red onion, very thinly sliced

2 carrots, peeled and shredded

⅜ cup julienned fresh mint leaves

⅜ cup julienned fresh cilantro leaves

Leaves from 1 head tender lettuce, torn
    into bite-sized pieces

1. For the dressing: In a large bowl, combine all the ingredients and whisk to blend. Set aside.

2. Bring a gallon of salted water to a boil in a stockpot. Add the squid and cover. As soon as the water comes back to a rolling boil, give the squid a stir and turn off the heat. Let stand for about 1 minute. Drain, rinse quickly under cool water, and add to the bowl with the dressing.

3. Marinate the squid in the dressing for 20 minutes, stirring occasionally. Add the onion, carrots, mint, and cilantro to the squid and toss gently. Divide the lettuce among 4 plates and spoon the squid salad over the lettuce.

# SQUID AND CHICKPEA TAGINE
# WITH HARISSA AND PRESERVED LEMONS

A tagine is both a savory stew and the North African conical-shaped clay cooking pot in which the stew is traditionally cooked. Any heavy pot with a cover can be used to make this tagine.

A recipe for Preserved Lemons is provided, but the process takes one month; preserved lemons can also be purchased. Serve this dish on a bed of couscous made with chopped dried apricots, toasted almonds, and grated lemon zest.

2 tablespoons olive oil

1 onion, diced (about 1 cup)

3 garlic cloves, crushed and minced

2 pounds squid, cleaned (see page 320) and cut into rings

2 tomatoes, chopped (about 1 cup)

¾ cup dry white wine

1¼ cups chicken broth

One 15-ounce can chickpeas, drained and rinsed, or ¾ cup dried chickpeas, soaked overnight and cooked until tender (about 2½ hours)

⅓ cup finely chopped Preserved Lemons (recipe follows)

1 to 2 tablespoons Harissa, to taste (recipe follows)

¼ cup chopped fresh cilantro

Salt to taste

1. In a heavy pot, heat the olive oil over medium heat. Add the onion and cook, stirring occasionally, until soft and beginning to brown. Add the garlic and cook for 1 minute, then add the squid and stir briskly. Add the tomatoes and cook 1 minute longer.

2. Add all the remaining ingredients except for the cilantro and salt. Bring to a boil, reduce the heat to a steady simmer, cover, and cook for 30 minutes, or until the squid is fork-tender. Add the cilantro and season with salt; simmer 2 to 3 minutes longer.

## PRESERVED LEMONS

8 to 10 organic lemons, scrubbed

Kosher or sea salt as needed (about ½ cup)

1 tablespoon black peppercorns

1 tablespoon coriander seeds

Freshly squeezed lemon juice as needed (about ½ cup)

1. Cut each lemon into 6 lengthwise sections from the top to within ½ inch of the bottom, taking care to leave the pieces attached. Fill each cut with as much salt as it will hold. Place the lemons in a sterilized wide-mouth quart jar, adding a few black peppercorns and coriander seeds as you go. Compress the lemons when adding them until no space is left.

2. Add lemon juice as needed to reach almost to the top of the jar. Cover the jar tightly. Let the lemons stand at room temperature for 1 month, turning the jar upside down periodically to distribute the salt and juices.

3. To use the lemons, remove from the brine and rinse well. Once opened, store in the refrigerator, where they will keep up to 6 months.

## HARISSA

MAKES ½ CUP

In Tunisia, where harissa originated, the local Aleppo peppers are dried and coarsely ground with salt and olive oil, giving this chile paste its distinct flavor and texture. I'm lucky enough to have a small Middle Eastern grocery within walking distance of my house that sells moist, coarsely ground Aleppo pepper. For my taste, this creates a harissa whose grainy texture and sweet, hot, tart flavor rise above the pack. Ground Aleppo pepper is also available on the Internet.

½ teaspoon cumin seeds

2 tablespoons coriander seeds

¼ teaspoon caraway seeds

4 tablespoons ground Aleppo pepper

Pinch of ground cinnamon

1 garlic clove

Large pinch of coarse salt

2 tablespoons olive oil

Freshly squeezed juice of ½ lemon,
    preferably a Meyer

Hot water as needed

1. In a small dry sauté pan or skillet, toast the cumin, coriander, and caraway seeds over a medium-low heat until lightly darkened and fragrant, about 2 minutes. Grind in a spice grinder or mortar and stir in the Aleppo pepper and cinnamon.

2. Using a mortar and pestle, pound the garlic and salt together to form a paste. Mix in the spice paste, olive oil, lemon juice, and enough hot water to form a thin paste. Store in the refrigerator in a covered container, with a thin layer of oil poured over the surface of the harissa, for up to 1 month.

SQUID

## FRIED SQUID WITH SWEET PEPPERS, HOT CHILES, AND SHREDDED GINGER

More squid is landed in Point Judith, Rhode Island, than any other port on the Eastern Seaboard, so naturally squid is a local favorite. Batter-fried squid tossed with chopped pickled Italian peppers is a popular dish at beachside clam shacks; the vinegar and spice of the pickled peppers season the squid.

For a lighter version of Point Judith–style squid, use a dusting of flour and cornstarch for a tempura-like coating and make a quick pickle with fresh peppers. Early fall is a great time for this recipe; the markets are full of a variety of sweet peppers and hot chiles. I like to use thin-skinned sweet salad peppers, such as gypsy, banana, or sweet Italian peppers, but a variety of colored bell peppers as can be found in most supermarkets are fine. Mix the sweet peppers with an equal amount of mildly hot fresh chiles, such as New Mexico, Anaheim, poblano, pepperoncini, or wax peppers. Choose a variety of colors for eye appeal.

Note that to reuse the oil for deep frying seafood, strain it through a fine-meshed sieve, let cool, and refrigerate.

1 tablespoon olive oil

¾ cup julienned sweet peppers in a variety of colors

¾ cup julienned mildly hot chiles in a variety of colors

3-inch piece fresh ginger, peeled and shredded or finely julienned

Juice of 1 lemon

½ cup cider or rice wine vinegar

½ cup water

1 tablespoon sugar

¼ cup coarsely chopped fresh flat-leaf parsley

Refined peanut or another high-heat oil for frying

½ cup all-purpose flour

½ cup cornstarch

1 tablespoon kosher salt

2 pounds squid, cleaned, with tentacles reserved and bodies cut into rings

1. In a large sauté pan or skillet, heat the olive oil over high heat until shimmering. Add the julienned peppers and chiles and sauté for 1 or 2 minutes. Add the ginger and sauté for 1 minute. Add the lemon juice, vinegar, water, sugar, and parsley. Bring to a quick boil and turn off the heat. Set aside and let cool to room temperature.

2. In a Dutch oven or deep fryer, heat 3 to 4 inches oil to 375°F. Place the flour, cornstarch, and salt in a large paper bag. Add the squid to the bag and shake well to thoroughly coat with the flour mixture. Remove the squid from the bag and shake off any excess. Fry in batches, not crowding the pan, for 3 or 4 minutes, or until golden brown. Let the oil return to the correct temperature between batches. Using a wire skimmer, transfer the squid to a wire rack to drain.

3. Spoon the peppers and some of their liquid over the freshly cooked squid and serve.

# STRIPED BASS, FARMED

After wild striped bass stocks nearly collapsed from overfishing and pollution in the 1980s, the fishery was severely restricted. The aquaculture industry responded by creating a **hybrid striped bass**—a cross between a female striped bass (*Morone saxatilus*) and a male freshwater white bass (*M. chrysops*). The result? A functionally sterile offspring that is hardy and quick growing and can be reared in freshwater.

Unfortunately, the hybrid striper is far less majestic in appearance and flavor than its wild parents. It has a shorter, stouter, more perchlike appearance than wild striped bass, and its stripes are broken and jagged. Yet with its consistent availability and freshness, mild flavor, and agreeable texture, the hybrid striper fits a niche.

Hybrid stripers are grown in ponds and tanks throughout the southern United States and California. The best-quality fish are raised in tanks where filtration, UV light, and ozone are used to offset the mossy flavor that is sometimes associated with pond-raised fish.

Farmed striped bass are usually marketed at one to three pounds, and are most popular in markets that appreciate whole-fish preparations. Hybrid stripers are common in Chinese markets, where they're found in live tanks as well as on the counter. They can also be found in Japanese markets, where they may be sold for sashimi.

Hybrid striped bass should be firm-fleshed, with a bright appearance and red gills. Live

## Wanted: Dead or Alive

Live fish and the tank they are in should appear healthy and fresh; by this I mean sparkling clean water and no dead fish. Fish that have chewed-up tails and fins, streams of skin hanging from their bodies, or obvious injuries such as blinded white eyeballs have been in the tank too long; they are stressed from crowding and bumping up against the spines of other fish.

Fish from crowded and dirty tanks will taste old even though they are alive. A freshly caught fish on ice will taste better than a live fish that has been in a crowded or dirty tank too long.

The same holds true for lobsters and crabs, although at times it is more difficult to determine whether a lobster or crab has been in a tank too long or the tank is dirty. Often a lobster tank will appear clean but has unwanted bacteria growing in it. If a crab or lobster's shell feels slimy and slippery, it has been in the tank too long or the tank is dirty; if the shell feels dry and coarse, the animal is fresh and the tank is clean.

Clams, mussels, and oysters generally do not do well in typical live tanks designed for retail stores. The tanks don't provide enough oxygen, so the animals quickly weaken, and even if they don't die, their flesh becomes mushy and soft. Specialty tanks built for mollusks allow water to cascade over the shellfish, keeping them damp and cool without actually submerging them. Buy live clams, mussels, and oysters from this type of tank, built specifically for mollusks, or buy them iced from the counter. Never buy shellfish stored in still, unaerated water as I sometimes see in Chinatown; they are guaranteed to be dead.

stripers and the tank they are in should appear healthy and fresh; by this I mean the water should be sparkling clean, with no dead fish floating around. Remember: Live fish that come from a dirty tank can taste like the water they've been held in. It is worth the extra money to buy live fish in Chinatown and have them cleaned for you. Fish on the counter are very likely to have died in the tank and been transferred to the counter.

### CHOOSING SUSTAINABLE SEAFOOD

Farm-raised hybrid stripers are grown in closed-system freshwater ponds, which have little impact on the environment. Fish meal is used in hybrid striped bass food, however, which impacts wild fish (see Fishing Down the Food Chain, page 48).

### CHOOSING HEALTHY SEAFOOD

Farmed striped bass are a low-fat source of protein—although lower in omega-3s than wild seafood—and are very low in saturated fats and free of environmental pollutants and parasites because they are grown in closed system tanks and do not eat live wild food.

### IN THE KITCHEN

Hybrid striped bass can be used for any whole-fish recipes, from baking in rock salt to steaming or frying. Chinese chefs like to steam a one- or two-pound whole hybrid striped bass. Japanese chefs prefer to buy the largest fish, which they usually slice and serve raw as sashimi (though its mild flavor is not the most highly regarded). Hybrid striper also maintains good texture in uncooked marinated dishes.

# STEAMED WHOLE BASS
# WITH GINGER AND SPRING ONIONS

SERVES 2 AS A MAIN COURSE

At the age of thirteen, my friend Freddy Fong came to the United States from a small Chinese village just north of Macao. Soon after he stepped off the boat, he began working in the fish markets of Oakland's Chinatown, where he still works today at the age of seventy.

Live fish is a specialty of the Cantonese cuisine Freddy grew up with. On a recent visit to China, Freddy found that most of the fish now available in his village are the same aquacultured species that are available in the United States. A recently introduced species, hybrid striped bass, has become very popular. Although the fish is new to the area, the most common cooking method, steaming, has been practiced for centuries.

In Cantonese cooking, strong spices are used to mask stale seafood. The freshest seafood is cooked simply with very few spices so that its natural fresh flavors are accentuated. Serve this dish with steamed rice and braised mustard greens seasoned with rice wine vinegar.

1 whole striped bass, 2 to 2½ pounds,
   cleaned and dressed (see page 33)
Kosher salt for sprinkling
8 or 10 spring onions or scallions
One 3-inch piece fresh ginger, peeled
2 tablespoons soy sauce
3 tablespoons Asian-style unrefined
   peanut oil
Cilantro sprigs for garnish
Black Bean Dipping Sauce (recipe follows)

1. Sprinkle the fish inside and out with kosher salt. Put 3 or 4 spring onions or scallions on a plate that will fit in your steamer and place the fish on top of them. Cut half the ginger into thin coins (a mandoline works well for this) and arrange them on top of the fish. Reserve the remaining onions or scallions and ginger for finishing the dish.

2. In a wok, steamer, or large pot, bring 2 or 3 inches of water to a rolling boil. Set the plate with the fish in a steamer basket or on top of a trivet, cover, and cook until the fish is almost opaque throughout, about 15 minutes.

3. You may serve the fish from its steaming plate or transfer it and its juices to a platter. Pour the soy sauce over the fish. Using the largest holes of a box grater, shred the rest of the ginger over the fish. Julienne the remaining spring onions or scallions and scatter them over the fish. In a small, heavy saucepan, heat the peanut oil over high heat until smoking hot, then pour the oil over the fish, ginger, and scallions. Garnish with the cilantro and serve with Black Bean Dipping Sauce.

STRIPED BASS, FARMED

329

# BLACK BEAN DIPPING SAUCE

¼ cup soy sauce

2 tablespoons rice wine vinegar

2 tablespoons dry sherry or Shaoxing wine

1 teaspoon minced jalapeño or
    serrano chile

1 teaspoon minced Chinese black beans

1 teaspoon sugar

In a small saucepan, combine all the ingredients. Bring to a boil and allow to cool before serving.

NOTE: Bamboo steamers or metal trivets that fit inside a wok for steaming are available in Chinatowns and many stores. An alternative is to use a plate positioned on three overturned heatproof cups inside a large pot.

# STRIPED BASS, WILD

The **striped bass** (*Saxone marone*) is a quick-growing voracious hunter that swiftly grows to twenty pounds, and may ultimately reach seventy-five pounds in weight. Sea green fades to silver along its sides, and eight dark lateral stripes decorate its flanks, giving the striper its name.

Stripers range along the entire East Coast, with the strongest concentrations found between Cape Cod and the Chesapeake Bay. During the winter months, the fishery focuses on the northern neck of Virginia and environs of Chesapeake Bay. In spring, schools of striped bass migrate northward to take up summer residence in the inshore coastal waters of Long Island Sound and southern New England. Chesapeake-area fish are most often taken by gill net, while stripers taken from its northern range may only be taken by rod and reel or fish trap. Stripers taken by these methods and then immediately iced by a conscientious fisherman are of incomparable quality.

Fresh striper fillets, usually sold with the skin on, are moist and sparkling in appearance; the color varies from translucent white to pink. The dark red hemoglobin-rich muscle tissue found just under the skin should be intensely red. Really fresh striper may have a rainbow sheen of color where the meat has been sliced across the grain. Fish with any obvious bruising or dry and discolored flesh should be avoided.

Whole striped bass are generally sold with the head on and gills and guts in, so all the signs of freshness are right there to read: a lively, full, firm appearance; bright bulging eyes and red gills; and firmness to the point of rigor. The naturally-occurring protective coating of slime should be clear and viscous, not clotted, curdled, or yellow.

Wild striped bass can easily be found in the fish markets of New England and the Atlantic states. It is sold across the country in upscale markets such as Whole Foods and fresh-fish markets. Striper is also very popular in restaurants. On the West Coast, it is considered a sport fish only and is not captured commercially.

### CHOOSING SUSTAINABLE SEAFOOD
Pollution and overfishing contributed to the precipitous decline of striped bass populations during the 1980s, bringing the species to the brink of commercial extinction. A controversial fisheries management plan was put in place, which implemented drastic measures.

Attesting to the plan's success, striped bass stocks have fully recovered from their formerly depleted levels and are once again important commercial and recreational fisheries. The Maryland striped bass is currently under review for MSC certification as a sustainable fishery.

### CHOOSING HEALTHY SEAFOOD
Striped bass is a very good low-fat, high-protein source of B vitamins, minerals, and omega-3 fatty acids, which lower blood cholesterol, have an anti-inflammatory effect, and enhance brain function, among other health benefits.

In the past, consumption advisories have been issued for striped bass from industrialized areas known to have sedimentary accumulation of organic pollutants such as PCBs and dioxin (see Persistent Organic Pollutants, page 417), the most notable being for striped bass spawning in the Hudson River. Water conditions have improved dramatically since Congress passed the Clean Water Act in 1972, and the levels of organic pollutants in stripers have declined significantly.

To avoid risk of exposure to pollutants, do not eat the oldest and very largest fish, and follow the suggestions on page 417 for reducing the risk of pollutants.

### IN THE KITCHEN
Striped bass is moderately fatty, with a large, firm flake and rich flavor, making it adaptable to many methods of cooking and recipes. Add a forgiving nature that lets it stay moist, and it's

no wonder the striped bass has become a favorite in the kitchens of America's restaurants.

Small fish, simply gutted and scaled, are moist and delicious when baked in rock salt. Skin-on fillets can be charcoal-grilled or sautéed; the skin crisps nicely under high heat and is edible. Skinless fillets are perfect poached, braised, or *en papillote*. Seldom parasitized, striped bass can also be used for raw fish preparations.

The rich flavor of striped bass pairs well with a variety of sauces and ingredients. Mild sauces bring out the ocean-sweet flavor of the fish, while stronger-flavored sauces complement rather than overpower.

The roe, cheeks, and liver of the striped bass are all considered delicacies today, but do read the suggestions for reducing exposure to pollutants (see Persistent Organic Pollutants, page 417). The bones are superb for making a rich-flavored stock thick with natural gelatins.

Early colonists who first fished striped bass were particularly enamored with the "marrow" found in the striped bass's head. The flesh of the fish was usually salted for the winter larder, while a meal was made of its head and the delicious substance found therein.

## STRIPED BASS AND SEASHELL PASTA BAKED WITH OLIVES, TOMATOES, AND GOAT CHEESE

SERVES 4 AS A MAIN COURSE

This is a nice one-dish meal for busy weeknights, because it allows the cook time to relax while the fish is in the oven. This recipe works well with any white fish, as well as salmon, opah, sturgeon, or even shrimp or scallops.

Be sure the pasta is cooked not quite al dente when it goes into the casserole so it does not overcook. Laura Chenel's goat cheese, which is available in most supermarkets, is perfect for this recipe: Its light, smooth, and creamy texture binds the tomatoes in a nice light sauce.

CONTINUED

12 ounces small seashell or other small
shaped dried pasta such as orecchiette

8 tablespoons olive oil

1 cup oil- or salt-cured black olives such as
kalamata or gaeta

1½ pounds tomatoes, seeded (see page 39)
and chopped, about 3 cups

½ cup chopped scallions, including light
green parts

Juice of 1 lemon

1 tablespoon minced fresh dill, marjoram,
or oregano

Salt and freshly ground black pepper
to taste

5 ounces mild fresh goat cheese such
as Laura Chenel's

Four 5-ounce striped bass fillets

¼ cup fresh bread crumbs drizzled with
olive oil

1. Preheat the oven to 350°F. In a large pot of salted boiling water, cook the pasta until not quite al dente, about 9 minutes. Drain and mix with 4 tablespoons of the olive oil; place in a 2½-quart ovenproof casserole.

2. Place the olives between clean kitchen towels and pound lightly with a mallet or saucepan; pick out and discard the pits.

3. In a medium bowl, combine the remaining 4 tablespoons olive oil, the pitted olives, tomatoes, scallions, lemon juice, and herbs. Stir to blend and season with salt and pepper. Pour the tomato mixture over the pasta.

4. Cut the goat cheese into small chunks and distribute evenly throughout the sauce, pushing some of the cheese well down into the sauce and leaving some on top. Nestle the fish into the sauce so it is not quite submerged, and sprinkle the bread crumbs evenly on top of the pasta and fish. Bake for 20 minutes, or until the sauce begins to bubble, the crumbs are browned, and the fish is cooked almost opaque throughout.

# STRIPED BASS WITH BRAISED FENNEL

One of the classic pairings in fish cookery is that of sea bass and fennel. Striped bass and fennel, both at their tender young best in the spring, shine in this simple but flavorful dish. It pairs nicely with braised artichokes, roasted asparagus, or sautéed sugar snap peas, along with some roasted potatoes.

2 small fennel bulbs, trimmed and cored
   (reserve fennel fronds for garnish)
1 organic lemon
2 leeks, white part only, halved lengthwise
   and rinsed
Kosher salt and freshly ground black
   pepper to taste
8 tablespoons olive oil
Four 5-ounce striped bass fillets
Juice of 1 lemon
½ cup dry white wine

1. Preheat the oven to 425°F. Using a mandoline or sharp knife, slice the fennel ⅛ inch thick. Cut the ends off the lemon, then cut it in half lengthwise. Slice the lemon halves into thin half-moons, and remove any seeds as you cut. Chop the leeks finely.

2. In a bowl, combine the fennel, lemon slices, chopped leeks, salt, pepper, and 4 tablespoons of the olive oil. Toss to mix. Press this mixture into the bottom of a 10-inch cast-iron skillet.

3. Heat the skillet over high heat until the fennel begins to sizzle, about 2 minutes, then bake for 10 minutes.

4. Season the striped bass fillet with salt and pepper to taste and place on the bed of fennel, skin-side up. Pour the remaining 4 tablespoons olive oil and the lemon juice over the fish and bake for 10 minutes per inch of thickness, or until almost opaque throughout.

5. Use a spatula to turn the fish and fennel mixture out of the pan and onto 4 plates. Stir the white wine into the pan juices, scraping up any of the loose braised fennel mixture. Bring to a boil and divide the pan juices evenly over the fish. Garnish with minced fennel fronds.

NOTE: If you're looking for even more flavor, the tapenade can be thinned with fresh orange juice and olive oil to make a nice sauce (see Orange-Scented Olive Tapenade, page 381).

## Trap Fishing on Narragansett Bay

I've known Al Glidden for twenty-five years, and during that time he has remained a fisherman set in his ways and proud of it. Al lives by himself in a small cottage looking out over the dunes to the Atlantic. Some of the best-quality fish we buy year in and year out comes from Al's fish trap, set in Narragansett Bay. His fish is always perfectly handled and impeccably fresh, arriving in San Francisco the afternoon of the same day it comes from the sea.

Al's a good fisherman and a fanatic about quality, but he has little time for the conventions of the business world. He throws most paperwork away after a few days, his packout slips detailing the fish he sends us are incomprehensible or nonexistent, and his billing system was developed before the advent of computers. When it rains at the South Shore, which is often, his phone doesn't work. So, the only communication we receive is likely to be boxes of fresh fish showing up at the airport.

He's infuriating in the way he does business and exasperating in his resistance to change, but when Al sends us glistening fish only hours from the sea, all the rest is forgiven. Not only does the first trap-fish of spring provide welcome relief from the days of winter storms and poor supply, but it has the ability to assuage some of the cynicism I develop through the winter months. And most important, it reminds me why I'm in the seafood business: an appreciation for the qualities of truly fresh fish and a resolve to sell only the best. In August, I took a trip with Al on the *Amelia Bucolo* to see what trap fishing is all about.

### THE *AMELIA BUCOLO*

At 5:30 a.m., I joined the crew of eight as they made final preparations to leave the dock. This consisted mostly of drinking sugary-sweet coffee, eating donuts, and trying to wake up while taking on ice. The sixty-five-foot steel-hulled flat-decked *Amelia Bucolo* is painted dull black from stem to stern and keel to mast. It looks as much like a coal barge as a fishing boat, but is perfectly fitted for the hard work of tending the fish trap. We steamed out the inner channel past the breakwater with two longboats that look as if they could have been used to chase whales in the nineteenth century and two small wooden skiffs in tow. Casting a glance at the orange orb sitting atop the dunes behind the salt pond, Al said, "It's gonna be wicked hot today."

About half an hour from the dock, old Joe, who was at the pilot wheel, asked me how I felt, letting me know that "this is the kind of sea that makes you sick, a big, smooth, oily lump and a roll." "Thanks," I said. Before long, we passed the point and came up on the trap just off Scarborough Beach. We quickly got busy, and I was able to think of something other than the "oily lump" Joe put in my head. "This is a place that has been fished in the same way for hundreds of years," Al said. Fish traps built of wooden stakes driven into the bay bottom were being used by Native Americans to fish squeteague, scup, and tautog when the first Europeans came to the shores of America. Today's fishermen tend traps constructed of cotton netting or a combination of stakes and nets, and use the same native names to describe the fish they catch.

The fish trap turned out to be a much larger and more complex operation than I had imagined. Anchored against the tides by twenty 1,000-pound anchors, the trap was set in about forty feet of water a quarter of a mile offshore. A hedge made of cotton lines, called the leader, ran perpendicular to the beach for twelve hundred feet. This interrupts the fish as they hunt the tide line, turning them away from shore to deeper water and into the trap. The "wings," two large walls of net, direct them into the funnel-shaped opening of the trap and into the "kitchen." The trap is a large shoebox-shaped labyrinth of net rooms, each named after various rooms in a house by some long-forgotten fisherman.

After the fish pass through the "parlor" they enter the "bedroom," or nozzle end of the trap. They are supposed to be inextricably trapped here, unable to navigate the maze back to freedom, but old Joe thinks they come and go as they please—the haul is really just the unlucky ones who happen to be in the trap when it's pulled.

"These traps work by simply confusing the fish," Al explained. "If they were just a little smarter they could find their way back out. It's kind of like young Jimmy here: The longer he's in the bar at night, the harder it is for him to find his way out." Jimmy had been the last onboard that morning, making a leap for the deck as we chugged away from the dock. He managed a sheepish grin.

## TENDING THE TRAP

The crew worked quickly and efficiently, unhitching the longboats and the skiffs. The two longboats have motor-driven winches to help pull, but most of the work is done by hand. We hitched one side of the trap's nozzle, where the fish are, to the *Amelia Bucolo*; the longboats and skiffs are dispatched to the other three sides. After twenty minutes of strenuous pulling and tying off on all four sides, the area allowed the fish became ever smaller, until Al called, "Ah, there's striper at home, finest kind." Other fish began to appear: bluefish, scup, shad, fluke. Suddenly, the net swarmed with fish and the water was alive. Even a few lobsters and a handful of spider crabs had somehow found their way in and were being bullied around in the melee.

CONTINUED

A huge thorny ray of close to two hundred pounds appeared, gliding across the surface. Old Joe simply reached out and grabbed his tail, threw a quick line around it, and hauled the ray to a standstill. With the help of the *Amelia*'s boom, the giant ray was easily raised up and over the edge of the net. Allowed to slide away into the green, he appeared unaware of his close call and unseemly treatment and slowly cruised away.

When fish began to jump and flutter across the surface, we stopped pulling. Seemingly hundreds of fish were contained in the small area left to them. A small dip net attached to the *Amelia*'s boom helped the crew brail, or scoop, the fish out of the trap and onto the deck. As the fish hit the deck, they jumped and thrashed in unison, a sparkling blizzard of seawater, scales, and fish. When the fish were all onboard and settled down, the crew waded through the pile, sorting, picking, and choosing. Scup, bluefish, and fluke went into separate boxes; tautog were chased out the scuppers because the season is closed. The largest stripers went into a box, while obvious shorts were thrown over the side. Anything close got measured, but even a half inch short sent them back to freedom; about 80 percent of the stripers went back.

That day was a poor day: A couple boxes of blues, scup, and shad, no money there; half a box of fluke and two hundred pounds of striper would be enough to pay the crew and fuel. Al, who owns the trap, would have to wait for another, better day.

When all the fish was onboard, the netting was released back into the sea and settled back into the maze that so easily fooled these fish. The sea was glassy smooth and undisturbed, with just a wisp of mist yet to burn off. The longboats were slowly rowed backed to the *Amelia Bucolo* and lashed in place. We headed back.

## SUSTAINABLE FISHING

On the way in, one of the crew sat down next to the fluke with a short, stubby knife, and started poking them one by one, first the vein near the gills and then again by the tail. "This way they bleed out and the meat stays nice and white for the sushi market," he explained. Everyone else finished sorting, icing, and cleaning up. The best thing about trap fishing, after the quality, is that everything comes up alive and can be released. By the end of the day about a hundred stripers, ten or twelve tautogs, a half dozen squeteagues, and the giant thorny ray had all been released alive. I lauded the crew for their care of the discard. "Earlier in the year when the scup were running heavy, we sometimes had to cut fifty thousand pounds loose," Joe said from the pilot house. "Regulations say we can only keep a thousand pounds a day. We got so tired of brailling we sewed a zipper in the side of the net so we could just open it up and let 'em go. At least when you're trapping, you can let 'em go. If we'd been a dragger, there'd have been fifty thousand pounds of scup floatin' belly up for the seagulls."

# STURGEON

Sturgeon first appeared on earth some 300 million years ago and had little trouble surviving two major mass extinctions in the eons that followed. For the hardy sturgeon, the demise of 95 percent of all marine life 250 million years ago and the subsequent fall of the dinosaur 65 million years ago caused barely a ripple. Little, in fact, would perturb this fish until just over one hundred years ago, when humankind deemed that salted sturgeon eggs—caviar—were a delicacy.

Caviar has been enjoyed in areas around the Caspian Sea for centuries, but the international appreciation of caviar is very recent. It wasn't until the late nineteenth century that the French first began importing Caspian Sea caviars, and only since the introduction of refrigerated transportation has the type of caviar we enjoy today—low-salt malossal—become popular.

In the late 1800s, Hudson River sturgeon was so plentiful it was referred to as "Albany beef," while in the western United States, white sturgeon caviar was served as a free bar snack much like popcorn and peanuts are today. But both the **Atlantic sturgeon** (*Acipenser oxyrinchus*) and the **Pacific Northwest white sturgeon** (*A. transmontanus*) were driven to the verge of extinction by the sudden worldwide demand for caviar. After the turn of the century, so few sturgeon were left that all the American sturgeon fisheries closed.

Today, wise management of the sturgeon fishery has returned a few Pacific Northwest sturgeon populations in Oregon and Washington to stable or increasingly abundant levels. The Columbia River is home to the largest population of white sturgeon, and the Willapa, Chehalis, Quinault, Queets, and other Northwest rivers also have healthy populations. Commercial and recreational fisheries alike are restricted to fish between forty-two and sixty inches long, which ensures that the largest breeding fish are protected. Northwest sturgeon populations have been successfully managed since the 1950s.

Until wild stocks are rebuilt, aquaculture appears to be the future of sturgeon and sturgeon caviar. Stolt Sea Farm of California now grows white sturgeon in an environmentally friendly manner and produces caviar of excellent quality under the Sterling Caviar label. Last year they sold eight tons of caviar and millions of pounds of sturgeon throughout the United States. Other farms in Florida and British Columbia are preparing to join Stolt in producing American sturgeon and caviar.

When buying sturgeon, look for white fillets with a bright yellow layer of fat on the backside and between the large, firm flakes of meat. Avoid muddy, mildewed, or musty-smelling fish or those with bruising.

Aquacultured sturgeon is available year-round. Wild sturgeon are at their peak of availability during the winter.

### CHOOSING SUSTAINABLE SEAFOOD

Although sturgeon can live for more than one hundred years and may produce 6 million eggs, they often don't mature until age twenty, may not breed every year, and are extremely vulnerable to overfishing, pollution, and habitat loss from dams. Today fifteen of the world's sturgeon species—including our own Atlantic sturgeon—are listed as endangered. Black Sea and Caspian Sea sturgeon are all endangered or threatened.

Scientists, fishermen, and fishing industry groups have finally realized that the sturgeon stocks in the Caspian and Black seas are on the verge of extinction. Many have begun lobbying governments to stop all sturgeon fishing before it is too late. In June of 2006, Romania, a top-five exporter of beluga caviar, announced a ban on all commercial sturgeon fishing for the next ten years.

NOTE: Caviar Emptor, a coalition of SeaWeb, Pew Institute for Ocean Science, and the Natural Resources Defense Council, has called for a halt to the international trade in beluga caviar and reduced export quotas for other endangered wild sturgeon. They have encouraged international funding for improved management and enforcement and petitioned the U.S. government to list beluga sturgeon under the U.S. Endangered Species Act, resulting in the U.S. ban on beluga caviar from both the Caspian and Black seas. As Americans consume 60 percent of the world's beluga caviar, this ban will have real impact on beluga sturgeon stocks.

## CHOOSING HEALTHY SEAFOOD

Wild sturgeons are bottom feeders and favor brackish areas and rivers where pollutants from both industrial and agricultural sources may accumulate. Some river systems where sturgeon are found, such as the Quinault, Hoh, and Queets rivers of the Olympic rain forest, are very clean; others, such as the Columbia, may not be. Guidelines for reducing the risk of pollutants can be found in the Glossary of Health and Safety Concerns (see page 411).

Aquacultured sturgeon are free of pollutants and parasites because they are grown in closed system tanks and do not eat live, wild food.

NOTE: Although sturgeon do not have scales, they do have large bony diamond-shaped plates called scoots on their sides and back. Because some people consider scoots scales, there is disagreement as to whether or not sturgeon should be prohibited for those with religious-based dietary restrictions.

## American Caviar

Caviars from the Caspian and Black seas are the finest in the world. The unctuous steel-gray beluga, the rich, nutty osetra, and the delightfully briny sevruga are without equal.

Unfortunately, these fine caviars have become an increasingly rarefied delicacy. That's because the sturgeons that produce them are endangered or threatened. The effects of pollution, loss of spawning habitat, increased poaching due to the economic havoc caused by the breakup of the Soviet Union, and overfishing have proven to be devastating to sturgeon populations. Some populations are nearing extinction.

The world body Convention on International Trade of Endangered Species (CITES) has agreed to restrict Caspian Sea caviar exports to a fraction of what they once were. Iran, long a producer of premium caviars, seems to be following procedures for monitoring and replenishing the Caspian sturgeon better than other countries.

One could make the argument, as some do, that sturgeon fishing in the Caspian and Black Seas should be stopped completely until the fish have had a chance to recover. The problem with this plan is that income from caviar sales supports not only hatcheries but law enforcement, without which illegal fishing and bootlegging of caviar would quickly take over. The social and economic reality of the situation creates a quandary that is hard to unravel.

While I can't recommend caviar from the Caspian and Black seas, I have no difficulty encouraging you to try the following sustainable American caviars and roes as an alternative. Only caviar from fish of the *Acipenseridae* sturgeon family can legally be called simply *caviar*; all others must be preceded by the species name—for example, "salmon caviar."

### HACKLEBACK STURGEON CAVIAR

**Hackleback sturgeon** (*Scaphiryhnchus platoryhnchus*), sometimes called the "shovelnose sturgeon," is the most abundant wild American sturgeon, a small, quick-growing fish native to the Mississippi/Missouri basin. The small black berry of hackleback sturgeon caviar can be quite delicious, but quality varies considerably by producer.

Confusingly, hackleback sturgeon caviar and paddlefish caviar are both marketed as American sturgeon caviar. Be sure to ask which you are buying; paddlefish caviar is the more highly regarded and expensive of the two.

## PACIFIC WHITE STURGEON CAVIAR

Caviar is produced from aquacultured Pacific Northwest white sturgeon (*Acipenser transmontanus*) under the Sterling Caviar label by Stolt Sea Farms of California. Several other small California farms also produce fine-quality caviar from Pacific sturgeon, sometimes marketed as "California osetra." These are excellent, carefully prepared caviars, the best grades of which are comparable to Caspian Sea caviars and are similar in flavor to osetra.

## PADDLEFISH CAVIAR

**Paddlefish** (*Polyodon spathula*) are cartilaginous cousins to sturgeons from the Mississippi-Missouri basin and the streams of Montana and Wyoming. Wild paddlefish are endangered, but Osage Catfisheries of Osage, Missouri, has sold aquacultured paddlefish and paddlefish caviar under the label American sturgeon caviar for thirty years. The gray-green osetra-sized berries are nicely flavored and the quality is consistent.

## SALMON CAVIAR

**Salmon caviar**, sometimes referred to as red caviar, is usually produced from the well-managed wild Alaskan fisheries. Chum salmon eggs, thinner-skinned and more tender than the eggs of other salmon species, produce the best-quality salmon caviar. The attractive orange-colored eggs are pearl-sized, with a nice salmon flavor.

## SIBERIAN STURGEON CAVIAR

**Siberian sturgeon** (*Acipenser baerii*) is one of the most commonly aquacultured sturgeons; it is grown in France, Italy, Uruguay, China, and, most recently, the United States. Caviar from Siberian sturgeon grown at the Mote Marine Research Laboratory in Florida has just entered the market. Another Florida farm and a British Columbia farm are slated to begin production soon.

## TOBIKO

Although not an American-produced caviar, tobiko is well known and commonly available in American restaurants and markets. Produced from the abundant **flying fish** (*Exocetus spp.*), the roe is harvested in Thailand and processed in Japan. Tobiko has little flavor but is appreciated for its bright, crunchy texture. It may be either red, black, or orange and is sometimes seasoned with wasabi, yuzu, ginger, Japanese plum, or hot chile.

CONTINUED

Sunburst Trout Company of North Carolina produces some of the most highly regarded rainbow trout caviar. Steelhead caviar, the saltwater version of rainbow trout caviar, may be produced from either aquacultured fish or hatchery fish returning to spawn. Trout and steelhead caviars have a vibrant orange hue, with smaller berries and a lighter, more delicate flavor than the similar salmon caviar.

**Whitefish** (*Coregonus clupeaformis*) is a wild freshwater relative of salmon. Whitefish caviar, sold as American golden caviar, is produced from fish caught under strict quotas from the lakes of northwest Montana. The small egg has a rich apricot hue, mild flavor, and crisp texture.

## IN THE KITCHEN

Sturgeon is a very firm and muscular fish that is best cooked by grilling, baking, or sautéing. Young sturgeon that live near the sea can be exquisitely flavored, while older fish caught upriver may taste of algae or mud. Farmed sturgeon is always mildly sweet and consistent in flavor.

The best sturgeon I've ever eaten was from the Quinault River. It was simply grilled and served with a delicious tomato, caper, and anchovy sauce spiked with red wine vinegar and mustard. The sauce was delicious but the sturgeon was so perfect, marbled with fat and rich in flavor, that the sauce only interfered. At first bite, I thought I was tasting a fat king salmon; then sweet herring and shad spoke up. I understood why sturgeon has been called "Albany beef."

Cold smoked and kippered sturgeon has long been popular in the Northwest and the delis of New York's Lower East Side. Mike Josephson of Josephson's Smokehouse in Astoria, Oregon, smokes sturgeon over alder wood. Juicy, sweet, and full of flavor, his cold-smoked sturgeon is light and airy but firm enough to slice paper thin. Mike's father, grandfather, and great-grandfather were all commercial sturgeon fishermen.

Sturgeon can be eaten in raw preparations; mince for sturgeon tartare or slice thinly and dress with olive oil and lemon for crudo.

A sturgeon has no bones, only a single central cartilaginous notochord. The marrowlike notochord, a primitive backbone, is edible; it is used in *koulebiaka*, a traditional Russian recipe of sturgeon baked in flaky pastry. The skin is too tough to eat.

# BROILED STURGEON WITH ROMESCO SAUCE

Sturgeon is the perfect choice for broiling. While lean, quick-cooking fish tend to steam before browning, the dense, fatty-fleshed sturgeon browns nicely while being basted in its own fat. Broiling allows those fats to drain away.

More than any other request, customers at our retail store want to know a really good sauce for plainly cooked fish. Romesco Sauce is just that, a delicious sauce for any simply cooked seafood, from grilled spiny lobster to sautéed cod. If at first glance the recipe appears to have a daunting number of steps—roasting almonds, charring peppers and tomatoes—don't worry; none are difficult. Try Romesco once, and I guarantee you'll come back to it time and again. Romesco can also be used to thicken and season a fish stew.

Olive oil for coating

Four 5-ounce sturgeon fillets

Kosher salt and freshly ground black
     pepper to taste

Romesco Sauce (recipe follows)

Preheat the broiler. Oil a room-temperature broiler pan. Coat the fish with oil and season with salt and pepper. Place the sturgeon, fat-side up (where the skin was removed), 4 to 6 inches from the heat source and broil for 3 to 4 minutes. Turn the fish over and continue to broil until the top is well browned and the fish feels firm to the touch, for a total of about 10 minutes per inch. If necessary, change the position of the broiler pan while cooking to evenly brown all the fillets. Serve with the Romesco Sauce spooned over the top.

# ROMESCO SAUCE

MAKES ABOUT 1 CUP

½ cup raw almonds

4 unpeeled garlic cloves

1 slice country-style bread, trimmed of
   crust and torn into small bits

2 tablespoons red wine vinegar

1 red bell pepper, roasted, peeled
   (see page 38), and chopped

1 tomato, roasted (see page 39)
   and chopped

2 teaspoons sweet Spanish paprika
   (pimentón)

½ teaspoon hot Spanish paprika (pimentón)

¼ cup fruity olive oil

Water as needed (optional)

About 1 teaspoon kosher salt

1. Preheat the oven to 275°F. Spread the almonds and garlic cloves on a baking sheet and toast until the almonds are golden brown when cut in half, 15 to 20 minutes; shake to turn once or twice so that they cook evenly. The garlic cloves should be soft. Remove from the oven and let cool. Soak the bread in the vinegar for 5 minutes.

2. In a blender or food processor, chop the nuts until they are a mixture of fine and coarse grind. Remove the nuts and set aside. Peel the roasted garlic and add to the blender or processor along with the bell pepper and tomato; puree for 10 seconds. Add the paprikas and vinegar-soaked bread and pulse until everything is well mixed. Add the nuts and then, with the machine running, add the olive oil in a slow, steady stream. Be sure the ingredients are moist enough to be easily turning over and thoroughly mixing so that the oil will emulsify with the other ingredients. Add a little water if needed. Process until the mixture forms a thick, coarsely textured, nutty sauce. Do not overprocess. Season with salt to taste.

NOTE: For a more authentic romesco, substitute three or four dried nora chiles and one or two jarred Spanish piquillo peppers for the paprika and red bell pepper. Both are available at the Spanish Table on the Internet at www.spanishtable.com.

# HOMEMADE SALMON OR STEELHEAD CAVIAR

The skein, or roe, of chum salmon eggs, called *ikura*, are available in Japanese markets and make an excellent salmon caviar. In early December, the steelhead come back to the Quinault River hatcheries on the Olympic Peninsula in Washington. There are always more eggs than needed for the next year's run, so at Monterey Fish we are able to sell steelhead roe for curing. Niloufer Ichaporia King, a friend who is a wonderful Indian cook and cookbook writer, makes steelhead caviar from Quinault River steelhead every fall and winter, which she sells to Bay Area restaurants. I always plan on having steelhead caviar for Christmas and New Year's Eve.

---

3 quarts lukewarm water (100°F)

1 cup kosher salt

1 skein salmon or steelhead roe
　(about 1 pound)

1. In a large glass or stainless-steel bowl, combine the water and salt and stir to dissolve the salt. Reserve half the saltwater bath in a clean bowl and immerse the entire skein in the remaining saltwater for 30 minutes.

2. Place a colander in the sink and adjust the tap to a gentle stream of the hottest water your hands can tolerate. Gently remove the skein from the saltwater bath. With a sharp knife, cut the skein open so the individual eggs are exposed. Cradling the skein in both hands, pass it back and forth under the gentle stream of hot water. The skein material will retract from the individual eggs, allowing them to separate and fall into the colander. After most of the eggs have fallen from the skein, discard the skein and any eggs still attached. Return the separated eggs to the reserved salt bath.

3. Pick through the eggs in the salt bath, removing and discarding any skein material that may still be attached to small bundles of eggs. When finished, the eggs should be individually separated and there should be very little skein material left in the water.

4. Allow the eggs to sit in the bath for 15 minutes. Tilt the saltwater to one side and gently agitate the eggs while slowly pouring off the water. This should remove any remaining skein material and broken eggs. Drain the eggs in a clean colander or strainer for 5 minutes. The eggs may appear opaque at this point, but they will become translucent. Place the drained eggs in sealed glass jars and refrigerate. The caviar will last at least 2 weeks.

# SWORDFISH

Forty years ago, swordfish was seasonally captured—predominantly by harpoon—and marketed locally. Today, technology and deepwater fishing methods have made the swordfish a worldwide commodity that's sold year-round. It would not be at all unusual to encounter Vietnamese swordfish in New York, South African swordfish in Los Angeles, or Caribbean swordfish in Seattle.

Although imported swordfish can be quite good, swordfish caught domestically at the height of the season always seems to have that little something extra. Late summer and fall is the best time of year for swordfish taken from the North Atlantic and Pacific coasts. In winter months, the best-quality swordfish comes from Hawaii, the southern Atlantic, and the Gulf of Mexico.

The highest-quality fish—and the most desirable from an environmental standpoint—is always harpooned swordfish, which is most often available during summer and fall. Few swordfishermen still use harpoons, although a few diehards still work out of ports in New England, the Maritimes of Canada, and southern California.

Fresh swordfish can range from creamy white to almost pumpkin orange, depending on the fish's diet. Although some people prefer one color over another, I've noticed very little difference in flavor based on color alone. Instead, the criteria I find to be most important are a tightly formed red blood line (indicating freshness), and on close inspection a fine, netlike marbling of fat throughout the flesh. This marbling gives the flesh a greasy feel and lots of wonderful flavor.

The blood line is the powerful, hemoglobin-rich red muscle tissue used for sustained swimming. It typically appears as a narrow, isolated section of red flesh in the lighter-colored cut of swordfish. The blood line is the prime indicator of freshness in swordfish: It should be tightly formed and ruby red in color; as the fish ages the blood line begins to stain the surrounding flesh and become less distinct. With further aging, extended exposure to air, or freezing, the blood line darkens until it becomes chocolate brown.

## CHOOSING SUSTAINABLE SEAFOOD

Even though an adult swordfish is capable of releasing 30 million eggs in a single spawning, technological innovation combined with unrelenting fishing pressure and a disregard for the sanctity of spawning grounds led to the near collapse of the North Atlantic swordfish in the 1990s. SeaWeb's "Give Swordfish a Break" campaign of 1998 helped focus public attention on the problem, and the international and federal organizations that regulate swordfish in the Atlantic reduced quotas and adopted area closures to protect juvenile swordfish.

Since then, the North Atlantic swordfish has staged a stunning recovery. By 2002, the swordfish was considered 94 percent recovered, and today the population is considered healthy.

Although swordfish in the Pacific are regulated by federal and state governments, no international agreement to regulate the harvest of Pacific swordfish exists at the present time. Svein Fogner of the National Marine Fisheries Service believes Pacific swordfish stocks to be healthy, pointing to the large average size of fish as a good indicator of population health.

There is considerable concern about the incidental bycatch of sea turtles, seabirds, and sharks associated with longlining, the type of fishing gear that predominates in the swordfish industry. Managers and fishermen in the U.S. swordfish fleet have made great strides in reducing bycatch in recent years through changes in regulations and modifications to longline fishing gear. The international fishery is often less conscientious, however, and continues to take high numbers of sea turtles and seabirds. A threatened species of particular concern is the giant Pacific leatherback turtle.

Environmental groups, citing the Endangered Species Act and the need to protect sea turtles, are now calling for a complete ban against longlining on the high seas, while fishery managers call for continued work on modifying longline gear and improving regulations. Meanwhile, the harpoon fisherman who produces the best-quality swordfish with the ultimate in sustainable fishing gear, zero habitat impact, zero bycatch, and 100 percent selectivity in its ability to choose mature fish receives little encouragement or support.

### CHOOSING HEALTHY SEAFOOD

Swordfish is an excellent high-protein source of antistress B vitamins, minerals (particularly selenium, which may help neutralize mercury toxicity), and omega-3 fatty acids, which have been shown to lower blood cholesterol, reduce inflammatory response, and enhance brain function, among other health benefits.

Swordfish, along with king mackerels, Gulf of Mexico tilefish, large sharks, and large tunas, have been cited by the FDA as the fish most likely to contain unsafe levels of mercury. The very oldest and largest fish are more likely to accumulate mercury levels exceeding the FDA's action level of one part per million (ppm).

FDA warnings for mercury in fish are aimed at pregnant women and young children, not healthy adults. Eating swordfish only occasionally presents little danger to an adult, but it is always best to eat a variety of different seafood that comes from different places. Refer to the mercury chart on page 405 for advice on how to select a mix of seafood that will balance your exposure to methylmercury, while still providing the health benefits of a diet high in seafood.

Because some wild fish may be susceptible to infective parasites, care should always be exercised when eating raw or lightly cooked seafoods (see Raw Seafood: How to Stay Safe, page 408).

NOTE: Swordfish have scales when they are young but they disappear as they mature, so there is disagreement as to whether or not swordfish should be prohibited for those with religious-based dietary restrictions.

### IN THE KITCHEN

Swordfish was one of the most common fish to pass through my mother's kitchen. Simple to cook and full of flavor, it seldom received any adornment other than a wedge of lemon. Unlike many restaurant chefs today, my mom always left the skin on and the blood line in; the fat next to the skin acts to baste the fish during cooking, and the stronger-tasting dark meat is delicious when fresh.

Swordfish is dense and firm, with a hearty, satisfyingly rich flavor. Serve swordfish from the charcoal grill with a Mexican salsa, or braise it in a red wine sauce with mushrooms, caramelized onions, and bacon. Even the pow-

## High-Tech Isn't Always the Best Tech

Some swordfish boats, in an attempt to extend the number of days they are able to stay at sea, use a high-tech refrigerated seawater system (RSW) to chill their fish. The brochure states the fish are stored at a constant optimal temperature of twenty-eight to thirty degrees for optimal holding capacity. But when low-tech humans are responsible for high-tech machinery, the results aren't always as predicted. If the fish is improperly handled, kept too long in refrigerated seawater, or if temperatures are allowed to fluctuate, the result is all too often mushy-textured, watery fish that lacks flavor. The best clue that swordfish may have been mishandled in a RSW system is a green, halolike discoloration of the flesh just below the skin or along the edge of the belly. I'm an advocate of plain old-fasioned ice boats that simply fill their hold with fresh ice—they always produce better-textured and -flavored fish than the new and improved model.

erful flavors of an Indian-style curry with yams or a Thai red curry won't overwhelm the flavor of swordfish.

In Sicily, whose surrounding waters are some of the richest swordfishing grounds in the Mediterranean, thinly sliced swordfish is wrapped around a stuffing of bread crumbs, raisins, and pine nuts, then grilled. Try this served with a blood orange and fennel salad or a salsa verde.

Swordfish can be used in any raw preparation; in nineteenth-century Japan, swordfish, and marlin were more popular as sashimi than tuna. The cuts of swordfish are similar to those of tuna, and can be divided into lean and fatty parts, just as you would tuna. The tastiest and fattiest part of a swordfish, whether raw or cooked, is the belly, which many cooks discard—a practice viewed by some as akin to throwing away $400-per-pound bluefin belly.

The marrowlike notochord, or primitive spinal column of the swordfish, taken from the center of the large backbone, can be cooked, as in recipes for sturgeon marrow, or (as I was recently surprised to learn) may even be eaten raw.

Irregular pieces of trim from the sword's tail and nape are often sold much more cheaply than steaks, and are excellent for brochettes.

S W O R D F I S H

# GRILLED SWORDFISH WITH CAPONATA

Although Caponata is usually sautéed in olive oil and served as a room-temperature relish, it also makes a great vegetable side dish. The fish, vegetables, and accompanying grilled bread for this recipe are all cooked on the grill—perfect for alfresco dining and easy on the cleanup.

Serve with thick slices of country bread brushed with olive oil and toasted over the fire. Rub the toasted bread with a halved clove of garlic, which will melt into the bread. Use about half a clove garlic for each slice of bread.

Four 5-ounce swordfish steaks

Mild-flavored olive oil for coating

Salt and freshly ground black pepper
   to taste

Caponata (recipe follows)

Prepare a medium-hot fire in a charcoal grill or preheat a gas grill to 375°F. Coat the swordfish with oil and season with salt and pepper. Oil the grill rack well and grill the fish, turning once halfway through the cooking process, a total of 8 to 10 minutes per inch of thickness, or until almost opaque throughout. Serve with Caponata on the side.

## CAPONATA

When I prepare Caponata on the grill, I start a small fire an hour and a half before I want the fire I will cook my swordfish over to be ready. When the small fire is ready, I cook the Caponata ingredients, then I add more charcoal to prepare a bigger fire to cook the swordfish.

1 eggplant, cut into rounds ½ inch thick

1 white onion, cut into rounds ⅓ inch thick

2 tomatoes (about 8 ounces)

½ cup olive oil

¼ cup red wine vinegar

¼ cup minced fresh flat-leaf parsley

2 tablespoons capers, chopped

½ cup green olives, pitted (see page 38)
   and chopped

Salt and freshly ground black pepper
   to taste

4 or 5 fresh basil leaves, cut into fine
   ribbons, for garnish

Prepare a low fire in a charcoal grill or preheat a gas grill to 325°F. Grill the eggplant, onion, and tomatoes until tender, 10 to 15 minutes. Transfer the vegetables to a plate and let cool to the touch. Chop the tomatoes and put them with all their juices in a bowl with the oil, vinegar, parsley, capers, and olives. Cut the eggplant and onion into ¼-inch dice and add to the bowl. Mix well and season with salt and pepper. Garnish with the basil.

## Harpooned Swordfish

My Uncle Emil grew roses all his life, but he also loved to fish. When he retired, he bought a low house pushed into the sand dunes on the Galilee side of the Point Judith–Galilee channel. His front deck stretched out into the water and became a dock, where he tied up a little fishing boat. Every day he went fishing, looking to hook flounder, tautog, and squeteague.

My first memory of Uncle Emil was him sitting on the front dock, looking as wiry and tough as a piece of dried cod, watching the swordfish fleet steam out the channel. They were harpoon boats all, no gill nets or longliners. I was seven at the time, and I thought my uncle was at least a hundred. "See that pulpit out front?" he said, pointing to the bow of one of the sword boats as it passed by. "That's where they stand when they stick the fish."

The sword showed up off the point in June every year and stayed around until October. The fish would sometimes come in so close that the fleet could day-fish: eat breakfast at home, go fishing, then return home to sleep in their own bed. Big sword lolled on the surface, warming up in preparation for deep-diving night feeding. With few natural enemies, mature swordfish were seldom concerned when a boat slid alongside—that is, until the man riding the pulpit leaned over and the harpoon struck home. Each fish was chosen for its size; no juveniles were taken, and there was no waste. Year after year, every New England market and restaurant featured beautiful, fresh swordfish through the summer and fall. When winter came, we switched to flounder and lobster.

CONTINUED

Sometime in the late seventies, an enterprising young fisherman out of Gloucester decided to try something different with swordfish. Longlines, used in other fisheries, were rigged with different hooks and bait and set in the deep long after the swordfish had disappeared for the season.

The experiment was such a success that *Boston Herald* headlines trumpeted "largest, most valuable catch of swordfish ever landed," and the stampede was on. Fishermen quickly realized that one longline boat could catch more fish than twenty-five harpoon boats. Boats were rerigged and new boats were built; depth finders and positioning technology were employed to track the fish. As the fishery went unregulated, a gold-rush mentality took over. Before long, swordfish were tracked to their wintering grounds off the continental shelf of Florida. So much fish was caught that prices plummeted, forcing fishermen to catch more fish to make the same profit. Boats stayed on the water for weeks instead of days. Once the sword's spawning grounds off Cape Hatteras were discovered, the end was near: juveniles, pups, spawning fish—everything was taken.

It was only a matter of three or four years until there wasn't a swordfish within two hundred miles of Point Judith. In ten years, the average size of Atlantic swordfish fell from 250 to ninety pounds, less than reproductive maturity. As swordfish stocks crashed, the swordfish captains that my Uncle Emil was proud to call his neighbors and friends fell on hard times. The crow's nests on their boats were empty, but the bar stools at the Dutch Inn were full.

Although North Atlantic swordfish stocks have recovered, the economic die has been cast in favor of big-production longline boats. It is unlikely that we will ever see the wholesale return of harpoon fishermen. Until the day that fishery managers see the wisdom of encouraging an environmentally friendly harpoon fishery through preferred quota management, I can only cast my vote at the marketplace. I buy harpoon-caught swordfish whenever I'm able, and I encourage chefs and consumers to do the same.

# TILAPIA

Tilapia is an environmentalist's dream and a cook's quandary. It is a freshwater fish native to Africa, and is now the fifth most popular seafood consumed in the United States. Tilapia is big business in the United States: We are the third largest producer, third largest consumer, and the largest importer of tilapia in the world.

As aquacultured in the United States, tilapia is gentle on the environment. A pure vegetarian that requires no animal protein, although most tilapia feeds do contain some, the fish is inexpensive to raise and is amenable to a variety of growing conditions.

The knock on tilapia is a muddy or mossy flavor. In addressing this problem, the United States and many quality South American farms use recirculating filtered-water systems. Fresh tilapia imported from many tilapia farms in Colombia, Costa Rica, Mexico, Brazil,

## Organic Seafood

Recently we've seen farmed salmon from Scotland and Ireland being marketed as "organic" in the United States. While this salmon does not qualify for the USDA organic label, it is not against the law to label it as such. Because the USDA's National Organics Program does not have standards for labeling aquatic species, it does not regulate or issue the organic label to farmed salmon.

But what is being marketed as organic salmon is not what most Americans have come to trust the word *organic* to mean. While Scottish and Irish salmon farmers must adhere to what we would call environmental "best practices," which is commendable, there is no guarantee that organic salmon are free of contaminants. The use of the synthetic coloring pigments canthaxanthin and astaxanthin is prohibited, but organic salmon farms still use pesticide, administered in the salmon's feed, to control sea lice. As well, European organic salmon has been shown to contain levels of PCBs and other organic pollutants similar to those that are found in nonorganic aquacultured salmon.

Currently the only seafoods that meet stricter USDA labeling standards for organic animals is tilapia—raised on a 100 percent organic vegetarian diet—and suprisingly, shrimp. USDA standards maintain that all the feed must be completely traceable as to origin—something that is impossible to do when carnivorous fish, such as salmon, are fed a diet based on wild fish.

It is relatively easy for tilapia growers to meet USDA organic labeling standards by feeding their fish a 100 percent organically grown vegetable based diet. But shrimp are predators and demand fish in their diet.

The old saw, "Where there's a will there's a way," certainly applies to two of the pioneers in the field of organic shrimp production. Permian Sea Organics of Texas and Ocean Boy Farms of Florida feed their shrimp fish meal manufactured from USDA-certified organically grown tilapia to produce USDA-certified organic shrimp.

and Ecuador are striving toward the same environmental standards as practiced in the United States, and their fish is generally of good quality. In Southeast Asia, however, the inexpensive and frozen tilapia is often plagued by mossy, muddy flavors caused by rainy-season runoff and algal blooms.

Tilapia fillets, which can be found in grocery

stores and markets throughout the country, should be white or slightly pink, with no drying or brown discoloration along the edges. Tilapia is often deep-skinned to remove the fat on the backside, which quickly oxidizes and discolors. Without this important visual clue to freshness, odor becomes even more important; check for mossy, muddy, or musty odors.

Niche U.S. growers concentrate on live fish for Asian markets and restaurants and very fresh fish for the sashimi market; both the emerald green and red hybrid varieties are popular, and their flavor is identical.

### CHOOSING SUSTAINABLE SEAFOOD
Tilapia grown in closed-system freshwater ponds and fed a diet based mostly on vegetable protein has little impact on the environment and wild fish.

### CHOOSING HEALTHY SEAFOOD
Although lower in omega-3s than wild and carnivorous seafood, aquacultured tilapia is free of environmental pollutants and parasites. Expect to see more tilapia marketed under the USDA organic label.

Tilapia with cherry-red fat on its back may be pretty but has probably been treated with tasteless smoke or carbon monoxide (see Carbon Monoxide with Your Sushi?, page 368). Taiwan-grown tilapia fillets labeled as sashimi quality are almost always treated with tasteless smoke.

### IN THE KITCHEN
Even though quality growers have addressed the problem of off flavors, the industry description of tilapia as "a cross between catfish and sole" is more wishful thinking than accurate description. Nevertheless, the soft white fish fillets with their very mild flavor have a certain appeal.

Tilapia can be cooked either as fillets or whole fish. It maintains good texture in raw and uncooked dishes. The bones can be used for stock but do not make a very flavorful broth, and their small size means it's usually more work than it's worth.

A friend of mine who spent time in Liberia tells me that tilapia is a popular fish in the countryside. Whole fish are split, threaded on a green stick, seasoned with copious amounts of red pepper, and basted with palm oil while roasting over an open fire. Apparently this has long been a popular way to cook tilapia in Africa—an excerpt from Joseph H. Reading's travel diary *A Narrative of African Travel* published in 1890 describes a similar scene:

*The next morning there were fresh fish for breakfast and they were good, too; the Gabonese cook cooked them by running a green stick lengthwise through them and then toasting them over the coals; if they fall in the ashes a few times before they are done, as they are quite likely to do, it makes no difference, the ashes are easily brushed off with the hand and the fish taste better when they have the flavor of the wood through them.*

# CRISPY TILAPIA
# WITH LEMON-ONION RELISH

Wild tilapia cooked over an open fire in the African bush may be delicious, but its good results could be difficult to duplicate at home. I discovered this method of cooking tilapia by accident, of course. One morning at the wharf, I decided to cook some particularly nice-looking tilapia fillets for breakfast. I put them in a nonstick pan with a bit of oil and turned on the heat; before the fish even began to sputter, I was called away. On returning, I discovered that I hadn't turned off the fire and the tilapia had been merrily frying along over medium-low heat for twenty minutes or more.

The fish was opaque white almost all the way to the top, meaning it was nearly cooked through even after only cooking on one side. I turned the fish over for a look and found the bottom a rich, burnished brown. Further investigation revealed the bottom to be crisp, chewy, and delicious, with a flavor I can only describe as baconlike—after all, pigs and tilapia are both fed a diet of corn. In any event, it gave the notoriously soft-fleshed, mild-flavored tilapia an intriguing texture and flavor. Serve this with steamed spinach or other greens, and a Liberian favorite, yams roasted in their skin.

**2 tablespoons refined peanut or another mild-flavored oil**
**Four 5-ounce tilapia fillets**
**Salt to taste**
**Minced fresh flat-leaf parsley for garnish**
**Lemon-Onion Relish (recipe follows)**

Put the oil in a large nonstick sauté pan or skillet. Season the fish fillets with salt and place them in the pan, skin removed–side down. Turn the heat to medium, give the pan a shake, then go to work on the rest of dinner. After a few minutes, the fish will be gently sizzling; in 10 minutes it will be briskly sizzling in its own rendered fat. Cook the fish, uncovered, for 20 minutes or more until the bottom is crunchy, chewy, and brown and the top is beginning to turn white and opaque. Turn the fillets over for 30 seconds to finish cooking the very top of the fillets. Divide the fish among 4 plates, crisp side up, and garnish with the parsley. Serve with Lemon-Onion Relish alongside.

# LEMON-ONION RELISH

1 tablespoon refined peanut or another
 mild-flavored oil

1 large or 2 small yellow onions, finely
 sliced (1 heaping cup)

2 tablespoons water

2 tablespoons dry white wine

2 tablespoons cider vinegar

2 teaspoons light molasses

2 large organic lemons

1 teaspoon kosher salt

Freshly ground black pepper to taste

1. In a heavy, medium sauté pan or skillet, heat the oil over medium heat and sauté the onions, stirring frequently, for 10 minutes, or until well browned and reduced to about ½ cup. Add the water and wine and stir to scrape up the browned bits on the bottom of the pan. Stir in the vinegar and molasses.

2. Cut the ends off the lemon, stand it on end, and cut the rind off lengthwise all the way down to the flesh. Lay the lemon on its side and slice it into coins, discarding any seeds as you cut. Add the lemon coins to the pan with the onions, season with salt and pepper, and simmer for 1 minute. Turn the heat off and let the mixture stand for 1 hour before serving.

TILAPIA

# TROUT
# AND CHAR

The rainbow trout's historic range is the Pacific coast from Alaska down to Mexico, but it has been introduced to freshwater streams and lakes worldwide and is now considered the world's most widely aquacultured species. Although no wild trout is sold in the United States, aquacultured trout is widely available. Small farms that specialize in local sales can be found in almost every state, but nearly 85 percent of the trout sold in the States is produced in Idaho's green and sheltered Hagerman Valley. Here, plumes of Rocky Mountain spring water gush from the black basalt canyon walls of the Snake River canyon at a constant 58°F. The sparkling-clear water is then channeled through cement raceways, where millions of young trout are raised for the American table.

While these domesticated trout may not display the same golden-hued beauty or possess the extraordinary flavor of a wild trout caught in the high Sierra, they're a nicely flavored fish in their own right. Fresh trout are typically grown to single-serving size and sold either as whole bone-in or boneless trout.

Fresh trout have an earthy, mineral-like aroma without any trace of mustiness. When shopping, open the belly and smell the inside. Trout should be plump, firm, and slippery, and its naturally-occurring protective coating of slime should be clear and viscous, not yellow, clotted, or curdled. Trout with sunken, tired-looking eyes, dull gray or dry skin, or a musty odor are old.

Char and trout are closely related members of the salmon family. The vast majority of Arctic char sold today is raised by fish farmers. First attracted by its beauty and incomparably flavored pink flesh, aquaculturists began growing Arctic char about ten years ago. More so than trout, farmed Arctic char stays true to the beautiful colors found in wild fish. Steel blue on the back, the char's sides glisten with silver and gold and are decorated with violet spots; the belly ranges from warm pink to sunset orange. The pink-fleshed char is usually grown to a size of two to three pounds and may be marketed either as whole fish or fillets.

Lake trout (*Salvelinus namaycush*), a wild char found in the Great Lakes, supports a commercial fishery of some importance, although demand for this fish isn't as great as it once was. A small amount of wild **Arctic char** (*S. alpi-nus*) is harvested from the far northern streams and lakes of Canada's Northwest Territories in the fall. Most of these fish are marketed to restaurants, and only occasionally do they find their way into fish markets. Although a very small fishery, Canadia Arctic char is currently under assessment for MSC certification as a sustainable fishery.

## CHOOSING SUSTAINABLE SEAFOOD

With few exceptions, trout and char farms raise their fish in tanks or concrete ponds located on dry land. Outgoing water is filtered and treated with ozone or ultraviolet, and the farms' waste products are recycled as fertilizer. Since 2004, the EPA has required permits and the monitoring of effluent from land-based aquaculture operations. These land-based systems are generally considered to be among the more environmentally responsible designs for aquaculture.

Like their salmon cousins, trout and char require a high-protein diet that is dependent on the capture of wild fish. However, farmers are actively working to reduce the amount of fish meal in their feed.

## CHOOSING HEALTHY SEAFOOD

Trout and char are both excellent low-fat sources of protein and a good source of B vitamins. Aquacultured trout and char are lower in omega-3 fatty acids than their wild brethren, but they still contain relatively high amounts of these fatty acids, which help prevent chronic heart disease, reduce inflammatory response, and enhance brain function, among other health benefits. Aquacultured trout and char grown in closed-system ponds and raceways are free of environmental pollutants and parasites.

Farm-raised char and red-fleshed trout and farmed salmon are fed a diet containing a synthetic version of astaxanthin, the naturally occurring red carotenoid pigment that gives wild salmon its color. Although synthetic astaxanthin is considered by some to be a health risk, it's also been marketed as an antioxidant. The FDA classifies astaxanthin as "exempt from certification," the safest category of food additives.

## IN THE KITCHEN

Trout and char are very closely related and can be treated similarly in the kitchen. Trout has a mildly earthy flavor; char is more interesting, with a hint of sweet salmon. Both fish are soft-textured, with a small, delicate flake.

Although trout and char aren't as rich or flavorful as salmon, they have many of the same characteristics. Both types of fish are able to hold their own with rich sauces or strong flavors, yet acidic ingredients such as citrus, fruit, tomatoes, vinegars, and capers work to brighten their flavor.

Aquacultured trout may also be eaten raw as tartare, while char makes a beautiful Italian crudo or citrus-marinated Peruvian tiradito.

The skin of trout or char can be left on during cooking and need not be scaled before being broiled, grilled, or sautéed to crispness.

Trout roe can be cured in the same fashion as steelhead or salmon roe. The eggs are light orange, with a fresh, delicate flavor, much better than salmon, in my opinion. Trout roe ("caviar") of very good quality can be purchased at upscale markets.

Smoked trout is also widely available and makes a tasty, quick, and easy snack or appetizer.

# STUFFED TROUT WITH A SHAOXING WINE-PEANUT SAUCE

SERVES 4 AS A MAIN COURSE

Trout can stand up to the strong flavor of Asian ingredients as well as any fish. Expand the recipe and substitute char or salmon if you like. Serve this flavorful dish with steamed rice or noodles and bok choy or other mild greens.

4 boneless whole trout, 8 to 10 ounces each

2 tablespoons Asian-style unrefined
    peanut oil

Salt and freshly ground black pepper
    to taste

Juice of 1 lemon

1 bunch scallions, including light green
    parts, julienned

2-inch piece fresh ginger, peeled and
    cut into julienne

2 large garlic cloves, thinly sliced

½ cup Shaoxing wine or dry sherry

### SHAOXING WINE-PEANUT SAUCE

2 tablespoons Shaoxing wine or dry sherry

3 tablespoons Chinese black vinegar or
    rice wine vinegar

2 tablespoons soy sauce

5 to 6 thin rings serrano chile with seeds

1 teaspoon toasted sesame oil

¼ cup freshly squeezed lime juice

1 teaspoon sugar

¼ cup dry-roasted peanuts, coarsely ground

1. Preheat the oven to 350°F. Rinse and dry the trout. Rub the trout inside and out with the oil and season the inside with salt, pepper, and lemon juice. Stuff the trout with the scallions, ginger, and garlic, dividing them evenly among the fish. Place the fish in a shallow baking dish and pour the wine over. Cover with aluminum foil and bake for 12 minutes. Uncover and bake for an additional 5 minutes, or until almost opaque throughout.

2. For the sauce: In a small bowl, combine all the ingredients and stir until the sugar is completely dissolved.

3. Serve the fish with the sauce spooned over.

# T U N A

Tuna has been taken from the sea for thousands of years by Mediterranean cultures, which have passed their fishing skills down through the generations. In modern times, however, the Japanese have roundly supplanted all others in their tuna consumption.

The ancient Mediterranean ritual of setting out tuna traps—the *mattanza*—still takes place every spring as giant bluefin migrate through the Straits of Gibraltar, but those fish now end up in Tokyo rather than Rome. Tunas are, without a doubt, some of the most amazing creatures in the sea. Their bullet-shaped bodies immediately convey a sense of speed; even the curvature of their eyeballs is hydrodynamically efficient. In addition, magnetic material found in the skull and a transparent window to the pineal gland allows these wide-ranging fish to determine the season as well as their position and direction during oceanwide migrations.

Tunas are the only warm-blooded fish in existence, both a blessing and a curse. They are speedy predators, able to hunt actively in a wide range of temperatures, but in order to supply their powerful muscles with oxygen they can never stop swimming. Like the *Flying Dutchman*, tunas are fated to travel the seas constantly, never stopping lest they suffocate. The iron-rich myoglobin muscle needed for this endless transfer of energy is what gives tuna its distinctive rich red color and savory beeflike flavor.

Color is the easiest criteria to use when choosing tuna. Quality tuna can be any shade from light pink to deep rich red. The color should be bright and clear. Avoid brown or maroon-colored tuna that is dull and flaccid looking. While poor-quality tuna is easy to recognize, the signs that distinguish high-quality tuna are more subjective. Even the most practiced of experts will often disagree on the grading of tuna. The three variables used to judge tuna are color, clarity, and fat content. Bright red color and good clarity are the characteristics most often appreciated in the United States. A fine, lighter-colored marbling of fat toward the skin and near the belly greatly improves flavor. High fat content is the characteristic most appreciated in Japan. The finest bluefin are not a deep red but rather pale pink in color, due to the fine webbing of white fat that permeates the red flesh. Tuna is graded as No. 1 grade, which is appropriate for sashimi; No. 2 grade, which lacks either color, clarity, or fat, but is still fresh, good-quality fish that can be used for searing or preparing marinated raw fish dishes; and No. 3, or "cooking grade," which is best thoroughly cooked.

The warm-blooded tuna can become very hot when fighting the hook; if not chilled rapidly after capture, which can be difficult when the fish is large, the tuna becomes "burned"—it literally cooks itself from the inside out. The flesh of "burned" tuna appears ash gray to white near the topmost part of the triangular-shaped fillet, which comes from the center of the fish. Burned tuna may be sold as "cooking grade" tuna, but I don't recommend buying it. The flavor is often poor.

As well, avoid tuna that has obvious small soft spots in the flesh, or a very distinct rainbow sheen across cut surfaces (see the discussion of kudoa and scombroid in Choosing Healthy Seafood, page 367).

No matter where you travel in the United States today, beautifully colored fresh tuna can be found on the menu or in the market. The most common tuna in the fresh market is the large, red-fleshed yellowfin, followed by bigeye and bluefin tuna.

## BIGEYE

**Bigeye tuna** (*T. obesus*) is the second most common tuna in the U.S. market. Caught in the deeper, cooler waters of both the Pacific and

Atlantic oceans, bigeye tuna typically has brilliant ruby-red flesh and a higher fat content than yellowfin. Although softer fleshed and more difficult to work with, the bigeye has a superior flavor that makes it a preferred species for sashimi and other raw preparations. Bigeye is also among the most desirable species for grilling, with its high fat content. Availability is year-round, but the best-quality bigeye comes from Hawaii during the winter season, which lasts from October through April. Both yellowfin and bigeye tuna are referred to as **ahi** in Hawaii.

## BLUEFIN, ATLANTIC

There are three different species of bluefin tuna in the world's oceans—two of which are caught in U.S. waters. The majestic giant **Atlantic bluefin** (*T. thynnus*), which may increase its weight by one billion times from birth to maturity, reaches a length of twelve feet and a weight of fifteen hundred pounds. Prime-quality Atlantic bluefins are caught in summer and fall off the Atlantic Coast; most are sold to Japan.

## BLUEFIN, NORTH PACIFIC

The **North Pacific bluefin** (*T. orientalis*) is the only bluefin tuna that is not considered overfished. Small-schooling Pacific bluefin tuna appear off the coast of Mexico and California during the summer and fall. Historically, seine fisheries have targeted these fish for the cannery, but a growing number are now being sold on the fresh market. U.S.-caught North Pacific bluefin tuna can be purchased fresh during late summer and fall.

Aquacultured bluefin is also sold. Bluefin farms off the coast of Baja California at Salsipuedes buy immature live northern bluefin tuna, which they fatten for the lucrative Japanese market. There are also bluefin farms in Australia, Atlantic Canada, and Spain—all areas that are known for their bluefin fisheries.

## YELLOWFIN

**Yellowfin** (*Thunnus albacares*), named for its bright yellow fins, is the most abundant tuna in the world's oceans, and the one most often found in U.S. markets. It is extensively fished on all three U.S. coasts, and large quantities are also imported from Vietnam, Trinidad, Brazil, Ecuador, Fiji, Indonesia, the Philippines, and many other countries. The yellowfin found in mainland U.S. markets is usually firm fleshed and lean with a deep, rich red color. American-caught yellowfins are at their peak availability from April through October; most yellowfin sold in the winter is imported from the southern hemisphere countries mentioned above.

### CHOOSING SUSTAINABLE SEAFOOD

Yellowfin and bigeye tunas are abundant. Both species mature early and grow quickly. Yellowfin populations are stable and for the most part not considered overfished.

Much of the fresh tuna that comes to market

## O-toro

Not long ago, the lean cuts of tuna (*akami*) were preferred for sashimi. But following World War II, the Japanese began embracing fat- and flavor-laden Western foods, and tastes changed. Today, the velvet-textured, rich-flavored fatty cuts of tuna (*toro*) are preferred. Most of the world's fattest, most expensive tuna—the tuna deemed No. 1 sashimi quality—is sold in Japan. The well-marbled, fattiest belly cut (*O-toro*) from a giant bluefin landed in Montauk will bring fifty dollars to one hundred dollars for a single one-ounce serving. Only a few of the world's very finest sushi bars are able to afford such a delicacy.

is caught by longline. The U.S. tuna longline fleet has made great strides in reducing bycatch; international fisheries, however, are often less conscientious. Troll and hook-and-line fisheries are the most environmentally friendly. As much as 50 percent of Hawaiian tuna is caught in this manner, and smaller amounts are taken in the Gulf and Atlantic fisheries.

Sixty percent of the world's yellowfin tuna comes from the Pacific, where stronger international management is needed. Giant super-seiners from Spain and Taiwan that are targeting immature fish for the cannery are one of today's greatest threats to future yellowfin populations.

Unlike yellowfin and bigeye, bluefin tuna is slow to mature. Heavy fishing throughout the 1970s and 1980s sent Atlantic and Southern bluefin populations into a severe decline, and bluefin population levels today are 20 percent or less of what they were just twenty years ago. Despite sophisticated international manage-

ment bodies for both Atlantic and Southern bluefin, both are listed on the International Union for Conservation of Nature and Natural Resources (IUCN) Red List of endangered species. The current status of bluefin populations may be largely attributed to the high value of the fish in the Japanese sashimi market, where one fish can command $100,000 or more. North Pacific bluefin populations are healthy, but the lack of management is a cause for worry there, given the status of the other bluefin populations.

### CHOOSING HEALTHY SEAFOOD

Tuna is one of the cold-water fatty fish that are extremely rich in heart-healthy omega-3 fatty acids, which help prevent heart disease, reduce inflammatory response, and ensure good brain function, among other health benefits. Tuna is also an excellent high-protein source of vitamin A and contains incredibly high levels of

## Carbon Monoxide with Your Sushi?

Fresh tuna, when exposed to the air, quickly loses its rich red color, eventually becoming an unappealing chocolate brown. In Japan, fresh tuna is frozen at ultra-low temperatures— 75°F—to maintain its red color. The energy and equipment needed to do this is very expensive, so it isn't practical in other countries where tuna is not such an important part of the cuisine.

In 1999, Bill Kowalski of Hawaii International Seafood patented a process to "fix" the color of tuna without freezing it. His process, labeled "tasteless smoke," uses state-of-the-art equipment to filter a "substantial amount of the particulate matter that imparts flavor from the smoke." What is left is 40 percent carbon monoxide. When treated with tasteless smoke, tuna maintains its red color for a very, very long period of time.

Some companies, mostly in the Indo-Pacific, taking this process one step further have begun using 100 percent industrial carbon monoxide to treat tuna. This enhances the natural color of tuna and prevents it from turning dark for an *unnaturally* long period of time, longer than it takes for the tuna to spoil.

The use of carbon monoxide deceives consumers and creates unnecessary risk by enabling tuna to remain fresh-looking far beyond the point at which typical color changes would indicate aging or bacterial spoilage. Officials say that packaging is labeled to indicate that the tuna has been treated. But the FDA doesn't enforce labeling at the retail level, and consumers don't see labels in restaurants or at sushi bars.

Tuna treated with carbon monoxide and tasteless smoke is most often sold at the retail level as individual vacuum-packed portions but may be displayed unpackaged. Restaurants and sushi bars use treated tuna because it is inexpensive, though top-quality places are unlikely to serve it. Although tasteless smoke—treated tuna is difficult to tell from fresh tuna, because the natural color of the tuna has simply been "fixed," the color of industrial carbon monoxide– treated tuna is changed, or "enhanced." Industrial carbon monoxide treatment changes tuna to an unnaturally bright, almost fluorescent, shade of strawberry or lollipop red.

antistress B vitamins, particularly B$_{12}$. It is also a very good source of selenium, which may neutralize mercury toxicity.

Members of the tuna family may produce histamines (see Scombroid, page 413) in their flesh if not properly handled. A very distinct rainbow sheen across the cut surface of a tuna steak is a sign of scombroid and should be avoided. Tuna seldom contain parasites that are of concern to human health. They may sometimes have a condition known as kudoa (see page 412) that, while not a threat to people's health, does adversely affect the texture of the fish.

The very oldest and largest tuna may accumulate mercury levels that exceed the FDA's action level of 1 ppm. It is best to eat a variety of seafoods; refer to the chart on page 405 to find a mix of seafood that will safely balance your exposure to methylmercury while still providing the health benefits of a diet high in seafood.

Any of the smaller tunas, such as **skipjack**, **bonito**, and **young albacore**, are low in mercury. In addition, younger tuna of any species are less likely to have bio-accumulated higher levels of mercury. Look for yellowfin, bigeye, and bluefin tuna steaks with a diameter of less than four inches—this indicates that they've come from smaller, younger specimens.

### IN THE KITCHEN

The flesh of tuna is similar to beef, a hybrid of both light and dark muscle—mixed bundles of fast and slow twitch fibers—making it one of the most densely textured of all fish. The lean tuna most often available in U.S. markets is ideal for lightly cooked preparations such as searing that leave it rare in the center. Quickly sauté or grill tuna steaks that have been dredged in spice—fennel seeds, coriander seeds, or a blend of spices—and serve with a simple tomato relish, a sweet-and-sour salad of orange and onion, or an anchovy-walnut vinaigrette. For an easy pasta, sauté chunks of tuna with fresh fennel and tomato.

Quick marinades that highlight the fine flavor of tuna are also excellent: Marinate small cubes of tuna in Asian or Latin ingredients (Hawaiian poke is a classic). A Mediterranean-style raw preparation, crudo, in which the fish is thinly sliced, dressed with olive oil and lemon, and then served immediately, is perfect for tuna. Braising or stewing also works well. A popular Basque dish pairs tuna with a stew of late-summer tomatoes and peppers.

The rich, stronger-flavored dark meat of tuna is isolated to one side of the loin. While many people enjoy the flavor of the darker muscle tissue—particularly when the fish is very fresh—it can easily be trimmed away.

The roe of tuna is salted and pressed as *bottarga*, an Italian delicacy that is thinly shaved and served over pasta. The tuna's skin is too tough to eat, and tuna bones are too strongly flavored to be used for making stock.

## Katsuobushi and Dashi

Katsuobushi (dried bonito flakes) is the Japanese name for a dried preparation of tuna that is one of the basic ingredients of Japanese cooking. Small skipjack tuna (oceanic bonito) are steamed, hung to be dry cured, and then smoked over a period of many months. The result resembles nothing more than a petrified block of wood, albeit one that is deeply rich in umami and other complex flavors.

Traditionally, an instrument similar to a wood plane or mandoline was kept on hand to shave slices of katsuobushi as needed for making soups and sauces or as a seasoning sprinkled over rice and noodles. In a nod to convenience, the whole-block form of katsuobushi is seldom seen today; rather, it is most often available already shaved. Sold in small bags in any Japanese food store, this form of katsuobushi resembles pink-brown shavings of cedar. Whether found in block form or shavings, however, katsuobushi retains its status as one of the primary ingredients in Japanese cooking.

Dashi, a stock made from dried kelp (konbu), and katsuobushi, forms the basis of most soups and sauces in Japanese cuisine. Dashi may seem seem like a simple ingredient on which to base a cuisine, but don't be deceived—centuries of knowledge and months of work have gone into making the katsuobushi from which dashi is made. Both dried kelp and katsuobushi are readily available in Japanese specialty stores.

## Dashi (Japanese Stock)

MAKES 4 CUPS

4 cups water
3-ounce piece konbu (dried kelp)
Large handful (1 ounce) katsuobushi
    (dried bonito flakes)

In a large saucepan, combine the water and konbu. Bring to a simmer over low heat. Just before the water boils, use a wire skimmer to remove the konbu. Add the katsuobushi and turn off the heat. Let stand until all the flakes have sunk to the bottom of the pan, about 5 minutes. Strain the stock through a fine-meshed sieve. For a deeper-flavored but less clear stock, cook the kelp and bonito flakes over very low heat for 15 minutes.

# SCATTERED-SUSHI SALAD

This is fun to eat and easy to prepare.

The type of sushi we most often see in sushi bars is rolled, or finger, sushi. Rolled sushi is popular because it showcases the dexterity and skills of the sushi chef—a big part of the sushi experience. But there is another type of sushi that is popular in Japanese-American homes and is perfect for those of us who would like to enjoy sushi at home but find its preparation intimidating.

*Chirashi*, or scattered sushi, is just that: fish and other ingredients that are artfully scattered on top of a bed of sushi rice. It's easy to make but still leaves plenty of room for artistic expression; you can use whatever ingredients you like and arrange by color, shape, and taste to make the dish attractive. This recipe is for a one-dish meal at home, but scattered sushi is perfect for a party; simply expand the recipe and add as many different ingredients as you like. Guests serve themselves as they like. Any raw or cooked seafood such as broiled eel (*unagi*) or salmon roe (*ikura*), as well as shiso leaves, fried tofu, or Japanese gourd strips, are all popular ingredients used in scattered sushi and are available at Japanese markets.

Serve with soy sauce and wasabi, or as is popular with some Japanese today, mix the soy sauce and wasabi with Mayonnaise (page 37) to make a sauce.

½ ounce dried shiitake mushrooms

1 large egg

Pinch of salt

4 to 5 ounces snow peas, trimmed

10 ounces medium shrimp

¼ cup sake

2 tablespoons mirin

1 tablespoon soy sauce

10 ounces tuna steaks

2 cups Sushi Rice (recipe follows)

1 carrot, peeled and shredded

1 Japanese cucumber, cut into ¼-inch dice

1 avocado, peeled, pitted, and diced

1 sheet toasted nori (seaweed processed into paperlike sheets)

1. Soak the shiitakes in warm water until softened, about 30 minutes.

2. Put the egg in a bowl and whisk with the salt. Lightly oil a small nonstick sauté pan or skillet and add a thin layer of about half of the egg, tilting the pan to create an egg crepe. Cook on both sides. Repeat to use the remaining egg mixture. Cut the crepe into 1-inch-wide strips, then cut crosswise into julienne. Set aside.

3. In a medium saucepan of salted boiling water, blanch the peas for about 30 seconds. Rinse in cold water, then pat dry and cut into julienne. Set aside.

4. In a small saucepan, combine the shrimp, sake, and mirin. Bring to a boil over high heat and

TUNA

371

immediately remove the shrimp, reserving the pan liquid. Let the shrimp cool, then shell it and slice in half lengthwise.

5. Stem the hydrated shiitakes and cut the mushrooms into julienne. Add the soy sauce to the reserved liquid in which you cooked the shrimp and simmer the shiitakes until all the liquid has evaporated, about 10 minutes. Set aside.

6. Prepare the tuna by slicing it into 1-inch pieces ¼ inch thick, as for sashimi.

7. Put the Sushi Rice on a platter, then sprinkle the carrot shreds and julienned egg over. Arrange the tuna and shrimp on either side of the platter, separated by the julienned snow peas. Place piles of cucumber, avocado, and shiitake mushrooms around the platter. With a pair of scissors, cut the nori into 1-inch-wide strips, then cut the strips crosswise into julienne, allowing them to fall over the platter of ingredients. Provide serving utensils and chopsticks.

## ■ ■ ■ SUSHI RICE ■ ■ ■

MAKES 3 CUPS

Using an electric rice cooker is the easiest way to be assured of achieving perfectly textured rice, but you may also use a saucepan.

6 tablespoons rice vinegar

1 teaspoon salt

2 tablespoons sugar

2 cups Japanese short-grain rice

2 cups water

One 3-inch square konbu (dried kelp); optional

1. In a glass bowl, stir the rice vinegar, salt, and sugar together to dissolve.

2. Wash the rice until the water runs clear, then drain in a sieve and set aside for 30 minutes so it can absorb some moisture. Put the rice in the rice cooker and cover with water; add the optional konbu and turn the rice cooker on. When the rice is cooked, turn off the cooker and let the rice stand to steam for 10 minutes.

3. Or put the washed rice, water, and konbu in a medium saucepan and cover with a tight-fitting lid. Bring to a boil over medium-low heat. Don't lift the lid—just listen for the sound of bubbling. When it boils, turn the heat to high and cook for 5 minutes. Turn off the heat and let steam for 10 minutes.

4. Empty the rice into a large, shallow bowl and discard the konbu. Sprinkle the vinegar-sugar mixture over the rice, one third at a time, while using a spatula to slice through the

grains of rice, separating and mixing them. Using an electric or handheld fan, gently fan the rice to help it cool while cutting and slicing the vinegar mixture into the rice. When it takes on a shiny gloss and has cooled down to room temperature, cover the rice with a damp cloth until needed. Sushi rice may be prepared up to 3 hours ahead but should not be refrigerated.

## CORIANDER-CRUSTED TUNA WITH HOT AND SWEET MANGO SALSA

SERVES 4 AS A MAIN COURSE

Tuna steaks, particularly from the lean yellowfin tuna, hold little excitement when they are cooked to doneness. In this recipe, the steaks are cooked until the coriander crust on the outside is just crisp and crunchy but the fish inside is still very rare—the best of both worlds.

3 tablespoons coriander seeds

1 teaspoon black peppercorns

½ teaspoon fennel seeds

Four 6-ounce tuna steaks, about 1 inch thick

Kosher salt for sprinkling

Grated zest of 1 lemon

2 tablespoons olive oil

Mango Salsa (recipe follows)

**1.** Using a mortar and pestle or spice grinder, coarsely crush the coriander, black peppercorns, and fennel seeds. Sprinkle the tuna on both sides with salt and lemon zest, and then sprinkle evenly with the crushed spices, pressing them into the flesh on both sides.

**2.** In a large cast-iron skillet, heat the oil over medium-high heat until it shimmers. Lay the tuna in the pan and cook for 1 to 2 minutes on each side, or until the spices are lightly browned and crisp. Transfer to a cutting board to let rest for a minute or two, then cut into ⅜-inch-thick slices and fan across the plates. Serve Mango Salsa alongside.

# MANGO SALSA

MAKES 1 CUP

Many varieties of mangoes come to market through spring and summer, and any of them will make a nice salsa for seafood. One of my favorites is the Ataulfo, an early-season variety that sometimes goes by the market name of champagne mango. These mangoes are smooth textured, with few fibers and a wonderful flavor. Mango salsa is delicious with salmon, halibut, yellowtail jacks or just about any other fish, lean or fat.

1 or 2 ripe mangoes, peeled, pitted, and
    cut into ¼-inch dice (about 1 cup)
2 tablespoons minced fresh cilantro
1 tablespoon minced fresh mint
2 serrano or jalapeño chiles, seeded
    and minced
2 tablespoons finely chopped red
    bell pepper

Juice of 1 lime (about 2 tablespoons)
½ teaspoon kosher salt

In a small bowl, combine all the ingredients and stir well. Serve immediately and use it all; it won't keep well overnight.

## Bobby's Bluefin: The Last Fish

On a cool September morning, Bobby Folsom, a friend of my older brother, settled into his seat on JAL flight 293 as it lifted off from Tokyo, carrying him back to Boston, 430,000 yen and quite a few experiences richer. Three days earlier, he had been to the Tsukiji fish auction to watch the frenzied bidding and collect the fat check that now sat in his wallet.

He still found it hard to believe that a single fish could be worth $40,000. It did weigh almost eight hundred pounds and was the most expensive and sought-after fish in the world—but $40,000! For one single fish! Bobby's giant Atlantic bluefin tuna had brought top dollar because it was the ultimate specimen. Chasing fatty bluefish and mackerel all summer and fall, it had packed on weight and fat, its bright red flesh rich with oils and flavor—the most coveted of all seafood for the Japanese sashimi market. In prime shape—if one considers a sumo wrestler to be in shape—its belly lining was white with fat and over a foot thick. The belly pieces would eventually be sold as o-toro for over $400 a pound in Tokyo.

Bobby had known right away when he hooked up that it was a big fish. After all, he had been fishing out of Point Judith for twenty-five years, ever since he was a teenager. When he got the tuna to the side of the boat, he could see by its shape and size that he had a valuable fish on the line. He hooked the steel leader to an empty beer keg and cut the fish loose. For the next four hours, he followed that shiny steel beer barrel around the ocean. He kept his rifle by his side and a sharp eye out for sharks. When he thought enough time had passed to let the fish cool down and burn off any lactic acid from the fight, he pulled the barrel on-board, eased the fish to the side of the boat—and shot it in the head three times.

Bobby winched the fish onboard, made two quick cuts so it would bleed out, and packed it in a salt-water-and-ice slurry. He then raced for shore to find more ice—lots more ice—and refrigeration. After cooling the fish to 33°F in the giant walk-in cooler at the fisherman's co-op, he went to work. He booked his tuna on a flight to Tokyo, and to make sure nothing went awry, he reserved a seat on the same flight for himself. Working inside the cooler, he built a giant coffin around the tuna, then injected the spaces around it with self-hardening, insulating foam. When the time came to leave for the flight to Tokyo, Bobby drove the fish to Boston himself.

## ATLANTIC TUNA TOURNAMENT

Not that many years before, when Bobby was a kid, the giant bluefins were much more common. He remembered walking the docks with his dad every year during the Atlantic tuna tournament and seeing thirty or forty giant bluefin of this size landed during the five-day tournament. The whole family would walk down to the docks at the end of the day to watch the boats come in and see who had been lucky. If a small white flag with a blue fish was seen waving from the flying bridge, that meant fish onboard. Sometimes, there was barely room for anything but fish in the cockpit.

The whole point of the Atlantic tuna tournament was to see who could catch the biggest fish. The largest fish were hoisted out of the cockpit by a crane and hung from a scale. The weight of each was recorded and its picture taken, the proud angler, rod in hand, standing by its side. Afterward, the fish was unceremoniously cut down into a waiting dump truck to be driven to the cat-food factory located at the far end of the wharf.

CONTINUED

The owner of the biggest fish received a beautifully polished walnut and brass plaque with his name inscribed on it and an all-expense-paid five-day holiday in Palm Beach, Florida. Everyone else received three cents a pound for their fish at the cat-food factory if they bothered to go pick up the check.

## THE REVEREND

Then came Sun Myung Moon, a young Korean visionary who knew opportunity when he saw it. He began offering dimes and dollars instead of pennies for the tuna landed in Point Judith. Keeping a low profile, the Reverend Moon was the only buyer on the dock for years, and during that time he made millions selling Point Judith bluefins in Asia at an enormous markup. The profits allowed him to establish his own church and become an international force in seafood. Today, the Unification Church, led by Moon, is firmly entrenched in every phase of the U.S. fishing industry, from catching and processing to retail.

By the 1980s and 1990s, the world had discovered the giant bluefins being landed in Point Judith. Today, white-coated Japanese lab technicians are the ones waiting at the dock. They arrive with vans outfitted with sophisticated equipment for testing fat content, color, histamine, and bacteria levels. The level of sophistication among local fishermen has risen in an equally steep curve. Some, like Bobby, realize that if proper care is taken with the right fish and the fish is marketed directly, it can make a difference of tens of thousands of dollars at the market.

## A RECORD . . . BUT AT WHAT PRICE?

The highest price recorded for a single giant bluefin at the Tsukiji auction was $173,600 for a 444-pound fish in 2001. When the rich, red, fatty flesh of this tuna was sold as sashimi in Tokyo's most elegant sushi bars. a single slice of sashimi sold for nearly one hundred dollars. As fishery scientist and author Daniel Pauly suggests in *In a Perfect Ocean*: "The bluefin's enormous price essentially dooms it: The fishery will be profitable to the very last fish."

If there is one large predatory fish that is capable of becoming extinct in our lifetime it is surely the giant bluefin that has ranged the North Atlantic and Mediterranean seas for perhaps millions of years. One has to wonder at this point in time if the management policies of the International Commission for the Conservation of Atlantic Tunas (ICCAT) will be sufficient to save the North Atlantic Mediterranean bluefin. It's estimated that since the establishment of ICCAT in 1969, North Atlantic bluefin populations have declined by more than 90 percent.

# TUNA, ALBACORE

After beginning life as free-floating plankton far out at sea, the **albacore** (*Thunnus alalunga*) quickly matures into a speedy predator capable of circumnavigating entire seas in search of food. The albacore can reach speeds in excess of fifty miles an hour with its aerodynamically shaped body, smooth skin, and pectoral fins that tuck away neatly into slots.

The most exciting and interesting albacore fishery takes place off the Pacific Coast of the United States from midsummer through fall. Huge schools of young migrating albacore first appear in the eastern Pacific off the coast of Baja California in midsummer; they then follow the food-laden upwelling of ocean currents northward along the continental shelf. A fleet of more than four hundred small boats troll for these albacore as they migrate through U.S. waters each summer and fall, catching thousands of fish by pole and line.

At about the age of five, albacore quit traveling and settle down in the deep waters far out to sea, where they lead a more sedentary existence. Mature albacore from throughout the Pacific have long been popular in Hawaii and on the West Coast, where they are referred to as **Hawaiian tombo** and used much like any other tuna. Albacore are also taken on the Atlantic Coast during the summer months.

Historically, Pacific coast albacore have been fished for the cannery, but they're now in ever-increasing demand as fresh fish during the summer and fall season. Japanese buyers have come to appreciate the tasty young albacore of our Pacific Coast, buying as much as half the year's catch for sashimi. There is a growing demand for fresh albacore on our own shores as well.

The albacore is unusual in that, unlike other tunas that become fatter and tastier as they mature, the albacore is at its healthiest to eat, fattest and best flavored, when it is a voraciously feeding youngster. The very plumpest and tastiest albacore, rich in omega-3 fatty acids, are the troll-caught Pacific Coast albacore of summer and fall. It also turns out that, unlike mature albacore, young troll-caught albacore are very low in mercury.

Fish markets in urban areas with large Japanese populations such as Honolulu, Vancouver, Seattle, New York, and San Francisco carry fresh albacore year-round; in other areas it may only be available during late summer and fall when Pacific Coast runs are under way.

Japanese fish markets are an excellent place to buy albacore: Because the albacore on sale is intended to be used as sashimi, these fishmongers are extremely conscientious about the quality.

Fresh albacore has a distinct and pleasant mineral-like smell that can only be described as the odor of steel. The surest sign of freshness in albacore is found in the darker, fatty meat isolated along one side; this should be ruby red in color. The leaner loin portion of the meat may vary from white to bright pink, depending on the diet of the fish.

### CHOOSING SUSTAINABLE SEAFOOD

Pacific Coast albacore is one of the world's most ecologically friendly fish choices. Fishery researchers generally agree that Pacific albacore stocks are healthy, and the Pacific Coast albacore fishery is enthusiastically endorsed as sustainable by all environmental groups. There is very little bycatch and no impact on fishery habitat, since albacore troll boats catch fish one at a time on individual hooks.

The more mature deepwater albacore, such as Hawaiian tombo, are fished by longline. Although U.S. fishermen have made great strides in reducing bycatch in longline fisheries, some international fisheries are less conscientious.

Unlike other tuna species, albacore do not swim with dolphins. For this reason, all of the world's albacore fisheries are considered dolphin safe.

## CHOOSING HEALTHY SEAFOOD

Cold-water fatty fish such as salmon and albacore are rich in heart-healthy omega-3 fatty acids (especially young troll-caught albacore), and health professionals advise eating them on a regular basis to help avoid chronic heart disease, reduce inflammatory response, and ensure good brain function. Albacore is also an easily digested high-protein source of B vitamins and minerals, particularly selenium, which may help reduce the effects of mercury.

Young troll-caught albacore from the Pacific Coast fishery have another thing in their favor: The Oregon State seafood laboratory has done tests showing that Pacific Coast troll-caught albacore of less than twenty-five pounds are very low in mercury. Ask your fishmonger for Pacific Coast troll-caught albacore.

If they are not quickly chilled after being caught, members of the tuna family may produce histamines in their flesh (see Scombroid, page 413) that can cause allergic response. A distinct and obvious rainbow sheen seen in the cross section of the cut flesh of albacore is a sign that the fish was not properly chilled after capture.

## IN THE KITCHEN

As with other members of the tuna family, the myoglobin-rich, stronger-flavored dark meat is isolated to one side of the loin in the albacore. While many people enjoy the flavor of the darker muscle tissue, particularly when it's very fresh, it can be easily trimmed away.

The albacore's mild flavor takes particularly well to poaching, but you can also use it in any of your favorite tuna or mackerel recipes. In Tahiti, albacore is one of the most popular fish used in the local specialty, *poisson cru*: a dish consisting of raw albacore steeped in a marinade of lime, coconut milk, tomato, onion, and cucumber. For an Italian flavor, add cooked albacore to white beans and then season with parsley, basil, mint, lemon, and a good extra-virgin olive oil.

The roe of albacore can be salted and pressed as *bottarga*—much as is done in Italy with other tuna or mullet roe—producing an Italian delicacy that can be shaved and served over pasta or salad. The skin of the albacore is too tough to eat, and the bones are too strong flavored to be used for making stock.

# ALBACORE CONFIT

MAKES 8 TO 10 CUPS

During the fall, when fresh troll-caught albacore is plentiful, take the time to conserve several jars of it. Not only do the jars look beautiful sitting on the shelf in your refrigerator, but the albacore inside is delicious and versatile. To make a quick and easy meal, break up the albacore and toss it with fresh-cooked green beans to serve over pasta, or toss in a niçoise salad. For tuna salad sandwiches, forget the mayonnaise and just mash the vegetables and albacore together with some of the juices.

One 3-pound albacore tuna loin

1 onion, sliced ⅛ inch thick

1 fennel bulb, trimmed, cored, halved, and sliced ⅛ inch thick

2 pimientos or red bell peppers, seeded and cut into julienne

8 to 10 black peppercorns, cracked

8 to 10 coriander seeds, toasted (see page 38)

½ teaspoon fennel seeds, toasted (see page 38)

2 bay leaves

2 lemons, thinly sliced and seeded

1 tablespoon kosher salt

¼ cup freshly squeezed lemon juice

¾ cup or more fresh fruity olive oil, plus more as needed

¼ cup olive oil

1. Preheat the oven to 250°F. Slice the albacore loin into 1-inch-thick steaks. In a medium bowl, combine the vegetables, spices, and lemons and stir to mix. Put half of the mixture in a shallow 4-quart baking dish. Arrange the slices of albacore on top and top with the remaining vegetable mixture. Sprinkle with and pour the lemon juice and the ¾ cup olive oil over all. Press everything firmly into the bottom of the baking dish with a spatula. If the albacore is not completely submerged in liquid, add more olive oil to cover.

2. Cover with aluminum boil and bake for 1 hour. Remove from the oven and let cool in the dish. (This gentle, low-temperature oven poaching keeps the fish moist and juicy.)

3. Evenly divide the ingredients among small glass jars and cover with the cooking juices. Add a touch of extra-virgin olive oil to cover and refrigerate for up to 10 days.

# BAKED ALBACORE WITH ORANGE-SCENTED OLIVE TAPENADE

Though packed with powerful flavors, tapenade doesn't overpower. While stronger-flavored swordfish, marlin, tuna, and mackerel pair well with tapenade, milder-flavored halibut, striped bass, and other delicately flavored fish can also be used in this recipe.

For an accompaniment, cut potatoes, yams, and beets into one-inch chunks, toss with olive oil and sea salt, and roast in a second baking dish alongside the fish for about forty-five minutes.

Four 5-ounce albacore steaks

Orange-Scented Olive Tapenade
   (recipe follows)

Juice of 1 orange

¼ cup dry white wine

2 tablespoons olive oil

GARNISHES

1 navel orange, segmented
   (see page 35)

Chopped fresh flat-leaf parsley

1. Preheat the oven to 425°F. Place the albacore steaks in an 8-cup baking dish and spread the Orange-Scented Olive Tapenade on top of them; pour the orange juice and wine around the fish. Cover with aluminum foil and bake until the fish is almost opaque throughout, about 10 minutes.

2. Remove from the oven and transfer the fish to 4 plates. Pour the liquid into a small saucepan and cook it over medium heat to reduce it to ¼ cup. Whisk in the olive oil and spoon the sauce over the fish. Garnish with the orange segments and parsley.

## ORANGE-SCENTED OLIVE TAPENADE

2 cups oil- or brine-cured black olives,
   such as kalamata or niçoise

2 anchovy fillets

2 tablespoons capers, rinsed

1 garlic clove

½ teaspoon Dijon mustard

1 tablespoon freshly squeezed orange juice

2 tablespoons olive oil

Grated zest of ½ orange

Fresh-cracked black pepper to taste

Minced fresh thyme to taste

TUNA, ALBACORE

381

1. Rinse the olives well and place between clean kitchen towels. Pound the olives lightly with a mallet or saucepan, then pick out the pits and discard.

2. In a food processor or by hand, chop the olives, anchovies, and capers until minced but with some texture. Using a mortar and pestle, pound the garlic to a paste. Stir in the mustard, orange juice, and olive oil, and then mix into the olive paste. Season with orange zest, black pepper, and thyme. To store, scrape the tapenade into a clean jar, float a little olive oil on top, and store in the refrigerator for up to 10 days.

## Concern over Mercury in Canned Tuna

America and Japan both have a love affair with tuna. Between the two countries, we catch, eat, buy, and import more tuna than all the other nations of the world combined. The big difference is in how it is served: The Japanese take their tuna raw with a little wasabi and soy, while we Americans favor ours with mayo on white bread.

Now, I have nothing against canned tuna—even James Beard considered canned tuna to be better than fresh. Since World War II, generations of American kids have grown up with canned tuna in sandwiches in our school lunch and in tuna casserole at night. Mom looked on it as healthy and easy.

Canned tuna became American comfort food—or at least it did until mercury cast a shadow of doubt on the prudence of Mom's choice of a healthy lunch.

The U.S. Food and Drug administration recently advised young children and women of childbearing age to limit consumption of canned white-meat albacore tuna because of elevated mercury levels. Light-meat canned skipjack tuna tests low for mercury (.12 ppm), whereas the milder-flavored, more popular white-meat albacore tuna averages three times those levels (.38 ppm). Yes, white-meat albacore tuna still falls in the moderate range for mercury levels, but the fear is that the most vulnerable members of society—small children still undergoing neurological development—are the ones most likely to eat lots of canned tuna. Children generally prefer the mild-flavored, white-meat albacore tuna variety.

The three tuna canneries that dominate the canned tuna market—Bumblebee, Star Kist, and Chicken of the Sea—prefer to can large mature albacore because large fish yield more meat per pound, and the meat appears solid white when cooked. But it is these larger, older, mature albacore that are most likely to test high in mercury because mercury is bio-accumulated over time.

Consumer concern over these recently released findings has encouraged a number of small independent canneries in California, Oregon, and Washington to begin marketing a safer alternative to the white-meat tuna found on the grocer's shelf. These canneries are packing small Pacific Coast albacore—fish from ten to twenty-five pounds—that have consistently tested low in mercury in studies done by the Oregon State seafood laboratory. These small-schooling Pacific coast albacore test at about one third the mercury level of the larger, older albacore preferred by the big canneries. Moreover, these young fish are feeding heavily to support their prodigious growth rate, which makes them considerably higher in heart-healthy omega-3s than their more mature brethren. Canned small albacore is therefore a truly healthy choice.

Some canneries have gone so far as to third-party certify each batch of fish as low mercury, stating so on the label, but any white-meat albacore tuna canned on the Pacific Coast of the United States is almost assuredly low mercury. Many of these "micro canneries" hand-pack their tuna so even though they may be more expensive, the quality is high and the cans are packed fuller than they can be by machine.

Light-meat canned tuna, which is skipjack, is as always a healthy choice, but if you want low-mercury white-meat albacore tuna that is safe even for young children and mothers-to-be, seek out albacore caught and canned on the U.S. Pacific Coast. Where can you find it? Low-mercury white-meat albacore is available under labels such as Pacific Fleet, Carvalho's, Dave's, Lazio, Vital Choice, Wild Planet; others can be found on the Internet. The label should read "low mercury," "minimal mercury," or "caught and canned on the U.S. Pacific Coast." The Whole Foods chain of grocery stores is expected to release a low-mercury canned white-meat tuna under their own label, and I wouldn't be surprised to see one of the big three canneries begin marketing a low-mercury white-meat tuna in the near future.

# WEAKFISH

The weakfish is actually two closely related species nearly identical in appearance. **Northern weakfish** (*Cynoscion regalis*) may wander as far north as southern New England, but are most abundant in the waters of the mid- and southern Atlantic states. The second species (*C. nebulosus*), often referred to as **spotted sea trout**, is found from the Carolinas south into the Gulf of Mexico.

Weakfish, a member of the drum family, is known for the loud drumming, chattering, and croaking sounds they use in echo-location and communication. When trying to attract a sexual partner, males make a purring sound by rapidly drumming their swim bladders.

When freshly caught, the weakfish's silvery sides and fins are highlighted with various iridescent gold reflections; small dark speckles on its back and flanks are responsible for its southern name of spotted sea trout. Sea trout average between two and ten pounds in the market.

The weakfish is considered great table fare with superior texture and flavor. However, it can spoil quickly and should be cleaned and iced right away to prevent it from earning the name bestowed on it by early Dutch settlers: weekvis, from the Old Dutch for "soft fish."

Fresh weakfish fillets should be translucent, with a lustrous sheen. The flesh is firm and dense, rebounding when probed with a finger; it should not appear soggy or waterlogged or have visible bruising, tears, or gaps. The darker red hemoglobin-rich muscle tissue should be intensely red. The two rows of red dots, one on either side of the fillet marking the muscle fibers that control the fins, should be tightly formed and intense; the color should not have bled into the surrounding lighter-colored flesh.

### CHOOSING SUSTAINABLE SEAFOOD

Although the northern weakfish has once again been delegated to the status of overfished (see Managing the Seas—An Impossible Task, page 386), the southern spotted sea trout is still considered abundant and is sustainably managed. It has benefited greatly from reduced fishing pressure and the use of bycatch-reduction devices in Southern shrimp fisheries that have dramatically reduced the catch of juvenile fish.

Weakfish seem resilient in nature; they mature at a young age and spawn repeatedly, producing millions of eggs. And that is why the rapid and precipitous decline in northern populations was such a surprise. The weak link may very well be its dependence on estuaries and seagrass beds as spawning habitat (see Too Much of a Good Thing, page 268).

### CHOOSING HEALTHY SEAFOOD

Weakfish is a good high-protein source of B vitamins and minerals and a moderate source of omega-3 fatty acids, which are said to improve the blood lipid profile, reduce inflammatory response, and ensure good brain function, among other health benefits.

Although some drums, such as spot, croaker, and black drum, tend to be heavily parasitized, weakfish are much less affected, though care should always be exercised when eating raw seafood (see Raw Seafood: How to Stay Safe, page 408).

### IN THE KITCHEN

One of the two weakfish species is available to you for great eating if you live anywhere from southern New England to Texas. Weakfish are closely related to the redfish of blackened redfish fame, and are equally as good in the kitchen. The soft-fleshed weakfish, with a long, tender flake, is moist and delicious. In Peru, the closely related corvina is one of the most popular fish for ceviche.

The bones of the weakfish make a very good stock but are moderately oily; simmer them gently for a short period of time and press the bones well to extract the juices. The skin, cheeks, roe, milt, and liver are all edible.

## Managing the Seas— An Impossible Task

When I began this book, I wrote that the weak-fish was "a bright spot in fishery management, as it has returned to historic levels of abundance and range." At the same time, I decided to leave lingcod (*Ophiodon elongates*), a mild-flavored West Coast species, out of the book because it had been overfished through much of its range and was seldom seen in the market anymore. But before ink could hit paper, the Northern weakfish was again designated "severely overfished" and the lingcod has rebounded to complete recovery. The cause of the weakfish's decline has yet to be divined, but the result is obvious to fishermen—there are few weakfish to be found, and severe restrictions will soon be implemented. On the other hand, for West Coast fishermen, lingcod will provide a much needed bright spot. The lingcod has rebounded to healthy levels many years sooner than was expected.

This comes as a reminder that nature is complex, fishery management is an inexact science, and humans may not be as important to the grand scheme as we might like to think. It takes more than just counting fish to determine what is happening in the sea. Climate change, pollution, oceanic conditions, the health of other species, human impact on rivers and wetland nurseries, and a myriad of other factors can all conspire to create quick and far-reaching change over which we have little or no control. The status of any of the fish in the sea can quickly change for better or worse, and humans are often relegated to being mere observers.

Unlike in the past when Pacific Coast lingcod were taken predominately by trawl vessels, today most lingcod is taken by hook and line. West Coast regulations, which severely restricted where trawlers can fish, have encouraged hook-and-line fishermen to go after the lingcod. Much as the haddock is the East Coast cod of the future, lingcod will become an ever more popular substitute for rockfish on the West Coast. Good-quality hook-and-line–caught lingcod is available from Alaska south to California.

# BAKED SEA TROUT WITH GREMOLATA-CRUMB TOPPING, SHIITAKES, AND ARUGULA

This crumb topping can be used when baking any kind of fish. It's particularly good with soft-fleshed fish, such as haddock, hake, whiting, or croaker and in particular the lingcod mentioned above; the crisp, crunchy bread crumbs provide textural contrast and flavor. Orange zest, chives, or other herbs make a nice addition to the topping.

When the fish is served on the bed of arugula, the heat from the fish wilts the greens. The sautéed shiitakes add flavor and texture. The shiitake is a very dry mushroom; any water that is released during cooking readily evaporates, which allows the mushroom pieces to easily brown and crisp rather than stew. I like to serve this dish with freshly cooked polenta.

3 tablespoons olive oil

1 tablespoon freshly squeezed lemon juice

Kosher salt and freshly ground black
    pepper to taste

Four 5-ounce sea trout (weakfish) fillets,
    about 1 inch thick

GREMOLATA-CRUMB TOPPING

1 cup fresh bread crumbs

1 tablespoon minced garlic

1 tablespoon grated lemon zest

¼ cup minced fresh flat-leaf parsley

1 tablespoon fish marinade (above)

1 tablespoon unsalted butter

1 tablespoon olive oil

4 ounces shiitake mushrooms, stemmed
    and chopped

8 ounces arugula

1. In a small bowl, combine the olive oil and lemon juice; whisk to blend. Season with salt and pepper. Reserve 1 tablespoon of the mixture for the topping. Place the fish in a baking dish, pour the remaining marinade over, turn to coat, and let stand for at least 15 minutes or up to 2 hours.

2. For the topping: In a shallow bowl, combine all the ingredients and stir to blend. Dampen the bread crumbs with a sprinkling of the reserved marinade. The bread crumbs should be slightly moist and crumbly, like wet sand.

3. Preheat the oven to 450°F. Remove the fillets from the marinade and roll them in the crumb mixture. Place the fillets on a baking sheet or broiler pan. Sprinkle any bread crumbs left in the bowl on top of the fish fillets.

4. Place the fish in the oven and bake for 12 to 15 minutes, or until the bread crumbs are toasted

and golden brown. If you're using fish fillets that are thinner than 1 inch (such as sole or John Dory), the cooking time may be shorter, so you may need to brown the bread crumbs under a preheated broiler.

5. While the fish is in the oven, cook the shiitakes: In a small sauté pan or skillet, melt the butter with the oil over medium-high heat and sauté the shiitakes for 8 to 10 minutes, or until browned and crisp. Divide the arugula among 4 plates and place the hot fish on top of the greens. Top with the sautéed shiitakes.

# WHELKS

**W**helks have been highly valued since ancient times, as much for the deep royal-purple dye they produce as for their food quality. Roman senatorial robes were colored with the dye extracted from whelks, and to this day there are places in the Mediterranean where purple dye is still processed from this creature.

The beautiful sun-bleached sienna-colored shell of the whelk can be seen washed up on Atlantic Coast beaches from Georgia to Maine. Often incorrectly referred to as conch, whelks are popular in East Coast cities with large Italian populations, where they're known as **scungilli**.

Unlike the vegetarian queen conch of Florida and Caribbean fame, whelks are carnivores, and they spend much of their time crawling around the ocean floor in search of clams, oysters, and other sedentary prey.

Also unlike the queen conch, whelks are abundant and well managed.

Two species of whelk are harvested commercially: the **waved whelk** (*Buccinium undatum*), a native of Maine and Canadian waters, and the **knobbed whelk** (*Busycon carica*), found from southern New England to Georgia. Little distinction is made between the two in U.S. markets, though waved whelks—which have a milder flavor—are the preferred whelk for export to France, England, Spain, and Italy, where they're very popular. In France, whelks often find their way onto the omnipresent *plateau de fruits de mer*.

## PERIWINKLES

**Periwinkles** (*Littorina littorea*) were introduced to Nova Scotia in the mid-1800s, most likely in an attempt by immigrants to introduce a popular working-class food to the region. They spread rapidly, becoming a common intertidal species as far south as New Jersey. Small-scale, commercial hand-harvesting of the abundant periwinkle occurs throughout its range, but production is limited due to low-market demand in North America. You may have to place a pre-order with your fish market.

### CHOOSING SUSTAINABLE SEAFOOD

Whelks are taken by trap throughout their range except in the waters of Georgia, where the fishery is by trawl. Horseshoe crabs, which are important to medical research, have been heavily exploited for use as bait in whelk traps.

In recent years, fishermen have modified their gear so that the bait can be reused, lessening the whelk fisheries' impact on the horseshoe crab population.

Whelk and periwinkle populations are considered healthy.

### CHOOSING HEALTHY SEAFOOD

Neither whelks nor periwinkles are subject to the pathogens that may affect filter-feeding bivalves. They are a good source of vitamin E, iron, copper, zinc, and selenium.

### IN THE KITCHEN

Whelks are most often cooked and removed from their shells before being sold; sometimes the meat is thinly presliced as well. Live whelks may be available at Chinese or Italian markets.

If whelks are purchased live, they should be cooked soon after purchase by gently boiling them in salted water for ten to fifteen minutes. At ten minutes, use a fork to try to remove the flesh from the shell. If it doesn't slide right out, return it to the water for further cooking, but be careful; if cooked too long, the flesh will toughen and be difficult to remove.

To prepare whelk meat, slice off the hard, horny operculum (a trapdoor the whelk uses to protect itself when retracted inside its shell) and discard. Cut the whelk meat in half lengthwise. The viscera and mouth parts will be obvious; cut these off and discard as well. Thinly slice the meat for salads, dice it for stir-fry, or mince for fritters and chowder. In Japan, whelk is simmered in sake and soy sauce, then chopped with vegetables before returning it to its shell to be baked.

Raw whelk meat used for ceviche or other preparations can be removed from the shell by slipping a thin knife down the inside curve of the shell and then cutting across the opening. This severs the muscle attaching the whelk to the shell.

Periwinkles are always sold alive in the shell.

Rinse them in a colander under cold running water, then discard any whose little trapdoor (operculum) is not securely shut. Be sure the periwinkles smell clean and briny. Cook them for two or three minutes in salted water or court bouillon. Serve with an aïoli or, if cooked in court bouillon, simply add a knob of butter to the broth and serve with country-style bread. The meat can easily be removed from the shell with a large pin or small fork.

## PERIWINKLES IN BLACK BEAN SAUCE WITH CHINESE SAUSAGE

SERVES 4 AS AN APPETIZER

If you like abalone or conch or clams, there is no reason you wouldn't like periwinkles. These delicious little curlicues are packed with flavor that can easily stand up to a black bean sauce. Lop chong, those hard red six-inch sausages hanging in the window of most Chinese markets, are easy to find—their sweetness is a nice counterpoint to the vinegar and chile in the sauce and gives the dish a little more substance. If you want to omit the sausage, add some Shaoxing or dry sherry wine to round out the flavor.

Serve the periwinkles with toothpicks for removing them from the shell as an appetizer. Or serve over fresh thin Chinese egg noodles (sometimes called Hong Kong, or chow mein, noodles) with braised Chinese broccoli for a complete meal.

2 tablespoons Asian-style unrefined
    peanut oil
1 tablespoon minced garlic
1 tablespoon minced fresh ginger
1 serrano or jalapeño chile, minced
4 scallions, sliced diagonally
2 Chinese sausages (lop chong), cut into
    ½-inch chunks, or 2 tablespoons

Shaoxing wine or dry sherry (optional)
2 tablespoons soy sauce
2 tablespoons rice vinegar
2 tablespoons fermented black beans,
    rinsed and coarsely chopped
½ cup water or chicken stock
2 pounds periwinkles

In a wok or large, heavy saucepan, heat the oil over medium heat and sauté the garlic, ginger, chile, and scallions for 1 minute. Add the sausages, soy sauce, rice vinegar, black beans, and water or stock. Simmer for 3 or 4 minutes. Increase the heat to high and add the periwinkles. Cover and cook for 1 minute, or until they appear to be falling out of the shell.

NOTE: Black bean sauce is a favorite accompaniment to seafood in Chinese restaurants. Squid, clams, shrimp mussels, salmon, and many other fish can be braised in black bean sauce.

# SALAD OF SPAGHETTI, WHELKS, OLIVES, AND CELERY

Whelks are extremely abundant in Narragansett Bay, where I grew up, only we knew them as "snails." It was one of the defining foods of the provincial cuisine I enjoyed in my youth. Snail salad was found on the menu of every restaurant, no matter how plain or fancy, and scungilli marinara was, and still is, a standard in the Italian restaurants of Federal Hill. Recently, I've seen restaurants trying to gentrify sea snails by calling them conch.

Although the snail salad of my youth was made with iceberg lettuce, canned olives, and coarse red wine vinegar, it provided the inspiration for this salad of spaghetti and whelks.

¼ cup olive oil

2 tablespoons freshly squeezed lemon juice

Kosher or sea salt to taste

Pinch of red pepper flakes

20 oil- or brine-cured black olives,
   such as kalamata

6 ounces whelk meat, cooked, cleaned,
   and sliced

1 to 2 stalks celery with tops, finely diced
   (about ½ cup)

½ teaspoon minced fresh oregano

1 tablespoon minced fresh flat-leaf parsley

6 ounces spaghetti, cooked al dente
   and cooled

Curly endive, escarole, frisée, or other bitter
   lettuce, chopped or torn, for serving

1. In a small bowl, whisk the olive oil into the lemon juice to make a vinaigrette; season with the salt and red pepper flakes.

2. Place the olives between clean kitchen towels and pound lightly with a mallet or saucepan. Pick out the pits and discard. Chop the olives coarsely and add the whelk meat, celery, oregano, parsley, and vinaigrette. Toss well and let stand for 1 hour.

3. Just before serving, add the pasta and toss again. Serve atop a bed of the bitter lettuce.

VARIATION: Octopus is an excellent substitute for whelk, as is squid or razor clams.

# WHITE SEA BASS

The **white sea bass** (*Atractoscion nobilis*) is the largest and most prized member of the drum or croaker family. Other drums of particular note are the Gulf of Mexico redfish, the Atlantic sea trout, weakfish, and corvina.

Until the mid-twentieth century, white sea bass was one of the most important fish species in California. Fishery department photos from the time show entire railway cars packed with well-iced sea bass on their way to market. Over time, however, degradation of spawning habitat, overfishing, and the demise of its favorite prey, the sardine, led to dramatic declines in California white sea bass populations.

When I first started selling fish in the 1980s, the white sea bass was a rarity. But today, thanks to a combination of good management and improved habitat, this fish has come roaring back.

The establishment of a hatchery program at Hubbs-SeaWorld in Carlsbad, California, and the banning of inshore gill nets have helped the white sea bass make great strides toward recovery. "They're definitely back," says state fish and game biologist Steve Crook, based in Long Beach. "There has been a tremendous natural recovery in the stocks."

The white sea bass changes color to match its mood: green-gold when hunting the kelp beds, flashy silver with iridescent-purple stripes when courting. Freshly caught, the white sea bass is gold and silver with purple highlights. The largest recorded catch is eighty-four pounds, but the average fish weighs from ten to thirty pounds.

The otoliths (ear bones) of the white sea bass have long been considered good luck charms and were used as wampum by early California Indians. Otoliths have been found in Indian middens throughout California, and even to this day many fishermen save these large calcareous ear bones for ornamentation and good luck.

Fresh white sea bass fillets should be translucent, with a lustrous sheen. The flesh will be firm and dense, springing back when probed with a finger; it should not appear soggy or waterlogged or have visible bruising, tears, or gaps. The darker red hemoglobin-rich muscle tissue should be intensely red. The two rows of red dots, one on either side of the fillet marking the muscle fibers that control the fins, should be tightly formed and intense; the color should not have bled into the surrounding lighter-colored flesh.

California white sea bass season takes place from June 15 through March 15; the heaviest landings are between July and October.

### CHOOSING SUSTAINABLE SEAFOOD

In 1994, gill-netting for sea bass was banned in shallow waters, reducing the number of immature and spawning fish taken. The banning of gill nets encouraged California fishermen to turn to hook-and-line gear, thus improving the quality of fish coming to market and creating an environmentally sound fishery to be proud of. As a result, there has been a dramatic increase in the average size and number of fish landed—good indications of a healthy, growing population. Following the resurgence of their prime prey, the sardine, white sea bass are actively repopulating northern California waters.

### CHOOSING HEALTHY SEAFOOD

White sea bass is a very good high-protein source of antistress B vitamins and minerals, particularly selenium, and is a moderate source of omega-3 fatty acids, which improve the blood lipid profile, reduce inflammatory response, and enhance brain function.

Although wild fish may be susceptible to infective parasites, white sea bass are seldom affected, though care should always be exercised when eating raw seafood (see Raw Seafood: How to Stay Safe, page 408).

## IN THE KITCHEN

Moderately fatty, with a large flake, white sea bass is tender yet firm enough to charcoal-grill if carefully handled. This is a versatile fish, taking well to any method of cooking, from steaming to broiling, and it accepts pairing with most ingredients. A braise or stew of sea bass can be delicious, and the sweet flavor of this fish matches particularly well with tomatoes and basil—both of which are at their peak during the height of the sea bass season.

The skin of the white sea bass must be scaled before cooking but is edible and delicious if cooked crisp, although strong flavored. The bones make a rich and flavorful stock. The darker-fleshed fat can be assertively flavored in large fish, so when your preparation calls for a mild-flavored fish (such as for curing or poaching or in raw preparations), choose smaller fish of under ten pounds.

## WHITE SEA BASS BROCHETTES WITH MOROCCAN CHARMOULA

SERVES 4 AS A MAIN COURSE

Moroccan charmoula, delicious with any fish from bluefish to salmon, can be used as a marinade, sauce, or both. It is one of my favorite sauces with grilled fish, but it's also very good with baked or broiled fish. The parsley and cilantro can be minced by hand for a relishlike consistency or chopped in a blender or food processor for a smoother texture. Serve this dish with couscous and tomato salad.

CHARMOULA MARINADE

2 garlic cloves

1 teaspoon coarse kosher salt

2 tablespoons freshly squeezed lemon juice

1-inch piece fresh ginger, peeled
   and minced

¾ cup fresh flat-leaf parsley leaves

¾ cup fresh cilantro leaves

2 teaspoons sweet Hungarian paprika

½ teaspoon ground cumin

½ teaspoon cayenne pepper

½ cup olive oil

4 tablespoons freshly squeezed orange juice

1½ pounds white sea bass fillets, cut into
   1-inch cubes

1. For the marinade: Using a mortar and pestle, grind the garlic and salt to a paste; add the lemon juice and scrape the mixture into a blender or food processor. Add the ginger, parsley, cilantro, spices, ¼ cup of the olive oil, and 2 tablespoons of the orange juice. Pulse to grind the herbs and mix everything, then turn the machine off and push the herbs down into the blade.

2. Turn the machine on low and drizzle in the remaining ¼ cup oil, alternately adding enough of the remaining 2 tablespoons orange juice to keep everything moving. Puree to a coarsely minced, thick sauce. Taste and adjust the seasoning.

3. Thread the fish onto skewers and arrange in a baking dish. Reserve a small amount of the charmoula to serve as a sauce and pour the rest over the brochettes. Mix well and marinate in the refrigerator for 2 hours.

4. Prepare a medium-hot fire in a charcoal grill, preheat a gas grill to 375°F, or preheat the broiler. Oil the grill grids and add the fish to the grill, or place the fish on a broiler pan 4 inches from the heat source. Grill or broil the fish for about 3 minutes on each side, or until almost opaque throughout.

5. Transfer the brochettes to plates and spoon the reserved charmoula over.

VARIATION: Other tasty additions to charmoula include fresh mint, a little chopped tomato, a few threads of saffron, or a pinch of ground cinnamon. Preserved Lemons (page 322) are particularly good in this recipe; add ½ cup finely chopped preserved lemons to the other ingredients.

# PERUVIAN TIRADITO OF WHITE SEA BASS WITH SOY DIPPING SAUCE

SERVES 12 AS AN APPETIZER

Peruvian fishermen have long salted and soused fish in lime to make ceviche, while tiradito is a more recent incarnation. The influence of the many Japanese immigrants who came to Peru in the nineteenth century is apparent in the way the fish is sliced rather than chopped, and ginger, soy, and other Japanese ingredients often find their way into tiradito. Other good fish to use in this preparation are fluke (summer flounder), aquacultured sturgeon, striped bass, albacore, and Alaska or California halibut—all environmentally sound choices as well.

The tiradito can be garnished with cold cooked yams and corn on the cob cut into thick wheels, or the typical garnish, *cancha*: panfried Peruvian hard corn, very similar to the American snack food known as "corn nuts." Vanessa Barrington, who did a wonderful job of testing the recipes for this book, suggested an easier-to-find alternative in boiled edamame.

1½ pounds white sea bass fillets

1 tablespoon coarse kosher salt

⅓ cup finely chopped celery with tops

⅓ cup finely chopped green olives

¼ cup finely chopped red bell pepper

½ cup freshly squeezed orange juice

½ cup freshly squeezed lime juice

SOY DIPPING SAUCE

1 red rocoto or serrano chile

1 garlic clove

1-inch piece fresh ginger, peeled

¼ cup soy sauce

Orange and lime juices reserved
    from marinade (above)

1. With a sharp knife, cut along either side of the dark blood line that runs down the center lateral line of the fillet. Discard the dark flesh. Trim away the thinnest edges and the belly flap, making sure to include the fine pinbones that reside just to the center of the belly meat. Each fillet has now been turned into 2 relatively uniform blocks.

2. Cut each block into ¼-inch slices and arrange on a chilled platter. Sprinkle with the salt. Scatter the celery, green olives, and bell pepper over the fish. Mix the orange and lime juice together, and pour three fourths of it over the fish, reserving the rest, ¼ cup, for the dipping sauce. Refrigerate for at least 15 minutes or up to 1 hour.

3. For the sauce: Using a mortar and pestle, pound the chile, garlic, and ginger into a paste. Stir in the soy sauce and the reserved orange and lime juices.

4. Serve the tiradito with the dipping sauce alongside.

# WRECKFISH

In 1987, a South Carolina fisherman attempting to recover lost gear in a deepwater canyon far off the coast brought aboard a grouperlike fish he had never seen before. It turned out to be the **Atlantic wreckfish** (*Polyprion americanus*), a species formerly considered unknown in the western North Atlantic. It was soon revealed that an undersea mount known as the Charleston Bump was deflecting warm Gulf Stream waters, causing an upwelling of nutrient-rich bottom water. Large numbers of big wreckfish had gone undiscovered because they were concentrated at depths that are usually food-poor.

The Atlantic wreckfish is a member of the temperate bass family and is closely related to the striped bass.

There are well-established fisheries for this species in the Azores and throughout the Mediterranean. The

Atlantic wreckfish is the exact same species as the highly esteemed **New Zealand grouper**, which is very popular in Asia and on the U.S. Pacific Coast, and is closely related to the Hawaiian sea bass (hapu'upu'u), one of the most highly regarded species for sashimi.

Atlantic wreckfish are available from mid-April through mid-January, while New Zealand grouper are available year-round.

The moist, succulent flesh is firm and pinkish, becoming white when cooked. The fresh fillets have a clean, fresh ocean smell, and should be translucent, with a satiny, lustrous sheen.

### CHOOSING SUSTAINABLE SEAFOOD

Wreckfish are well-managed and sustainable. They are caught by jigging, a form of hook-and-line fishing, and managed by individual fishery quota with limits on yearly allowable catch. There is a seasonal closure to protect spawning fish from mid-January to mid-April.

### CHOOSING HEALTHY SEAFOOD

Wreckfish is an excellent low-fat, high-protein source of B vitamins and minerals, particularly selenium, and is a moderate source of the omega-3 fatty acids said to improve the blood lipid profile, reduce inflammatory response, and enhance brain function. Caught in clean, deep offshore waters, the wreckfish is generally free of pollutants and parasites.

### IN THE KITCHEN

Wreckfish is moderately fatty, with a large, firm flake and a rich flavor. Like its close relative the striped bass, the wreckfish is adaptable to any method of cooking and many recipes. Its rich flavor pairs well with a variety of sauces and ingredients. Mild sauces complement its ocean-sweet flavor, yet stronger-flavored sauces don't overpower. The skin of the wreckfish is too tough to eat and is usually removed before cooking. The bones make a rich and flavorful stock.

## BRAISED WRECKFISH WITH A GOLDEN PAN SAUCE AND RED PEPPER–SAFFRON AÏOLI

SERVES 4 AS A MAIN COURSE

Braising wreckfish in turmeric and wine creates a golden pan sauce that is beautifully complemented by Red Pepper–Saffron Aïoli. Serve with parsleyed potatoes and green beans or a shaved fennel salad.

**Four 5-ounce wreckfish fillets, skinned**

**⅓ cup ground turmeric mixed with**

  **1 tablespoon kosher salt**

**2 tablespoons refined peanut oil or another**

  **high-heat oil for frying**

**2 tablespoons finely chopped onion**

1 cup dry white wine

½ cup water or Fish Stock (page 26)

1 tablespoon minced fresh chives or
flat-leaf parsley

Red Pepper–Saffron Aïoli (recipe follows)

1. Roll the fillets of wreckfish in the turmeric mixture until well coated on all sides.

2. In a large, heavy ovenproof sauté pan or cast-iron skillet, heat the oil over medium-high heat until shimmering. Carefully lay the wreckfish fillets in the pan, skin-side up. Cook for 1 to 2 minutes, then turn the fillets over, add the onion, and cook for 1 minute, or until the onion is sizzling and beginning to turn brown. Add the white wine and water or stock and simmer gently for about 5 minutes, or until the fish is almost opaque throughout.

3. Transfer the fish to 4 plates. Add the chives or parsley to the juices in the pan and cook to reduce to about ½ cup. Taste and adjust the seasoning and spoon Red Pepper–Saffron Aïoli evenly over the fish.

## RED PEPPER–SAFFRON AÏOLI

MAKES ¾ CUP

Large pinch of saffron threads

2 or 3 garlic cloves

¼ teaspoon coarse sea salt, plus more
to taste

Pinch of cayenne pepper or hot paprika

1 large egg yolk

1 teaspoon warm water

⅜ cup olive oil

⅜ cup refined peanut or another
mild-flavored oil

1 red bell pepper

1 tablespoon freshly squeezed lemon juice

1 tablespoon white wine vinegar

1. In a small sauté pan or skillet over medium heat, toast the saffron threads until they begin to curl, about 1 minute. Using a mortar and pestle, grind the garlic, saffron threads, the ¼ teaspoon salt, and the cayenne or paprika to a smooth paste. Transfer the mixture to a bowl or a food processor. Add the egg yolk and water and whisk or process until smooth. While constantly whisking or with the machine running, gradually pour in the oils, starting with just a few drops at a time; as the sauce begins to thicken, add the remaining oil in a slow, fine stream. If the aïoli becomes too thick, thin with a bit of warm water.

2. Cut the sides off the red pepper and shred the flesh sides on the large holes of a box grater; discard the skin. Drain the red pepper flesh well in a sieve. Whisk the lemon juice, vinegar, and bell pepper into the aïoli and season with salt to taste. It can be stored for several days in a clean jar in the refrigerator.

# HEALTH APPENDIX

Seafood is one of the most healthful foods we can eat, but as with all foods, eating seafood does carry an element of risk. Much of the information in this appendix addresses those elements of risk. I've tried to present all the information in a clear and balanced manner so the next time a seafood-related health scare hits the headlines you can refer to this appendix and make your own decision as to how serious that threat may be.

The appendix begins with the most important issue in the minds of health-conscious seafood consumers today: how to balance the benefits of omega-3s against the hazards of mercury. A discussion of omega-3s and mercury is accompanied by charts showing their levels in seafood.

We then continue with a glossary of health and safety concerns, which covers all worms, germs, and other piscatorial concerns imaginable. While the health glossary is often referred to throughout the text, seldom if ever will the average consumer be faced with the threats presented here. However, by understanding and learning to recognize the risks inherent in eating seafood, we are better able to minimize them.

## OMEGA-3S AND MERCURY: A BALANCING ACT

### Omega-3s: Benefits Found in Seafood

Omega-3 fatty acids, essential to life and good health, protect against disease and can treat illness. They prevent heart disease, have been shown to be beneficial to those with Type 2 diabetes, and chronic diseases involving the immune system such as rheumatoid arthritis, asthma, psoriasis, eczema, and some allergies. They encourage healthy brain function, help prevent depression, and ward off age-related macular degeneration, which is a major cause of impaired vision in older adults.

Research indicates that children born to mothers consuming higher quantities of omega-3-rich fish are health-ier at birth and exhibit higher IQs and better health later in life. The omega-3 fatty acids help in the development of the child's brain, nervous system, immune system, and retinal system. Authorities recommend that pregnant and nursing mothers eat a well-balanced diet that includes fatty fish two to three times a week to ensure proper childhood development (see also Omega-3s, Mercury, and Pregnancy, page 407).

Omega-3s are found almost exclusively in seafood, and thousands of studies, clinical trials, and books have detailed their benefits. Dr. Joyce Nettleton, a nutrition consultant, writes the PUFA (polyunsaturated fatty acids) newsletter at www.fatsoflife.com, which summarizes professional articles and discusses research on the health benefits of omega-3 fatty acids.

The chart on page 404 depicts the comparative amounts of omega-3s in each species rather than the exact amounts. Spawning activity and diet may cause the fat content of individual fish and shellfish, and thus the omega-3s, to vary greatly from season to season. The body fat of a Boston mackerel in early spring may be only 3 percent, while the same mackerel after fattening through the summer may attain a body fat content of 21 percent, a sevenfold increase in both body fat and omega-3 fatty acids.

### SOURCES OF DATA

Detailed measurements of omega-3 fatty acid levels in seafood can be viewed at the USDA National Nutrient Database web site at www.ars.usda.gov/ba/bhnrc/ndl, or the easy-to-use Nutritiondata web site at www.nutritiondata.com, which is based on USDA data.

## Mercury in Seafood

All living organisms that evolved with the planet Earth contain trace quantities of mercury. Elemental mercury is washed into streams and the sea, where bacteria convert it into organic mercury, which can enter the food web. At the same time, plants and other organisms are busy converting organic mercury back to inorganic compounds. This constant cycling of mercury from elemental to organic and back again has occurred for eons.

Until the Industrial Revolution, the natural process of rivers washing mercury from rocks, volcanic activity, and forest fires were the greatest sources of mercury entering the environment. Today, coal-burning power plants, waste incinerators, and chlorine-production plants are responsible for greatly increasing the amount of mercury entering the atmosphere.

What we do know is that mercury in the food supply can lead to neurological problems and birth defects. We know that fetuses and infants are especially vulnerable to the effects of mercury. But what we do not completely understand is what safe long-term low-dose exposure levels for adults are.

In the past, standards for mercury exposure were determined by observations gathered from industrial accidents in Iraq, Japan, and Sweden. Only recently has the type of mercury found in seafood (mercury cysteine) been identified. Initial studies have found that the mercury found in seafood may be less toxic than the form of mercury on which fish consumption advisories have been based. As well, a number of studies have found that the essential element selenium, high amounts of which are found in ocean fish, neutralizes the toxic effects of mercury in the human body. This may be the reason why studies have never shown an epidemic of child developmental problems in coastal populations whose diets have been comprised in large part of seafood.

A U.S. National Academy of Sciences report in 2000 examined the dangers of mercury and concluded that the risk of harm from the intake of mercury from eating fish for the majority of people was low. It is unlikely that mercury is a threat to a healthy adult who eats a normal and varied diet. In many cultures around the world, fish are a much greater part of the diet than in the United States. In Japan, for example, seafood consumption is four times higher than in the United States, and for centuries the very largest tunas, those most likely to bio-accumulate large amounts of mercury, have been a favorite Japanese food without causing apparent problems.

However, the risk of mercury exposure to pregnant women, infants, and children cannot be minimized. The ever-increasing amount of mercury entering the environment presents a grave risk to future generations. It is our responsibility to utilize the technologies that exist to

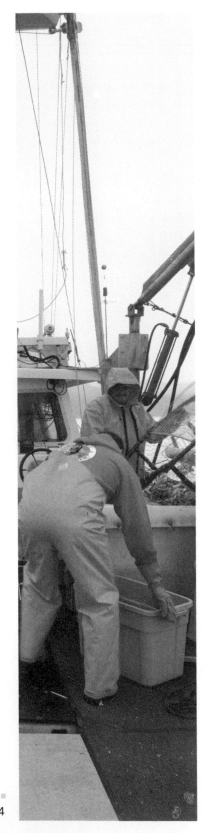

| Species | Omega-3 Level | | | | |
| --- | --- | --- | --- | --- | --- |
| | Low | Low to Moderate | Moderate | High | Very High |
| Anchovies | ▓ | ▓ | | ▓ | ▓ |
| Black Sea Bass | ▓ | ▓ | ▓ | | |
| Bluefish | ▓ | ▓ | ▓ | ▓ | |
| Butterfish | ▓ | ▓ | ▓ | | |
| Catfish | ▓ | ▓ | | | |
| Clam | ▓ | | | | |
| Cod | ▓ | ▓ | | | |
| Crab | ▓ | ▓ | | | |
| Crayfish | ▓ | | | | |
| Croaker | ▓ | ▓ | | | |
| Dory, John | ▓ | | | | |
| Grouper | ▓ | ▓ | | | |
| Haddock | ▓ | | | | |
| Hake | ▓ | ▓ | | | |
| Halibut, Alaska | ▓ | ▓ | ▓ | | |
| Herring | | | | ▓ | ▓ |
| Jack, Amberjack, Yellowtail | ▓ | ▓ | ▓ | ▓ | |
| Jack, Hamachi | ▓ | ▓ | ▓ | | |
| Lingcod | ▓ | | | | |
| Lobster | ▓ | ▓ | | | |
| Lobster, Spiny | ▓ | | | | |
| Mackerel, Boston | ▓ | ▓ | ▓ | ▓ | |
| Mackerel, King | | | | ▓ | ▓ |
| Mackerel, Pacific | | | | | ▓ |
| Mackerel, Spanish | | | | ▓ | |
| Mahimahi | ▓ | | | | |
| Monkfish | ▓ | | | | |
| Mussel | ▓ | ▓ | | | |
| Octopus | ▓ | ▓ | | | |
| Ono or Wahoo | ▓ | | | | |
| Opah | ▓ | ▓ | | | |
| Oyster | ▓ | ▓ | ▓ | | |
| Pollock, Alaska | ▓ | | | | |
| Pollock, Atlantic | ▓ | ▓ | | | |
| Rockfish | ▓ | | | | |
| Salmon | | | | ▓ | ▓ |
| Sand Dabs | ▓ | | | | |
| Sardines | | | | ▓ | ▓ |
| Scallops | ▓ | | | | |
| Shad | | | | ▓ | ▓ |
| Shrimp | ▓ | ▓ | | | |
| Skate | ▓ | | | | |
| Snapper | ▓ | ▓ | | | |
| Smelt | ▓ | ▓ | ▓ | | |
| Sole or Flounder | ▓ | | | | |
| Squid | ▓ | ▓ | | | |
| Striped Bass, farmed | ▓ | ▓ | ▓ | ▓ | |
| Striped Bass, wild | ▓ | ▓ | ▓ | | |
| Sturgeon | ▓ | ▓ | ▓ | ▓ | |
| Swordfish | ▓ | ▓ | ▓ | ▓ | |
| Tilapia | ▓ | | | | |
| Tilefish | ▓ | ▓ | ▓ | | |
| Trout or Char | | | | ▓ | |
| Tuna, Albacore, large | ▓ | ▓ | ▓ | ▓ | |
| Tuna, Albacore, young | | | | ▓ | ▓ |
| Tuna, Red | ▓ | ▓ | ▓ | | |
| Weakfish | ▓ | ▓ | | | |
| Whelks | ▓ | ▓ | | | |
| White Sea Bass | ▓ | ▓ | | | |
| Whiting | ▓ | ▓ | | | |
| Wreckfish | ▓ | ▓ | ▓ | | |

| Mercury Levels | | | |
|---|---|---|---|
| **Negligible** (nondetectable to 0.15 ppm) | **Low** (0.16-0.30 ppm) | **Moderate** (0.31-0.55 ppm) | **High** (above 0.55 ppm) |
| Anchovy | Black Sea Bass | Bluefish | Jack, Crevalle, Gulf |
| Butterfish | Bluefish, Atlantic | Bluefish, Gulf | Mackerel, King |
| Catfish | Grouper, Atlantic Red | Grouper | Shark, Mako |
| Clam | Halibut, Alaska | Grouper, Black, Gulf | Swordfish |
| Cod, Alaska | Mackerel, Spanish, Atlantic | Lobster, Maine | Tilefish, Gulf |
| Cod, Atlantic | Monkfish | Mackerel, Spanish, Gulf | |
| Crab | Ono or Wahoo | Marlin | |
| Crayfish | Rockfish | Tuna, Albacore, large | |
| Croaker | Snapper | Tuna, Red, large | |
| Flounder and Sole | Striped Bass | | |
| Haddock | Tilefish, Atlantic | | |
| Hake | Weakfish (Seatrout) | | |
| Herring | | | |
| Lingcod | | | |
| Lobster, Spiny | | | |
| Mackerel, Boston | | | |
| Mackerel, Pacific | | | |
| Mahimahi | | | |
| Mussel | | | |
| Oyster | | | |
| Pollock | | | |
| Rockfish (deepwater species) | | | |
| Sablefish | | | |
| Salmon | | | |
| Salmon, canned | | | |
| Sardine | | | |
| Scallops | | | |
| Shad | | | |
| Shrimp | | | |
| Skate | | | |
| Squid | | | |
| Tilapia | | | |
| Trout or Char | | | |
| Tuna, Albacore, young, Pacific | | | |
| Tuna, canned, light | | | |
| Whiting | | | |

SOURCES OF DATA

National Marine Fisheries Service (Hall et al). 1978. Survey of trace elements in the fishery resource report.

The occurrence of mercury in the fishery resources of the Gulf of Mexico report. 2000. www.duxbury.battelle.org

FDA Monitoring Program. 1990–2004. Mercury concentrations in fish. www.cfsan.fda.gov

USEPA: National listing of fish and wildlife advisory fish tissue database. www.epa.gov/waterscience/fish

USDA nutrient database. www.ars.usda.gov/ba/bhnrc/ndl

Alaska Department of Environmental Conservation fish monitoring program 2004. www.dec.state.ak.us/eh/vet/fish.htm

Oregon Sea Grant: Mercury in Oregon bottom fish. 1972. www.seagrant.oregonstate.edu/sgpubs/onlinepubs/i01003.pdf

Oregon State University Seafood Laboratory in Astoria (Michael Morrissey): Mercury in albacore. 2004

Florida Fish and Wildlife (Douglas Adams): Mercury levels in estuarine fishes of Florida. 1989–2001 significantly reduce industrial mercury pollution entering the environment, regardless of the cost.

The chart on page 405 depicts the average level of mercury, in parts per million (ppm), as found in various seafoods. Compiled from numerous samples, the chart expresses an accurate picture of the comparative levels of mercury found in each species, but the exact amount of mercury found in individual fish or shellfish may deviate considerably from the mean average. This is particularly true of species that test at the highest end of the scale, such as swordfish and shark.*

Mercury levels below .15 ppm are negligible; .16 to .30 ppm is low; .31 to .55 ppm is moderate; seafood with levels above .55 ppm should not be eaten by young children, women considering pregnancy, or pregnant and nursing mothers. The FDA-recommended action level for restricting the sale of seafood is 1.00 ppm mercury.

### MERCURY STUDIES

Determining acceptable levels of long-term low-level mercury exposure is complicated by individual responses and the subjectivity of symptoms, but there are two ongoing science-based studies.

The first study, conducted by a research team from the University of Rochester led by pediatric neurologist Gary Myers, follows a subject base of 779 pregnant women and their children in the Seychelles Islands. The subjects typically ate fish on average twelve times per week. The study, published in the journals *Neuro-Toxicology* and *Lancet*, determined that after comparing the fifteen hundred children born during the study with a control group in the United States, "There is no evidence of neurodevelopmental risk from prenatal methylmercury exposure resulting solely from the consumption of ocean fish."

The second study, referred to as the Faroe Islands study, was reported in the February 2004 issue of *The Journal of Pediatrics*. Conducted by a research team from the Harvard School of Public Health led by Philippe Grandjean, the study found "neurological anomalies" in some of the children in the study.

Faroe Islanders consume pilot whales that contain high levels of both PCBs and mercury while containing only small amounts of selenium, an element that is thought to sequester mercury and reduce its detrimental effects. The entire whale is consumed soon after capture, creating a pulse effect of exposure to a witch's brew of PCBs and mercury. Lacking the protective effect of the high amounts of selenium found in finfish, it is possible this atypical Western diet may exacerbate the neurodevelopmental effects of mercury.

In 2004, the FDA and EPA lowered the safe threshold level of mercury in the blood of pregnant and nursing mothers from 20 micrograms per liter to 5.8 micrograms per liter. Citing the Faroe Islands study findings of neurodevelopmental anomalies in the fetuses of mothers with mercury levels of 58 micrograms per liter, a tenfold safety level was deemed appropriate.

The FDA and EPA now recommend that pregnant and lactating women not allow mercury levels to rise above 5.8 micrograms per liter of blood. The EPA has determined that a safe level for mercury as measured in hair is one part per million. Methylmercury is eliminated from the body via bile and stool; most mercury leaves the body within months.

---

* *Some of the most important factors that affect mercury levels in seafood are not reflected in available data. It is well known that larger, older fish and fish captured near notable mercury "hot spots," such as coal-burning power plants, chlorine production facilities, and offshore oil-drilling platforms accumulate higher levels of mercury. Seldom has this pertinent information been compiled or correlated in survey data. More extensive surveys and improved sampling methods would go a long way toward helping us understand the issues of mercury in seafood.*

## Omega-3s, Mercury, and Pregnancy

Fish and shellfish are an important part of a healthy diet for all people, especially pregnant women and young children. Scientific evidence has shown that omega-3 fatty acids, found exclusively in seafood, are essential to the complete development of the brain, nervous system, immune system, and retinal system during pregnancy and the first two years of life.

However, fetal growth and infancy are the periods in human development when exposure to methylmercury poses the greatest threat to the nervous system. Methylmercury easily crosses the placenta, and the mercury concentration may rise to 30 percent higher in fetal red blood cells than in those of the mother.

More studies are needed to understand the effects of mercury on human development and determine acceptable low-dose, long-term exposure levels, but common sense tells us that the developing fetus and infants are especially vulnerable. Prudence dictates that pregnant or nursing mothers and those trying to become pregnant should follow the FDA guidelines that recommend eating omega-3-rich seafood while avoiding fish testing high for mercury.

Pregnant and nursing mothers and those trying to become pregnant should:

- Avoid the largest long-lived predatory ocean fish, such as swordfish, marlin, large-sized tunas, king mackerel, and Gulf of Mexico tilefish. Also, Spanish mackerel, barracuda, conger eel, grouper, jacks, and bluefish over ten pounds should be avoided. The FDA fish consumption advisory for commercial fish can be found at the FDA's center for food safety and nutrition at www.cfsan.fda.gov.
- Avoid wild freshwater fish such as whitefish, pike, pickerel, walleye, and lake trout, which are more likely to be contaminated with mercury and other pollutants than saltwater fish. Recreationally caught fish from bays and inshore estuaries may be tainted by mercury runoff from abandoned mines or industrial sources. Fish-consumption advisories for recreational fisheries can be found at www.epa.gov/mercury/advisories.htm.
- Choose the following fish, which are very high in omega-3 fatty acids yet contain nondetectable to very low levels of mercury. The best choices for pregnant and nursing women are all species of wild salmon, anchovies, sardines, shad, sablefish, butterfish, Boston mackerel, Pacific mackerel, bonito, and herring. Other very good choices are Pacific troll-caught albacore, small skipjack tuna, and small red-meat tuna of less than thirty pounds (see page 382 for choosing small-sized tuna).
- Choose aquacultured fish with higher levels of omega-3s and nondetectable to very low levels of mercury: Trout, char, sturgeon, barramundi, hamachi, and kampachi are high in omega-3s, while catfish and tilapia have moderate levels of omega-3s.
- Choose seafood that contains low to moderate levels of omega-3s and nondetectable to very low levels of mercury: cod, pollock, haddock, hake, flounder, sole, croaker, spiny lobster, crab, squid, scallops, shrimp, clams, oysters, mussels, and farmed crawfish. (Pregnant women, young children, and those with compromised immune systems should refrain from eating raw shellfish; see Raw Seafood: How to Stay Safe, page 408.)
- Choose canned light-meat tuna or low-mercury Pacific troll-caught albacore (see Concern over Mercury in Canned Tuna, page 382).
- Eat a variety of seafood from different locations. Refer to the charts on pages 404 and 405 to find a mix of seafood that minimizes exposure to methylmercury while providing the health benefits of a diet high in omega-3 fatty acids.

Not long ago, raw seafood in the United States consisted of oysters or clams on the half shell served at the water's edge, an abbreviated selection of previously frozen sashimi at the local sushi bar, and the occasional dish of ceviche in Latin restaurants. Today, in contrast, fresh seafood is sourced from around the world and presented in raw seafood recipes from a dozen different cuisines and served in restaurants and homes throughout the country.

Contrary to popular perception, only 5 percent of all foodborne illnesses are seafood related, but as raw seafood becomes a greater part of our diet, seafood-associated illnesses become of greater concern. Raw seafood today is as safe as it has ever been, but there are risks. The best way to avoid seafoodborne illnesses is to heed the sensible precautions that follow, many of which pertain to cooked seafood as well.

### Eating Raw Finfish Safely

In the United States, it is extremely rare for individuals to become ill from consuming finfish. Carefully prepared in a clean environment, even *raw* finfish is almost never a source of human illness. Other than bacterial cross-contamination from other foods, poor hygiene, or dirty conditions, the greatest threat from eating raw or lightly cooked finfish is the possibility of ingesting a worm. Fewer than thirty cases a year are reported in the United States, yet the possibility of finding a live worm in our fish has such a sinister connotation that a disproportionate amount of attention is paid to this rare occurrence.

To avoid cross-contamination:

- Purchase seafood from a clean shop with knowledgeable employees. Seafood meant for raw consumption should never be displayed in such a way that other foods can drip on them, come in contact with them

accidentally, or cross-contaminate them in any way. Employees should wash their hands or change gloves before handling raw seafood, and utensils should be used for handling only one type of seafood. Be particularly wary when buying food in stores where poultry, which often contains salmonella, is displayed near cooked seafood or seafood meant for raw consumption.

- Practice safe hygiene at home; wash cutting boards, knives, utensils, and your hands with hot, soapy water before preparing seafood meant for raw consumption.

To avoid parasites:

- Choose only the freshest fish, preferably those that have been dressed immediately on capture, a practice common to hook-and-line fisheries. Most parasitic worms reside in the belly cavity and migrate into the flesh only after the fish dies.

- Select open ocean species such as the various tunas, billfish, wahoos, large mackerels, and opahs, which are seldom infected with parasites of concern. Aquacultured sturgeon, salmon, trout, char, sea trout, hamachi, kampachi, barramundi, daurade royale, and catfish do not eat live wild food, so are always free of parasites.

- Avoid wild freshwater fish, such as whitefish, pike, perch, and lake trout; tapeworm is endemic to these fish.

- Learn to identify the culprits in fish; they are visible to the naked eye and easily recognizable (see Parasitic Worms, page 412).

- Prepare raw fish at home carefully. Slice fish into fine batons, cubes, or slices no more than a quarter inch thick and examine the flesh as you cut. Be particularly vigilant in examining the belly meat, as most parasites are found in and around the belly cavity. The top loin, farthest away from the belly, is far less likely to harbor parasites.

- Examine with extra care the following species, which are some of the most popular fish used in raw dishes: Pacific rockfish, wild Pacific salmon, all halibut (Pacific, Atlantic, California), and Atlantic fluke.
- "Candle" your fish, as is sometimes done in commercial cutting houses. For the super-cautious: Place the fish fillet on a piece of clear Plexiglas and hold it over a naked 100-watt lightbulb—any parasites in the flesh will be highlighted.

The FDA recommends freezing fish to −31°F for fifteen hours, or −4°F for seven days to prevent illness.

## Eating Raw Shellfish Safely

While only 5 percent of all foodborne illnesses are seafood related, 85 percent of those illnesses can be traced to eating raw mollusks: filter-feeding shellfish, such as clams, mussels, and oysters. Naturally-occurring bacteria that thrive in a salty environment, marine toxins related to algal blooms (see "Red Tide" Marine Toxins, page 415), and pollution-related viruses and bacteria that enter shellfish harvest areas with runoff after heavy rains can all be responsible for illness.

Local, state, and federal health agencies regularly monitor shellfish beds and farms. Water and shellfish samples are taken from shellfish harvest areas weekly and analyzed for the presence of natural toxins and pathogens. Harvest areas are closed if contamination or algal blooms are detected and as a precaution during heavy rains.

The shellfish that are at risk for cross-contamination only are shellfish other than mollusks, which are commonly eaten raw; lobster and abalone; and those mollusks of which only the muscle and not the viscera is commonly eaten, such as sea scallops and geoduck clam. Otherwise, there are no inherent risks in eating these kinds of shellfish raw.

To avoid shellfish-related pathogens and illness:

- Buy shellfish from a reputable dealer who practices good sanitation and displays National Shellfish Sanitation Program (NSSP) tags with all mollusks. The NSSP requires mandatory tracking of harvest location and dating of all commercially harvested shellfish to ensure that the harvest has taken place in waters that are certified to be safe at the time of harvest. The harvest of contaminated shellfish by ill-informed recreational harvesters is responsible for the great majority of shellfish-related illnesses.
- Give first preference to locally grown shellfish, which doesn't have far to travel.
- Eat raw shellfish only at restaurants that appear clean, professionally managed, and busy—even better, ones you are familiar with and where you have confidence in the abilities of the chef.
- Remember, the old maxim to eat shellfish only during the cool-weather "r" months—those months with an "r" in their spelling—is based on experience. The warm waters of summer encourage algal blooms and the growth of pathogens, while warm weather and inadequate refrigeration after harvest may contribute to their growth.
- Avoid raw shellfish preparations at buffets or large catered events, where they are more likely to have been handled by unskilled labor, prepared in a rush, or not properly refrigerated.
- Avoid raw shellfish in poor areas of the world where the public sanitary system may be inadequate to the needs of the population. Be particularly careful in the tropics, where the incidence and seriousness of pathogens is much greater than in temperate seas.

The FDA recommends cooking shellfish to 140°F; freezing is ineffective in preventing illness from viruses and bacteria. Red tide–related toxins are not deactivated by cooking or freezing. To be safe, pregnant women, young children, individuals with diabetes, cirrhosis, leukemia, AIDS, or chronic disease, and those who take immunosuppressive drugs or chemotherapy should not consume raw shellfish at any time.

NOTE: Depuration, widely practiced in Europe, is a technique whereby shellfish are held in tanks and allowed to filter water that has been purified with ozone or ultraviolet light. This allows the shellfish to completely rid themselves of viruses, bacteria, and red tide–related pathogens. Few farms in the United States depurate their shellfish, but look for this to become a much more common practice in the future.

## Finfish Health and Safety Concerns

In the United States, it is extremely rare for individuals to become ill from consuming finfish. Even raw finfish, carefully prepared in a clean environment, is almost never a source of human illness. Contrary to popular perception, only 5 percent of all foodborne illnesses are seafood related—and 85 percent of those cases involve shellfish.

Globally, the most often reported and most serious illness related to finfish is ciguatera, a disease that's very rare in U.S. waters. Another cause of finfish-related illness is scombroid, or histamine, poisoning—a relatively benign condition that is caused by improper handling. Bacterial cross-contamination from other foods and improper hygiene is probably the most common cause of illness in raw, smoked, and prepared fish dishes; and finally, there is the illness that affects us the least, yet scares us the most: parasitic worms.

### CIGUATERA

Ciguatera is similar to paralytic shellfish poisoning (PSP), in that marine algae are the source of the natural toxins responsible for the poisoning. Cases of ciguatera have been reported from Hawaii, extreme southern Florida, and the Caribbean. Most U.S. waters, however, including the northern Gulf of Mexico and southeast Atlantic Coast, are not associated with the illness. Symptoms generally include nausea, vomiting and diarrhea, tingling or numbness, itching, and hot-cold sensory reversal. At high levels, the toxins may cause difficulty breathing or even respiratory failure from muscular paralysis. There's no treatment, but symptoms usually subside within a few days.

Ciguatera is most commonly found in reef-dwelling tropical species, particularly those that prey on other fish. Barracuda, moray eels, and the various jacks should be avoided in all parts of the Caribbean; large groupers, snappers, and other species may also bio-accumulate dangerous levels of ciguatera toxins by eating smaller fish. Small fish are safer for this reason. The toxins are most heavily concentrated in the fish's liver, gonads, and other viscera, and these parts should be carefully avoided. Cooking or freezing does not inactivate the toxins, and there is no known antidote. The only solution is avoidance.

Reef disturbances such as hurricanes or wharf construction seem to encourage algal blooms, increasing the likelihood that ciguatera will develop. Local fishermen are generally familiar with suspect reefs, and some area governments also issue advisories on reefs that are known to be toxic. If you're fishing in unfamiliar tropical waters and you plan to eat your own catch, a rapid-test kit called the Cigua-Check can be purchased online.

### GEMPYLOTOXIN

The wonderfully rich flavor of escolar (*Lepidocybium flavobrunneum*) and oilfish (*Ruvettus pretiosus*) has made both species menu favorites from Miami to Seattle. Caught in the South Pacific and Gulf of Mexico, escolar and oilfish—of the Gempylidae, or snake mackerel, family—contain waxy esters in their fatty tissue, similar to those found in the fat substitute Olestra. These indigestible waxy esters have powerful laxative properties that affect people to varying degrees.

The most disturbing part of this illness is its complete lack of associated symptoms: You can be affected without warning at any time or in the most inappropriate place, and the results can be quite embarrassing. Some people believe that oilfish, which can be identified by its pineapple-like skin, is the greater culprit. To be safe, however, you should eat no more than a five-ounce serving of either fish at one time. Freezing and cooking have no effect on gempylotoxins.

### KUDOA

This common infection of marine fish by parasitic protozoa poses no threat to human health, but it does adversely affect the fish's texture and appearance. Found in the muscle tissue of many marine species, including tuna, hake, sand dabs, halibut, and aquacultured salmon, kudoa makes itself known only after the host fish dies, at which point the microscopic protozoa begin producing enzymes that attack the host's flesh. Sometimes referred to as "soft spot syndrome," because of the obvious presence of soft, suppurating spots in the flesh of infected fish, the parasites can be destroyed by thorough cooking or freezing. Kudoa is the major reason why much of the tuna destined for the sashimi trade is frozen.

### LISTERIA

Listeria is ubiquitous in nature, and its control depends heavily on the maintenance of clean processing facilities and proper handling. Although listeria is found much more commonly in foods other than seafood, the bacteria's ability to resist cold temperatures makes it a concern to the seafood industry. Cold-smoked fish—uncooked fish that is stored for relatively long periods of time under refrigeration—is the most likely seafood-related vector.

Listeriosis usually causes mild flulike symptoms in healthy adults, but it may have serious manifestations in infants and people who are immunosuppressed; pregnant women should be particularly careful, because the disease may cause miscarriage. When purchasing smoked fish in a vacuum-packed package, check to be sure that the packaging has not been breached.

### MERCURY

See Mercury in Seafood, page 403.

### PARASITIC WORMS

We live in a parasite-filled world: All animals and plants—even the soil—harbor numerous parasites, most of which we never notice. There are a few that under certain circumstances may affect human health.

Specifically, four parasites in seafood are a cause for concern: two types of roundworms commonly called cod worms and herring worms, and two broadfish tapeworms. These worms all go through a similar complicated life cycle that involves living inside a crustacean, a fish, and a mammal, in that order, to reproduce. For this reason, these parasites and the fish they infect are most abundant where there are significant populations of fish-eating mammals. Seals, sea lions, Alaskan grizzly bears, and raccoons are all definitive hosts. These parasites are known to occur in the flesh of cod, flounder, haddock, fluke, Pacific salmon, rockfish, herring, monkfish, and other fish.

#### Roundworms (*Nematodes*)

Cod (*Anisakis simplex*) and herring worms (*Pseudoterranova decipiens*) are approximately three quarters of an inch to one inch long and are the thickness of pencil lead. One species is brown or red, making it quite easy to see. The other is white and may be coiled into a tight, bull's-eye-like circle, making it more difficult to notice. Both species can be found in a variety of fish and, as well, the occasional squid.

If a worm is accidentally ingested, in most cases it will simply pass through the digestive system with no ill effects. On rare occasions, a live worm may attempt to attach itself to the stomach or intestinal wall. When this happens, the attendant stomach pain and nausea may be misdiagnosed as appendicitis or an ulcer. Termed anisakiasis, for the family of worms responsible, this malady, though unpleasant, is very rare. Both cod and herring worms are incapable of surviving in humans and are eventually digested. Like other parasitic worms, cod worms are destroyed by thorough cooking or freezing.

### Tapeworms

As noted above, two varieties of tapeworm commonly infect fish and can be contracted by humans. One (*D. latum*) is found both in freshwater species and in anadromous species, like salmon, which spend part of their life in freshwater. Healthy populations of Alaskan bears serve as the definitive host in Alaskan watersheds. The marine tapeworm (*D. pacificum*) uses marine mammals like sea lions and seals for definitive hosts, and is apt to be found anywhere such mammals are present.

The larval stage measures from four to five millimeters in length and appears as a large, cream-colored rice grain–shaped cyst embedded in the flesh of fish. The disease is often asymptomatic, although symptoms of stomach distress or anemia may sometimes occur. Infection is usually diagnosed by the presence of tapeworm eggs in the stool, and antihelminthic drugs are then administered as treatment. Tapeworms are destroyed by thorough cooking or freezing.

### PERSISTENT ORGANIC POLLUTANTS (POPS)

See page 417.

### PFIESTERIA

Pfiesteria, a microscopic marine organism that is an indicator of deteriorating water quality, kills millions of fish each year from Delaware to Alabama. While consuming affected fish won't instigate any symptoms, pfiesteria can cause symptoms of allergy and neurotoxin poisoning in humans if it becomes airborne.

### RAW FINFISH

See Eating Raw Finfish Safely, page 408.

### SCOMBROID

Scombroid fish poisoning, also known as histamine poisoning, is a mild disease of short duration. The most common symptoms are facial flushing, itching, and rash, although nausea, vomiting, and headache may also occur. Often, the first sign of the illness is a distinctly sharp, peppery, or metallic taste, along with a tingling or burning sensation in the mouth.

The toxins associated with scombroid poisoning are formed during cleaning, when bacteria normally found on the skin of live saltwater fish can spread to the fish's flesh, where they encourage certain proteins to produce histamine-like allergens. While scombroid fish—members of the tuna family that are warm-blooded and therefore difficult to chill quickly—are particularly susceptible, mahimahi, bluefish, escolar, and other fish have also been implicated.

Scombrotoxin is not easily detectable, so you'll have to rely on the good handling practices of your fish dealer. Seafood contaminated with histamine does not look or smell spoiled, and the effects of histamine poisoning are not diminished by freezing or cooking. In most cases, treatment with an over-the-counter antihistamine such as Benadryl is enough to produce relief.

### VENOMOUS SPINES

While more than one hundred species of fish can inflict venomous stings, only a few are likely to be encountered in fish markets. During handling, venom may be injected through dorsal, anal, or pelvic spines, resulting in mild to moderate pain and swelling. All Pacific Coast rockfish are venomous, though some seem to be more so than others. Catfish, scorpion fish of New Zealand, and some sharks have venomous spines. Skates of both the Pacific and Atlantic coasts have venomous spines on their wings, although these are usually removed before sale.

Those who are repeatedly stung by the above fish, usually fishermen and fish handlers, may develop a serious allergic reaction to the venom. Being stuck by the spine of any fish can lead to serious bacterial infection, including septicemia (bloodstream infection). All deep wounds from a fish spine should be washed immediately, then soaked in heavily salted water (½ cup salt to ½ gallon very hot (120°F+ water) for 5 minutes. Change the water and repeat at least twice. If pieces of spine remain in the wound or infection occurs, see your doctor immediately.

## Shellfish Health and Safety Concerns

According to the FDA's Center for Food Safety, raw shellfish is responsible for 85 percent of all seafood-related illnesses. Bacteria, viruses, and marine toxins that are accumulated by filter-feeding mollusks such as clams, mussels, and oysters cause most seafood-related illnesses. For specific ways to avoid ill effects from ingesting shellfish, see Raw Seafood: How to Stay Safe, page 408.

### ALLERGIES

Allergy attacks are much more likely to be triggered by ingesting shellfish than fish, with crustaceans—shrimp, crab, crayfish, and lobster—being the most common causes of allergic reactions. Cross-reactivity is also common, meaning that a person with an allergy to one crustacean is likely to be allergic to the others as well.

Common symptoms of fish and shellfish allergies include skin rash and itching, upset stomach along with cramps or swelling, and wheezing and shortness of breath. An over-the-counter antihistamine such as Benadryl will usually relieve symptoms.

#### Sulfite Allergy

Processed seafoods such as surimi, fish sticks, and frozen fish sandwiches often contain chemicals that are used to preserve, add flavor to, or change the texture of seafood. The most common of these—and the most frequent cause of allergic reaction—is sodium bisulfite, followed by sodium tripolyphosphate. Nearly all processed seafoods are treated with these chemicals, as are many unprocessed scallops and shrimp.

### BACTERIA

Certain naturally-occurring bacteria in the marine environment have been associated with gastroenteritis, with raw mollusks, such as oysters and clams, being the most common vector. These bacteria have also been known to infect open wounds in swimmers.

*Vibrio vulnificus* is a serious infection threat to anyone with diabetes, cirrhosis, or a compromised immune system, since septicemia may result. It's found predominantly in the warm coastal waters of the Gulf of Mexico during the warm-water months of May through September. Gastroenteritis symptoms usually appear within twelve to twenty-four hours. Vibrio bacteria are destroyed by thorough cooking.

*V. parahaemolyticus* is more widespread but less dangerous. Sporadic cases are reported along all the coasts of the United States, but the majority of infections occur in the Gulf Coast states. Symptoms of gastroenteritis usually appear within twelve to twenty-four hours. The bacteria are destroyed by thorough cooking.

### CROSS-CONTAMINATION

Cooked seafood such as crabmeat and shrimp should never be displayed in such a way that uncooked foods can drip on them, come in contact with them accidentally, or cross-contaminate them in any way. Be particularly wary when buying food in stores where poultry, which often contains salmonella, is displayed near cooked seafood or seafood meant for raw consumption. Be sure to practice safe hygiene at home: Wash cutting boards, knives, utensils, and your hands with hot soapy water before preparing cooked seafood or seafood meant for raw consumption.

### HEPATOPANCREAS

The hepatopancreas, commonly called crab butter, lobster tomalley, or crayfish fat, depending on which shellfish you're eating, is considered a delicacy by many people. Although the hepatopancreas appears to be fatty flesh, it is actually a gland that performs the function of both pancreas and liver, producing digestive enzymes and filtering impurities from the blood. If chemical contaminants such as PCBs and dioxin are present in the environment, they will accumulate in the hepatopancreas. In addition, naturally-occurring toxins associated with red tides have been known to accumulate in the hepatopancreas of crabs.

## MERCURY
See Mercury in Seafood, page 403.

## PERSISTENT ORGANIC POLLUTANTS (POPS)
See page 417.

## RAW SHELLFISH
See Eating Raw Shellfish Safely, page 409.

## "RED TIDE" MARINE TOXINS
Some microscopic marine algae produce small amounts of naturally-occurring biological toxins. Under normal conditions, these algae are simply part of the marine food web, but when ocean conditions are favorable, usually during the warmer summer months, an algal bloom may occur. Although these algal blooms are usually referred to as "red tides," they can appear as red, brown, green, or yellow stains on the surface of the sea. Filter-feeding mollusks such as clams, oysters, or mussels, which are not susceptible to these toxins themselves, may ingest and accumulate the toxic algae in their viscera. Trouble occurs when infected shellfish are eaten by humans.

Red-tide shellfish poisoning may cause neurological and or gastrointestinal symptoms that include tingling, numbness or burning of the mouth, drowsiness, fever, reversal of hot and cold sensations, diarrhea, and other gastrointestinal symptoms. Since cooking or freezing do not inactivate the toxins and there is no known antidote, the only solution is avoidance.

Most shellfish poisoning occurs when recreational harvesters, who aren't native to the location, disregard official quarantines or local traditions of safe consumption. I could not find any reported cases of shellfish poisoning in the United States from aquacultured shellfish, which makes up almost all the mollusks you will buy in the store.

## Amnesiac Shellfish Poisoning (ASP)
Symptoms may include disorientation and memory loss. The toxin associated with ASP is an unusual amino acid called domoic acid, which can be found in the Atlantic, from the Gulf of Maine north, and along the entire Pacific Coast (rare south of Oregon). The toxin is transmitted most commonly by filter-feeding mollusks, but it may also be contained in the viscera of Dungeness crabs as well as anchovies and other filter-feeding fish. If algal blooms or the conditions that encourage them are present, commercial fisheries are monitored for domoic acid.

Domoic acid was not understood to be the cause of amnesiac shellfish poisoning until 1987, when the first case of ASP was documented. Yet ASP inspired one of most memorable Hollywood thrillers ever filmed. In the summer of 1961, hundreds of crazed birds attacked the seaside town of Capitola, California, crashing through glass windows and attacking people on the ground. Alfred Hitchcock, who frequently vacationed nearby, was fascinated by the incident and included newspaper clippings about the Capitola attack in his studio proposal for *The Birds*. It is now believed the birds had contracted ASP from eating shellfish containing domoic acid.

Amnesiac shellfish poisoning is particularly serious in elderly patients.

### Neurotoxic Shellfish Poisoning (NSP)

This disease, found in the Gulf of Mexico and the South Atlantic bight, is both gastrointestinal and neurological in nature, but is far less serious than either PSP or ASP.

### Paralytic Shellfish Poisoning (PSP)

Paralytic shellfish poisoning is found in the northeastern and northwestern coastal regions of the United States, and is the most serious type of red-tide marine toxin from a public health perspective. Severe cases may result in respiratory paralysis and death if respiratory support is not quickly provided. Thanks to strong regulatory programs designed to prevent exposure, there have been very few outbreaks of PSP in the United States.

### VIRUSES

Norwalk virus is the most common fish-related cause of gastroenteritis. Associated with fecal pollution, it strikes twenty-four to forty-eight hours after ingesting contaminated shellfish. Symptoms include nausea, vomiting, diarrhea, headache, and low-grade fever. Viruses are destroyed by thorough cooking.

Hepatitis A virus is transmitted much in the same way as Norwalk virus and produces similar symptoms, though it may also be immediately followed by jaundice. The incubation period is about four weeks, making it difficult to trace the origin of most infections, but typically the virus is contracted by eating raw shellfish. Unlike other types of hepatitis, hepatitis A is not a chronic infection. Viruses are destroyed by thorough cooking.

Industrial and agricultural pollutants such as dioxin, PCBs, and pesticides like DDT have made their way into the food web over the years. There is evidence that exposure to these chemicals over time may affect reproduction and childhood growth and development, as well as creating a lifetime cancer risk. Although many of these chemicals are no longer in use, they are slow to degrade and are still found in the soil, aquatic sediment, plants, and animals.

Today, the main source of human exposure to these compounds is through the consumption of fatty foods, such as meat, fish, poultry, eggs, milk, and milk products. Federal and state government agencies monitor contaminant levels in fish and shellfish. When levels exceed action levels, contaminated bodies of water are closed to commercial fishing or an individual species of fish is banned from the commercial marketplace. However, funds for more complete testing and enforcement need to be allotted. Recreational and subsistence anglers, pregnant women, and children who eat large amounts of sport fish caught from inshore contaminated waters are at greatest risk.

Many of these chemicals are being slowly buried by sedimentation. They are found in much lower levels in human tissue and our food supply than in the past, but there are still freshwater lakes, streams, and inshore waters where PCBs in particular may contaminate fish. Advisories for all states can be found at epa.gov/waterscience/fish/states.htm.

To reduce exposure to POPs:

- Avoid wild freshwater fish, such as whitefish, pike, pickerel, walleye, and lake trout, and marine fish taken from inshore industrialized areas prone to pollution.
- Avoid highly predatory marine fish that travel to inshore waters to prey on large amounts of smaller inshore fish. Consumer advisories have been issued for bluefish, striped bass, and weakfish taken from inshore industrialized areas. To reduce the risk of exposure from these fish, choose small fish of five pounds or less.
- Avoid the fatty tissues of fish where POPs accumulate. Remove the skin, and trim the darker fat found underneath the skin and along the sides and belly before cooking.
- Do not eat the tomalley, or butter (see Hepatopancreas, page 414) of lobster, crab, or crayfish, or the liver or other viscera of finfish.
- Serve less fried fish. Frying seals in pollutants that might be in the fish's fat, while grilling, broiling, poaching, or cooking in a grill pan allows fat to drain away.
- Choose fish that spend most of their life far from the shoreline, such as salmon, tuna, opah, halibut, cod, and haddock. Fish from Alaska and the South Pacific tend to be free of POPs. An extensive study of Alaska seafood in 2004 reported nondetectable to very low levels of POPs in Alaskan seafood.
- Eat a variety of seafood originating from different locations.

# FISHING AND AQUACULTURE METHODS APPENDIX

The way we capture and culture fish and shellfish greatly affect the health of the world's oceans and its denizens. One of the most important aspects of choosing sustainable seafood is knowing how that seafood was caught or raised and understanding a fishing or aquaculture method's impact on fish and the environment. Throughout the text I often refer to fishing and aquaculture methods, inferring that some are more sustainable than others. This appendix will guide you and help you understand each method and its effect on the environment.

Unsustainable methods of fishing damage coral and rock reefs or seagrass beds, areas of the sea that act as nursery and protected areas for fish, known as **essential fish habitat**. This type of fishing is also nonselective, and catches immature fish and nontarget species, which are then discarded as **bycatch**. In the United States alone, 2.5 billion pounds of fish as bycatch are discarded at sea every year, most of it dead or dying, upsetting prey-predator relationships and biodiversity.

Sustainable methods of fishing catch the target species and little else—waste and bycatch are minimal. These methods of fishing do not damage essential fish habitat, those areas of the sea necessary to fish for spawning, feeding, and growing to maturity.

Aquaculture may affect wild fisheries and the environment—some methods of aquaculture allow fish to escape into the wild, spread disease, pollute the surrounding seas, and use wild forage fish for food inefficiently, all adversely affecting wild fisheries. Others are less harmful simply either because growers use "best practices" in an attempt to lessen their impact on the environment and wild fisheries, or the species being cultured—such as shellfish—is inherently environmentally friendly.

## Fish and Shellfish Capture

### FISHING METHODS

#### Gill-Netting

A **gill net** is a curtain of netting that hangs in the water suspended by a system of floats, weights, and sometimes anchors (see illustration A on page 419). Fish swim through the virtually invisible monofilament netting, and are entangled when their gill covers or spines are caught in the webbing. While habitat impact is generally not an issue, bycatch of nontarget species is of concern. **Trammel nets**, popular in Europe, are a type of gill net with two or three curtains of net; they can have very high rates of bycatch.

Giant **drift gill nets** are not anchored to the bottom. They drift freely and were once widely used to target tuna, billfish, squid, and salmon on the high seas. This fishing method is banned because of its high bycatch of seabirds, marine mammals, sea turtles, and sharks. A coastal Pacific drift gill net fishery for swordfish has been successful at ameliorating bycatch through regulation and gear innovation.

Inshore gill netting for many species, such as Florida pompano and California white sea bass, has been banned because of issues of bycatch and overfishing.

With careful regulation—mesh size, when and where set, how often tended, etc.—gill nets can be a sustainable method of fishing. Salmon fishermen are able to target a specific river or run of salmon while avoiding other potentially less healthy runs. Herring and mackerel fishermen are able to select a year class of fish rather than take entire schools. Large-mesh monkfish gill nets allow small species to escape and are easier on habitat than trawling. **Tangle nets**, a type of gill net that entangles salmon by the teeth, can be used to target hatchery fish or healthy wild salmon runs while avoiding or releasing steelhead or endangered salmon runs.

### Hook and Line

**Trolling**, **pole and line**, **rod and reel**, **hand lining**, **jigging**, and other terms are used to describe selective methods of fishing where the fish are individually hooked and can be quickly handled. Nontarget bycatch can be easily avoided or released, and there is little or no impact on fishery habitat. Salmon, wreckfish, haddock, cod, striped bass, black sea bass, halibut, rock-

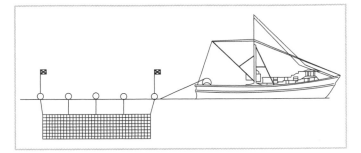

A. A GILL NET SUSPENDED IN THE WATER

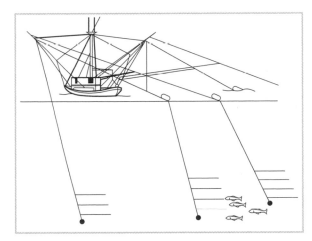

B. TROLLING FOR SALMON

fish, snappers, and any other fish taken by this method are always of the highest quality.

Trolling, which refers to the towing of artificial lures or natural bait from a moving boat, should not be confused with trawling (see illustration B above).

**Longlines** consist of a single long main line to which is attached a number of branch lines and baited hooks. Although technically hook and line, longlining generally takes place on a much larger scale than other hook-and-line methods of fishing. It is one of the world's major methods of catching fish.

Depending on the target species, a longline can be anchored on the bottom or suspended by floats in the water column. **Bottom longlines** are used to catch

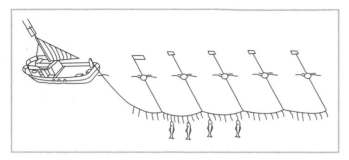

**A.** TYPICAL LONGLINE GEAR

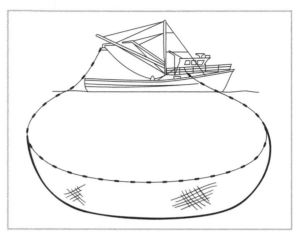

**B.** A PURSE SEINE SET AROUND A SCHOOL OF FISH

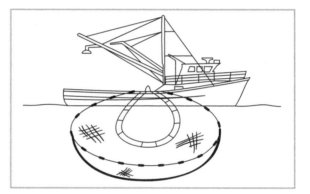

**C.** THE SEINE NET IS "PURSED" AND READY TO COME ABOARD.

cod, halibut, and other bottom fish, while **pelagic longlines** are used to catch fish higher in the water column such as swordfish and tuna.

Although longlining is not as environmentally friendly as other hook-and-line fishing methods, it has minimal effect on bottom habitat. Bycatch of seabirds, sea turtles, sharks, marine mammals, immature, and other fish has been greatly ameliorated by improved gear and regulation in American fisheries. Other countries that are less conscientious about adopting sustainable harvesting practices continue to have an impact on seabirds, sea turtles, sharks, marine mammals, immature, and other fish.

## Harpoon

Harpooning, used extensively in the whaling days, is still practiced today to catch surface-swimming swordfish and tuna. They are thrown by hand or shot by mounted guns, each tipped with a barb that is attached to a line with a buoy at the end. Each fish is individually selected, so only mature fish are taken; there is no bycatch or habitat impact. **Powerhead spear fishing** by underwater divers, seemingly as selective as harpooning, has been the cause of overfishing when used to target aggregations of spawning grouper and snapper in the southeast Atlantic.

## Purse Seine

A purse seine is a wall of netting used to encircle an entire school of fish. A drawstring cable is used to pull, or purse, the net tight at the bottom, enclosing the fish in a large pouch. The entire net can be hauled onboard, or small dip nets can be used to scoop out the fish, a process called **brailing**. Seines are used for capturing fish that congregate in large schools near the surface, such as tuna, salmon, squid, herring, mackerel, or sardines.

Purse seines do not affect bottom habitat. Bycatch is usually not an issue in small-scale purse-seine fisheries such as those for herring, squid, or salmon. Bycatch and the targeting of immature tuna by industrial-scale tuna seiners is a serious concern. The incidental capture of dolphins by tuna seines led to a U.S. federal regulation creating "dolphin-safe" tuna.

### Trawling

Trawling, responsible for the largest percentage of commercial fish landings, can be simply described as towing a funnel-shaped net through the water. It can be used to harvest bottom-dwelling fish when dragged along the ocean floor, or pelagic species when fished off the bottom in midwater.

**Bottom trawls** are used to harvest cod, haddock, monkfish, Pacific rockfish, sole, scallops, shrimp, and many other species. Bottom-trawling reduces fish and plant diversity on the bottom and selects for faster-growing fish. Trawling reduces the overall health of an ecosystem and adversely affects the viability of individual species.

Bottom trawls are very destructive when used over rock or coral reefs. **Rock hopper** bottom trawls equipped with large rubber tires that allow them to roll over reef obstructions are notorious for destroying this important fish habitat.

When bottom trawls are used over a soft mud or sand bottom, particularly in shallow areas subject to frequent storms, there is little evidence of long-term adverse effect to the habitat. Flounders, shrimp, and scallops often favor this type of bottom, although bycatch can still be an issue of concern.

**Midwater trawls** are used to capture herring, pollock, whiting, hake, squid, and other fish that swim in the water column. They are towed through the water between the surface and the bottom, and do not come in contact with the bottom or damage the bottom habitat. Midwater trawls are used to target schools of fish; the percentage of bycatch to target fish can be low.

### Traps

**Floating fish traps** constructed with netting are held in place with anchors and floats. Fish enter the mouth, are directed through a series of ever-restrictive mesh boxes, and become entrapped when they reach a mesh cage at the end. Because captured fish never come into direct contact with the net, they are in perfect condition and can either be harvested or released live.

**Reef nets** are used in the Pacific Northwest. Migrating adult salmon are directed over a shallow net, which is then lifted so the fish spill into holding pens. This is a selective and environmentally responsible method of fishing.

**Weirs**, similar in design to floating fish traps, consist of stakes driven into shallow water bottom. Fences direct fish to swim voluntarily into successively smaller enclosures, where they are easily captured.

**Wire-mesh fish traps** are generally small submerged wire cages baited to attract fish and hold them alive until fishermen return to haul in the gear. Traps lie on the bottom—either singly or in a row. A rope runs from the trap to a buoy floating at the surface, allowing fishermen to locate their gear.

The sablefish fisheries of Alaska and Canada that utilize traps are sustainable and environmentally friendly. In the Gulf of Mexico and the Caribbean, where traps are the most common method of fishing for reef species, widespread improper and illegal use has led to the destruction of coral reefs and the overfishing of spawning and immature grouper, snapper, and other reef species. Wire-mesh fish traps have been banned in the southeast Atlantic and are being phased out in the Gulf of Mexico. These traps are still being used extensively in the Caribbean.

### SHELLFISH HARVESTING METHODS

### Diving

The hand harvest of shellfish by divers may have a range of impacts. The well-regulated Pacific Northwest geoduck fishery is an example of a well-regulated sustainable diver fishery, while on the other hand, the illegal harvest of California red abalone led to the demise of the

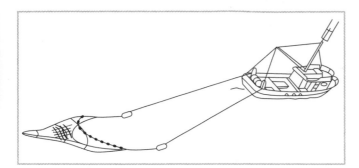

**A**. A TRAWLER DRAGGING THE BOTTOM

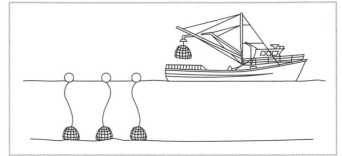

**B**. SETTING A LINE OF SABLEFISH TRAPS

commercial fishery. The jury is still out on the oft-praised diver scallop fishery of Maine that began in 1992. Some believe stocks have been diminished by divers taking too many previously unavailable older scallops. These scallops form a reproductive bank responsible for replenishing stocks.

### Dredge

A dredge is a metal rectangular frame with a rake on the bottom to which a bag-shaped net of metal rings is attached. The frame is connected to a towing cable and dragged along the sea floor, raking scallops, clams, and occasionally oysters into the metal bag. Pressurized jets of water may be used to assist the dredge, loosening the bottom and stirring up deep-burrowing clams.

Dredging is most destructive to fishery habitat when used over reefs such as those formed by oysters. When used over a mud or sand bottom, it stirs up food from the substrate and encourages the growth of filter-feeding animals such as scallops. However, repeated dredging adversely affects the diversity of flora and fauna in an area, as fast-growing plants and animals take over the habitat. Dredging may also capture flounder and other bottom dwellers as bycatch.

### Traps and Pots

Traps and pots are made of wire mesh, and have one or more funnel-shaped openings, which include specially

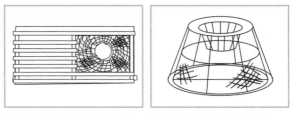

**C**. A DOWN-EAST LOBSTER POT

**D**. A PACIFIC NORTHWEST SABLEFISH TRAP

designed escape vents for undersized animals. They lie on the bottom, either singly or in a row. A rope runs from the trap or pot to a buoy floating at the surface. This allows fishermen to locate and retrieve their gear.

Shellfish traps used to catch lobsters, crabs, and shrimp are regarded as environmentally friendly. Unintended bycatch and undersized shellfish can be released often without harm. Habitat impact is minimal when traps are used on a soft, sandy bottom. Sensitive coral and rock reef can be harmed by shellfish traps being hauled in or moved by ocean swells and tides.

### Tongs

Various types of rakes are used to manually harvest clams and oysters. Basket rakes are equipped with wire-mesh baskets to hold the catch, and bull rakes have very long handles for operation from a skiff. Bycatch is of no concern, and habitat damage is minimal.

# Fish and Shellfish Culture

## FISH AQUACULTURE

### Open Ocean Net Pens or Cages

**Floating net pens** or submerged cages enclose fish, which can be fed and harvested at will. Most open ocean aquaculture takes place in floating net pens in coastal waters. The federal government is currently promoting offshore **submerged cage** aquaculture. Salmon is the primary species grown in open ocean net pens, but tuna, cod, halibut, hamachi, and other fish are also grown in this manner.

Growing fish in open ocean net pens and cages can pollute the ocean bottom and surrounding waters, encourage the spread of disease and parasites to wild fish, and allow the escape of nonindigenous fish that compete with wild stocks. Of great concern is the fishing pressure placed on **wild forage fish**, such as anchovies, sardines, and mackerel, used to manufacture feed and the impact their removal from the food web has on wild predatory fish.

Conscientious growers raise fish at lower densities, frequently replace netting and other materials used to enclose fish, and evaluate the condition of the wild forage stocks used in their feed.

### Ponds, Tanks, and Raceways

Coastal **saltwater ponds** are most often used to grow shrimp, while inland **freshwater ponds**, **tanks**, and **raceways** are used to grow catfish, tilapia, sturgeon, trout, and other species. The water in ponds and tanks is aerated with pumps, while raceways simply divert free-flowing water from a natural river or stream through a channel and then back into the waterway.

The construction of saltwater shrimp ponds in Asia has led to the widespread destruction of mangrove forests and other important coastal habitats. At this time, most countries have realized the folly of destroying important wild fish nursery areas and have forbidden the construction of new shrimp farms in mangrove swamps. Wastewater, if untreated, can pollute oceans, streams, and groundwaters. In the United States and increasingly in other countries, farmers treat wastewater and monitor nearby water quality.

**Closed-system** ponds and tanks filter and recirculate water within the system. These land-based systems are generally considered to be among the most environmentally responsible designs for aquaculture. Almost any species, including salmon and shrimp, can be raised in a closed system, but energy costs to recirculate, filter, and chill the water are high.

Shrimp, trout, striped bass, sturgeon, salmon, and trout raised in this manner require feed manufactured from wild forage fish. Tilapia, catfish, and carp are raised on a grain-based diet. Conch and abalone, which graze on seaweed, may be raised in ponds or tanks.

## SHELLFISH AQUACULTURE

### Beach Culture

Filter-feeding shellfish, such as clams, mussels, and oysters, are an important component of a healthy marine environment. Wherever these shellfish are grown, water quality improves. Beach culture has only minor effects on the beach and its community.

### Suspended

Filter-feeding oysters, mussels, and clams may be grown suspended in the water on ropes or in mesh bags on racks (the "rack-and-bag method"). Suspended methods of aquaculture are faultless in that they do not have an impact on habitat or other species, they take pressure off wild stocks, and no wild fish are used for food.

# BIBLIOGRAPHY

Auerbach, Paul S. *A Medical Guide to Hazardous Marine Life.*
St. Louis, MO: Mosby Year Book, 1991.

Bacchella, Adriano. *Pesci del Mediterraneo.* Rome: DIAL, 2005.

Cost, Bruce. *Asian Ingredients.* New York: Quill, 2000.

Davidson, Alan. *North Atlantic Seafood.* New York: Viking Press,
1979.

Doerper, John. *Shellfish Cookery.* Seattle: Pacific Search Press,
1985.

Halstead, Bruce W. *Poisonous and Venomous Marine Animals.*
Princeton, NJ: Darwin, 1988.

Hoese, Dickson H., and Richard H. Moore. *Fishes of the Gulf of
Mexico.* College Station, TX: Texas A&M University Press, 1998.

Kennedy, Diana. *The Essential Cuisines of Mexico.* New York:
Clarkson Potter, 2000.

Love, Milton. *Probably More Than You Want to Know about the
Fishes of the Pacific Coast.* Santa Barbara, CA: Really Big
Press, 1996.

Love, Milton S., Mary Yoklavich, and Lyman Thorsteinson.
*The Rockfishes of the Northeast Pacific.* Berkeley, CA:
University of California Press, 2002.

Manooch, Charles S. *Fishes of the Southeastern United States.*
Raleigh, NC: North Carolina Museum of Natural History, 1984.

McClane, A.J. *Encyclopedia of Fish Cookery.* New York: Holt,
Rinehart and Winston, 1977.

McGee, Harold. *On Food and Cooking.* New York: Scribner, 2004.

*New Zealand Fishing Industry Board Guide Book to New Zealand
Commercial Fish Species.* Wellington, N.Z.: Printgroup, 1994.

Nettleton, Joyce. *Seafood and Health.* New York: Van Nostrand
Reinhold, 1987.

Rodgers, Judy. *The Zuni Cafe Cookbook.* New York: W.W. Norton,
2002.

Sakanari, Judy A., Mike Moser, and Thomas L. Deardoff. *Fish
Parasites and Human Health.* La Jolla, CA: California Sea
Grant College, University of California.

Saran, Suvir. *Indian Home Cooking.* New York: Clarkson Potter,
2004.

Shimbo, Hiroko. *The Japanese Kitchen.* Boston: Harvard Common
Press, 2000.

Stein, Rick. *Complete Seafood.* Berkeley, CA: Ten Speed Press, 2004.

Trang, Corrine. *Essentials of Asian Cuisine.* New York: Simon &
Schuster, 2003.

Waters, Alice. *Chez Panisse Vegetables.* New York: HarperCollins,
1996.

Wolfert, Paula. *The Slow Mediterranean Kitchen.* Hoboken, NJ:
John Wiley & Sons, 2003.

## ON THE INTERNET

Atlantic States Marine Fisheries Commission www.asmfc.org/

FishBase. Froese, R. and D. Pauly, editors. 2006.
http://filaman.ifmgeomar.de/search.php

Hawaii Seafood Buyers Guide www.hawaii.gov/dbedt/seafood

Fats of Life Newsletter & PUFA Newsletter www.fatsoflife.com/

U.S.FDA Center for Food Safety. The "Bad Bug Book"
www.cfsan.fda.gov/~mow/intro.html

Nutritiondata.Com www.Nutritiondata.com

Monterey Bay Aquarium's Seafood Watch Program
www.mbayaq.org/cr/seafoodwatch.asp

Seafood Business Magazine www.seafoodbusiness.com/

NOAA's National Sea Grant College Program
www.seagrant.noaa.gov/colleges/colleges.html

National Oceanic and Atmospheric Administration Fisheries Science
Centers www.nmfs.noaa.gov/science.htm

# INDEX